Sowing Seeds

"A small-town, plain coat–wearing Mennonite from rural Iowa sails to India to share the gospel in a land teeming with anticolonial activism. His journey to the other side of the globe—and back—is a fascinating missiological story, expertly told by R. Bruce Yoder."

—**DAVID SWARTZ**, professor of history at Asbury Seminary and author of *Facing West: American Evangelicals in an Age of World Christianity*

"As the first executive secretary of the Mennonite Board of Missions and Charities (MBMC), Joseph Daniel Graber played a crucial role in shaping mission initiatives. He advocated for the proposition that each church should function as a mission outpost. His legacy encompasses the promotion of a diverse and global Mennonite identity. Graber's leadership markedly expanded the church's international mission activities, and he was instrumental in advancing postcolonial mission strategies. This noteworthy scholarly contribution is essential reading for those who uphold the mission of God in the world."

—**NELSON OKANYA**, leadership consultant and former president of Eastern Mennonite Missions

"In this well-written and carefully researched biography of a Mennonite missionary couple, Joe and Minnie Graber, R. Bruce Yoder presents a minority perspective on the high era of US missions in the mid-twentieth century. We learn how Mennonite mission leaders challenged their denomination's ethnocentrism and developed an engaged approach to the world that was at the cutting edge of questioning colonial mission practice and pioneered a global partnership approach."

—**KIRSTEEN KIM**, PhD, Paul E. Pierson Professor of World Christianity and associate dean for the Center for Missiological Research at Fuller Seminary

"J. D. Graber was the face of missions for many twentieth-century North American Mennonites. And now, in turn, R. Bruce Yoder offers us the face of J. D. Graber—his origins, his love of Christ and the church, and his passion for God's reconciling work in the world. This long-anticipated study fills an important gap in our understanding of Mennonite mission history and the growth of Anabaptist faith families around the world."

—**JAMES R. KRABILL**, mission worker and administrator (1976–2018) with Mennonite Board of Missions, now Mennonite Mission Network

"*Sowing Seeds* tells the remarkable story of J. D. and Minnie Graber, whose shared vision helped shape the global Anabaptist movement. With clarity and depth, R. Bruce Yoder captures the Grabers' bold call for every congregation to be a mission outpost and the Grabers' conviction that faithful mission requires humility, justice, and partnership across cultures. Starting with the Grabers' experience in India, we can trace their evolving understanding for how to share the gospel through equitable relationships. Their legacy continues to inspire those committed to God's reconciling work in the world. This book is a vital resource for leaders who want to bear witness to the way of Jesus in our diverse, interconnected world."

—**DAVID W. BOSHART**, president of Anabaptist Mennonite Biblical Seminary

"Through R. Bruce Yoder's clearly written and thoroughly researched biography of J. D. Graber, we discover the twentieth-century transformation of Anabaptist missions from a Eurocentric and paternalistic enterprise into a world Christian movement calling for decentralized, interdependent, and contextualized understandings of what it means to be a Mennonite. As one of the most important leaders in Mennonite missions, Graber's legacy for the goals and values of postcolonial mission work continues to reverberate today. Yoder is to be commended for sharing Joe and Minnie Graber's story in such a thoughtfully analyzed—and enjoyably readable—way."

—**TROY OSBORNE**, dean and associate professor of history at Conrad Grebel University College and author of *Radicals and Reformers: A Survey of Global Anabaptist History*

Sowing Seeds

J. D. Graber and the Vision for Global Anabaptism

R. Bruce Yoder

HERALD PRESS
Harrisonburg, Virginia

Herald Press
PO Box 866, Harrisonburg, Virginia 22803
www.HeraldPress.com

SOWING SEEDS

Library of Congress Control Number: 2025939872
International Standard Book Number: 978-1-5138-1670-8 (paperback);
978-1-5138-1672-2 (ebook)
Printed in United States of America
Cover and interior design by Merrill Miller

29 28 27 26 25 10 9 8 7 6 5 4 3 2 1

Contents

In Memory of Wilbert R. Shenk,
who conceived of this biography
and insisted that it come to fruition.

Foreword

ONE APPROACH to characterizing this remarkable biography of an influential twentieth-century Mennonite church leader is to frame it as an account of two different sermons given at the same church in Elkhart, Indiana—one delivered in 1925 and the other in 1976. In the first sermon, the newly commissioned Mennonite missionary Joseph D. Graber expressed a colonialist view of mission that assumed the superior perspective of Western Christians to the non-Christian people they were seeking to convert. In the second sermon, the retired mission leader Joe D. Graber asserted instead a postcolonial understanding of mission that adapted to the work of God already unfolding in communities engaged by missionaries. If the first sermon emphasized the conversion of unbelievers, the second sermon stressed the conversion of mission workers. This book shows us how Graber made it from the first sermon to the second during a half-century of adventurous mission and innovative leadership.

R. Bruce Yoder, a consequential Mennonite mission leader himself, tells the story of Graber's lifelong transformation toward collaboration and partnership in mission, including the renunciation of colonizing and ethnocentric habits of thinking and practice. This story of Graber's personal growth and development as a Christian disciple and spiritual leader both instructs and inspires. At the same time, Yoder also contextualizes Graber's unfolding life within the context of Anabaptist communities and institutions that shaped him and which were themselves undergoing dramatic change. From Graber's studies in Mennonite educational institutions such as Hesston College and Goshen College to his connections with regional Mennonite conferences such as the Western District Amish Mennonite Conference and the Franconia Mennonite Conference to his leadership roles in church agencies such as Mennonite Central Committee and the Mennonite Board of Missions and Charities, Graber's life and leadership embodied the limits and possibilities of twentieth-century Mennonite institutions. Yoder also shows how during Graber's career such institutions responded to global events like the Great Depression, World War II, and the Cold War, which constrained the resources and revised the implementation of Anabaptist mission programs.

The relationship between Graber's personal growth and institutional change is enlivened in Yoder's telling by Graber's leadership communication skills—the sermons, pamphlets, editorials, and correspondence by which he sought to influence the direction of change in the church networks he served as a bishop, an administrator, and an advocate. Navigating hostility to mission programs from traditional Mennonite leaders while addressing anxiety about the influence of modernism from mission supporters, Graber displayed a rhetorical savvy rooted in careful listening and well-crafted arguments, along with public speaking and preaching skills honed during a homiletics course at Princeton Seminary.

And yet what stands out most in this story of mission leadership and social change is the deep and humble curiosity that Graber displayed throughout his life: curiosity about the audiences to whom he was speaking or writing, curiosity about the cultures and communities served by the mission programs he administered, curiosity about emerging new paradigms for postcolonial mission, curiosity about unacknowledged prejudice and privilege that posed obstacles to authentic mission, curiosity about the weather and the natural world to which it belonged, curiosity about the lives of his friends and family members.

Graber's posture of curiosity about the contexts in which the mission of the church unfolded, along with a willingness to adapt to changing contexts, altered his own worldview, as exemplified in the dramatic contrast between the two sermons delivered at Prairie Street Mennonite Church bookending his career as a church leader. But Graber's humility and curiosity, expressed through persuasive public communication, also influenced the character of Mennonite mission programs and strengthened the flourishing of a global Anabaptist community beyond the grip of Western colonialism and less constrained by Protestant conflicts between modernism and fundamentalism. May the publication of this biography during the five-hundredth anniversary year of the Anabaptist movement arouse new curiosity about the possibilities for Anabaptist mission in the twenty-first century, informed by the paths to mission discovered in the twentieth century by visionaries like Joseph D. Graber.

—Gerald J. Mast
Series Editor, Studies in Anabaptist and Mennonite History

Introduction

The Story of a Mission Visionary

ON SUNDAY morning, April 4, 1976, the service at Prairie Street Mennonite Church in Elkhart, Indiana, focused on the congregation's mission involvement in its local community.[1] Unsurprisingly to the members, the preacher that morning was Joseph Daniel Graber, Joe or J. D. for short. Joe was a veteran missionary, a former executive secretary of the Mennonite Board of Missions and Charities (MBMC), and a longtime member and leader at Prairie Street.

The congregation had an extensive and illustrious history of innovative leadership in the Mennonite Church. Its founding in 1871 was linked to the emergence of the Mennonite Publishing Company, and the Mennonite Evangelizing Committee, the earliest precursor of MBMC, was formed there in 1882.[2] Prairie Street members organized the Mennonite Church's first Sunday evening Young People's Meetings, youth gatherings that became common in Mennonite congregations in subsequent decades, as well as the Elkhart Institute, which became Goshen College in 1903.[3] The congregation was instrumental in choosing the Mennonite Church's first foreign missionaries in 1899.[4]

If those gathered for the April 4 service were expecting Joe to laud their church's history of faithful witness, however, they were mistaken. His sermon was instead a challenge to the congregation. As he encouraged those gathered that morning to participate in outreach, he urged them to change the way they understood their place in God's mission in the world. "We are so ethnocentric," he lamented, challenging them to widen their horizons.[5] Despite nearly a century of mission activity at the time of Joe's sermon, the Mennonite Church still was primarily made up of white people of European descent. Joe argued that God was already at work among the peoples whom the congregation had often thought of as the objects of missionary outreach: the poor, the oppressed, the homeless, the lost, the discouraged, those considered "uncivilized," and people of color in places like India, where Joe had started his missionary career. Jesus would be more at home among them than at Prairie Street, which existed in a society of conspicuous consumption and corruption, Joe suggested.

Thus, Joe preached, God's mercy for the people gathered that Sunday morning for worship was perhaps more notable than God's love for those traditionally on the receiving end of missionary intervention. Indeed, he said, to argue that Jesus loved other peoples as much as he did the faithful at Prairie Street was to say it backward. "We should say that we are glad that Jesus loves the people who are underprivileged and lost, and who are in great need, and that even in his great mercy Jesus loves and cares for us," he declared, however undeserving of that mercy the relatively affluent and monocultural North American middle-class Mennonites might be.[6] Humility should be the congregation's posture as it sought to reach out to the world in mission, he argued, voicing a perspective that grew out of gratitude for God's mercy.

In his half century as a church leader, Joe had always expressed the view that missionary engagement in the world was an important responsibility of a faithful church. Throughout his career, he argued that the Mennonite faith had something of value to offer the world and that establishing new Mennonite churches rooted in the Anabaptist heritage was a faithful and positive contribution in the world, in North America and around the globe. The world needed the Christian gospel, and missionaries played a significant role in communicating the message.

Yet his 1976 sermon was different than the missionary day sermon he had delivered at Prairie Street fifty-one years earlier, in 1925, shortly before he and Minnie (Swartzendruber) Graber, his wife and colleague, departed for their first term of missionary service in India.[7] In that sermon, entitled "Why I Am a Christian," Joe had identified those among whom missionaries worked as heathen and described them as living in ignorance and torturing their bodies to find peace of soul. It was the duty of the missionary, indeed of all Christians, to provide the message that would remedy their plight. This earlier sermon was subsequently published in the Mennonite Church's weekly *Gospel Herald* and reproduced as a tract by MBMC.[8]

The 1976 sermon was markedly less pejorative in tone, arguing that God was already at work among those whom missionaries sought to serve and warning against ethnocentric attitudes. God was at work "wherever injustice is trying to be mitigated, wherever the hungry are being fed, wherever there is a healing program, wherever there is something that is good that is going on."[9] It was up to the missionary to discern what God was doing, identify with it, and reveal the saving Christ "by word and by deed, in lifestyle and in character, by witness and by service."[10]

Clearly, more than a half century of missionary experience and reflection had changed Joe and his vision of what constituted faithful missionary witness. The question of why and how such a change came about is answered by the story of his life and ministry.

This biography tells the story of Joe's work, including the development of his vision for the church's engagement in the world and the impact his leadership had on the Mennonite Church. Joe and Minnie served as missionaries in India from 1925 until 1942, after which Joe served in executive leadership at MBMC from 1944 until 1967. He was the first Mennonite mission executive to have extensive overseas experience. As a firsthand observer of the Indian independence movement that Mohandas K. Gandhi helped lead, he understood better than most Western missionaries the need for new, postcolonial attitudes and approaches. During his tenure at MBMC, Joe expanded the Mennonite Church's work in regions around the world. In many of those places, churches took root that continue to shape the global Anabaptist/Mennonite movement in the twenty-first century.

Joe also developed a vision of mission renewal in North America, of churches engaging their local communities in mission outreach. A gifted communicator, he spoke widely at gatherings and in churches across North America. His challenge to every congregation to conceive of itself as a mission outpost resulted in many new Mennonite Church congregations.

Perhaps the most significant facet of Joe's vision was his desire to see Mennonites be transformed from a largely mono-ethnic people of European descent to a movement spread across the globe including people of diverse ethnicities and cultures. He drew on the work of anthropologists, linguists, and missiologists to call on North American Mennonites to overcome their ethnocentrism and appreciate all cultures as fertile ground for the emergence of authentic expressions of the faith. Joe encouraged missionaries to balance the religious assumptions of their sending church with those of the people and cultures among whom they ministered. He was ahead of his time in recognizing the need for what might be described as missiological and theological contextualization.

In North America, Joe sought to make space for ethnic minorities and their faith assumptions in a Mennonite Church still overwhelmingly beholden to a Swiss-German ethnic identity and related religious assumptions. With growing intensity during the middle decades of the twentieth century, he pushed the Mennonite Church to make room in its thought and practice for groups that did not emerge from a European Mennonite heritage. Joe was eager for the church to be enriched by their presence. The ensemble of identities now present in the twenty-first-century Anabaptist/Mennonite movement is the result of the work of leaders of many different ethnic, cultural, and linguistic backgrounds. This reality would no doubt cause Joe to rejoice.

As the principal architect and advocate of MBMC's post–World War II expansion, Joe widened the geographical, ethnic, and cultural breadth of his church and of the global Anabaptist movement to which it belonged. In so doing he helped a church shaped by a sectarian sense of separation to increase its engagement in the world via the mission paradigm.

The modern mission movement and the Mennonite Church

North American Mennonites like Joe were relative latecomers to the modern missionary movement. That movement emerged from the era of medieval European Christendom, which (in contrast to the theology that Mennonites would embrace) assumed a unity of church and state.[11] In the subsequent centuries, the Christian faith combined with imperial or national interests to promote ecclesiastical and colonial expansion. By the end of the fifteenth century, the Christian kingdoms of the Iberian Peninsula had conquered the last regions held by Muslims and turned their attention to conquest in Africa, the Americas, and Asia. To gain state sponsorship to evangelize these "new" lands, Roman Catholic popes issued papal bulls that legitimized colonial expansion and gave Portugal and Spain control over church affairs in conquered territories. Missionary efforts allied with European conquest, so that the goal of Christian expansion became part of the justification for the subjugation of peoples, resources, and lands.

To be sure, missionaries and the church sometimes pushed back against the colonial systems and their mentalities. Sixteenth-century missionaries in the Americas like Antonio de Montesinos and Bartolomé des Las Casas condemned colonists for brutalizing and enslaving the indigenous peoples and ignoring their missionary obligations.[12] In 1622, the papacy created the *Congregatio de Propaganda Fide* to regain control of the church's mission initiatives and circumvent state control of the clergy. It sought to develop indigenous clergy that would be accountable to Rome instead of to Spain and Portugal. Colonial authorities and their allies resisted such efforts, and significant development of indigenous church leadership would only happen much later. Given the seeming dominance of colonial structures and attitudes during the age of European global expansion, it is remarkable that pockets of Christian faithful emerged among indigenous peoples around the world.

Protestant mission activity gained strength later than its Roman Catholic counterpart. Seventeenth-century Protestants sent chaplains with explorers, traders, and soldiers who spread out across the globe. Often sponsored by the state or a trading company, chaplains were responsible for the spiritual care of the Europeans, and they sometimes ministered to indigenous peoples as well. Pietists, especially the Moravians, provided many of the early Protestant missionaries sent from Europe. Like their Roman Catholic counterparts, they encountered opposition from European colonists who were settling on indigenous lands, often enslaving or pushing out native peoples. Eventually Protestants developed a mission strategy that relied more on the work and support of lay persons than on state-sponsored clergy. The rise of mercantile capitalism increased disposable income for some church members who then pooled their wealth to form voluntary missionary societies that sponsored work in the colonies of European powers. Such societies became especially prominent in the United States.[13] Nineteenth-century advances in global transportation and communication further encouraged the expansion of the Protestant mission movement. That century was the heyday of the modern mission movement and saw the first stirrings of mission work among North American Mennonites.

By the early twentieth century, though, cracks had appeared in the framework of Christendom and colonialism alike. The subsequent world wars of the twentieth century gave the lie to the notion of Western superiority. Missionaries were hardly exempt from paternalistic attitudes and assumptions about Western superiority. As they carried the gospel message to the far corners of the globe, they sometimes collaborated in educational, social, and commercial efforts that allied them with colonial governments. Even so, their mission work set in motion a process that would ultimately leave religious agency in the hands of indigenous Christians. True to their Reformation roots, Protestant missionaries translated the Bible into vernacular languages, work that depended on collaboration with native speakers.[14] The reliance on local language speakers and the new vernacular translations meant that indigenous religious assumptions were embodied in the burgeoning Christian communities. Indigenous evangelists who knew local cultures and languages were more effective than their Western counterparts, reinforcing local expressions of the faith. The emergence of independent nations from what had been European colonies was coupled with a similar emancipation of the newer Christian communities from Western norms and structures.

The crumbling of Western colonial rule and the increasing weight of the Christian movement in other parts of the world changed core assumptions about Christianity. Western missionaries had benefited from colonial structures for access to land and the peoples whom they sought to evangelize. But their schools and promotion of Western values had also planted the seeds of nationalist movements. Many nationalist leaders had studied in mission schools, where they gained knowledge, skills, and ethical frameworks necessary to resist colonial systems. As newly independent nations took over mission institutions like schools and hospitals and restricted Western missionary access to their populations, nationalists critiqued European Christendom and rejected mission activity for its complicity with colonialism and its imperialistic and racist assumptions. Critics of missionaries charged them with "cultural imperialism" and colonizing the "consciousness" of the peoples among whom they worked.[15]

Far from being delegitimized, however, Christianity exploded in strength during the second half of the twentieth century in many of the lands that European powers had colonized. Even in places like China, where the communist state sought to suppress the movement, communities of Christian faith persisted. By the end of the century, while European Christendom had faltered, the Christian movement overall had simply evolved, adding new forms of the faith and shifting demographically from the North Atlantic to the former missionary lands of the Global South.

Such changes have made the framework of "world Christianity" a helpful way for scholars and other observers to understand the phenomenon of the world Christian movement. Today one cannot conceive of Christianity, a global religion with diverse expressions, as uniquely Western or even as centered in the West. At the beginning of the twentieth century, approximately three-quarters of the Christians in the world were in Europe and North America.[16] By the end of the century, nearly two-thirds of the faithful resided across the Global South where new forms of the faith had emerged.

The discourse that describes the relatively new phenomenon of world Christianity provides a helpful framework for the story of Joe and Mennonite mission activity. It emphasizes the multicultural, polyvocal, and complex character of a faith with multiple centers of influence, power, and authority.[17] It puts the focus on indigenous responses—the way local communities around the world have appropriated and transformed the faith—and on the global interconnections that made possible, and continue to nurture, a movement in which a diversity of religious expressions and the common identity of a world religion are interdependent parts. Without the missionary vision of a global Christian community, the gospel would not have been introduced to localities around the world. Without the contextualization of the faith and identification with it by people in those localities, creating new expressions of the faith, Christianity would not exist as a world religion.

Joe Graber's lifetime of mission activity with the Mennonite Church spanned the period when the Christian movement, and the Anabaptist stream within it, underwent changes that ultimately led to the world Christianity framework of today. His 1925 sermon at Prairie Street Mennonite echoed the assumptions of a missionary who was Eurocentric by default. By 1976, however, his call for humility reflected a thoroughly global, postcolonial understanding of mission work.

The Mennonite Church, the largest of several Mennonite/Anabaptist groups in North America, lacked a strong missionary tradition when Joe began his missionary career. However, a mission awakening across the church had begun a few decades earlier, in the late nineteenth century, and Joe's career coincided with an acceleration of that trend in the middle decades of the twentieth century.

Mennonites looked to the sixteenth-century Anabaptists as the genesis of their church. Anabaptism was a dynamic movement that quickly grew and spread across Europe from its diverse beginnings in the 1520s.[18] With time, though, the missionary zeal of the new movement lessened.[19] Persecution sapped the energy of some groups, and they withdrew into tight-knit communities suspicious of the world.[20] Others found themselves abandoning their earlier missionary impulse in exchange for religious toleration.

That trend away from mission work continued when European Mennonite immigrants to North America arrived in earnest by the early eighteenth century as part of European colonization efforts. They left persecution behind and found a measure of prosperity in their new home.[21] They understood Christian faithfulness primarily as adhering to their religious community's discipline and practices; thus, transmitting the faith became mostly a matter of nurturing the young people of their own Mennonite congregations rather than making disciples of others.[22] Humility, the opposite of worldliness, became a mark of Mennonite piety and identity that encouraged separation from the world.[23] The confident nature of the prevailing Protestant mission impulse seemed to contradict the core standard of Mennonite humility, which encouraged a posture of being the "quiet in the land."[24]

During the heyday of the modern mission movement of the mid-nineteenth century, however, some North American Mennonites began to balance their focus on humility and separation from the world with an emerging missionary vision. A newly formed conference in Pennsylvania started sending financial assistance to their counterparts in Europe to support Dutch Mennonite mission work.[25] This more progressive group (in the sense of embracing trends from contemporaneous Protestant churches) became part of a movement that founded the General Conference Mennonite Church, which was a separate denominational structure from the Mennonite Church until 2002, when they merged to create two national denominations (Mennonite Church USA and Mennonite Church Canada).

Toward the end of the nineteenth century, the Mennonite and Amish Mennonite conferences that would combine to form the twentieth-century Mennonite Church also started to catch the missionary vision. Such interest was evident in the ministry of John S. Coffman, whose itinerant preaching across the church during the last two decades of the nineteenth century nurtured revival, inspired young people, and helped the church start to conceive of evangelistic meetings as faithful expressions of the church's work.[26] In 1882 some mission advocates established the Mennonite Evangelizing Committee to assist congregations that found themselves geographically isolated from the church, while others formed the Benevolent Organization of Mennonites in 1894 to establish home and foreign mission work.[27] The Evangelization Committee and the Benevolent Organization reconstituted as the Evangelizing and Benevolent Board in 1896, precursor to the Mennonite Board of Missions and Charities, which was created in 1906.[28]

The growing energy for mission engagement reached a significant milestone at century's end with the Mennonite Church's first foray into foreign mission activity. George Lambert, who later became a member of Prairie Street Mennonite Church for a time, made a round-the-world trip from August 1894 to July 1895 that included travel to India.[29] Upon his return he advocated for establishing missionary work in India, where he eventually returned to distribute aid donated by

Mennonites during the famine of 1896–97.[30] After the second trip he graphically described the suffering of the Indian people and continued to encourage starting mission initiatives, particularly among orphans.[31] The tragedy of the Indian famine and Mennonites' generous response to it added to their awareness of and interest in missionary intervention in the world. The first Mennonite Church missionaries to foreign lands embarked for India in February 1899.[32] Twenty-six years later Joe and Minnie became part of this burgeoning mission activity when they sailed to India to start their missionary careers.

The move toward missionary engagement with the world in which Joe and Minnie participated entailed a significant change from the historic posture of Mennonites. Humility and separation from worldliness had long been the preferred Mennonite ways to embody faithfulness vis-à-vis a fallen world that needed redemption, but that also represented a threat to the Mennonite faith community. While mission-minded Mennonites presumed a similar understanding of the world as sinful and needing redemption, they proposed a different relationship to it. They assumed they had something valuable to offer the world and a faith-motivated imperative to do so.[33] One might characterize the older Mennonite model of faithfulness as protective in nature and the newer model as oriented toward engagement. Engagement Mennonites moved into the world with the expectation that they could be agents calling a fallen world to faithfulness. Protective Mennonites, on the other hand, saw the world as something to protect the faith community from; they gave greater weight to the dangers of worldliness and relied more on maintaining separation. Joe and Minnie were engagement Mennonites who were comfortable with the Mennonite Church's increasing encounter with the world through Christian missionary activity.

A growing missionary imperative was part of a larger shift among North American Mennonites toward the selective embrace of larger Protestant trends. Earlier Mennonite immigrants from Europe and succeeding generations had maintained their faith identity through strong attachments to local religious communities. Members' identities were reinforced by their shared religious traditions, use of a German dialect, family connections, and sectarian sense of distinctiveness. In the absence of the stark persecution that had hounded them in Europe, though, it was relatively easy for Mennonites who were so inclined to appropriate values from the wider North American society, including a tendency toward forward-looking optimism. As many Mennonites progressively shed their identity as immigrant communities and integrated into North American society, their traditional German dialect started to give way to the English that was necessary to interact with neighbors and the wider community. Mennonite publishing initiatives like John Funk's periodical *Herald of Truth* and the development of Sunday school materials allowed church leaders to communicate their ideas and values well beyond local congregations.

The establishment of a central "General Conference" with wide North American participation increased the institutional nature of the Mennonite Church and was indicative of the move toward formal organizational structures (The Mennonite Church's "General Conference" should not to be confused with the similarly named General Conference Mennonite Church, a separate Mennonite denomination). Mennonites established homes for the aged and for disadvantaged children and created mission boards to facilitate domestic and international mission activity. The emergence of Mennonite-affiliated schools provided trained leaders for these new, more modern forms of church work.

With a publishing house, mission board, centralized conference structure, and other emergent institutions, the Mennonite Church was, in measure, embracing engagement over protection. While still theologically and culturally distinct in many respects, it was coming to resemble other North American Protestant denominations in important ways.

Over the middle decades of the twentieth century this new way of being the church lent momentum to Joe and his mission-minded colleagues. The Mennonite Church's weekly periodical *Gospel Herald* provided a medium for rallying readers around mission programs, which it featured prominently from its first issue in 1908. Between 1916 and 1947 the *Herald* contained a monthly sixteen-page mission supplement before, starting in 1948, providing six pages of mission news and promotion with each weekly issue.[34] With wide circulation and readership among the faithful, the *Herald* was an indispensable tool to inform, motivate, and build common ownership of the mission task.

The resulting consolidation of resources and energy in MBMC's institutional structure during Joe's tenure made domestic and international expansion possible on a scale that local congregations or regional conferences could not have implemented on their own. The time was ripe for a new missionary vision and the marshalling of energy and resources to propagate, sustain, and embody it. More than anyone else, Joe provided that vision.

About Joe—and Mennonite mission

This biography seeks to illuminate the importance of Joseph Daniel Graber for the broader Mennonite/Anabaptist church. An influential Mennonite leader during the middle decades of the twentieth century, Joe was both a product of his times and a visionary who helped shape the direction of Mennonite identity and engagement with the world. He inspired a generation of mission practitioners and, as the first full-time executive secretary of MBMC, expanded the boundaries of the Mennonite Church.

A biography is a way to introduce Joe and his vision to contemporary readers, present an informative account of mid-twentieth-century Mennonite mission work, and provide essential historical context for the emergence of twenty-first-century North American Mennonite/Anabaptist mission identity. A biography is useful for charting an individual life and describing its religious, social, and cultural contexts, identifying meaning and significance in the relationship and interaction between the two.[35] History through the lens of an individual can become more human, vivid, and accessible than might otherwise be the case if one prioritizes institutions, ideas, or nation-states.

Joe's vision, as it developed, reflected the influence of several factors: his upbringing, experience as a missionary in India, relationships within the larger Protestant mission movement, work as MBMC executive secretary, encounters with the processes of decolonization, and dialogue with the broader Mennonite/Anabaptist community. Joe's leadership stimulated conversation and practice that sought to meld Mennonite priorities with contemporary mission theory and practice during a period when North American Mennonites were formulating anew what it meant to be Mennonite and Anabaptist. This also happened to be a period of decolonization throughout the Global South.

Seeking to chart a path of faithful mission activity in a changing world, Joe articulated his vision in the church press and through speaking and teaching assignments.

Joe's influence on the Mennonite/Anabaptist movement was broad and enduring. As a mission executive, Joe spoke for MBMC, established policy, made decisions about how to employ institutional resources, and maintained active collaboration with leaders of other Mennonite mission agencies and Mennonite Central Committee (MCC). His many roles gave him a platform to articulate his vision and the means to advance it. In collaboration with other leaders and agencies, Joe oversaw a significant increase in MBMC's international footprint during the period of decolonization. Domestically, his promotion of the idea of each church as a source of mission work (encapsulated in the slogan "a mission outpost for every congregation") was instrumental in the emergence of new congregations in the years after World War II. The domestic and international legacy of Joe and his ministry is significant for understanding the evolving topography of Mennonites in North America and the emergence of the global Mennonite/Anabaptist movement in the twenty-first century.

Joe's contributions to the Mennonite Church were significant, but naturally they were only one piece of a much larger narrative of increased Mennonite engagement in the world during the middle decades of the twentieth century. While Joe was arguably the most influential mission leader across the Mennonite/Anabaptist movement in North America during that period, he was one of many leaders and practitioners who advanced the mission cause and the expansion of the global Anabaptist movement. The General Conference Mennonite Church and other North American Mennonite/Anabaptist denominations also increased their mission activities and are important parts of the larger story. Mennonite Central Committee expanded its footprint in the post–World War II decades as well. While Joe collaborated widely with other Mennonite agencies, he worked primarily within the program of the Mennonite Church, the denomination to which he belonged, and its mission agency, Mennonite Board of Missions and Charities.

Vocationally Joe was a missionary, a mission agency administrator, and a mission visionary, so this book is about mission. While Joe always worked within a church context, the word *mission* has different meanings that are not necessarily religious in nature.[36] For example, institutions such as corporations, nonprofits, government agencies, and congregations may adopt mission statements that identify their purpose. Among Christians, *mission* often also refers to initiatives that reach beyond themselves and the boundaries of their Christian communities to minister to and with persons or groups that are different in some way from themselves. Confusion easily arises when Christian churches, institutions, or individuals reference their "mission" without clarifying which of these two options they mean. A church might have a mission statement that focuses both on ministry that is oriented inward to reinforce its life and identity *and* on ministry that is oriented outward and reaches beyond its own boundaries. The second of those orientations was Joe's life work.

When Joe used the word *mission*, he typically used it to describe ministry oriented beyond the boundaries of the church. He meant ministry in, for, and with the world outside of North American Mennonite faith communities. For instance, he encouraged the church to dedicate at least half of its resources to mission initiatives and to limit the use of its resources for institutions and programs such as schools and congregational activities that were meant primarily to serve Mennonites. Following Joe's usage, in this book the word *mission* refers to that outwardly focused ministry of the church in international and domestic spheres.

Chronologically, the story begins with Joe's early years growing up in an Amish Mennonite family and church in Iowa, from which he emerged with a commitment to the faith and to mission activity. A high school and undergraduate education at church institutions exposed Joe and Minnie to the wider Mennonite community and led to two terms of missionary service in India, where they faced new challenges of culture, colonialism, leadership, and mission theory and practice. Called to be the first remunerated executive secretary of the Mennonite Board of Missions and Charities in 1944, Joe became the most important mission leader in the Mennonite Church for the next twenty-seven years. He oversaw the expansion of his church's international mission reach, the search for postcolonial mission approaches, the campaign to introduce new Mennonite congregations in communities throughout North America, and the appropriation of partnership as a mission paradigm.

My hope is that this story of Joe's life and work will increase the reader's understanding of Mennonite engagement with the world during the twentieth century, Joe's legacy as a missionary and mission leader in the Mennonite Church, and the dynamics of an expanding worldwide Anabaptist movement at the start of the postcolonial era. Involvement in mission work provided a way for Mennonites with a seclusionist predisposition to begin moving into the world without forsaking their faith values. Joe's leadership during that time nurtured commitments that reverberate in the church's mission activities and evolving mission identity to this day. His advocacy for creating new churches rooted in diverse contexts around the world planted seeds of faith communities within ethnic traditions and cultures that were new to the Anabaptist movement, raising questions about religious identity in the movement that have only become more important over time.

Joe's life thus can help us better understand the Mennonite Church in North America and the emergence of the global Anabaptist movement to which all Mennonites now belong. As a member of a denomination that is a twenty-first-century successor to the Mennonite Church and as someone whose vocational roles span the areas of mission practitioner, theorist, and historian, I hope this biography increases, in at least some measure, the awareness and significance of Joe and his vision.

ONE

From Iowa to the World

A Mennonite Education and a Call to Mission

AS YOUNGSTERS, Joe and his older brother Chris developed their own language, which they called "Grabish." The hours they spent working together on the family farm near Noble, Iowa, provided time for such inventiveness.[1] Structurally their language was simple; they used English but pronounced the words backwards. This was enough to keep their conversations private and spark the interest of those within hearing distance. The brothers used Grabish to converse during the buggy ride of four and a half miles to church, to entertain themselves, and to provoke their sisters, who could not understand it. The Graber family's telephone was on a "party line," as was common at the time; inquisitive neighbors could listen in and keep up on the news of the families who shared the line. By speaking their own language, the brothers frustrated neighbors' attempts to follow their conversations when one called home to speak with the other.[2] Their father, Daniel Graber, initially suspected that his sons were simply speaking nonsensically, and so he devised a test. He had one son sit on a chair and translate a passage from a book into the private language, while the other, some distance away, translated it back into normal English.

Situated so that he could see the passage, Daniel found that the translation was correct and that his boys were in fact communicating with each other.

The household of Daniel and Fanny (Conrad) Graber was marked by linguistic ability. Daniel's parents had come from the Alsace region of France, so Joe grew up speaking an Alsatian dialect of German at home.[3] Fanny also spoke French, having immigrated to North America from the French-speaking part of Switzerland. Daniel, as minister of the Sugar Creek Amish Mennonite congregation, located in Henry County near Wayland, Iowa, might preach in German or English. But he always prayed in German, even after English became the primary language of church services during World War I.

With the national mobilization for war among all strata of society, popular hostility against pacifist (and overwhelmingly ethnic German) Mennonites, who resisted participating in the war and in some cases voiced support for the German side, was strong. Some in the Wayland community accused the Sugar Creek congregation of being pro-German because of its stand against the war. They defaced the church building with yellow paint and boycotted the businesses of church members.[4] There was pressure for German-speakers to conduct their affairs in English and play down their German background so as not to be associated with the enemy. By that time, though, Joe had a solid base in German. While attending high school at Hesston Academy in Kansas in 1921, he reported to his father that his German teacher had charged him with leading the class through its review of the parts of speech.[5]

Joe's linguistic abilities were only part of the heritage from his early years that would help prepare him for a vocation of service to the church and its mission activity. In their home his parents provided a nurturing space that upheld and encouraged a commitment to Christian service. The Grabers also valued education, and thanks to their church's growing interest in establishing educational institutions that would instill Mennonite values, Joe was able to take college courses at Hesston.

Hesston was where Joe met his life partner, Minnie Swartzentruber, and developed skills that would serve him as a mission practitioner and theorist. Hesston, and to a lesser extent Goshen College (which he later attended), offered him exposure to and involvement with the larger Mennonite Church. Joe became familiar with issues such as the doctrinal debate between fundamentalists and modernists, the movement to establish norms to protect the church from worldliness, and the growing Mennonite impulse to engage the world through mission initiatives. The need for teachers at Hesston and Goshen colleges and for missionaries in the India field would provide concrete options within developing institutional structures, helping Joe and Minnie channel their vocational discernment as they made decisions about their future.

The Graber family in church and mission

Joe was the second-generation descendent of Amish Mennonite families who had immigrated from the Alsace region of France. The Graber name appears to have originated in Switzerland, from which several families immigrated to Alsace.[6] Christian Graber arrived in Washington County, Iowa, in 1856. The first Euro-American settlers there had arrived some two decades earlier to land that had been the home of the Ioway, Otoe, Sauk, Meskwaki, and Sioux peoples.[7] Mennonite settlers typically established farms. Those arriving directly from Europe were often fleeing the compulsory military service to which their sons would have been subjected.

Christian's son Daniel, Joe's father, was born two years after the family arrived.[8] Daniel married Fanny Conrad in 1891.[9] Fanny's parents were from France, but she was born in Switzerland and held Swiss citizenship before the family immigrated to Wayne County, Ohio, in 1886 when Fanny was fourteen years old. Daniel and Fanny settled on the Graber family homestead, where Daniel had grown up and where Joe would spend his childhood.

Joe grew up in a home and church that were becoming increasingly invested in mission initiatives. Participation in Sugar Creek Mennonite Church, where Daniel had been active since his youth, was a significant part of the family's identity and life. Amish Mennonite settlers who arrived in the 1840s and 1850s established the congregation alongside the Methodist, United Brethren, and Baptist churches in the area.[10] The Amish were a branch of the Mennonites that had taken a more rigid position with respect to discipline and the maintenance of certain worship, dress, and polity traditions. Among those who immigrated to

North America, two streams emerged: the Old Order Amish and the more progressive Amish Mennonites, who more readily adapted their practices over time.

The Grabers and the Sugar Creek congregation were part of this more progressive group, which eventually became part of the Mennonite Church. The Amish Mennonites in the area around Wayland instituted regular church services in homes in the mid-1850s and in 1871 built their first church building on a plot outside of town. Involvement in the Protestant Sunday school movement was one of the adaptations happening among the Amish Mennonites by the 1890s, and Daniel was an early leader, having been ordained preacher in 1893.[11] He and the other Sugar Creek leaders reported an average attendance of 140 participants in Sunday school programs in 1894. Sunday school offering collections during that period supported mission causes such as responding to the massacres of Armenian Christians and famines in India.[12] Sugar Creek would later provide financial support for Joe and Minnie's ministry in India, holding its first missionary day when they left for India in 1925.[13]

Daniel's mission work beyond Sugar Creek gave Joe additional exposure to his future vocation. Daniel was on the board of the Mennonite Gospel Mission in Kansas City. Started in 1905, it was one of the early Mennonite urban mission initiatives, and the workers there ministered in a variety of ways: street evangelism, prisoner visitation, neighborhood Sunday schools, and medical assistance.[14] Child welfare became a primary concern, and the mission established a children's home in 1917. The basement of the Graber house became a storage depot for two or three wagonloads of canned goods and vegetables that supporters in the area donated for the Kansas City mission and home each year.[15] Daniel also served as secretary of the Western District Amish Mennonite Conference and was among the first evangelists appointed by the conference. Such responsibilities took him away from home for extended periods when Fanny and the children did much of the farming, a labor-intensive, horse-powered activity at the time. The family was accustomed to Daniel's sharing about his various ministry experiences, and Christian service was a strong family value. Visitors were frequent at the Graber household, and visiting missionaries represented an ideal to follow.

Joe later remembered that there had never been a time when he did not consider himself a Christian.[16] At thirteen he made a public confession of faith, became a member of the church, and was soon leading singing and teaching Sunday school.[17] The Graber household participated fully in the Sugar Creek congregation, and family prayer and hymn singing were routine. The family ate meals together three times a day with supper lasting an hour or more as Daniel shared news about extended family, the local community, and the world. Before meals everyone except Chris, Joe's brother, prayed in turn, in German, and then Chris prayed after the meal.[18]

Daniel was a lover of music, which he taught in the church and to his children.[19] Music accompanied his work on the farm. Joe liked to milk the cows, keeping rhythm with a song. He sang "Nearer, My God, to Thee" if he was tired, and "We're Marching to Zion" if he wanted to get done in a hurry. Music would always be an important part of his life.

The Daniel and Fanny Graber household provided spiritual grounding that was conducive to the development of Christian vocation. Both Joe and his brother Chris became ordained ministers in the Mennonite Church and served in Mennonite institutions. Sisters Esther, Lena, and Verna all served in Christian mission and service agencies.

Hesston

Daniel and Fanny Graber had not gone to high school, but they valued formal education and sent Joe and his siblings to school. In his youth Daniel had wanted to attend school but was not able to do so.[20] As an adult he read widely, often into the late hours of the night.[21] Among other material, he read the books his children brought home from school. Although he lacked formal education, Daniel sat on the board of a local bank, was a businessman, and worked with the poor and widows in the community.[22] He was active in the local community and understood the importance of education. Daniel and Fanny sent their children to high school during a period when many in the Mennonite community questioned the value of doing so. Chris, Joe, and Verna attended Hesston Academy or College in Hesston, Kansas, and Lena did her high school education at Goshen College Academy in Goshen, Indiana.

Joe demonstrated a desire for learning from an early date. During routine work on the farm, he would find ways to exercise his mind.[23] He worked at memorization and sometimes carried a book to read when there was a lull, such as when the horses in the fields needed a rest.[24] Joe completed his first year of high school at Wayland while helping his father with the farm work and then finished at the newly established Hesston Academy, studying there from 1919 to 1922.[25] The Hesston experience would be formative for Joe's evolving sense of vocation and eventual mission commitments.

Mennonite Church leaders established the Hesston Academy and Bible School (later Hesston College and Bible School) in 1909. By then they had been discussing the need for a Mennonite school west of the Mississippi River for over a decade.[26] The church's Goshen College provided educational opportunities for those further east but was far from the Mennonite settlements west of the Mississippi River. The General Conference Mennonites had founded Bethel College in Newton, Kansas, in 1887, but significant cultural and theological differences existed between that denomination and the groups that were forming the Mennonite Church. Many from the General Conference

Iowa students and fans at Hesston Institute. Joe is in the first row, seated, on the far right. MCUSA ARCHIVES

group had emigrated from Ukraine, where they had governed their own settlements. This governance required active involvement in local civic institutions. As such they were less separatist than their Mennonite Church counterparts and more comfortable with involvement in local political structures. The General Conference Mennonites also were ecumenically minded and had a congregationalist polity. The Mennonite Church was more distrustful of worldly involvements and over time had invested a good deal of authority in district conferences. Its leaders felt the need for an educational institution other than Bethel that would provide training more in accordance with their denomination's deeply held faith convictions and ecclesial understandings.

In March 1909, when Joe was eight years old, Daniel Graber received a letter from Tillman M. Erb, a primary leader in the establishment of the new Hesston school, informing him that building would start on the campus the following week.[27] While this was good news it also presented a challenge, since J. D. Charles was leaving his position as superintendent of the Kansas City mission to take on a teaching role at Hesston. Tillman and Daniel were members of the Kansas City mission board, and they would have to adjust the date of their board meeting to accommodate the change to a new superintendent. Six months later, in September, the Hesston Academy and Bible School opened. It offered several courses of study: teachers' training, a secondary school track, Bible school, and eventually a college-level program.

Hesston provided families like the Grabers a place to educate their young people in a context that sought to strengthen their identification with the Mennonite faith. As more Mennonites engaged the world in mission initiatives and felt the encroaching influences of American society, their young people sought educational opportunities, and new church institutions needed trained leaders and staff. At the same time, some church leaders became especially concerned with protecting the faithful from harmful worldly influences and reinforcing simplicity and modesty. When Tillman Erb asked for the Missouri-Iowa district conference's endorsement for the new school, the conference agreed conditionally, resolving, "If the school will be kept free from popular games, instrumental music, worldly minded teachers and other influences which stand in the way of spiritual progress, it shall have our sympathy, our support and our prayers."[28]

The wider ecclesial context of American Protestantism helped to shape changes in Mennonite identity and, in turn, influenced the course of Mennonite educational institutions like Hesston Academy. Particularly influential was the teaching of the Holiness movement that the inner spiritual life would show itself in outer simplicity. Adapting that perspective to Mennonite mores, some church leaders taught against neckties as symbols of worldliness and urged uniformity in plain dress to distinguish the faithful from the world.

Also influencing the Mennonite Church and its institutions was the fundamentalist–modernist debate, which peaked in the 1910s and 1920s. Fundamentalism was a Protestant movement that spanned denominational lines in the early twentieth century. Arguing that theological liberalism undermined the authority of the Bible, fundamentalists sought to reinforce correct doctrine by identifying core Christian beliefs, such as the inerrancy of scripture, the virgin birth of Jesus, a substitutionary-atonement understanding of salvation, the authenticity of Jesus' miracles, and the physical resurrection of Jesus. A primary characteristic was a militant defense of these tenets and fierce attacks on those whom they considered liberals or modernists. Mennonites' biblicist orientation and acceptance of orthodox positions likely made many of them more comfortable with fundamentalism than with modernism.[29]

The early decades of the twentieth century saw a significant push to reinforce correct doctrine in the church. Influential leader Daniel Kauffman published three volumes on biblical doctrines and, as editor of the *Gospel Witness* and later the denominational weekly *Gospel Herald*, emphasized orthodox belief, running a monthly doctrinal supplement in the latter outlet.[30] He and other church leaders sought to protect the church from modernist or liberal theology. Historians of North American Mennonites note, however, that for Mennonites who took up the fundamentalist battle cry, the issue was just as much cultural as theological.[31] Many Mennonites were looking for ways to resist the modernizing tendencies that seemed to threaten their conservative religious traditions. Indeed, for those who sought to protect their faith communities from worldly influences and change, fundamentalist rhetoric must have felt relevant and opportune.

Discord between Mennonite fundamentalists and those willing to consider new ways of thinking and of faithfulness led to institutional paralysis at Goshen College while Joe was a student at Hesston. On the fundamentalist side there was unease and then growing alarm at the theological pedigrees and progressive tendencies of faculty and students at the college.[32] J. E. Hartzler, president from 1913 to 1918, was a graduate of the liberal Union Theological Seminary. Former students who challenged church leadership and suggested the need for reform in the church seemed to indicate that Goshen was a place that birthed rebels. For traditionalists seeking to protect the church, the proper role of the college was to educate the church's youth in Mennonite ways and denominational orthodoxy and to safeguard them from dangerous worldly or modernist influences. This perspective clashed with pedagogical concerns to provide an education in which students wrestled with contemporary ideas. The Mennonite Board of Education, which exercised authority over the church's schools, sought to ensure that the college remained faithful to church teaching by, for example, barring textbooks with unscriptural doctrine.

Seeking to respond to criticism, Goshen's faculty adopted a statement in 1918 that affirmed its support of the church's principles and "distinctive doctrines."[33] Later, critics claimed that the faculty had not lived up to its pledge of loyalty, particularly by not adhering strictly enough to the church's regulation garb, straight-collar coats for men and bonnets and prayer head coverings for women. The situation was such that in some circles merely being a Goshen graduate was sufficient reason to disqualify one from service or employment in church-related institutions. Campus morale plunged. Finding the situation untenable, the Mennonite Board of Education closed the school for the 1923–24 school year and hired a new president, who reopened the college the following year with almost entirely new faculty.

Similar concerns about liberal theology and modernist tendencies were in play at Hesston Academy. Tillman Erb and his colleagues typically sympathized with such concerns and, perhaps more importantly, understood that to garner support and attract students, the school would have to embody the conservative values of the church. The publication announcing the founding of the new school at Hesston was clear. It would "be under the control of the church and equipped with

Joe worked as one of the town's telephone switchboard operators while a student at Hesston. MCUSA ARCHIVES

Hesston Literary Group in 1920. Joe is second from right, standing. MCUSA ARCHIVES

officers and teachers who are in perfect accord with the faith and practices of the church."[34] Once the school was open, the faculty taught and modeled the church's doctrines, including an emphasis on plain attire and the defense of orthodox belief in the face of the modernist challenge.[35] In addition to providing academic training, Hesston Academy and Bible School sought to cultivate in Joe and his fellow students a commitment to the church and its teachings and practices.

Joe's time at Hesston helped him develop habits and skills that would serve him well later as a leader. He had never before lived away from his childhood home, and his journey to Hesston in 1919 was his first long-distance train trip. Joe was impressed that his father entrusted him with a checkbook, which he used to help pay for living expenses and school fees.[36] At Hesston Joe spearheaded the building of a temporary gymnasium, edited the academy's newspaper, and became president of his class.[37] He had strong work habits, finding time and energy to work as a night operator at the local telephone switchboard and at a store during school holidays.[38]

Joe put particular energy into cultivating his writing and oratory skills. He was active in Hesston's literary society, which had a mission

***Hesston College Journal* staff 1919–20. Joe, standing second from left, was its first student editor.** MCUSA ARCHIVES

to advance "literary culture" and "create an active interest in public speaking and debate."[39] It met monthly for lectures and to debate issues. On top of his course work and many other responsibilities, he accepted public speaking opportunities, coached other orators, and wrote and edited articles for the *Hesston College Journal*, serving as its first student editor.[40] Later, as a student at Goshen College, he was editor of the *College Record*, president of his literary society, president of the Young People's Christian Association, and a member of the music and athletic organizations.[41]

Joe must have distinguished himself as a writer and editor, since he received an invitation to become editor of the Mennonite Church publication *Christian Monitor* while he was still at Hesston.[42] He did not take on that role, which would have required him to move to Scottdale, Pennsylvania, but his writing and oratory skills would serve him well later in life when he traveled widely to advocate for mission activity and wrote hundreds of mission reports and editorials for the *Gospel Herald* and other church publications.

Minnie Swartzendruber

Joe's future spouse, Minnie Swartzendruber, was already enrolled at Hesston by the time he arrived in Kansas. Minnie's family was from an established Amish Mennonite community in Johnson County, Iowa, but moved across the state to Eagle Grove, where they were part of a new Mennonite settlement.[43] Minnie was born there in 1902, one of nine children of Elias and Sarah (Knepp) Swartzendruber. Elias and Sarah had grown up in the Amish Mennonite church and were among those who eventually assimilated into the Mennonite Church.[44] The Eagle Grove settlement prospered for a time but eventually fizzled as families moved away, and the church disbanded.[45] This was not unusual. There was considerable mobility among Mennonite communities as people moved for economic or family reasons, and congregations consequently sprang up, grew, declined, and disbanded.[46] In 1910 the Swartzendrubers moved on to Versailles, Missouri.[47] In the absence of an ongoing Mennonite community at Eagle Grove, two of their children had married outside the faith.[48] Elias and Sarah moved to Versailles in order to raise their children in a Mennonite community and increase the possibility that they would remain in the church. In 1923 the Swartzendrubers moved again, this time to Manson, Iowa.

Like Joe's family, Minnie's family lived by farming and was very involved in church activities. On the farm Elias Swartzendruber enjoyed raising horses and had a reputation of being gifted mechanically. There was never anything "out of order" at the Swartzendruber farm.[49] Elias was ordained deacon in 1884, and at Eagle Grove he preached for the congregation when no ordained preacher was available.[50] He and Sarah cultivated a Christian environment in their home and supported mission work.[51] Like many Protestants in early twentieth-century America, Elias read travelogues that encouraged the idea that America, and its missionaries, might make a positive contribution in countries around the world.[52] He led daily family devotions in the morning, and the family was active in their church community. Missionaries visited the church, creating awareness of the growing Mennonite engagement in mission initiatives.

Minnie participated in church activities, and even had thoughts of being a missionary to China, but she waited to join the church until she had left Versailles and was at Hesston. Reflecting on her faith journey later in life, she reported that one factor had been that she and her friends detested wearing bonnets, which they associated with being Christian. She also resisted the feeling of being coerced during church revival meetings. At Hesston she found that she was the only person there who had not made a decision to be a Christian, so everyone was praying for her.[53] When C. F. Derstine came to do revival meetings, she stood and made a public confession of faith.

Minnie attended Hesston from 1918 to 1922, completing high school (having already taken correspondence courses in Versailles) and also taking college-level courses. As a youth she was interested in history and English literature and hungry for an education.[54] She remembered that she "just couldn't get enough books to read."[55] Minnie's classes at Hesston included a wide range of subjects such as psychology, philosophy, and Greek.[56] She was able to explore her strong literary interests. Reading the English Romantic poets, she especially enjoyed Wordsworth, was less enamored of Shelley, and found that Keats made her sleepy.[57] After Hesston she continued her college education via correspondence courses and at Goshen College.[58]

Courtship and engagement

Joe and Minnie started their courtship during the 1920–21 school year. Minnie was already close friends with Joe's sister Verna, who also started attending Hesston in 1918 and lived just across the hall. Joe and Minnie met when he arrived a year later, but it was not until the following year, their junior year, that the two started "keeping company."[59] The three of them often spent time together during Joe's first year at Hesston, but Minnie thought it inappropriate to date the brother of a close friend.[60] She felt that she needed to choose between Verna and Joe, so she chose Verna that year. The next year, however, Joe asked her to be his date to a church service at Alexanderwohl Mennonite Church, where the Hesston choir, of which both were members, was scheduled to sing. Hesston students had to ask their counselor's permission to go on a date, but Minnie forgot that rule until she was sitting on stage and noticed her counselor in the audience. She assumed that she would be disciplined, but the counselor never broached the issue. After that Joe and Minnie were together frequently, sometimes several times a week. Since neither of them had a car, they often went out with other couples who had cars.

Picnic at Hesston in 1922. Joe to the far right and Minnie to his left.
MCUSA ARCHIVES

The year was cut short for Minnie when a basketball injury resulted in a wound and a life-threatening tetanus infection. She was hospitalized, and her mother Sarah came to help care for her. As the illness was in its most serious stage, Sarah heard a voice say, "Saved to serve." Minnie's recovery seemed to begin from that point.[61] Minnie returned home to Versailles to recuperate for the remainder of the year, but later in life she remembered her recovery as having instilled in her the sense that she was "saved for a special purpose."[62]

The next year, as seniors, Joe and Minnie dated regularly but faced the prospect of an unknown future after graduation. They took long walks along the railroad tracks that led from Hesston to Newton, and they shared their dreams with each other.[63] After high school graduation in May, both were planning to do more training. Minnie was trying to choose between nursing and teaching and decided to search for a teaching job in the meantime. Joe wanted to continue studying to get his college degree. Facing the prospect of being separated and having years of training ahead of them, they decided—or, as Minnie later remembered, mostly Joe decided—that they would not get engaged. They also would not write to each other for a while. Minnie described their departure from Hesston after graduation as the saddest day of the year for her. She returned to Versailles to a teaching job while he left for home for the summer.

Things soon changed course, however. By the first week of June, Joe had written a deeply repentant letter to Minnie.[64] He feared that he had misrepresented his feelings on departing from Hesston and wanted to correct any misunderstanding. He certainly did not want their friendship to diminish; quite the contrary, he wanted it to become warmer and deeper. In addition, he had had a change of heart about writing. He now thought that they should write to each other. For the next year, when Joe was back at Hesston taking college courses and Minnie was still in Versailles, they corresponded regularly. In the spring Minnie visited Hesston for a few days on a trip to Colorado.[65] They had a chance to take long walks together again. On May 23, 1923, during one such walk down the railroad tracks in a wooded area, Joe proposed. They were engaged. After that their letters to each other became more frequent. "We had so much to say to each other," Minnie recalled later about their engagement.[66] For the next sixteen months they continued to live far apart, and letters had to suffice, although Joe spent Christmas break visiting the Swartzendrubers at Versailles in December 1923. During the 1924–25 academic year they both attended Goshen College, where Joe completed his college degree. They married on June 28, 1925, a few days after Joe finished his last college class and not quite five months before they left for their first term as missionaries in India.

Mennonites engaging the world

His time at Hesston and later at Goshen College increased Joe's exposure to the wider Mennonite community and the issues it was facing during the first decades of the twentieth century. One debate concerned disagreements between young emerging leaders and the established church leadership about leadership practices and the future of the church. North American Mennonite relief workers in France following World War I had initiated the Young People's Movement, which led to three Young People's Conferences and a biweekly periodical, *The Christian Exponent*, published from January 1924 to September 1928. Those involved were openly critical of what they considered slow-moving, antiquated church leaders who, they argued, had failed to prepare Mennonite young men to face conscription into the armed forces during the war.[67] The relief workers sought more opportunities for qualified younger leaders and more Mennonite interaction in the world through increased mission and relief activity.[68]

On the continuum between engagement Mennonites and protective Mennonites, participants in the Young People's Movement were on the far end of the engagement side. They sought urgent change. Critical of church leadership, which they accused of being overly conservative, traditional, and autocratic, they pushed for more immediate engagement with the world. Perhaps unsurprisingly, then, they encountered resistance from some church leaders.

In September 1920, while Joe was returning for his second year of studies at Hesston Academy, he coincidentally met and conversed with Orie B. Gerig on the train ride to nearby Newton.[69] Gerig was teaching for the year at Bethel College in Newton and was the great-nephew of Sebastian Gerig, bishop at Sugar Creek Mennonite Church, Joe's home congregation. Orie was also a leader in the Young

People's Movement.[70] The conversation with Gerig startled Joe. In a letter to his father, he wrote of Gerig's strong critique of church leadership and church institutions. Gerig had criticized certain leaders by name and had complained that younger, more capable leaders were ready to take the reins but that the "old men" were in the way. Joe concluded that Gerig's approach was "radically wrong" and feared that the movement would "result in a split in the church."[71] Gerig's criticisms often had an acerbic tone and, judging by Joe's reaction, must have been quite strong.[72]

Their conversation on the train ride to Newton led to an even more uncomfortable exchange the following spring after the Mennonite Board of Missions and Charities had rejected Gerig's application to serve as a missionary in India. Gerig wrote to Joe because one reason given for the rejection was a report of Gerig's attacks on some church leaders during their conversation on the train to Newton.[73] Gerig argued that what he had said should have not disqualified him and asked what exactly Joe had passed along to church authorities. Joe responded that as a young person contemplating service in the church, he felt that it had been his prerogative to discuss Gerig's critiques of the church and its leadership with others at Hesston—yet he doubted that this was a decisive factor in MBMC's decision.[74] In the ensuing exchange of letters Gerig insisted that Joe enumerate in writing the charges that Gerig was accused of bringing against the church and its leaders, so that he could clear his name.[75] Joe, on the other hand, preferred that the two meet in order to clear up any misunderstanding. It appears that in the end neither happened. Eventually estranged from the Mennonite Church, Gerig went on to an illustrious career at the League of Nations and the US State Department, where he helped with the organization of the United Nations.[76]

The exchange with Gerig suggests that Joe at the time aligned himself with the conservative mainstream of the Mennonite Church. Hesston was part of that mainstream. On the one hand, it was a modern, church-related educational institution. On the other hand, it valued nonconformity and resisted the perceived dangers of worldliness, modernist theology, and precipitous change. While Gerig and his fellow Young People's Movement were too radical for Joe in the early 1920s, during the following decades the next generation of Mennonite leaders, including Joe, would increase the church's witness in the world through mission institutions and the relief work of Mennonite Central Committee. Joe's response to Gerig demonstrates that while he favored more engagement with the world through mission activity, he was loyal to the church and its institutions and hesitated to promote anything that might split or weaken it.

Theologically, too, Joe was in tune with the critique of modernist theology evident among church leaders and at Hesston. Hesston Bible teachers such as J. B. Smith and J. D. Charles appropriated aspects of fundamentalism in order to combat modernist or liberal theology and its modernist cultural influence, which they considered to be a danger to the church.[77] The college promoted the Scofield Reference Bible, a favorite of fundamentalists, and sold it to students through its bookstore.[78] In the *Hesston College Journal* and later in the *Goshen Record* Joe wrote editorials to address the fundamentalist–modernist debate and proclaimed the errors of the modernists and liberals.[79]

Joe was a fan of three-time Democratic presidential nominee William Jennings Bryan, a gifted orator who by then had fully pivoted from politics to the speaking circuit. By the 1920s Bryan was a prominent religious figure who criticized liberal theology and Charles Darwin's theory of evolution. Joe read Bryan's theological writings and subscribed to Bryan's monthly newspaper, *The Commoner*.[80] In the sermon Joe delivered at Prairie Street Mennonite Church eleven days before leaving for India, he twice referred to Bryan, the only religious authority he mentioned.[81] Given Bryan's place in American society at the time, it is not surprising that Joe and fellow Mennonites would follow his thought and writing. Willard Smith, a close friend and eventually Joe's brother-in-law, became somewhat of an expert on Bryan, lecturing and writing about him and his theology.[82] As a college student and then as a newly appointed missionary, Joe may have leaned progressive in his commitment to engage the world through mission activity, but he remained in line with the cautious mainstream of the Mennonite Church, which was suspicious of worldly or modernist theological influences.

Joe's mistrust of modernism resembled the approach of some other emerging Mennonite Church leaders of his generation who likewise used conservative or fundamentalist rhetoric. In 1937 Harold S.

Bender suggested that "'all the American Mennonite groups' held to 'conservative evangelicalism' and were 'orthodox in the great fundamental doctrines of the Christian faith.' He added that Mennonites felt 'sympathy' as they watched 'the great reaction against modernism in America known as the fundamentalist movement.'"[83] Later, after calling fundamentalism the "'greatest danger' threatening the Mennonitism of some North American Mennonite groups," Bender noted that he still counted "himself as thoroughly fundamental."[84] Guy F. Hershberger seemed to strike a similar balance, lamenting that fundamentalists did not hold to a scriptural peace witness that would have consistently followed "their Christ-centered religion and their Bible," with which he otherwise seemed to sympathize.[85]

If Joe found himself in step with the mainstream of the Mennonite Church theologically, his attitude was more nuanced toward the church's attempts to build bulwarks against worldliness and to enforce universal standards of plain attire. In their courtship-era letters, he and Minnie expressed at different times surprise, frustration, and resignation over such attempts. One summer when he was home from Hesston, Joe planned to attend the Bluffton College Men's Glee Club program at the General Conference congregation just down the road.[86] He decided against it, however, because others did not approve of such things. Glee clubs were popular among students but apparently too worldly for many Mennonites. Just the year before, the Mennonite Board of Education had discontinued intercollegiate athletics and off-campus glee club tours at Goshen College in an attempt to curtail inappropriate student entertainments and reinforce conservative values.[87] After attending a Thanksgiving service at a Presbyterian church while a student at Goshen College in 1924–25, Minnie wrote of the beautiful organ music. The Mennonite Church considered an organ too worldly for a worship service, but it had enhanced a worshipful experience for her. "Surely beauty isn't antagonistic with the gospel is it?" she mused.[88] Minnie had been surprised in 1921 when she returned to her home congregation in Versailles, Missouri, to find the men wearing plain coats and the women wearing capes.[89] It had not previously been a general practice there. She and Joe were incredulous about a ban on wristwatches, but Minnie quit wearing her watch nonetheless and bought a watchcase in which to carry it.[90]

Ultimately, Joe and Minnie chose to show deference to the church by accommodating themselves to its practices, even when they were not personally convinced of their value. Loyalty to the church was likely one of several factors in play as Joe and Minnie considered vocational options that were open to them in Mennonite Church circles.

Vocational discernment and the missionary call

Vocational discernment had been a frequent topic during Joe and Minnie's courtship and engagement. For Mennonite women who desired to prepare for a profession, the options were limited at the time. Minnie had to decide whether to be a nurse or a teacher.[91] From early in his life, Joe sensed that he would be a preacher and a missionary.[92] While Mennonite young men of the day did not face the limitations of their female counterparts, certain vocations were simply not on the table. Joe imagined that if he were not a Mennonite, he might have applied to study law at the University of Chicago and contemplated running for public office.[93] Daniel Graber had also entertained thoughts of becoming a lawyer.[94] Joe's oratory and writing capacity, intellectual aptitude, relational skills, and leadership qualities would likely have made him a gifted lawyer.

By the time he was a student at Hesston, however, people were starting to suggest that he prepare for this or that role in the church, and Joe began leaning toward teaching as his life's calling.[95] Hesston principal Daniel Bender and other faculty approached him about teaching at Hesston once he had finished his time there as a student. Sensing a call to preaching or missionary work at the same time as pursuing a teaching vocation was not a contradiction. Mennonite ministers of the time typically pursued another occupation to earn a living.

S. C. Yoder, who would soon become president of Goshen College and anticipated needing new faculty there, also asked Joe about his availability.[96] The Mennonite Board of Education had chosen Yoder to reopen the school following its year-long forced closure, and he was looking for teachers who were loyal to the church and its doctrines. Yoder was from Iowa and taught Bible courses regularly during Hesston's January Special Bible Term.[97] He drew on those connections to recruit a number of young leaders to fill positions at the newly reopened college starting in the fall of 1924.[98] Yoder wrote to Joe that he was looking for competent teachers who loved the church, were loyal to it, and would be able to withstand the criticism from the liberal elements of the church.[99] He obviously thought that Joe fit that description. The opportunity to teach at Hesston or Goshen would have marked a change in Daniel Graber's plans for Joe, as he had assumed that his son would return to Iowa, teach close by, and help out on the family farm in his free time.[100]

In addition to teaching at Hesston or Goshen, serving as a missionary in MBMC's India field was an emerging possibility in Joe and Minnie's vocational discernment. Professors at Hesston encouraged students to participate in mission activity, and Joe and Minnie had been members of the foreign mission band there.[101] Both faculty and student groups organized mission programs on campus and in the community, including organizing Sunday schools and establishing new congregations. Mission classes were part of the course offerings. MBMC missionaries visited campus and addressed the students, especially during commencement celebrations. Such exposure seems to have stimulated student interest, since a number of Hesston graduates contributed to Mennonite service and mission work internationally during the first decades of the school's existence.[102] While at Hesston Joe and close friend Willard Smith, who would marry Joe's sister Verna, applied to Mennonite Central Committee to do relief work in Europe.[103] MCC declined their offer, citing their young age.

Joe and Minnie had started talking about missionary work in India during their engagement. Long-time MBMC India missionaries P. A. Friesen and George Lapp started lobbying them to look "toward India" as they made vocational choices.[104] On furlough in Hesston in 1923, Friesen seemed so anxious that they not hesitate long to accept a position in India that Joe wrote to Minnie, "Really, the compass is beginning to point quite markedly toward India, isn't it?"[105] During the summer and fall of that year it seemed clear that they were moving in that direction.[106] Later, however, there was reason to reconsider. The option to teach at Hesston or Goshen was on the table, and being far away from family for extended periods of time gave them pause. For a while in 1924 Joe planned to accept a position as head of the mathematics department at Goshen College.[107] A letter from George Lapp in the spring of 1924 seems to have had a decisive impact in the other direction, however.[108] Fellow Goshen student Nelson Litwiller, a close friend who was preparing for his own missionary career in Argentina, also encouraged Joe and Minnie toward a missionary vocation.[109] The need was great. The call seemed strong. Both Joe and Minnie felt a conviction that they should accept.

If the call was clear to them, it must have seemed less so to some family members. After Minnie's mother read Lapp's letter, Minnie reported that she laid it on the davenport and was silent for an hour.[110] When she finally spoke, her mother reminded Minnie that a newly reopened Goshen College would need teachers. Goshen president S. C. Yoder was also general secretary of MBMC, so Joe wrote to him, laying out his and Minnie's convictions about the call to India.[111] Yoder was disappointed that the college would lose a prospective teacher, but he affirmed Joe and Minnie's call and assured them of his blessing were they to choose to go to India. When Lapp's letter arrived, they were still over a year from their wedding day and eighteen months from their November 1925 departure for India. There would be challenges to overcome before their departure, but the die appears to have been cast.[112] In the end family members did not oppose their going.[113] They were on their way to India.

Left to right: Minnie and Joe, Minnie Kanagy, and Nelson and Ada Litwiler at their commissioning as MBMC missionaries in May 1925 at Weavers Church in Harrisonburg, Virginia. Joe and Minnie were engaged but not yet married at the commissioning. Their wedding took place the following month. MCUSA ARCHIVES

TWO

First Missionary Term

Indian Mennonite Mission in a Colonial Era

DURING THE weekend of May 21–22, 1932, Joe was among the many who descended on the Metamora Mennonite Church in Illinois. They came from points across the United States and Canada for the three-day annual meeting of the Mennonite Board of Missions and Charities. He had arrived from India the month before after a first term of six and a half years of missionary service and would spend the next two years studying at Princeton Seminary. The meeting in Metamora brought together representatives and workers from the board's ten city missions and five charitable organizations as well as from numerous conference mission boards and their own city missions and organizations. Missionaries on furlough from the foreign fields attended, as did the members of the board and its various subcommittees. The annual meetings were not simply a time for board and committee work. Sermons and reports brought inspiring news from foreign and domestic fields and outlined visions for the future.

Joe addressed the annual meeting at Metamora, as missionaries on furlough typically did. After a term of service in India, he had something to say. In his farewell sermon upon departing for India six and a half years earlier, he had outlined a foundational missionary task of witnessing to Christian faith and hope. That theme remained constant in his thinking, but the details of his argument had changed after his first term in India.[1] The traditional depiction of indigenous peoples as uncivilized and pitiful heathen in the earlier sermon disappeared in favor of a description of fellow Indian Christians who had come to know that God loves them and who merited fellowship with their North American Mennonite brothers and sisters. Facing the crowd gathered at Metamora, Joe drew a contrast between a mission approach that sought fellowship with Indian Christians and one that assumed oneself or one's culture to be superior to others.[2] He strongly criticized attempts to create sympathy for mission work by depicting Indians in pitiful conditions or as "poor, black heathen" and reminded the gathering that the "white heathen of North America" were just as much in need of Jesus. Joe warned his audience against attitudes of "white supremacy" and noted that, despite the images they might have seen in Sunday school, Jesus was probably not white.[3] It must have been a striking message to a crowd that was almost certainly all white and largely homogeneous in its ethnic identity. It also indicates that Joe's first term of missionary service in India convinced him that there were issues of discrimination and equity that MBMC needed to address in its work.

New experiences, a new place, and a new language

On November 25, 1925, Joe and Minnie left New York City on the passenger steamship *City of Lahore* for their first term of missionary service. They arrived in Dhamtari, located in the Central Provinces of what was then British India, on December 31. Dhamtari was the center of the Mennonite Church's India work. The voyage was uneventful, except for the rough seas they encountered while crossing the Atlantic. The rolling and pitching of the ship left both Joe and Minnie seasick and once sent them tumbling across the deck.[4] The seas were calm for the rest of the trip across the Mediterranean to Port Said, then through the Suez Canal and the Red Sea, and finally across the Indian Ocean.[5]

For missionaries, a long sea voyage was an important time of transition between their home culture and the cultures in which they worked. Joe and Minnie had a period of five weeks between their intense period

***City of Lahore*, the ship on which Joe and Minnie sailed in 1925 for their first term as missionaries to India.** MCUSA ARCHIVES

of preparation in North America and their integration into the responsibilities of language learning and ministry in India. There was time for reading, interaction with fellow passengers, and other pastimes. Minnie and Joe took advantage of an abundance of books aboard the ship to read authors such as Mark Twain and Joseph C. Lincoln.[6] Most of the sixty-one passengers aboard were Protestant missionaries of one sort or another, and Joe and Minnie got to know them.[7] Ecumenical relationships were an important dynamic for the Protestant missionary movement, and the missionaries organized daily devotional meetings and Sunday services, taking turns providing leadership. Playing shuffleboard on deck was a popular recreational activity.[8]

Throughout his life Joe demonstrated an innate curiosity about the world. Engaging new situations and ideas was no less important to his formation than was his formal education. He was a person of many eclectic interests. For example, sailing to India provided ample opportunity for Joe to cultivate what his son Ronald later described as his deep interest in weather patterns.[9] His letters to family, friends, and colleagues throughout his life often included a paragraph reporting precipitation, seasonal changes, or weather predictions.[10] Writing to family in Iowa from aboard the steamship, he reported the changing wind directions and weather conditions.[11] Joe also kept track of the ship's daily latitudinal and longitudinal coordinates and studied the sky at night, noting the shifting positions of Venus, the North Star, and the Big Dipper. He befriended the ship's chief engineer and accompanied him below deck to see the engines, water distiller, dynamo, and refrigerator plant; he even later submitted an article about the ship to the Mennonite Publishing House's *Youth's Christian Companion*, a weekly magazine geared toward the interests of Mennonite young people. Upon arriving in India, he was fascinated with a small ice machine that missionary George Lapp had in the village where the Lapps lived.[12] In his first letter from India to family back in the United States, Joe described the machine and the way it worked, drawing a schema to further explain the technology involved. Given Joe's acute curiosity and wide interests, it is no wonder that people described him as a good conversationalist.[13] His desire to understand the world and the way things work was a trait that would be useful as he analyzed and guided mission work in the years to come, always looking for innovative approaches that would respond to the needs of a changing world.

Upon arrival in India, Joe and Minnie's first task was to learn Hindi. This was the primary focus of their first year, during much of which they lived with veteran missionaries George and Fanny Lapp at Ghatula, a mission station about seventy kilometers southeast of Dhamtari.[14] Along with P. A. Friesen, George had been instrumental in convincing Joe and Minnie to become missionaries to India; he recognized Joe's leadership qualities and shortly after the Grabers arrived to Ghatula described him as a visionary.[15] The Lapps' teenage daughter, Harriet, also was pleased with the arrival of the Grabers. Reflecting on their time at Ghatula, she remembered idolizing Joe and Minnie because they were so gentle and well-spoken. Upon hearing Joe sing she noted, "At last we have a missionary who is a good singer!"[16] In Ghatula, in addition to getting to know the Lapps, Joe and Minnie had opportunity to work with a language tutor and to become accustomed to life in central India. With its Devanagari script and influences from Persian and Arabic, Hindi was not an easy language for North American Anglophones to learn and was certainly quite different from the German and French with which Joe and Minnie were familiar. Nevertheless, by July they understood Hindi well enough that their tutor no longer used any English in his sessions with them.[17]

Missionary protocol required Joe and Minnie to demonstrate that they could minister in Hindi. Along with other foreign mission agencies working in central India, MBMC missionaries had established a system to evaluate language competency.[18] It entailed a series of oral and written tests meant to measure progress and efficiency. Joe and Minnie took their first oral exams in September 1926 and passed easily.[19] Joe had the top score in their year-one cohort of twenty-nine students, which included missionaries from the various foreign missions in the region, and Minnie had the second-highest score. In early October they passed their first written exams. This time Minnie had the best score of the group, and Joe came in second.[20] By December both had taken on some mission responsibilities, which afforded them language practice and reduced their studies with a tutor to afternoon hours.[21] That month, a year after they had arrived in India, Joe preached his first sermon in Hindi.[22] By the end of July 1927, only eighteen months after arriving, they had already finished the material for the third year but were waiting for the opportunity to take the second-year exams that September.[23] They both eventually mastered the language and were among the best, if not the best, MBMC Hindi linguists in India.[24]

THIRD HINDI.

Candidates' names and Missions.	Written.								Oral.					
	Mudra Rakshas.	Ramayan.	Shad Darshan Darpan.	Unseen, Hindi.	Grammar.	English-Hindi.	Esasy.	Total.	Reading, Scripture.	Conversation.	Address.	Grand Total.	Percentage.	Class.
(Maximum Marks.)	50	50	50	50	100	100	100	500	50	150	100	800	100	
Rev. J. D. Graber, A.M M.	41	36	43	45	80	64	75	384	46	138	93	662	82·7	I
Mrs. J. D Graber, A.M.M.	44	33	31	42	68	72	95	385	45	138	90	658	82 2	I
Miss C V. Baxter, U.C.C.M.	43	33	30	30	73	50	62	321	40	100	80	541	67·6	II

One candidate failed in one written paper, and one in one written paper and the total of the written examination

As new missionaries Joe and Minnie proved to be gifted language learners, earning the top scores on their exams during three years of Hindi language study. MCUSA ARCHIVES

Ministry in India

The Mennonite Church's involvement in India had begun with the aid it sent in response to famine at the end of the nineteenth century. The result was a significant institutional footprint there. Reports of ongoing need, particularly among children orphaned by the famine, and the desire of a growing number of North American Mennonites to start international mission work combined to motivate the Mennonite Evangelizing and Benevolent Board (MEBB) to send its first missionaries to India in 1899.[25] In 1906 the MEBB merged with another Mennonite mission board, the Mennonite Board of Charitable Homes and Missions, to form the Mennonite Board of Missions and Charities.[26] Not long after, in 1908, MBMC established the American Mennonite Mission (AMM), the organizational structure through which MBMC missionaries worked in India. Missionaries established the Mennonite Church in India as a conference in 1912.

The first Mennonite missionaries in India had planned to open an orphanage and a hospital as a way to develop community ties and establish a church. Another famine in 1900 meant that for a time they continued to focus instead on famine relief. The famine only increased the number of orphans, and missionaries eventually opened their orphanage and hospital, becoming responsible for the children in their care. As the children matured, the need to educate and prepare them for a vocation naturally arose, so the missionaries organized schools and training in the various trades.[27] By 1932 both the boys' and girls' orphanages in Dhamtari had been converted into boarding hostels for middle school and high school students. Missionaries added a leprosy sanatorium to their healthcare ministry and opened village schools as an evangelism strategy. Medical care had become an important part of mission practice during the nineteenth and twentieth centuries, with leprosy as a prime concern, and schools also were part and parcel of the Protestant missionary movement.[28]

Alongside their work of evangelization and establishing the church, therefore, Mennonite missionaries worked in a variety of institutional settings. Each year the AMM missionaries elected a managing committee, which directed mission activities. Responsibility for mission work fell under the purview of a variety of departments (medical, educational, evangelistic, industrial, auditing, translation, language,

Joe traveling by train, in the engine. MCUSA ARCHIVES

etc.). AMM planned and implemented mission strategy in India and decided how to allot financial resources as well as where to place missionaries. By the time Joe and Minnie were on the scene, there were seven mission stations, seven local congregations, ten charitable institutions, fourteen schools, one hospital, and five dispensaries. During their first term in India, Joe and Minnie were appointed to a variety of ministry assignments spanning the wide array of work in which AMM was involved.[29]

In September 1926 the Grabers moved to Dhamtari, where they took up their initial official duties. In theory, they were to continue spending half of their time perfecting their Hindi and the other half in mission work.[30] In reality, the demands of the day-to-day work often reduced the time and energy they had for language study. Joe took on the responsibility of overseeing the carpentry school and taught classes in the high school.[31] With the upcoming furlough of the missionary in charge of the high school, more of the school-related tasks would fall to Joe.[32] The carpentry school had twenty students, twelve on government-funded scholarships and eight on scholarships that the mission provided.[33] British colonial governments often contributed funding for mission schools, and AMM received about a third of its educational budget from government sources.[34] The government paid the salary of the carpentry school's only instructor and donated a set of tools to every graduate. As per government policy in this case, half the students were non-Christians.[35] The students' training included making furniture from the region's beautiful teak wood.

Minnie's assignment was the supervision of the AMM "Bible women" in Dhamtari. Bible women were native women evangelists, typically supervised by female foreign missionaries; they were an integral part of Protestant mission strategy in the late nineteenth and early twentieth centuries.[36] Their command of local languages and cultures and their access to homes that foreigners could not enter were invaluable. In its various mission stations during this period AMM employed thirty Bible women, six of whom worked in Dhamtari.[37] They visited homes in town and in fifteen surrounding villages. Minnie met with the Bible women in the morning for prayer and accompanied them on their evangelizing visits.[38] They found mostly women and children in the homes they visited, and they made friends, told Bible stories, shared the gospel, and invited people to consider the merits of the Christian faith. Minnie would eventually have many institutional responsibilities as well, such as managing the AMM Babies' Home and the Widows' Home at the Balodgahan station.[39]

Besides their official responsibilities, Joe and Minnie took up other tasks that came with being missionaries. They had to be ready to lead prayer meetings and Bible studies, and Joe received invitations to

Joe, second from left, with friends (names unknown). Christmas 1927.
MCUSA ARCHIVES

preach at the Mennonite churches. The February after their move to Dhamtari, the congregation there chose Joe to be its pastor, adding considerably to his assignment during the two years that he held that post.[40] Maintaining the mission institutions took time and effort too. When the need arose to enlarge the boys' hostel and provide new quarters for its warden, the job fell to Joe.[41] He played the role of contractor, arranging for materials and labor to build the enlargement and then overseeing the work to ensure its quality. He sought funding for the project from the Young People's Christian Associations at Mennonite colleges.[42] In addition, people came to Joe and Minnie seeking medical assistance. Neither of them had formal medical training, but when health professionals were not available, they stepped in to provide basic care such as cleaning and dressing wounds and dispensing simple medications.[43] The population welcomed this sort of nonprofessional medical care, and even missionaries who were not doctors or nurses had their own medical bags.[44]

The multiple departments and committees of AMM created administrative work that required time and attention. Joe sat on two committees that visited and evaluated the various mission stations and their institutions. One was the Educational Survey Committee, which advised the mission on ways to make its schools more practical, both as educational institutions and as a means of evangelism.[45] The other was the committee that audited its missionaries and institutions each year.[46] Joe also served as president of the Chhattisgarh Area Missionary Association, a group of mission agencies in Chhattisgarh, the region where the AMM mission field was located.[47] Writing and editing articles submitted to the *Gospel Herald* was an added ongoing task.[48]

One common method of evangelization among missionaries in India was "touring": visiting villages that did not have a Christian presence to share the gospel. Traveling with Indian evangelists, missionaries made two-to-six-week excursions from Dhamtari into the interior, typically living in a tent since other accommodations were not available.[49] Roads and paths off the main highways were often impassible to vehicles, so they used ox carts for transportation. Missionaries took along their medical bags to alleviate suffering and treat diseases. In addition to sharing Bible stories and evangelistic sermons, they addressed other topics including health, education, and agriculture, often using pictures and sometimes a stereopticon with slides to communicate their message.

The Grabers spent the first two months of 1928 on their inaugural extended tour.[50] Joe found that people were generally eager to gather for his preaching and were agreeable, but that they did not often respond with moves to associate with the Christian faith or join the church.[51] Convincing people of their need for the Christian faith was no easy task, since it meant religious as well as social disruption for converts. The seemingly unproductive nature of Christian witness in central India was a source of frustration for the Grabers and their missionary colleagues, who worked for years for what seemed like modest results. But such work was Joe's preference. When he was able, he limited his responsibility for schools and other institutions so that he could spend more of this time in village evangelism.[52]

Yet evangelism continued to be only one of the many hats Joe wore. He took over responsibility for the Shantipur (City of Peace) Leper Home when its resident doctor left for furlough in the summer of 1928. Shantipur, located five miles outside Dhamtari, became a home base for the Grabers through the end of their first term, even though they spent months at a time at other stations replacing colleagues who were on vacation or furlough. During the Grabers' tenure the Shantipur home served between 160 and 190 residents in varying stages of leprosy.[53]

Although not medical professionals, Joe and Minnie could do much to help. MBMC missionary doctors Christian D. Esch, Florence Cooprider Friesen, or George D. Troyer saw to the major medical work while the Grabers helped to dress wounds, give injections, and sometimes even diagnose leprosy cases.[54] Treatment for leprosy consisted of oral administration of potassium iodide, weekly injections of hydnocarpus oil, and topical application of trichloroacetic acid.[55] Joe reported that for the year 1930, staff administered 3,681 injections and dressed around 15,000 ulcers.[56] Administrative tasks to keep the institution running and manage the 120-acre farm that the leprosy patients worked fell to the Grabers, and Joe served as liaison with government health officials.[57] The spiritual care of the leprosy patients naturally fell to the missionaries, and Joe was pastor of the Shantipur congregation. During Joe and Minnie's assignment at Shantipur, on May 29, 1930, their first child, Ronald, was born.

Son Ronald was born during the Grabers' first term of missionary work in India. MCUSA ARCHIVES

Challenges of the colonial context

India, the "jewel" of Great Britain's colonial empire, had been a part of its imperial map for nearly two centuries. Formal government control of the colony grew over that time. Initially, the British East India Company enjoyed an official sanction to gain supremacy over other European powers in the region, especially the French, and benefited from a trade monopoly meant to pay for the colonial endeavor as well as to channel wealth back to English coffers. By the end of the eighteenth century, however, the trading systems were no longer lucrative enough to finance the troops, infrastructure, and profits necessary for the endeavor.[58] Direct payments from Indians to the British in the form of indemnities, tributes, and subventions from Indian princes, as well as taxes from those territories that the company governed, became the primary sources of colonial income. The British shifted India's economic systems to increase wealth extraction, impoverishing India and enriching the colonizers.

The British East India Company was eventually supplanted by a direct colonial governing system that relied on troops, mostly Indians trained and paid by the British, to quash outbreaks of resistance, thus maintaining a milieu of intimidation. The colonial project also cultivated a mirage of Western superiority that sought to legitimize white rule over Indian people of color. The regime had a place for a minority of educated and elite Indians (a co-opted aristocracy and those who filled civil service roles) who benefited in some way from its existence. It also provided enough infrastructure such as roads, railroads, and telegraph networks to keep the enterprise running.

Missionaries depended on the colonial government for permission to live in India and relied on its infrastructure to do their work. To the extent that they perpetrated colonial attitudes and practices, missionaries and their institutions reinforced the malevolent aspects of British

The MBMC missionary family in India in 1930. Joe sixth from left in the back row. Minnie and Ronald fifth from left in the second row of adults. MCUSA ARCHIVES

rule. To the extent that their churches, schools, hospitals, dispensaries, rural development projects, and social uplift initiatives empowered Indians and their communities, missionaries helped create a path toward decolonization and independence.

As they worked in a wide range of AMM ministries, Joe and Minnie started to question how colonial ways of being and working influenced mission activitiy. They developed deep and meaningful relationships with missionary colleagues and Indian coworkers, but they were troubled by what they understood as a paternalistic attitude on the part of some AMM missionaries and a lack of equity between missionaries and Indian Mennonites. Too often, it seemed to them, missionaries treated the Indians as children, even disciplining them as such. Their concerns echoed those of noted missionary, missiologist, and ecumenist Lesslie Newbigin, a contemporary of the Grabers, who was similarly shocked at the troubled relationships between Western missionaries and Indian Christians upon his arrival to India in 1936.[59]

AMM had not escaped the colonial mentality of the Indian context.[60] With relatively comfortable houses and comparatively generous incomes, foreign missionaries lived at a much higher economic level than their Indian counterparts.[61] When the congregation in Dhamtari selected Joe as its pastor, that process represented the first time it had solicited and obtained permission from AMM to choose its own pastor, instead of having AMM make the appointment. The fact that the congregation passed over the three veteran missionaries who lived in Dhamtari to choose the newly arrived Joe was a not-so-subtle indication that all was not well between the missionaries and church members.[62]

Joe was also troubled by the way some missionary literature seemed designed to encourage pity for Indians by highlighting their dire needs and lack of formal education or by assuming Indians were spiritually or morally deficient.[63] In his address to MBMC's annual meeting a month after his return to North America, Joe argued that such a tactic was wrong and only produced a "feeling of complacent race superiority."[64] Instead, he argued for an approach that recognized Indian Christians as brothers and sisters with whom missionaries and North American Mennonites could be in fellowship. He lamented that the Indian church leaders were not in attendance at the annual meeting to speak for themselves.

Joe's call for more equitable relationships with Indian Mennonites was a result of his and Minnie's ministry experience in India, but it also reflected trends within the larger Protestant missionary movement. Missionaries of all stripes depended on the British imperial systems of travel, communication, and trade, but the malevolent influence of the colonial enterprise on missionary attitudes and practice motivated pleas for more equity and partnership between foreign missionaries and indigenous Christians.[65] Indian church leader V. S. Azariah's famous presentation to the World Missionary Conference at Edinburgh in 1910 was a case in point.[66] Azariah was founder of the Indian Missionary Society and would become an Anglican bishop.[67] After expressing gratitude for the hardships and sacrifices of missionaries who had brought the gospel to India, he criticized the racial attitudes of paternalism and superiority that he observed among missionaries and pleaded for friendship and cooperation instead.

The period between the two world wars saw a flurry of activity that sought to increase understanding and fellowship across cultural differences, so much so that mission historian Dana Robert has suggested designating the 1920s the era of "world friendship."[68] Indigenous Christians and like-minded missionaries organized visits of Westerners to churches in the Global South and of indigenous church leaders to Western countries while also supporting publications written by non-Western Christians. Second- and third-generation indigenous Christians began to move out from under the paternalism and dependency of mission systems. Mennonite missionaries arrived in India later than many of their foreign missionary counterparts, but by the time Joe and Minnie were on the scene, an increasing number of Indian Mennonites were ready to move to a more mature relationship with AMM and with the missionaries who had nurtured them up to that point.

The issue of colonial attitudes among missionaries, and initiatives to increase mutuality and equity between Western and Indian Christians, played out within the context of the larger movement for self-rule in Indian society. While the British were successful in quashing rebellions during the nineteenth and early twentieth centuries, the need for troops and other colonial resources to repeatedly suppress opposition suggests that anticolonial sentiment was always present.

As India became integrated into global telegraph and shipping lines and educated Indians traveled more easily around the world, news that encouraged political awareness filtered back to the subcontinent: Ireland's resistance to British rule, for example, and movements for more autonomy in the settler colonies of Africa and Canada.[69] British rule was not invincible. The Indian National Congress had been in existence since 1885. It demanded political and economic concessions over the next decades and eventually became a political party. The colonial government slow-tracked change but over time provided for more representation of Indians in governance structures, introduced reforms meant to inch the country toward the practice of representative government, and opened access to high-level civil service posts. Activists worked to change economic policies that benefited Britain to the detriment of India.

While the British envisioned a protracted process toward some form of autonomy, Indians were growing impatient. In 1915 Mohandas Karamchand Gandhi returned to India from South Africa, where he had worked as a lawyer for twenty-one years and had developed his political views. His leadership in the decades to come would be decisive for the success of the nonviolent movement for self-rule that resulted in India's independence. World War I increased expectations of change. More than two million Indians participated as combatants and support staff on the side of the Allies, and the British government appreciatively indicated that it was preparing a new package of reforms. Expecting measurable advancement toward self-rule, Indians felt insulted when the British again slow-tracked progress after the war. Gandhi and others led an increasingly determined protest movement that included work stoppages, boycotts, and noncompliance with the colonial government's taxes. Sometimes they landed in jail for their efforts.

Joe and Minnie arrived during this tumultuous interwar period when Indians were losing patience with the slow pace of decolonization. The Grabers were conscious of the movement for self-rule in India and became increasingly convinced of the need for AMM to extricate itself from the colonial systems with which foreign missionaries were entangled. Mennonite missionaries' reactions to the independence movement were mixed, with some recognizing its legitimacy and effectiveness and some fearful that chaos and anarchy would result from an end to British rule.[70] Missionaries reported that during periods of heightened nationalist activity, evangelizing became more difficult.[71] Villagers increasingly saw North American missionaries as colonial agents and Christianity as a foreign religion that should be boycotted.

Joe was initially skeptical of the breadth of Gandhi's influence in India.[72] Later, however, he noted that the movement's strategy of using nonviolence, passive resistance, and civil disobedience to embarrass and cripple the colonial government had spread through all sectors of society.[73] He came to believe that the movement contrasted favorably with the policies of Western powers, arguing, "The program of Gandhi in India, based as it is on non-violence and a belief in passive suffering, is a good deal nearer Christianity than some of the imperialistic and capitalistic policies of our own country."[74] In the AMM's 1930 annual report Minnie wrote that the movement had successfully embarrassed the government, but that some nationalists had resorted to violence; by year's end there had been numerous arrests and the jails were crowded.[75] It was becoming increasingly clear to the Grabers that the colonial systems were neither justifiable nor sustainable.

Furlough and Princeton Seminary

The Grabers left India for their first furlough in March 1932, after nearly six and a half years in India. They traveled back to North America, passing through Europe to visit some of Joe's extended family in France.[76] They resided temporarily in Manson, Iowa, staying with Minnie's family. Furloughs were a time for reconnecting with extended family and visiting churches to report on mission work and to raise funds for future mission endeavors. Sometimes missionaries also used their time back in North America to continue their education.

Joe wanted to do seminary-level studies and intended to enroll at the Biblical Seminary in New York.[77] MBMC secretary S. C. Yoder recommended either that institution or the Moody Institute in Chicago for missionaries who wanted to pursue further studies.[78] Those Mennonite leaders who criticized MBMC and its missionaries often did so by charging that missionaries were too modernist in their theology. The Biblical Seminary in New York and the Moody Institute were two institutions that were spared by those critics. Upon applying to the former, however, Joe found that the economic realities of the Great Depression meant that there was little in the way of scholarship assistance.[79] He switched his focus to Princeton Seminary, where he found a more amenable financial situation.[80] Another plus for Princeton was that Noah Oyer, Harold Bender, and Chester Lehman, Mennonite leaders of Joe and Minnie's generation whom they admired, had studied there.[81] A one-year plan of study turned into two when MBMC decided to delay the Grabers' return to India because of a financial shortfall.[82] Minnie and Ronald remained in Manson for the first year, and Minnie took a Bible correspondence course through Bethany Seminary in Chicago, but the family was together at Princeton for the second year.

Joe at Princeton, January 1933, during his and Minnie's first furlough, his first year of studies there. At Princeton he did not wear the plain coat, where he decided it would be conspicuous, the opposite of simple attire. MCUSA ARCHIVES

Joe's time at Princeton Seminary was an opportunity to increase his competency in several areas, and he worked especially on his oratory skills. Classes the first semester included the gospel of John, systematic theology, homiletics, New Testament Greek, English Bible, apologetics, and ecclesiastical history.[83] Separated for an extended period for the first time since their engagement, Joe and Minnie corresponded regularly. The twenty-five extant letters that Joe wrote to Minnie during the fall of 1932 devote significantly more space to the topics of preaching and public speaking than to the other subjects that he was studying.[84]

At Princeton Joe studied under Andrew Blackwood, an innovative and influential homiletics specialist, who made a strong impression on him.[85] While colleagues had often experienced Joe as a gifted speaker, he thought that much of the preaching he had done up to that point was of poor quality.[86] He was also concerned that too often Mennonites did not preach well, lamenting, "All a man needs to make a splurge in the Mennonite Church is to have the gift of gab, be radical on a few points, have an overdose of self-confidence, and then shoot."[87] Anxious to change that dynamic, Joe wanted to build his sermons soundly with solid biblical study and thoughtful reflection and present them in a stimulating and fruitful way. Using gestures and voice inflections and finding a proper balance between intellectual discourse and popular speech were some of the things he worked to improve.[88] He saw his goal as achieving the correct blend of the scholar and the revivalist, a combination he believed even a Mennonite farmer would enjoy. Joe strove to be at the same time interesting, effective, and inspirational.[89]

The study furlough provided ample opportunity for Joe to practice his ideas about preaching and public speaking. Princeton was not far from Pennsylvania, and late in the fall of his first year he started receiving invitations to address Mennonite churches and young peoples' meetings in the Franconia Conference in eastern Pennsylvania. By the beginning of the twentieth century a few mission activists there had initiated activity in the conference, which sanctioned the creation of a Board of Missions in 1917.[90] Still, the transition to a mission mentality did not enjoy the wholehearted support of the leadership even in the 1930s.

By November members of Franconia Conference had learned that Joe was nearby, and invitations soon followed. An acquaintance from

Doylestown, Pennsylvania, helped arrange an invitation from Bishop Abraham O. Histand to preach at Doylestown Mennonite Church.[91] The weekend of the Doylestown visit, Joe met Melvin Bishop, pastor of Blooming Glen Mennonite Church, and Leidy Hunsicker, a chorister at Blooming Glen.[92] Such sympathetic contacts were essential for Joe's visits. Franconia Conference leadership sought to control the influence of visiting speakers, and a bishop's approval was necessary for an invitation.[93] Joe found that most of the older generation of bishops did not yet favor mission initiatives.

Hunsicker acted as a kind of booking agent for Joe, inviting him to Saturday and Sunday evening singing services that Hunsicker helped to plan and lead.[94] Joe typically preached a sermon and shared about the India mission work, and Hunsicker organized the singing. Joe was grateful that he was not in charge of these gatherings since the programs sometimes included special singing, by quartets, for example. Special singing was frowned on by the bishops and prohibited by Franconia Conference.[95] The singing services drew mostly young people and attracted large crowds. Joe reported attendances in the hundreds and noted that even the aisles and vestibules of the churches or chapels were often filled.

Leaders who supported mission work invited Joe to preach at their congregations on Sunday mornings, and he often also spoke in an adult Sunday school class as well as to the children. Joe eventually received so many invitations to speak that he sometimes had to decline to have enough time to complete his work at Princeton. He found these weekend visits to be energizing and encouraging since there was strong support for mission activity among the young people. For Franconia leaders who wanted to legitimize and increase mission awareness and activity in their churches, Joe provided a helpfully engaging and motivating voice.

Joe's visits to Franconia Conference saw the first articulation of what would later become a significant mark of his career as a mission advocate and visionary: the vision of mission outreach in every congregation. A group of Franconia young people had started Sunday schools in areas not served by a church.[96] The year before the Grabers' furlough these mission activists had rented meeting places and started regular church services at two new mission outposts. They were especially concerned to reach two minority communities, Italian immigrants and African Americans. The young people leading the initiative arranged for visits by sympathetic Franconia Conference bishops to baptize converts and reported regular attendance of as many as one hundred people in some places. The practice was to drive out to the communities to gather people and lead prayer meetings during the week and worship services on Sunday. Joe was impressed with the initiative and was disturbed when he learned that bishops in the area opposed this work as well as other evangelistic services. Referring to their opposition he wrote to Minnie, "Some people will have to give an account of some things in [at] the judgement!"[97]

Joe visited the Rocky Ridge and Finland outposts with the young people spearheading these initiatives and encouraged them to continue their efforts. His advice was to work within the limits imposed by the hesitant bishops but to find ways to challenge their intransigence. "By hitting the rim of the circle once in a while it would gradually enlarge," he thought.[98] James and Rowena Lark were early members of the Rocky Ridge congregation. The Mennonite Church would call the Larks to lead its mission work in Chicago in 1944, the same year that Joe would become executive secretary of MBMC and James would become the first African American bishop in the denomination.

The visits to Rocky Ridge and Finland stimulated Joe's imagination about local mission work in North America. He wrote to MBMC treasurer Vernon Reiff, "Some of the Franconia Bishops are opposed to these Sunday Schools out in the hills some of the younger members are running, but I personally feel like encouraging that sort of a thing as much as possible. In fact, if I have any outstanding conviction about Mennonite Mission Work it is that each congregation we have should have one or more Mission Sunday Schools. There are un-churched and un-evangelized areas within easy reach of practically every Mennonite congregation, I feel sure."[99] As secretary of MBMC in the decades following World War II, Joe would envision and lead MBMC's push for "a mission outpost for every congregation," a slogan that caught hold across the Mennonite Church and resulted in a flurry of mission activities and new congregations.

Because of accusations of modernism or liberalism against some MBMC missionaries and against Princeton Seminary, Joe had less occasion to speak at churches in Lancaster Conference, the other large Mennonite Church conference in eastern Pennsylvania. The bishops there were part of the traditional or protective element of the church who sought to counter the modernist or liberal tendencies that they thought were threatening the church. MBMC was one of many Protestant mission agencies caught up in the fundamentalist–modernist debate. Mennonite missionaries in India had for several years faced accusations of being modernists. In 1929 the Virginia Conference criticized the India mission, arguing for "more emphasis on preserving the orthodox position of the church," and a year later the Lancaster bishops called on MBMC to "send only missionaries trained in institutions 'beyond question as to orthodoxy and soundness.'"[100]

MBMC and the India missionaries acted to alleviate concerns about their supposed modernist leanings. MBMC formulated a doctrinal statement for missionaries to sign. It affirmed "full sympathy with the doctrine and principles of the Mennonite Church" and promised to "deny and oppose the doctrines of Modernism."[101] Missionaries staked out critiques of modernist and liberal theology and articulated them in the church press.[102] On furlough in 1929, veteran missionary George Lapp defended himself point-by-point in a meeting with the Lancaster bishops that resembled an interrogation.[103] As a college student Joe had allied himself with the fundamentalists by agreeing with many of the critiques of modernist theology. He did not consider himself or his fellow India missionaries to be modernists. He understood, however, that he had to navigate the controversy and was relieved to find that his professors at Princeton went out of their way to demonstrate that they were not modernist in their beliefs or teachings.[104]

While Joe was convinced of Princeton's orthodoxy, the Lancaster bishops were not.[105] He spoke at a Lancaster congregation during his first year at Princeton, but ten days later the board of bishops banned congregations from inviting him to speak at their services.[106] At a meeting in February 1933, they cited critiques of Princeton, found it to be too modernist, and banned congregations from inviting Joe to minister in Lancaster Conference since he was a Princeton student.

Joe was not able to itinerate in Lancaster Conference, but he did maintain cordial relationships with many Lancaster leaders. Some would have arranged for him to speak at their churches but apologized for not being able to do so.[107] Others, who were not aware of or who did not choose to respect the ban, did invite Joe, and he politely found ways to decline their invitations. In April 1934 Joe attended Lancaster Conference's annual mission meeting, despite the conference's decision to deny him the opportunity to speak. Afterward he reported to MBMC that he had a frank but cordial conversation with Bishop John Mosemann, a leading critic of MBMC's India mission for its supposed modernist tendencies. Mosemann held open the possibility of allowing Joe to speak in Lancaster Conference sometime in the future, saying that he hoped that Joe would conduct himself in such a way during his upcoming term in India that the doors might be open for him during his next furlough. Joe was able and willing to defend his point of view, in this case about Princeton Seminary's orthodoxy, while at the same time maintaining good relationships with those with whom he disagreed, a skill that would serve him well throughout his career.

Returning to India, or not

Joe and Minnie saw their decision to become missionaries in India as a vocational choice for the long term, but there were both institutional and personal challenges that needed to be addressed as they contemplated a second term. The economic crisis known as the Great Depression interrupted what had been a period of steady growth of financial resources available for the India mission work.

The Mennonite constituency's rising prosperity and growing interest in mission activity had meant a stream of new donors to the mission cause. During most of the 1920s, the rate of increasing support for MBMC outpaced that of other Protestant mission agencies.[108] By 1933 MBMC reported a net worth of $1,228,491, which included real estate, buildings, annuity funds, endowment funds, and special project funds.[109] Real estate included mission properties in North America, India, and South America as well as farms and other properties that had been passed to MBMC as charitable donations.[110] Endowment funds existed to provide for specific projects, and annuity funds delivered interest to annuitants and became estate donations to MBMC upon their death. MBMC invested such funds in loans, typically within the Mennonite constituency or to Mennonite-related charitable institutions and local mission boards. MBMC's overhead costs were extremely low since the only paid administrative staff was the treasurer; much of the other administrative work fell to unpaid executive committee members such as the president, Daniel D. Miller, or the secretary, Sanford C. Yoder. Undesignated interest from checking accounts and annuity funds covered overhead costs, so that MBMC could assure donors that all the funds they contributed would be used for mission work.

The financial crisis stalled the steady growth of financial resources. The constituency had less to contribute, and some who had taken loans from MBMC had to defer payment.[111] The early 1930s also saw resettlement of Mennonite refugees from the Soviet Union, which diverted funds that might otherwise have been used for MBMC initiatives. Meanwhile, droughts during the period meant Mennonite farmers had less disposable income.[112] Cash contributions had reached a peak of $281,737 in the fiscal year that ended in March 1930, but they decreased to $160,223 by 1934.[113] Even in 1930, MBMC ended that fiscal year with a deficit for the first time in its history.[114] Then in 1933 a sharp decrease in the value of the dollar only made it harder to meet the budgets in India and South America.[115]

MBMC responded to the financial crunch in several ways. Missionaries in India and South America took a 10 percent cut in allowance, mission stations and institutions reduced expenditures, and work that could be deferred was set aside for a later opportunity.[116] In the spring of 1931, MBMC delayed closing its books on the March 31 fiscal year deadline in order to allow for special Easter offerings, hoping to avoid the need to close the year with a deficit.[117] The India mission reduced its budget in 1931 and again in 1933, closed two schools, and canceled pay increases for AMM employees.[118] MBMC decreased the number of missionaries it planned to send overseas and, for the first time in its history, canceled sailing arrangements that had already been made for outgoing missionaries.[119] Furloughs for missionaries in the field were delayed, in some cases for several years, to reduce travel costs.[120] Articles in the *Gospel Herald* outlined the dire situation and warned that current work would have to be severely curtailed if the constituency did not respond with sacrificial giving.[121] For the first time, a series of ads appeared in the *Gospel*

Herald explaining MBMC's annuities and inviting people to consider investing in them.[122] The treasurer and executive committee arranged the budget expenditures into manageable amounts or "shares," such as the cost of supporting a teacher or evangelist for one year, and invited donors to buy these shares.[123]

While this strategy met with notable success, the MBMC budget had to undergo an additional 25 percent cut in July, August, and September of 1933, with cuts of up to 20 percent continuing for subsequent months through the following June.[124] Joe and Minnie did their part by instructing MBMC to suspend their allowance while they were on furlough.[125] Their income was limited to Joe's Princeton scholarship and what he received as honoraria for speaking engagements.

Meanwhile, Joe and Minnie had experienced a period of personal doubt about their future in India in light of the issues of discrimination and inequity that seemed to be intractable parts of mission activity in a colonial context. Joe was convinced of the need to reform AMM's way of working but found the mission structures and habits intransigent and doubted he could effect change, especially as a relative newcomer working with seasoned missionary colleagues.[126] Those with many years of experience in India found newer missionaries to be overly idealistic and naïve, and they resisted change. Whether there was a viable way to move the India mission work in a positive direction was a real question for the Grabers.[127]

Even if questions remained, Joe and Minnie soon regained their zeal. The message of a visiting speaker at Princeton proved instrumental. In early December 1932, New Jersey governor Harry Moore spoke on the responsibilities of a minister and the importance of living wholly and entirely for Christ.[128] Moore's address seems to have been providential for Joe as it led to a recommitment to ministry wherever God would direct him, in India or elsewhere. In addition, his itineration visits to Franconia Conference, by himself at first and as a family once Minnie and Ronald joined him at Princeton, were stimulating and encouraging. The Grabers found interest and energy for missions there, especially among young people.

In the end, the financial crisis delayed but did not prevent their return to India for a second term. The Grabers had been scheduled to return to India in the spring of 1933, but MBMC's financial crisis meant that their furlough lasted two years instead of one.[129] In February of 1934, despite the ongoing financial difficulties, MBMC decided to send the Grabers, along with Fred and Millie Brenneman, to India that summer.[130] Brenneman was a doctor, and there was no doctor on the field at the time. The AMM sorely needed the Grabers to shore up some administrative tasks for which no one else was available. When the letter of invitation came from MBMC secretary S. C. Yoder asking Joe and Minnie to return to India, they accepted.[131]

THREE

Back to India

"Indigenization" and Other Missiological Challenges

ON AN AUGUST Wednesday evening in 1936, Joe and Minnie moved the table out of their dining room and spread rugs on the floor in preparation for their evening guests.[1] With the coming of the rain after the hot dry season, temperatures in August were moderate and the countryside was once again green. It was a good time to entertain. The Grabers had invited three Indian colleagues and their families to share the evening meal. As was the custom in rural India at the time, they sat on the rugs as they ate and socialized.

The family of K. D. Ram was among the guests. He was the instructor at the American Mennonite Mission's carpentry school for which Joe was responsible. Ram and his family were preparing to leave Dhamtari as he was a government appointee and was being reassigned to a school in Nagpur, two hundred and ninety kilometers away.[2] To the delight of the group, one of Ram's children recited in clear and perfect Hindi a few stories that she had learned in kindergarten. Commenting on the evening, Joe noted with pleasure that everyone was much at ease and that the children, who were of similar ages, especially enjoyed themselves. Indian tradition valued hospitality, expressed by the phrase

Joe supervised the American Mennonite Mission's carpentry school. Back row are graduates circa 1936. Joe seated second from right. K. D. Ram, seated far left, was head instructor. He and his family were friends of Joe and Minnie. MCUSA ARCHIVES

atithi devo bhava from the Hindu Upanishads, meaning "Let thy guests be unto thee a god."[3] Having been on the receiving end of generous hospitality, Joe and Minnie enjoyed responding in kind. They placed a high value on forming and maintaining positive relationships with their Indian and missionary colleagues, a priority that became equally important in the way that they went about their missionary roles.

Relational mission engagement

Prioritizing relationships seemed to come naturally to the Grabers. Their intuitive sense of the importance of connecting spiritually and emotionally with their Indian colleagues sustained them during difficult times and had a long-term impact. Joe and Minnie expressed great appreciation for the support and comfort of Indian friends when they received news of the death of parents and siblings in North America and could not travel back to grieve with their families.[4] They sought ways to increase mutuality with their Indian colleagues and invited them into their homes to socialize and eat together.[5] Such socializing had not been common practice among missionaries previously but was becoming more common with those of the Grabers' generation.[6]

Joe had a warm relationship with J. W. Samida. A fellow teacher at Dhamtari Academy, the Mennonite high school, Samida became the academy's first Indian principal.[7] The Samidas lived next door to the Grabers, and the families were close. Joe valued the relationship and gave Samida his own Hindi Bible inscribed with a heartfelt message upon leaving India in 1942. Decades later Eleanor, Joe and Minnie's daughter, and her husband, Alan Kreider, met Bishop Shant Kunjam, who was their interpreter at the 1997 Mennonite World Conference in Calcutta. Upon learning that Eleanor was Joe's daughter, Kunjam clasped his hands in joy and showed them his Bible. "Look here," he said, "This is your father's Bible that Mr. Samida gave to me just before he died. It was a special blessing for me in my ministry. The blessing passed from your father through Samida to me. My family reads from this Bible every day at our morning prayers."[8]

Joe was committed to developing and maintaining deep friendships and good working relationships such as he had with Samida. He strove to encourage positive professional and interpersonal rapport with fellow missionaries and Indian colleagues.[9] He was especially appreciative of Indian leaders who, when debate at church conference meetings became heated and divisive, would intervene to call for a time of prayer and worship in an attempt to seek divine guidance. Joe described such times of collective prayer as key to the ongoing ministry cooperation within the church and between the Indian church and the North American missionaries.

The focus on relationships became an important missionary posture during a period when nationalists were challenging colonial assumptions and institutions but when there was not yet clarity about what the future would be and how mission energy might be expressed in the new era. Joe and Minnie were convinced that a change in the tenor of the relationships between missionaries and indigenous Christians was necessary. Already early in their first term they had expressed discomfort with what seemed like an attitude of paternalism on the part of missionaries.[10] Indeed, the pioneer missionaries had often literally played the role of parents to children whom they took into their orphanages. Church members, many of whom had passed through the orphanages or AMM schools, often found employment in a mission institution, making the missionaries also their employers.

By the time Joe and Minnie arrived on the scene there were mature Christians in the church who were ready to leave behind those paradigms of parent and employer in favor of more equitable and mutual relationships. The increasingly determined push for decolonization in the wider social context added a sense of urgency. Prioritizing closer relationships between missionaries and Indian Christians challenged the colonial assumptions present in divisions between Westerners and Indians and laid a foundation for a future that was still unclear. At the missionaries' annual business meeting in November 1937, Minnie led a session on the subject of "How [to] foster a closer fellowship with the Indian people, spiritually and socially."[11] Conscious of the urgency of working for more equitable relationships with Indian colleagues and appreciative of their spiritual and collegial rapport, Joe and Minnie took an innovative relational mission approach, even as more traditional missionary institutions and assumptions had not yet given way.

Chosen for leadership—secretary of AMM and bishop

Joe and Minnie's second term in India was a period of deepening relationships and, for Joe, new leadership roles. His fellow missionaries, the Mennonite Board of Missions and Charities, and the Mennonite Church in India all recognized gifts that motivated them to call him to leadership. Joe responded as he had over the previous decade when the church called him to mission roles:he accepted.

At their annual business meeting in November 1936, Joe's colleagues chose him to be secretary of AMM, a post that he would hold for four years.[12] It was up to the missionaries to choose a managing committee and its officers to direct AMM's affairs.[13] MBMC reserved the power of final approval of the secretary but typically approved AMM's decision. The president held the power of attorney, but the secretary implemented and explained mission decisions and policies. On a day-to-day basis the secretary was the face and arm of AMM, the primary liaison with MBMC, the person to whom missionaries turned when they needed assistance, and the one who dealt with government officials and regulations. As secretary Joe coordinated the discernment and articulation of policy on several missiological issues that came to the fore in the years leading up to World War II.

Meanwhile, the Mennonite Church in India chose Joe for roles of spiritual oversight. Already during the Grabers' first term the Sundarganj congregation in Dhamtari had selected him for a two-year term as pastor.[14] The selection of a new bishop was on the church's agenda in February 1939, and Joe was among those for whom the Indian delegates and missionaries voted; he and an Indian colleague received the greatest number of votes.[15] A second round of votes did not provide the required two-thirds majority for either candidate, so the conference opted to make the decision using the time-honored Mennonite practice of drawing lots. The lot fell to Joe, although the conference did not ordain him bishop until its annual meeting the following December.[16]

Given his administrative authority as secretary of AMM and his spiritual authority as bishop, Joe now had a platform from which he could influence mission theory and practice. During their first term Joe and Minnie had been cautious about taking initiative or critiquing

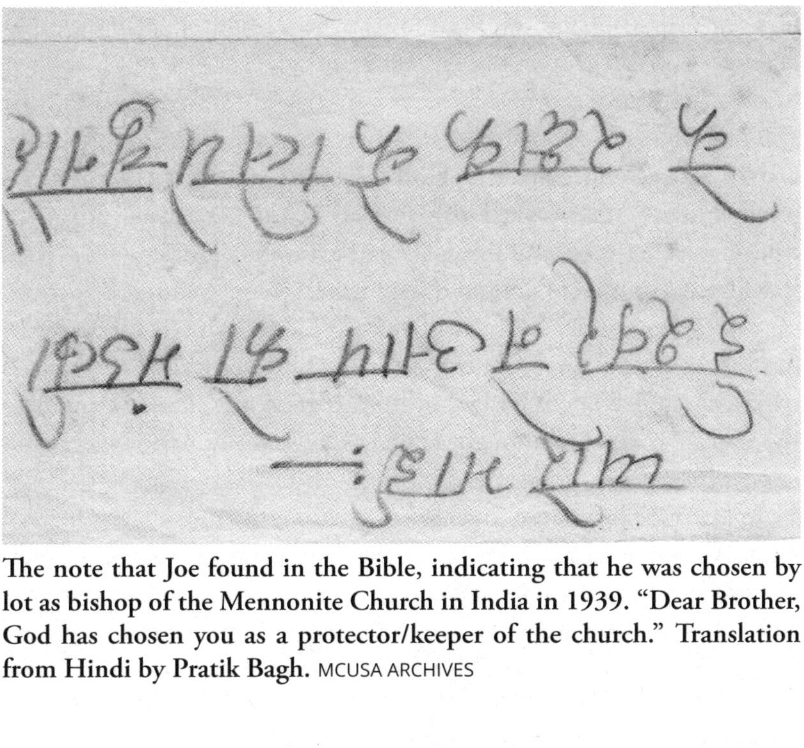

The note that Joe found in the Bible, indicating that he was chosen by lot as bishop of the Mennonite Church in India in 1939. "Dear Brother, God has chosen you as a protector/keeper of the church." Translation from Hindi by Pratik Bagh. MCUSA ARCHIVES

the approach of their missionary colleagues and of AMM in general.[17] The second term was different. By mid-term only twelve of the thirty-eight active missionaries had been working in India longer than Joe and Minnie.[18] The Grabers were now veterans and could more boldly innovate and develop their own approaches.[19] This, along with the confidence that the Indian church, his missionary colleagues, and MBMC showed in him, encouraged Joe to take on the challenge of leadership in India during the pre–World War II period.

Indigenization and missionary–Indian relationships

The Grabers' preferred approach resembled what missionaries and missiologists called indigenization. The concept emerged as a goal in nineteenth and twentieth century Protestant mission thinking but was difficult to implement in colonial contexts. Indigenization derived in large measure from Henry Venn and Rufus Anderson's three-self theory, which they articulated in the mid-nineteenth century.[20] They proposed that mission activity should develop indigenous churches, which they defined as self-financing, self-administering, and self-propagating churches free of dependence on Western resources. With the establishment of such churches, Western missionaries could move on to other regions where the church did not yet exist.

After the European powers carved up the African continent at the 1884–1885 Berlin Conference, however, the imperial spirit intensified and spilled over into the work of missionaries. Paternalistic assumptions resulted in missionaries retaining control of churches decades after they had established them. Additionally, churches in colonized lands often lacked the resources to maintain the institutions and church structures that missionaries had founded. Some missionaries used this as justification to argue that churches were not ready for indigenization. As nationalist movements for political independence gained strength in the twentieth century, though, churches in Asia and Africa also began to seek their independence.

In India the first decades of the twentieth century were a transitional time of nascent decolonization. There was growing frustration with the slow progress towards self-rule in the aftermath of World War I, when the British had promised movement in that direction, with the presumption that India would follow the dominion model of Canada,

Australia, and New Zealand. The British parliament ceded some power with the 1935 India Act, which gave the provinces a semblance of autonomy through the vote but kept the central government in the hands of loyalists.[21] The paternalism and racism endemic to colonial control of India generated deep animosity toward Westerners as a whole. In the minds of many Indians, there was no difference between the British, other Europeans, and North Americans. All personified colonialism.

While Mennonite missionaries were not normally implicated directly in the structures of the colonial state, they were entangled in the colonial culture. Missionaries' roles as employers of church members, their control of mission funds, schools, and hospitals, and their status as white Westerners placed them in positions of power over their Indian colleagues and left them open to accusations of complicity with the colonial systems, sometimes justifiably so.[22] The situation complicated relations between foreign mission agencies and Indian churches as the former sought to implement processes of indigenization. In the early 1930s, the German Evangelical Mission Society, which worked some four hundred kilometers northeast of Dhamtari, adopted policies to move the church it founded toward indigenization and away from dependency.[23] Church members objected to the subsequent disruption of their economic well-being, used nationalist language to accuse the missionaries of colonialism, and withdrew to form their own church independent of the mission society.

The establishment of an indigenous church had been a clear objective from the beginning of MBMC's work in India. Still, and even though indigenization was a goal of missionaries of all stripes, what exactly it meant and how best to achieve it remained open questions.[24] Missionaries regularly articulated some form of the three-self theory and envisioned an Indian Mennonite church that would be "wholly Indian in tradition, policy, and expression" and free of foreign domination and support.[25] Working as colporteurs, evangelists, and Bible women, Indian Christians were the primary actors in the establishment of the church, and the first Indian deacons were ordained after the AMM organized the India Mennonite Conference in 1912.[26] The conference was a separate structure from AMM with membership that included missionaries, church leaders, and congregational delegates. It had decision-making power over church affairs but not over AMM. In its annual business meeting in 1921, AMM resolved to shift responsibilities for its work to Indian personnel whenever possible, but the process was gradual and the practical results few.[27] Missionaries found it difficult to cede responsibility. Finally, in 1931 the first Indian pastor was chosen, and eight years later five of the ten Mennonite congregations had Indian pastors.[28]

Joe provided leadership during the 1930s, when decolonization was gaining force in Indian society and in ecclesial circles. Indian Mennonites were part of the larger push for self-rule, and their desire for a shift of control to indigenous hands within church and mission structures intensified.[29] Divisive conflict and the breakdown of relations between Indians and Western missionaries was a real possibility. Joe and Minnie had noticed how AMM structures and ways of working conveyed a sense of paternalism. Their attempts to cultivate more equitable relationships with Indian colleagues was one way they sought to address the situation. Joe sensed the implication of the independence movement before many of his missionary colleagues did. Recognizing the resolve and legitimacy of the Indian church's desire, he sought adequate responses.[30] He was impressed with the maturity of Indian church leaders and was confident that they were up to the task of guiding the church wisely and faithfully.[31]

With the agreement of his colleagues in November 1937, Joe asked MBMC to authorize the formal transfer of ownership of church buildings from AMM to the church.[32] He argued that hesitancy to do so risked giving the impression that AMM was "unsympathetic towards the natural development of the church."[33] Later the same year the missionaries suggested transferring to the church the responsibility for managing Mennonite primary schools and awarding AMM scholarships.[34] They also requested that the church appoint Indian leaders as pastors instead of appointing missionaries. Indian Mennonites wanted deeper changes, however, and asked to be incorporated into all AMM committees, including the all-important managing committee.[35] Such a move would introduce Indians into the decision-making structures of AMM and require a modification of its constitution.

The transfer of spiritual authority and of the ownership of church buildings to the Indian church conference moved forward. Indian leaders progressively took over more of the pastoral posts, and MBMC approved the transfer of properties to the Indian church, although the details of making the decision and its implementation took time.[36] The Indian legal processes were cumbersome, and the work of transferring both church and mission-related properties to the Mennonite Church in India was not completed until 1975.[37]

However, the church's request to integrate Indians into AMM committees did not go forward. It was a question upon which missionaries and Indian church leaders simply disagreed, and Joe and his colleagues decided against the proposal.[38] They had the power to do so since they controlled the AMM and its resources. The missionaries' reasoning was that it was in the best interests of both church and mission agency that the two remain organizationally separate. AMM, wrote Joe, sought to follow the example of Paul, focusing on direct evangelism beyond the context of the established church and to the ends of the earth. Integration of Indians on all committees could lead to an amalgamation of church and mission agency, tempting the mission agency to become permanent in one place and forget its provisional nature. This logic was consistent with mission theory that assumed mission structures to be temporary and transient, allowing missionaries to move on to uncharted territory after the establishment of an indigenous church. Differences of opinion between Indian church members and North American missionaries remained unresolved. Missionaries were troubled enough by the situation to request that MBMC send a delegation to help the two sides resolve their differences.[39] MBMC agreed to do so but found it impossible because of the outbreak of World War II.

Joe's defense of the decision to refuse to integrate Indian Mennonites into the mission agency structure appears incongruous with the priority he placed on strong collegial relationships with Indian colleagues. Allowing for more involvement of Indians in AMM committees would have modified the mission structures to formalize collaboration, shared missionary power with Indian church leaders, and been more consistent with the Grabers' relational mission focus. Joe appears to have sensed as much. In both the letter informing MBMC secretary S. C. Yoder of the decision against integration and in his official report, Joe took pains to affirm the importance of cooperation, closer fellowship, and the rejection of racial discrimination in relationships with Indian colleagues.[40]

Whether because of colonial assumptions that tended to maintain separate social circles for Indians and Westerners, a hesitancy to give up power, or the intransigence of traditional mission practice, AMM under Joe's leadership decided against integration of Indians into its committees in 1939. It was clear that the colonial era was coming to an end, but it was not yet clear how mission should happen in a new age. In this case there was disagreement about how institutional structures needed to be adjusted. Joe seemed to understand that mission practice had entered a period of flux. He wrote to Yoder, "We do not consider this problem is solved. We have reached a particular stage. We cannot stay but must seek the further guidance of God. He will point the way."[41]

Seven years later, in 1946, Joe and AMM reversed direction and helped implement the changes that the Indian church had requested. They incorporated Indians into the missionary business sessions, and together Indians and missionaries wrote a new, albeit provisional, constitution that integrated Indians into the mission agency and changed the name of the American Mennonite Mission to the India Mennonite Mission.[42] By then Joe was executive secretary of MBMC, and he was pleased with the new constitution and the more collaborative structure that it provided.

Missionary vocation and family life

Joe and Minnie worked for most of their first term in India without children, but with Ronald's birth two years before their first furlough and the arrival of Eleanor early in the second term, family dynamics played a greater role in their mission engagement. In addition to the new leadership roles, Joe and Minnie continued the day-to-day missionary work of their first term.

The added responsibilities of motherhood did not relieve AMM's women missionaries of their missionary responsibilities.[43] To allow time for ministry they typically employed household help: a cook, a nanny, and perhaps a gardener and errand man. Minnie taught part-time in the Bible department of Dhamtari Academy and worked with the Bible women, visiting households to share songs and Bible stories and to invite people to Christian faith. When Minnie did evangelistic work with the Bible women in the villages around Dhamtari, Eleanor sometimes accompanied her, perched on the back of Minnie's bicycle.

The condition of some roads and paths made the going difficult. Eleanor remembered having to walk alongside when deep sand bogged down the bicycle, and Minnie was forced to dismount and push.

Joe had a range of responsibilities that included teaching, pastoral tasks, and supervision of mission institutions. He was the head teacher in the Bible department of Dhamtari Academy, supervised the carpentry school and the boys' dormitories, and participated in the pastoral ministry of the local Mennonite congregation along with Indian church leaders and the other missionaries.[44] At the academy he taught a variety of classes and was principal for several years.[45]

Dhamtari Academy was a secondary school that played an important part in the AMM mission strategy. Schools of all sorts were a typical feature of the missionary movement, although not everyone agreed about their usefulness to the missionary task. Some argued that the provision of education was a ministry in itself, since it helped students and society to advance socially and economically. Others contended that schools were useful to the extent that they were a means of evangelization or of training for church leaders. Still others opposed schools altogether, seeing them as an unfortunate drain on personnel and financial resources that would have been better focused on more direct methods of evangelization.

Joe was among those who argued that schools were a useful means to evangelize and strengthen the church.[46] He noted that early on missionaries had neglected to provide formal theological and biblical training for church leaders in India, in part because they came from a Mennonite community in North America that relied on leaders who did not have such training.[47] The Indian church, he argued, did not have a long-established Mennonite tradition that produced leadership and consequently needed formal training for its leaders. Dhamtari Academy helped fill this need with its multitrack program: teacher training, a typical secondary education track, and religious training for Christian teachers and ministers.

Joe taught courses having to do with Christianity, Christian ministry, and the Bible. Some of his students would become teachers and leaders in the church, and he was pleased to arrange supervised practical ministry experiences for them. During school vacations he took groups of students, accompanied by Indian church leaders, to the

Joe with some of his students in Dhamtari, India, in October 1936.
MCUSA ARCHIVES

villages around Dhamtari, where they taught and evangelized.[48] This was in the tradition of missionary touring, but in this case involved young people who would later become leaders in the church. Students were eager for such opportunities, and Joe was pleased with their enthusiasm and dedication. Touring by missionaries had not produced the large number of converts that missionaries had envisioned, but Joe was encouraged that young Indian Christians, who were well prepared to evangelize in their home culture, were excited to step into such ministry roles.

There were also Hindu and Muslim students in his classes. Dhamtari Academy was open to students of all faiths even though classes in Christian faith and Bible were part of the curriculum. Students who were not Christian could opt out of the religion classes, but most did not.[49] Joe considered this an opportunity to present the Christian faith to some who would not otherwise be exposed to Christianity.[50] He enjoyed interacting with the questions and ideas of his Hindu and Muslim students, even though he never reported that any of them became Christian. Joe translated the gospel of Matthew into Hindi for his Bible students, describing Jesus with the culturally appropriate term *pundit*, from the Sanskrit term *pandit*, which referred to a religious teacher.[51]

His eclectic interests and abilities were useful assets when Joe was faced with the various other tasks that might befall a missionary. For example, pioneer missionary J. A. Ressler had introduced telephone technology to Dhamtari when he installed a system to communicate between mission stations in 1905.[52] Adding new stations and maintaining parts of the system fell to Joe during periods of the Grabers' tenure.[53] New stations meant raising poles, stringing wire, and installing new phones. Maintenance of the system was perhaps even more of a challenge. The poles typically followed roads, and when the axles of passing oxcarts periodically broke, drivers found the telephone poles to be temptingly easy replacements. Joe saw to the ongoing need to replace poles and wire and to repair telephones.

For Ronald and Eleanor, life in Dhamtari as young children was in some ways similar to that of children in North America, and in other ways quite different. The Graber family enjoyed picnics along the Mahanadi River, which flowed southeast of the town, or at the edge of the jungle, spots that provided cool relief from the heat.[54] Ronald had a bicycle to get around the neighborhood and Touser, the family's pet dog, to tag along. Another of the family's pets, however, was of a more exotic nature. It arrived in a wooden box on the head of a porter from the train station, marked simply as a gift from Reverend Menzel. The Grabers had met Emil Menzel, of the Reformed Mission, in Darjeeling, a "hill station" (as high-altitude resort towns were called) where missionaries of different denominations had opportunities to socialize. Joe and Menzel were both connoisseurs of humor, and Menzel was a notorious jokester with an interest in plants and animals.[55] Upon opening the box Joe was astonished, and the woman who brought it horrified, to find a mature live python nearly seven feet long.[56] Minnie wanted nothing to do with it, but Joe kept it in a cage in the cow stable by the carpentry school, took it out for a "walk" periodically, and fed it a live rat once a month. When Ronald was away at boarding school, Joe kept him apprised of how the two pets were doing.

The challenge of providing schooling for missionary children in India was significant, and boarding schools were a common solution.[57] AMM missionaries sent their children to English-language boarding schools in Darjeeling, Landour, or Kodaikanal, several days travel from

Eleanor and Ron in Darjeeling, India, where they attended boarding school. 1939. MCUSA ARCHIVES

Dhamtari. These hill stations had a more temperate climate than did the region around Dhamtari, where the intense heat of the dry season drained missionaries' stamina; temperatures from March to June rose to between 99° and 108° Fahrenheit (37° to 42° Celsius). Missionaries typically escaped for a month or two to these hill stations, where higher elevations provided a temperate climate for rejuvenation and spending time with their children who were in school there.[58]

Joe and Minnie sent Ronald and Eleanor to the Mount Hermon School in Darjeeling. At the beginning of the school year, one or two of the missionaries would accompany the group of children who attended Mount Hermon on the multiday train trip of one thousand kilometers (620 miles) into the Himalayas.[59] The group traveled third class, in a car with perhaps four wooden benches and the same number of ceiling racks for luggage, although passengers also occupied those sometimes.[60] Space was at a premium; not everyone was lucky enough to have a place on a bench for either the waking or sleeping hours. The students and their adult chaperones arranged themselves among the assorted pieces of luggage that passengers brought onboard: lunch baskets, trunks, suitcases, bedding rolls, bags, sun helmets, and bundles of all kinds. Cinders and soot accumulated in the car during the trip, and

Minnie noted that the eager students looked like little chimney sweeps by the time they arrived at the destination. The transfer between train stations in Calcutta was an ordeal, as the chaperones struggled to make sure everyone and their various pieces of luggage were accounted for amidst the hustle and bustle. The final leg of the trip, from Siliguri to Darjeeling, was via a narrow-gauge railroad that switchbacked its way up into the mountains, often leaving travelers feeling seriously queasy or downright sick.

Joe and Minnie typically spent time in Darjeeling each year. Minnie stayed for several months, and Joe joined her and the children for part of that time.[61] They and their AMM colleagues A. C. and Eva (Harder) Brunk shared the ownership of a cabin near the Mount Hermon School. Darjeeling provided opportunities for fellowship with missionaries of other churches and for family activities uninterrupted by the myriad of missionary responsibilities at Dhamtari. The academic calendar allowed the children to be home in Dhamtari during the temperate part of the year and for the Christmas season, and their parents were able to lodge near the boarding schools during their hill visits, thus reducing the amount of time parents and children lived apart. The experience of being separated for months at a time was naturally traumatic for both the younger children and their parents but seemed to be the best way to provide the schooling that would help the children to reintegrate into their home societies as adults and allow their parents to fulfill their missionary duties. Ronald started attending boarding school when he was five years old and Eleanor when she was six.[62]

Being far from extended family presented another challenge for the Grabers. Both Joe and Minnie's fathers passed away during their time in India, as did several of their siblings and extended family members.[63] Such news came via telegraph, and the distance between India and North America meant that Joe and Minnie grieved these life transitions together but far from their extended families and meaningful end-of-life rituals. They found Indian coworkers to be sympathetic and helpful during such times but described these periods of mourning as some of the most difficult of their missionary experience. The Grabers were grateful to be able to attend the funeral ceremonies of Joe's mother, who passed away in June of 1943, while they were in North America for their second furlough.[64]

If missionary life presented certain challenges to family life, the India experience contributed to long-term vocational fulfillment for the Grabers. Upon departure from India, Joe became executive secretary of MBMC. Minnie served as president of the MBMC's Women's Missionary Sewing Circle Organization, later the Women's Missionary and Service Auxiliary. Ronald became a surgeon and a member of the American College of General Surgeons, spending his career as a medical missionary at the MBMC hospital at Aibonito, Puerto Rico. Eleanor and her family served two decades as missionaries in the United Kingdom.

Missionary trials and group conversion

Evangelization has always been a difficult goal in India. Even Western missionaries who put a premium on building relationships found Indian culture to be challenging. The most responsive persons to Christianity tended to be from lower castes or tribal groups that were marginalized in the ancient and proud religion of Hinduism.

Within the context of such a challenge, the conversion of groups of people—caste groups or villages, for example—was part of the social context of India in the early twentieth century and became a matter of missiological discernment and strategy for Joe and Minnie and their missionary colleagues. Western Protestant mission theory and strategy had assumed that conversion to the Christian faith was primarily an individual matter, even if the history of the Christian movement included many instances of group conversion.[65] India brought the idea of converting whole groups of people back into Protestant missionary experience and strategy as people made collective decisions and came into the Christian faith as extended families, villages, or other social groupings.[66]

The possibility that missionaries might be able to encourage and channel such movements was only heightened when the Indian jurist and social reformer Bhimrao R. Ambedkar became convinced that the Hindu tradition was not an asset in the social advancement of marginalized classes. He announced in 1935 that he would not die a Hindu and invited the "untouchables" to follow his lead.[67] Writing to MBMC in February of the following year, Joe estimated the followers of Ambedkar to number about fifty million and noted that there were many around Dhamtari whom missionaries would happily welcome into the church.[68]

News of Ambedkar's statements was heartening for missionaries who were discouraged at the slow rate of growth of the Indian church. Missionary evangelistic touring was a high priority but produced relatively few converts, especially when one considers the significant time, energy, and personnel dedicated to the endeavor. The Mennonite Church in India had grown to 1,411 members between AMM's beginnings in 1899 and the end of 1936.[69] Most of these members had received assistance via Mennonite orphanages or primary schools.[70] Missionaries sounded an upbeat tone in their reports and letters to the home church, balancing a hesitancy to share their disappointment about the slow rate of church growth with the desire to be honest with their supporters. Frustration was evident, however, as they discussed, meditated, and prayed at their gatherings.[71] Responding to her father's inquiry about success among Hindus, Minnie wrote, "We are not satisfied with the results in our evangelistic work. And we have to say it with great humility because we feel that a great deal of the trouble lies with us—it must because surely God's promises are the same if we only appropriate the power."[72]

There was a creeping temptation to question if the North American church's support of the mission had been worth the effort. The constituency in North America was supportive, but articles such as "To What Purpose Is This Waste?" in the *Gospel Herald* suggest an undercurrent of questioning that sought a response.[73] Collecting yearly reports for MBMC, Minnie described missionary Alma Smucker's reaction when she found that it was once again time for a report. "How can I do it?" she asked as tears filled her eyes.[74]

Given their disappointment with the church's slow rate of growth, the Grabers and their colleagues followed the news of recent "mass movements" (as the phenomenon of group conversion came to be known) with interest. Joe was encouraged; he and others reported signs and expectations that a large influx to the Mennonite Church would happen soon.[75] AMM opened a new mission station in the district of Drug, home to many Satnami people, a group of agriculturalists descended mostly from the caste of leather workers, whom missionaries had long hoped would be the source of a mass conversion to Christianity.[76] Missionary A. C. Brunk accompanied J. Waskom Pickett, a Methodist missionary and expert on mass movements, on a study tour of such movements in southern India in October 1934. The following year AMM undertook a survey of the different castes in its own mission field, hoping the results would assist them in effecting a movement into the church along caste lines.[77] Back in North America on furlough in 1936, missionary S. J. Hostetler addressed the annual MBMC meeting on the theme of "Soul Winning Methods that Have Proved Successful in India," explaining mass movements and a number of the reasons that they would likely soon take place in the AMM field.[78] He described the advantages of group conversion: that new Christians did not have to experience social dislocation and did not become dependent on the missionary compound for their livelihood.

Hopes for a large influx into the Mennonite Church were in vain, however. Despite the enthusiasm evident in letters and reports, the mass movement phenomenon eluded the missionaries. At a meeting of the Mid-India Christian Council, where Pickett was speaking, missionary George Lapp rose and asked in an impassioned way, "Dr. Pickett, why does not that sort of thing happen here?" The question was born of long-building disappointment.[79] Hoping to assist missions such as the AMM that were not benefiting from the group conversion dynamic, the Mid-India Christian Council organized a study of Christian missions in mid-India.[80] The study, entitled *Christian Missions in Mid India*, attempted to identify how and why mass movements started, what made them successful church growth events, and what mission strategies might encourage them.

While the *Mid India* study lauded the three decades of effort to establish an Indian Christian community that could in turn propagate the faith, it offered a critical appraisal of AMM's methods.[81] Missionary support of the Christian community, the report argued, had caused Christians to see themselves as a people apart, a community that benefited from the mission but was separated from its own people. The economic and social advantages that AMM provided had created a dependent church membership, people who often left their villages to move closer to a mission station but who were not interested in evangelizing. In addition to creating dependency, AMM planning, organization, theory, and institutions had produced isolated conversions, whereas other types of thinking and organization would have been more conducive to the conversion of whole groups in their natural social units. Since AMM-style mission programs were common among missionaries in India, the AMM served as a case study of general discontent with established mission practices.[82]

The *Mid India* study likely overstated its case, since there were notable instances of Indian Mennonites who evangelized others and since mass movements were not part of the social fabric everywhere in India. But Joe and Minnie and their colleagues took the critiques to heart. They sought to improve their understanding of their context and adjust their mission practice accordingly. Joe was not one to cling to traditional strategies when it seemed clear that they were not working. He eagerly pursued fresh and innovative ways to move forward. He argued for trying to convince new converts to stay in their home villages to decrease social disruption, hoping that they would witness to other members of their family and caste.[83]

In the late 1930s, under Joe's leadership and with MBMC's blessing, AMM decided to open another field where they would apply newer mission theory and practice.[84] The goal was to discontinue strategies that had not worked in the region around Dhamtari and to try new approaches. Missionaries would increase their mobility and do more direct evangelistic work, decreasing time and energy spent working with charitable institutions and schools. Joe and his colleagues decided to prioritize work among groups in which there were indications that people were willing to hear and receive the gospel. Of all the possible factors, such as location, language of the people, and demography, the likelihood of a positive response to the missionary message was to be the guiding principle when deciding where to put their efforts. AMM considered several areas—one in the west of India (in modern-day Pakistan), two in Bihar, and two in West Bengal—before deciding on a region in Bihar that had been a former Methodist Episcopal Mission field.

Mission theology

Joe did not develop a systematic mission theology, but by the end of the Grabers' second term themes had emerged from his work and writing. The lack of a formal mission theology was a characteristic of the larger missionary movement in which matters of method and strategy had dominated missionary discourse. The need for theological formulations would garner attention in the decades that followed.[85] As a college student and early in his missionary career, the fundamentalist–modernist debate was an important framework for Joe. He evaluated theological stances on their repudiation of modernism.[86] He still rejected modernism after sixteen years of missionary service, but other themes that seemed more pertinent to the needs of the church in India and in North America replaced that framework in his theological reflections.

An important newer focus was what Joe termed "universality."[87] By this he meant not only that the gospel was for all peoples of the world, but also that mission was the responsibility of all believers, not just of designated missionaries. All Christians needed to be able to witness to the hope that was within them.[88] For Joe, the universality of the gospel motivated the church in every place to mission.

Two other themes that Joe highlighted were the importance of the Holy Spirit and the significance of faith. It was the Spirit that motivated the ministry of the apostles and led to the establishment and spread of the church in the New Testament.[89] It continued to be the divine presence that convinced, emboldened, and made effective the preaching of believers. The Spirit also was there to guide the believer, leading and directing in the face of opportunities and disappointments, doors that opened and closed. For Joe, faith was an adventurous trusting in God through which believers were assured of the sufficiency and efficacy of the gospel. Such trust was only possible if the believer had experienced faith and seen it in the lives of others.[90] Faith could propel the believer forward with endurance in the face of the inevitable hardships and suffering that were always part and parcel of the missionary task.

Finally, Joe argued that missionaries had to take into account the particular context in which they worked. In this respect, he was among those who anticipated what would become a major discussion after 1960, when new generations of missionaries would refer to the concept of contextualization. For Joe differences of race, language, standard of living, religious expectations, or ways of thinking resulted in different expressions of biblical faithfulness and missionary method.[91]

One of the ways that Joe engaged such differences was through comparative analysis of the doctrines and practices of Christianity,

Hinduism, and Islam. In articles for the church press he described and compared understandings of sacrifice, creation, God, humanity, worship, and sin, taking seriously the particular context of Indian culture and social life.[92] Of the three major approaches to the theology of religions—exclusivism, inclusivism, and pluralism—Joe fit most closely in the exclusivism category, arguing that there was no compromise about salvation, which was through Jesus Christ.[93] He also rejected as "utterly inadequate" the suggestion that Christianity might be the fulfillment of a non-Christian religion.[94] His exclusivism was nuanced, however, with sympathy and respect for people of other faiths and their religious needs and understandings, even when those needs and understandings differed from his own.

Innovation for a new day

The Grabers' second term in India fell during a period of growing doubt about traditional mission approaches, prompting questions about how to move forward. This was true of the larger missionary movement and for Joe personally as he took on the challenges of indigenizing mission structures and the expectations for church growth that the mass-movement phenomenon encouraged. Structures and approaches that had seemed to work earlier or that had depended on colonial structures would not work and would lack credibility in the postcolonial era.

J. Waskom Pickett's 1933 book *Christian Mass Movements in India* had analyzed the phenomenon of group conversion and suggested that missionaries of all stripes would have to rethink their basic assumptions and ways of working.[95] Group conversions seemed to encourage Indian Christians to maintain strong ties with their social groups, increasing their evangelistic influence and resulting in a Christian faith that was more thoroughly Indian in its patterns and customs. Mission practice centered too heavily in mission institutions, often tied to paternalistic and colonial ways of working, had resulted in dependency. Pickett argued that missionaries had not adequately adapted their methods to the Indian situation. His study provided a potent argument for Joe and other Mennonite missionaries who were seeking to understand why their efforts to increase the size and strength of the Indian Mennonite Conference were not more fruitful.

Christian Missions in Mid India, the study that specifically critiqued AMM's mission approach around Dhamtari, evaluated mission practice in light of Pickett's recommendations. As such it sought to explain why Mennonite missionary work had not benefited from group conversions and what approaches needed to be set aside or adopted to be more successful. Joe's description of AMM's new approach for its new field in Bihar was in line with these proposals for new ways of working.[96]

Donald McGavran, a missionary from the neighboring Disciples of Christ mission, was a leading member of the *Mid India* study team and a close friend and colleague of the Grabers. He wrote the first chapter of the published report as well as the conclusion, "How the Church Grows in Mid India," and was the sole researcher for two of the nine regions of the study.[97] After a missionary career in India, he would become the primary visionary for the Church Growth movement among North American missionaries and missiologists. During his time as executive secretary of MBMC, Joe would maintain a relationship with McGavran, consult him about mission strategy, and recommend his books to missionaries. While he and his MBMC colleagues did not always follow the lead of McGavran or his Church Growth associates, even identifying weaknesses and dangers of the approach, McGavran became an important interlocutor for Mennonite missionaries as they formulated and implemented their mission approaches in the post-colonial era.[98]

The Grabers' experience of working in India during a time of questioning and reorientation help to explain the missiological commitments that emerged later in Joe's career. His call for a posture of fraternal relationships with Indian Christians and his critique of white supremacy at the MBMC annual meeting in 1932 can be understood as a response to what he experienced as a pattern of paternalism in relationships between North American missionaries and Indian Christians.[99] The apprehension about whether to integrate Indian Christians into AMM structures is indicative of the pre–World War II years. It was becoming increasingly clear that formal colonial control of India was coming to an end, but missionaries had not yet let go of structures that embodied colonial assumptions and practices. New structural models that encouraged more equitable relationships needed to be envisioned and established, a value that Joe subsequently promoted when AMM adjusted its constitution and name to integrate Indian members into its committees.

The questions that grew out of studies of the group-conversion dynamic provided the opportunity to set aside traditional mission approaches that were not fruitful and to envision new ways of working. For the first time Joe clearly articulated the importance of social and cultural contexts, arguing that people should be able to come to Christian faith from within their particular settings, without severing ties to family and home context. During the interwar years missionaries were increasingly recognizing the value of anthropology for their work, and Joe was among those who encouraged appropriating the tools of that discipline in subsequent decades.[100] Instead of being tied to administrative roles in educational or healthcare institutions in centralized mission stations, he argued, missionaries should be more mobile, able to move to where there were mission opportunities and to spend time evangelizing and establishing the church. As a mission administrator and visionary, Joe would develop further his ideas about the importance of local social and cultural contexts for mission theory and practice and would move MBMC away from a reliance on mission stations and the "brick and mortar" institutions that typically populated them.

Theologically, ministry in India precipitated a shift in Joe's thinking, from focusing on the fundamentalist–modernist debate to themes that seemed more pertinent for the church's missionary vocation. The Indian context during the interwar period, immersed as it was in the beginning stages of decolonization and missiological debates, served as a kind of incubator for Joe, providing experience and prompting discernment that would be foundational for his missiological commitments during the dawning postcolonial era.[101] He would soon become MBMC's first full-time executive secretary and be able to start implementing those commitments and new ones as well.

FOUR

"New Day in Missions"

MBMC International Expansion in the Postcolonial Era

ON DECEMBER 13, 1951, the executive and missions committees of the Mennonite Board of Missions and Charities met jointly for an all-day meeting in the large meeting room at the board offices at 1711 Prairie Street in Elkhart, Indiana. Attendees had routine business and interviews with prospective missionaries to attend to, but the primary focus of the day was the expanding footprint of the board's mission engagement around the world.[1]

With the help of a large world map hung for the occasion, Joe led the group in an overview of the places where MBMC missionaries were active and potential new regions of expansion. Overseas ministries had increased over the past half decade, and work started long ago in India and Argentina now shared the world map with Puerto Rico, Belgium, and Japan. Joe hoped to add more European countries, was investigating possibilities in Taiwan (then Formosa), and would visit Uruguay and Brazil in a few weeks to explore options there.[2] Mennonite work among people of Jewish descent was increasing in North America and in a few months would motivate a proposal to send missionaries to Israel.[3]

The focus of this December meeting is remarkable. As the so-called "quiet in the land," many Mennonites had been late to embrace the energy of the Protestant missionary movement. By the mid-twentieth century, however, MBMC embraced the progressive missionary posture of a church convinced that its faith tradition had something important to offer the world.[4] Plotting geographical expansion on a large world map might now seem uncharacteristically imperialistic for a church that shunned violence and sought to personify an ethic of nonresistance. However, it was a typical exercise within the Protestant missionary movement.[5]

Likewise, in his preaching and teaching Joe appropriated the common missionary language of "gospel crusade" and the apostle Paul's imagery of the "good soldier" who exemplified obedience, discipline, and loyalty in favor of advancing the kingdom of God.[6] He was quick to point out, though, that the battle was against evil and that a nonresistant posture was integral to Christian faith and Mennonite mission activity.[7] Any hints of imperial design were tempered by his strong message that mission activity had entered a new day; colonial assumptions and practices had to be left behind. A few weeks after the meeting in Elkhart, Joe was in Argentina, reminding missionaries there of the importance of indigenization and the need to cede positions of leadership and power in the church to their Argentinian colleagues.[8]

The first decade of Joe's leadership at MBMC would be characterized by an interplay of these impulses: a strong missionary call to spread the Christian gospel around the world, a sense that the Anabaptist/Mennonite tradition had something important to offer the world, and a determined resolve to find postcolonial missionary approaches for the new day.

Princeton again, China, and a new challenge

In 1942, after their second term of eight years, it was again time for the Grabers to go on furlough. World War II had thrown the world into crisis, however, and missionary work was not spared. In the colonies of the Allied powers, missionaries from Axis countries were interned for varying amounts of time, and passenger sea travel slowed almost to a halt as the Atlantic and Pacific Oceans became contested.[9] MBMC warned its missionaries that travel was becoming difficult.[10] Some would have to remain in India past their furlough dates.[11] Off of the India mainland's eastern coast Japanese forces took Burma, and North American missionaries there fled, traversing India in hope of finding passage home.[12] There was fear of an imminent attack, but in the end the war on the mainland was limited to a short-lived invasion along the Burma–India border. Although travel within India was restricted, missionaries went about their work as best they could and prayed for a swift end to hostilities.[13]

Joe and Minnie had planned to depart for furlough in early January 1942, but when the United States entered the war their passage was canceled.[14] They put off their furlough plans, not sure if they would be delayed for a time or for the duration of the war.[15] In April, however, they got word from the American consul urging nonessential workers to leave; officials were organizing an evacuation ship to the United States.[16] It would be the last chance to travel back for the foreseeable future. After consulting among themselves, the AMM missionaries

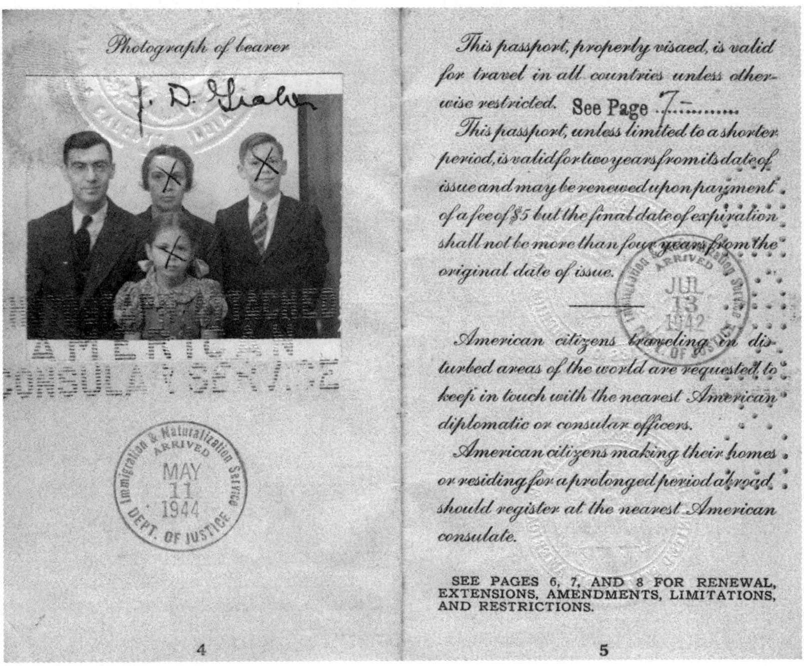

The photo page of Joe's passport delivered at the US Consulate in India in 1941, at first used for the entire family and later for his travel alone.

MCUSA ARCHIVES

decided that those whose furlough was due should take advantage of the opportunity. The Grabers, three other families, and one single missionary departed on May 31.[17]

The journey from India to New York on the *SS Brazil* took six weeks, sailing through water contested by Allied and Axis powers. The ship left Bombay with over 1,100 people aboard, having been stripped of furniture and other amenities to be retrofitted as a troop ship with metal three-tier bunks placed tightly together.[18] Reinforcing the sense of danger, the shipping company refused passage to women who did not have a pair of slacks, in case passengers were forced to abandon ship mid-ocean by descending a ladder on the side of the ship with the wind blowing skirts in every direction. Holding fast to the Mennonite dress codes of the day, veteran missionary Sarah (Hahn) Lapp, seventy-two years old at the time, at first refused unequivocally to accept the dictate, relenting to make a trip to a Bombay bazaar to acquire slacks only after considerable pleading by her colleagues.

The ship's crew followed wartime protocols, as the danger was real. It was a harrowing six weeks. For much of the way they traveled in a naval convoy with other ships, taking a zigzag course in blackout conditions to avoid attack.[19] The crew had sealed and covered the portholes with tar and took the light bulbs out of their sockets every night. Even lighting a match at night was prohibited. Fresh water for washing or laundry was rationed, one bowl per day per passenger, after which salt water was the only option. There was an outbreak of measles, which both Ronald and Eleanor contracted along with seventy-eight others, including many other children on board. There were also fifty cases of whooping cough. The ship's rules stipulated that passengers carry lifejackets at all times, and there were periodic drills to practice finding one's assigned lifeboat or raft and for the gunners to practice firing their weapons. Joe and twelve-year-old Ronald were assigned to a cabin in the men's section of the ship while Minnie and Eleanor's cabin was in the section designated for women and children. At one point the periscope of a submarine appeared, and the bridge ordered depth charges to be released. Their explosions shook the ship, but there was no attack.

The missionaries met at night on the top deck to sing and pray and to encourage each other. Joe took these opportunities to study the positions of the stars, trying to discern the ship's location since its trajectory was secret. Approaching North America, there was a warning of German attack submarines patrolling the coast, so the ship docked at Bermuda for a few days before continuing to New York, arriving safely on July 13.[20] Sarah Lapp had been spared the indignity of donning slacks.

The Grabers spent the next year at Princeton, where Joe finished his bachelor of divinity degree. As he had during the previous study furlough, he itinerated in eastern Pennsylvania on weekends, preaching and sharing about the India work.[21] This time Lancaster Conference did not bar him from speaking in its congregations.[22] During breaks in the school year, MBMC called on Joe to provide leadership for events such as young people's conferences and church gatherings.[23] As he was finishing studies in the spring of 1943, the Mennonite Publication Board asked Joe to serve as editor of the church's periodical *Gospel Herald*.[24] Daniel Kauffman had been editor since its inception in 1908, and after thirty-five years at the helm, he was set to retire in December 1943. The board was looking for his replacement. Joe declined the invitation, citing his primary calling and interest in mission work.

In the fall of 1943, Joe traveled to China with Samuel Goering on an exploratory visit sponsored jointly by MBMC and Mennonite Central Committee. The goal was to lay the groundwork for new relief and mission work in the country.[25] Other North American Mennonite and related denominations had worked in China since early in the century, and there was a push in the Mennonite Church to enter the country.[26] Articles about China appeared in the *Gospel Herald*, and people had started to donate money for the work. MBMC's Relief Committee envisioned collaborating with the American Friends Service Committee (AFSC), which was already working in China.[27] The Relief Committee proposed sending one of its newly conceived Mennonite Service Units, groups of young people who would serve benevolently and minister in practical and spiritual ways.[28]

Joe and Sam left for China in August, traveling in a roundabout way via New Orleans, Panama, Peru, Argentina, South Africa, and India due to the war raging in Europe and the northern Atlantic Ocean.[29] From India they flew over the Himalayas into the part of China not occupied by the Japanese. It was a high-risk endeavor because of the altitude and chronically bad weather.[30] They arrived to Kunming in western China in early November.[31]

Joe and Sam explored possibilities for work in various regions but reported significant challenges. Although the Japanese military occupied the eastern regions of China up to the Yellow River, MBMC and MCC expected it to retreat eventually, leaving behind opportunities for relief work.[32] Joe and Sam found that a relief unit might serve in Henan and Kwangtung provinces, which were experiencing a severe famine because of the war.[33] Possibilities for establishing new mission work were also evident.[34] There were many deterrents, however. The war situation increased prices astronomically, leading to an inflation rate of about 10 percent per month.[35] With the Japanese occupation of Burma, there was no way to get significant amounts of material aid into the country. A renewed advance by Japanese forces during the spring of 1944 added to the obstacles. Given such complications, Joe and Sam recommended gathering resources to enter China later, after the logistical and financial situations had improved. They returned to India, where Joe took on the responsibility of managing the MCC famine relief work in Calcutta for a few months, and Sam traveled to Bombay to wait for sea passage back to North America.[36]

Joe's work in Calcutta was cut short when MBMC asked him to become its executive secretary. S. C. Yoder had served twenty-three years in the role, which was part-time and not remunerated, but his health was declining.[37] He balanced his extensive involvement in church activities, including MBMC responsibilities, with his role as president of Goshen College. By the mid-1940s, MBMC had expanded beyond its beginnings as a networking hub for the India work and a few domestic initiatives. There were now fifty-eight missionaries working in India and Argentina. In North America MBMC owned five charitable institutions, operated eight city missions, and provided varying degrees of support for a dozen other conference-based mission initiatives.[38] After the financial crisis of the 1930s, donations had increased significantly, surpassing $800,000 per year as the war neared its end.[39] This, combined with a slowdown in work because of the war, meant that funds were accumulating in MBMC's accounts. Interest was high among the constituency. Four decades of mission activity, ongoing mission publicity in the church press, and the recent venture of funding and

Left to right: Daniel D. Miller, MBMC president 1920–35, Joe, Sanford C. Yoder, MBMC secretary 1921–44. Joe succeeded Yoder, becoming MBMC's first full-time general secretary in 1944. MCUSA ARCHIVES

organizing Civilian Public Service work had created significant momentum to engage the world in new ways previously unimaginable in Mennonite circles. MBMC was in expansionist mode, and the workload required full-time executive leadership for the first time in its history.[40]

The choice appears to have fallen quite naturally on Joe. The executive committee wanted someone who had mission experience and a proven track record, who instilled confidence, and who was a gifted mission advocate among the constituency.[41] Joe's strong Hindi skills and his knowledge of the India work were important for the complicated transitions that would need to happen for the church there to emerge from mission patronage. In February 1944 a cable arrived from the MBMC Executive and Relief Committees instructing Joe to return to Elkhart from Calcutta.[42] It is not clear that Joe was then aware that MBMC would ask him to take on the new role, but he packed quickly and arrived in Bombay in time to travel to New York with Sam. At the annual meeting in June, Joe became executive secretary, the role that would give him a platform to become the most prominent mission visionary and promoter in the Mennonite Church over the next two decades.[43]

Expansion

When Joe took on the executive role of secretary in July 1944, he brought fresh energy and a new vision to the church's mission activities. He was MBMC's first full-time executive secretary, and the Mennonite Church was prepared for a period of postwar expansion. International endeavors in India and Argentina had sown the seeds of churches that were maturing and produced a generation of missionary experience in new cultural contexts. Enterprising leaders and lay people at home had followed the example of the Mennonite Home Mission in Chicago and ventured out of their rural enclaves to do outreach in several urban areas.[44] They started Sunday schools, evangelistic work, and homes for orphans and the elderly across the continent, from eastern cities like Philadelphia, Altoona, and Toronto to Midwestern places like Detroit, Peoria, Kansas City, and Wichita, and in western cities like Portland and Los Angeles. The impulse to protect the faith community through isolationist tendencies of separation from the world had weakened over the first half of the twentieth century. Increasingly Mennonites considered mission activity an appropriate way to engage the world.

While the former generation of leaders had been cautious after the financial crisis of the depression years, Joe was convinced that the church needed to move ahead and branch out with confidence that God would provide the necessary resources.[45] He sensed the same optimism in the church and was convinced that by launching out with faith and vision, he could build on the work of earlier decades to move into new mission expansion.[46]

Joe's optimism corresponded with an increase in activity and collaboration on several endeavors across the Mennonite Church after the war. The Mennonite Publishing House expanded its capacity and publishing footprint during this period, local churches founded new congregations, committees established new church-affiliated primary and secondary schools, and Mennonite Central Committee activity grew at a steady pace.[47] The desire to expand and commit more of the church's personnel and financial resources to mission initiatives was part of this larger impulse.

Within the North American mission community other churches and mission agencies were at the beginning of a similar growth spurt. Evangelical, independent, and Free Church groups underwent postwar mission expansion, and the North American portion of Protestant missionaries sent internationally increased from about one-third of the total early in the century to more than 70 percent of the total by 1969.[48] Those groups soon outpaced the mainline denominations that had spearheaded the missionary movement during the nineteenth century. The initiatives of the "Great Century" of missions had resulted in new churches, and by the mid-twentieth century mainline Protestants were more focused on relationships with those "younger churches" than on plans for expansion. The Mennonite Church entered the international mission movement later, at the turn of the century, and MBMC had fewer such relationships to attend to.

Joe focused both on maintenance and expansion. He worked to expand international missions into new places and to develop healthy postcolonial relationships with the MBMC-founded churches in India and Argentina that were in the process of becoming autonomous, meaning independent of North American missionary control.

By 1944, as World War II was approaching its end, a reservoir of energy and resources had accumulated since MBMC had not been able to send missionaries or initiate new work overseas. In accordance with its pacifist convictions, the church had financed the Civilian Public Service (CPS) program to allow its young men to opt for civilian service instead of military service. This experience taught Mennonites to give, and donations increased accordingly. Contributions to MBMC rose from $128,106 and $183,705 in 1940 and 1941 to $539,184 and $653,660 in 1943 and 1944. This included funds for mission work, relief, and CPS.[49] Meanwhile, the war had slowed mission expenditures due to the disruption of travel and material scarcity. Funds built up in MBMC's accounts, and its financial position had never been better.

At the same time, an increasing number of Mennonites were interested in Christian service. CPSers had left their home communities and seen new parts of the world, and many went on to complete college degrees.[50] Many would not return to the farms in their home communities. Instead, they found vocational opportunities that propelled them into the wider society, looking for ways to engage the world via the framework of Christian mission. With this abundance of financial and personnel resources, the future of mission activity seemed bright in the Mennonite Church. Looking back during retirement years on the post–World War II period, Joe reflected, "The pump had been primed!"[51]

As he settled into his new role in the summer of 1944, Joe began laying the groundwork to increase MBMC's international footprint. With the church's pronounced mission interest, he saw the need for a "larger vision, wider outreach, and expanding programs."[52] By 1947 MBMC had a five-year *Plan of Advance* to send sixty-three new full-time missionaries and twenty short-term missionaries, more than doubling its missionary force and budget.[53] The newly established program of Mennonite Service Units was growing fast and required fifty-six summer workers that year. Plans to open work in England, Belgium, and Uruguay were developing, and there seemed to be prospects for work in Japan, Poland, Hungary, and Italy. The plan also called for a 25 percent expansion in mission activity in North America. Even with these lofty goals and the rising costs of international work, Joe urged the church to further increase its missionary activity, trusting that God would provide the money and people to follow through.[54]

Joe's belief that the church should proactively engage the world from a missionary perspective grew out of his spiritual and theological convictions. He had chosen the text of 1 Peter 3:15 for the sermon he preached just before he and Minnie sailed for India in 1925, reminding his audience of the Christian's responsibility to "be ready to answer to every man that asketh you a reason for the hope that is in you with meekness and fear."[55] Eighteen years later, after serving two terms in India, his sermon to MBMC's annual meeting was just as adamant about the church's responsibility to share the good news.[56] He gave three reasons for mission work: the experience of grace compelled Christians to testify to that experience, Jesus commissioned the disciples to go into all nations to teach and baptize, and Christians were to show compassion for those who are suffering, physically or spiritually. Furthermore, he argued that ongoing mission outreach would keep the church alive and growing. The best way to preserve the living community of faith was to propagate that faith in response to Jesus' instruction to preach the gospel to the ends of the earth.[57] Propagation of the faith, Joe argued, was the church's central and unique task and would not only result in the establishment of the church in new places but would also bring spiritual and intellectual enlightenment as well as economic advancement to people in need.[58]

Mission expansion relied on personnel just as much as it did on financial resources, and the young people of the church were the natural source of mission workers. The older generations were able to donate money, but Joe noted that those who would become workers would be mainly the young people.[59] He kept abreast of the issues of the youth, was a frequent speaker at their events, and contributed to *Youth's Christian Companion*, the church's monthly magazine dedicated to its youth.[60] Joe knew there was enthusiasm for mission work among this demographic and warned that this energy would be wasted

Joe, third from left, with staff at the Young People's Institute at Laurelville Mennonite Church Center, Pennsylvania, 1948. MCUSA ARCHIVES

Joe, middle of the back row, with staff at the Young People's Institute at Laurelville Mennonite Church Center, Pennsylvania, 1955. Note the change in dress patterns between 1948 and 1955. MCUSA ARCHIVES

if the church did not provide productive outlets for it. He sought to create structures that would allow young people to contribute, provide them with mission experience, prepare them to further serve the church, and strengthen the church's outreach. Joe was confident that many would experience a call to lifetime service and that even those who did not could serve for a shorter period. He advocated for the slogan "At least one year of service for my church," and noted that if everyone gave just one year, the collective effort would be a tremendous contribution of service and witness.[61]

In addition to his speaking assignments and articles in *Youth's Christian Companion*, Joe was secretary of missions education and led MBMC's missionary training events. In the missions education program he sought to reach every strata of the church through MBMC publications and programs, believing that children were the most impressionable audience and that the church could plant seeds of future commitment while they were still young. He and his colleagues scheduled MBMC's missionary training opportunities and the yearly meetings of the fledgling national Mennonite Youth Fellowship (MYF), both of which focused on young people, to occur alongside the annual MBMC meetings.[62] This was to provide cross-fertilization between youth programs and the church's mission work. If the church's mission engagement was going to expand, it would need its youth for current and future work. Cultivating interest within that demographic was part of Joe's vision of mission expansion.

In the late 1940s, donations for mission activity leveled off and decreased slightly while account surpluses disappeared as costs rose and MBMC made good on its plan to expand. Joe's conviction that the church should continue to branch out did not waver, however. He continued to urge Mennonites to increase their support, move forward in faith, be faithful stewards of their resources, and invest more of their incomes in mission activity.[63] Joe advocated for planned, systematic, and sacrificial giving for mission initiatives.

Despite fluctuations in donations, with Joe's leadership and the commitment of the constituency, the expansionist program continued. In 1953 MBMC calculated that the total contributions for mission work in the church amounted to less than 4 percent of the combined income of its constituency.[64] Conveying a sense that the church could do better, the annual meeting reaffirmed greater outreach and urged church members to increase their contributions. In the early 1950s special year-end appeals reminded donors of budget deficits, and money usually arrived to fill in the gaps.[65] Through it all, MBMC expanded its international footprint, adding Puerto Rico, China, Japan, and Belgium to the long-established work in India and Argentina during the first five years of Joe's tenure as secretary.[66] By 1954, a decade after Joe took the reins of leadership, England, France, Israel, and Brazil had been added to the list, and the number of missionaries serving internationally had risen from fifty-eight to one hundred and thirty-six.[67] Disbursements for international mission work totaled $343,458, quite an increase from a total of $149,236 in 1944.[68]

While reflective of broader trends within the missionary movement during the 1950s, this expansion was also a product of Joe's vision and guidance. Other Western Mennonite agencies sent missionaries to new areas as well, joining MBMC in laying important groundwork for the growth of the global Anabaptist movement.[69]

Settling in for the long haul

Joe, Minnie, Ronald, and Eleanor settled in to life in Indiana after Joe took on the executive secretary role at MBMC. It was a difficult adjustment, as Joe and Minnie wanted so badly to go back to India.[70] While it is not clear exactly when MBMC informed Joe of its desire that he remain in North America, Minnie learned of the change quite abruptly. During Joe's travel to China from fall 1943 to spring 1944, she, Ronald, and Eleanor lived in Goshen, Indiana. Minnie spoke in churches about MBMC's India work and finished her college education at Goshen College. As she was taking one of her final examinations, Dean Harold S. Bender interrupted the test to inform her that she and Joe would not be returning to India. This was understandably distressing for her, and afterward she questioned Bender's judgment in informing her in that manner. When Joe started his new role the family moved to Elkhart, Indiana, where MBMC bought a house close to its office for them to live in.[71]

Elkhart was far from Noble, Iowa, where Joe had grown up, and from Manson, Iowa, where Minnie's family had finally settled. But they visited those places from time to time and took advantage of speaking assignments to connect with family and friends there.[72] Paying fifty dollars to each of his siblings, Joe purchased their inherited portions of twenty acres of timber land at the homestead in Noble that his father had bought in 1880.[73] The plot had been a source of fence posts and firewood but had no agricultural value.[74] Joe had many happy childhood memories of that land and so was pleased to have it for sentimental reasons and to be able to eventually pass it on to Ronald.

The executive secretary role was a temporary assignment at first, and Joe and Minnie expected to serve in India as missionaries once again. MBMC reappointed Joe on a yearly basis, and for a time he and Minnie held out hope that "next year" they would return.[75] On an administrative visit to India in 1946, Joe wrote to Minnie and the children that he felt sick at seeing the garden of their former house neglected, with most of the banana and papaya trees gone and the remaining ones looking sickly.[76] He wished that they could return, which he noted was still possible. Nevertheless, he went through the personal effects that they had left behind, arranging to send a trunk with quilts, silverware, and linens back to Elkhart and disposing of other items such as dry goods, mosquito nets, and pillows.[77] In conversation with missionary and Indian colleagues, Joe noted the other option, that perhaps his place was back in North America where the need to promote the mission cause was strong. He and Minnie weighed the pros and cons.

The Grabers' situation changed in 1948, six years after the end of their second term in India, when the MBMC Executive Committee definitively declared its preference that they remain in Elkhart.[78] The final decision was an adjustment since they had chosen missionary work as their lifelong vocation. MBMC was growing, however, and Joe's contribution as chief executive and Minnie's subsequent work as president of the Women's Missionary and Service Auxiliary (formerly the Women's Missionary Sewing Circle Organization) would prove important for the church's growing missionary vision. If their hearts were still in many ways longing for India, they found important and fulfilling ministry in North America too.[79] By the end of 1950, they were building a house in Elkhart and had resigned themselves to not returning as missionaries.[80]

Several of Joe's siblings were in northern Indiana, so there was a familial support system that helped make Elkhart a good place to settle.

Brother Chris lived in Goshen, where he worked for Goshen College and Mennonite Mutual Aid and served as pastor of Goshen College Mennonite Church.[81] Joe's sisters Mary (Zook) and Verna (Smith) were close by; Mary's family had a farm not far from Elkhart, and Verna was a professor at Goshen College. Esther, the youngest sibling, became Joe's assistant at MBMC, eventually living just around the corner from Joe and Minnie. The siblings were close, and their families enjoyed gathering for monthly potluck meals and to celebrate special occasions.[82] Conversation ranged across a wide variety of subjects from church affairs to world events and even politics. Verna's husband Willard, who had become a close friend and was by then professor of history at Goshen College, often voted Republican while Joe leaned Democratic.[83] During those years the Zook farm was a favorite destination. Aunt Mary invited them for holiday meals there, and it was a place where Joe and Ronald hunted rabbits.[84]

Ronald was twelve years old when the Grabers left India, and Eleanor was six. The rest of their growing-up years would be in North America. Ronald finished high school at Hesston Academy in Kansas, as his parents had done, completed his college education at Goshen College, and went to medical school at Northwestern University.[85] At Hesston he met his future wife, Esther Rose Buckwalter. They attended college together and married in August 1952 before moving to Chicago the following month.[86] They lived at MBMC's mission to Mexican immigrants in the city, and Joe was pleased that they were active in ministry there during Ronald's medical studies.[87] Jane Elizabeth was born to Ronald and Esther Rose in July 1953, making Joe and Minnie grandparents.[88]

Eleanor attended Elkhart public schools but did her last year of high school at Hesston Academy. She developed her musical talents early and was already teaching piano lessons as a high school student.[89] Upon arriving to Hesston, the only class that Eleanor had left to take to meet the requirements for graduation was a course on Kansas history. Instead, she took college courses and never did receive a high school diploma.[90] She finished her college studies at Goshen College, focusing on music. Joe and Minnie were glad that Ronald and Eleanor could benefit from education steeped in Mennonite faith values, as had they, and that they were close to Elkhart during their college years.[91]

MBMC's expanding international work added significant international travel to Joe's responsibilities and increased the amount of time spent away from his family. During the eight years between November 1946 and November 1954, Joe traveled nine times to visit missionaries or explore new sites, typically spending from two to five months during a given trip visiting multiple countries and regions.[92] Those trips took him away from Elkhart and the family over the Christmas and New Year's holidays four of those eight years.

Minnie and Joe during Joe's first decade as executive secretary for MBMC. MCUSA ARCHIVES

Joe's extended absences must have created difficulties for Minnie. She did not drive but got around Elkhart on her bicycle and, when Joe was traveling, depended on others when she needed to venture further away. She had to see to tasks that were normally his during those times, such as keeping the furnace fired.[93] Joe reminded Eleanor, who still lived at home when his international travel increased significantly, to help with the furnace, wash the dishes, and generally assist Minnie with household chores.[94] When Ronald was nearby at Goshen College, Joe asked him to look after certain tasks, such as maintenance of the family car, during long trips abroad.[95] Joe's absences left a void. Looking back decades later, Minnie noted that he was the better nurse when Ronald or Eleanor was sick.[96] He played the role of hairdresser, washing Minnie and Eleanor's hair. While he washed the dishes, as he often did, he would ask Eleanor to play the piano, which he seemed to greatly enjoy. When he was gone for long periods of time, they missed him.

Minnie accepted the need for Joe's international travel, however. She and Joe shared a vocational commitment to missions. Minnie filled in sometimes, visiting churches to talk about missions, especially the work in India, when Joe could not respond to an invitation because he was traveling.[97] They played the roles of advisor and confidant for each other, exchanging concerns and advice about her work with the Women's Mission and Service Auxiliary or with evangelistic initiatives in Elkhart and the decisions he had to make about personnel or missiological issues.[98] When Joe traveled at year's end, Minnie saw to getting his Christmas greetings to foreign missionaries sent.[99]

If Joe was absent for significant amounts of time, he was a good letter writer, sometimes providing what amounted to a journal or diary of his activities. He described flights in great detail, noting the aircraft type, altitude, turbulence, delays, and airline food.[100] In truth, though, Joe did not like to fly.[101] It frightened him, and he would ask for sleeping pills if a flight was more than four hours or so. He preferred trains. Writing from Japan in December 1949, he wrote of the layers of clothing necessary to keep warm and told of hearing the theologian Emil Brunner preach.[102] Visiting India in 1951, Joe reported that the cooking among the missionaries had "taken a new lease on life" since they had received a few copies of the new *Mennonite Community Cookbook*.[103] He appreciated good food and had learned to savor curry and Darjeeling tea in India. His favorite meal, however, was chili con carne and pie; he loved chocolate and was keen on ice cream.[104]

Sometimes communication lagged when one depended on letters. Both Joe and Minnie expressed frustration when they did not receive letters during Joe's travels. From Manila in December 1949, Joe wrote, "I've not had a scratch from you since I left."[105] Likewise Minnie chided Joe when he failed to write often enough, in January 1952 complaining that she had written four letters to him and had not received even one in return. Frustrated, she wrote in the postscript: "Can't you do something to see I get a letter!"[106] In such cases Joe was quick to defend himself, assuring her that he really had sent letters her way faithfully, despite the heavy demands of these around-the-world visits.[107] Minnie often did not include the date on the letters she sent, leading Joe in one response to write, "The date, as usual, was missing."[108] Most of their letters got through in a timely manner, however, and they kept each other apprised of activities and expressed affection for each other as well as regret for the necessity of spending so much time apart. With gratitude for a letter from Minnie, Ronald, and Eleanor describing their Christmas celebration while he was in Japan, Joe wrote, "That was a lovely letter. I shed some joy-tears reading it and was so thankful for you all."[109] Another year, after he had missed yet another Christmas, Minnie wrote, "Every time I turned around I thought of you and wished you here."[110]

Joe also kept up with Ronald and Eleanor as he traveled the world, writing about his varied experiences and the interests he shared with each one. In letters to Ronald, he wrote of the planes and ships he took and the places through which he passed. Writing from Eritrea, for example, he described the Wright Whirlwind engines of the plane he was on, its passenger capacity, and how it compared to the Avro York aircraft that had taken him from London to Cairo. He also wrote of the makes and models of the camera equipment he carried, his own as well as equipment he was taking for missionaries whom he would visit. From Tokyo Joe told of getting a photo of General McArthur and seeing jet aircraft fly for the first time.[111] Ronald wrote to his father of activities at Hesston Academy and Goshen College, described concerts he attended, kept Joe apprised of his medical school applications, and (during one of Joe's visits to India) announced his engagement to Esther Rose.[112]

Joe and Eleanor's letters contained news but often dedicated significant space to their common love of music. Eleanor wrote about performances for which she was preparing and records she had bought but also about school, sometimes reporting the scores of sports events.[113] Writing from Rome in December 1950, Joe described for her a symphony concert that he had attended and included a diagram of the concert hall to show how close his seat was to the stage.[114] He had been able to watch the conductor's face during the concert. Joe wrote that he was brought to tears by the performance of the strings during the second movement.

He took a whole paragraph to describe the last movement:

> The last piece was most unusual. It had a lot of sound effects and was really difficult. It had passages of touching beauty—sometimes only the strings, sometimes only the woodwinds, sometimes only brass, and all combinations. The climax built up in a series of about half a dozen crescendos. These were characterized by loud drumbeat and crashing of cymbals, followed by the softest, sweetest music imaginable. When the final crescendo did come it sounded like heavy artillery. Even the huge organ, just behind us, was put on full alert and everyone was blowing, hitting, and raining everything they had with might and main. It was the most spectacular crescendo I've ever heard. It literally brought the house down; and it was a sell-out too. I did not see a single vacant seat.[115]

Joe's trips must have been exhausting. He would sleep for hours after arriving home from international travel.[116] Catching up on sleep was not the first, or even second, thing that happened upon Joe's arrival back home, however. First came a change of clothes and getting his travel clothing washed. Travel in planes and trains left one's clothing smelling strongly of cigarette smoke in those days, and a good wash was necessary.[117] Then came time for Joe and Minnie to sit at the kitchen table to catch up, to share news of what had transpired in Elkhart during his absence and of what he had experienced in his travels. While work was waiting at the office or elsewhere, Joe and Minnie seem to have successfully carved out time for themselves, together, despite the multiple demands on both.

The new day

Joe's tenure as executive leader at MBMC coincided with significant changes on the world stage and in mission theory and practice that would impact his vision for the church's international mission expansion. He, along with his Mennonite coworkers and colleagues in the larger Protestant mission movement, often referred to this time as a "new day" in missions. Processes of decolonization and the macropolitical shifts of the Cold War had both practical and ideological implications. Newly independent states sometimes restricted access to missionaries, and nationalist movements accused them of being instruments of colonial hegemony, occasionally threatening to expel them. With governments moving to establish social services, mission schools and hospitals would no longer provide the justification for large numbers of missionary teachers, doctors, and nurses. From an ideological standpoint, the racism and oppression of colonial systems were clearer than ever in the postcolonial era.

Joe was among those mission visionaries who accepted such change and sought to set aside colonial practices and assumptions in favor of more equitable relationships and ways of working. In the new day, the expansionist zeal of Joe and the Mennonite Church mission movement had to be expressed in new, postcolonial ways.

If the Grabers' experience in India had highlighted their appreciation for indigenization and the need for more equitable relationships and new mission strategies, Joe's interaction with mission literature and conversations in the larger Protestant mission movement provided language and missiological frameworks that helped him chart the way forward. Well-read in the literature of the day, he recommended and sent articles and books on mission strategy and indigenization to the missionaries he supervised.[118] He and other MBMC executive committee members subscribed to the *International Review of Missions* and *World Dominion*, two of the most influential missiological journals of the day.[119]

Such literature provided grist for Joe's thinking as he articulated a vision for MBMC's expansion. Early in the century, English missionary Roland Allen had issued a strong critique of Western mission strategy, but it was not until processes of decolonization became inevitable during the World War II period that many took such critiques to heart.[120] By the mid-1930s, mission scholars and leaders were suggesting that the rise of nationalist movements and changes in the economic, social, intellectual, and religious systems in lands where missionaries worked meant that they needed to adjust their programs and approaches.[121] During succeeding years newly free and sovereign nation-states began throwing off the yoke of colonialism. Scholars warned of a decline in the importance and influence of missionaries and an increase of resentment among colonized peoples, who associated Christianity with colonial systems. Local Christians were now better placed to have an influence in society and would adjust their churches and programs, founded largely on Western models, to suit their own realities.

Reflecting Joe's experience in India, critics suggested that mission schools and hospitals had become more important than the churches they were supposed to reinforce and had diverted missionaries' attention from their primary task of calling into existence indigenous churches. Since institutions required technical and financial resources that outstripped those of the churches, they risked becoming unconnected to the church's witness. It was time for missionaries to focus more energy on founding and nourishing Christian communities. Those communities could be an ongoing source of service and witness for generations to come, irrespective of whether they owned or controlled educational or healthcare institutions.

As World War II was ending, Joe recognized the salience of the postcolonial shifts that were on the horizon. International mission work was entering a new phase. Missionaries would have to cede to national Christians the power they had held over mission programs and decisions. Even as he started his tenure as secretary in the summer of 1944, it was clear that in India government officials would tighten control of missionary visas and that Indian Christians would increasingly make the decisions about foreign missionary work.[122] After India became independent in 1947, MBMC missionaries reported growing antagonism to Western mission work in Indian society.[123] They no longer felt free to go on evangelistic tours, fearing the government would expel them. It was clear that it would soon be up to the church to continue the mission activities that North American missionaries had initiated.

Joe led the process of turning over control of the entire American Mennonite Mission apparatus to the Mennonite Church in India, doing so over the objections of many of the missionaries, who doubted that the church was ready for the move. He was convinced that maintaining a foreign-controlled entity in a place where there was an established national church was not a credible way of working in the new day.[124]

In a series of four articles in the *Gospel Herald* under the title "The New Day in Missions," Joe outlined the impact of the changing contexts for Mennonites' mission engagement. Mission work had been too closely tied to colonialism for a century, and the passing of colonialism had ushered in a new era.[125] The case of China was the notable example, and Joe described how missionary complicity and involvement in the Opium Wars and other Western imperial abuses tainted Christian ministry and severely compromised missionary efforts. He warned of the dangers of collaboration or association with governments of any kind.

Missionaries also needed to adjust their understanding of race, Joe argued. He cited Mordecai Johnson, the president of Howard University, who observed that a billion people of color had emerged from colonial subjugation to attain national independence during the decade of the 1940s.[126] Missionaries needed to recognize the change this represented and how the colonial context had previously influenced their attitudes. Their goal, Joe argued, should be to strive to be a partner and helpful brother instead of the patriarchal father of the colonial era. If missionaries accepted discredited racial practices such as the creation of white minority rule that had developed at the time in South Africa, their missionary message would fall on deaf ears.

Joe staked out new mission practices. Missionaries needed to cooperate fully with indigenous leaders who would now have more say in mission policy and administration.[127] Just as John the Baptist had recognized that Jesus' importance would increase as his own decreased, so, Joe wrote, mission structures needed to be ready to step aside and even disappear if necessary. In India and Argentina MBMC missionaries needed to cede responsibility and authority to the indigenous church. In new fields, such as Japan, missionaries would work to make the church indigenous from the very beginning, affirming its stature as an authentic Christian community and avoiding the contentious process of turning over foreign-controlled structures and institutions.

Missionaries in the new day would be servants instead of executives, directors, or bishops.[128] They would need to have a clear sense of call, especially since they would no longer have the status they often enjoyed during the colonial era. Also important would be a sound experience of salvation and a solid faith. Having less institutional power, their usefulness would be primarily as a spiritual resource. Finally, missionaries would need to have a greater willingness to sacrifice. Gone were the days when they could have a standard of living dramatically higher than that of those among whom they worked. Their credibility would depend on identifying with the people they wanted to serve and living a simpler, less materialistic lifestyle than that of their predecessors.

Geopolitical concerns added urgency to the move to transfer responsibility to local church leaders. With the outbreak of the Korean conflict, the Cold War was heating up and nationalist movements unfriendly to North American missionaries continued to emerge. There was an apocalyptic edge in the air as the possibility of a third world war loomed in the background. In October 1950 the *Gospel Herald* quoted Mennonite leader Harold S. Bender as stating, "The human race stands terrified on the rim of an abyss."[129] There was no time to lose. Missionaries might soon find it difficult or impossible to reach some lands, as had been the case during World War II. The new day demanded that missionary-initiated churches and their leaders assume responsibility and that MBMC and its structures not be indispensable, since the day might come when North American-based foreign mission activity would no longer be possible.

Advances in systems of communication and transportation were also factors in the new day and facilitated MBMC expansionist designs. The time required to communicate with and visit locations around the world decreased dramatically. Travel time between continents involved hours in airplanes instead of weeks on oceangoing vessels. In late 1950 Joe embarked on a visit to MBMC mission fields and to several prospective fields, stopping in England, Belgium, France, Italy, India, Hong Kong, and Japan.[130] He used a special around-the-world airline ticket, which was less expensive than passage on the much slower-moving passenger ships. Such efficiency aided MBMC's international expansion.

Among national leaders and the missionaries he supervised, Joe used the new day nomenclature to communicate the significance of postwar changes and to build consensus about the need to modify mission practice. After MBMC approved the amalgamation of the Indian

Joe and Minnie traveled to and from India by sea, but by the time Joe started traveling as executive secretary of MBMC, air travel had become a more efficient option. MCUSA ARCHIVES

church and the American Mennonite Mission, collaboration between the church and missionaries broke down when the two groups could not agree on how to move forward. Joe traveled to India to set up a unification commission to get them working together and to chart a path forward. The day after the first meeting of the commission, he preached the sermon at the church's annual conference and chose to speak on the theme "Behold I make all things new," from Revelation 21:5. He stressed that it was a new day for the church and challenged Indians and missionaries to increased devotion and sacrifice as the unification moved forward.[131]

In the months and years that followed, Joe repeatedly shared his vision for the church in the new day. In communication with missionaries and Indian leaders alike, he urged them to support the unification process wholeheartedly, arguing that in the postcolonial context dissolving institutional barriers between missionaries and nationals was the only viable way forward.[132] Whether in MBMC's older fields of India and Argentina or in new fields like Japan, Joe stressed that the new era required unreserved collaboration, mutuality between missionaries and national believers, a focus on the well-being of the church, and a decreasing emphasis on mission institutions.[133] The fruit would be stronger relationships between missionaries and nationals, deeper spirituality, greater dedication to the church, a more focused vision, and a renewed stress on evangelization.

For MBMC the new day nomenclature became a way to recognize the postcolonial context and the reassessment of mission theory and practice that it required. As a gifted communicator, Joe provided a framework through which missionaries and national leaders alike used the new day terminology to reflect on their new context and articulate an appropriate way forward. They highlighted missionary values such as identification with local believers through simple living, the importance of relationships, and the priority of the church over the traditional focus on mission institutions like schools and hospitals.[134] Taking their cue from Joe, missionaries and national leaders considered their new context, discerning what it meant for mission practice and theory in their letters and articles for the church press. Joe's skills as a visionary and communicator helped his leadership at MBMC bear fruit. Reflecting on the new day provided a way for the church, its mission agency, and its missionaries to engage the new postcolonial context in productive and appropriate ways.

Mission strategy in the new day

The Grabers' India experience, the Protestant mission discourse of the period, MBMC's Mennonite/Anabaptist heritage, and the challenges that missionaries faced in a growing number of places around the world all provided grist for reflection about new mission strategies. The value that Joe and Minnie had given to the relationships they built with Indian colleagues carried into the new day as Joe encouraged missionaries to identify with those among whom they ministered instead of living on mission stations as a class apart. Indigenization too continued to be a strong priority as missionaries sought to establish self-administering, self-financing, and self-propagating churches.

The tumult of the World War II aftermath radically altered the context for global mission work, however. Ceding power to missionary-planted churches and their leaders, and setting aside paternalistic ways of working now featured a postcolonial ideological component on top of the more practical motives for indigenization. The *where* and *why* of mission activity also evolved. Work in Europe developed in the context of historical Christendom, a shift from the focus on traditional missionary fields in the Global South that required a reassessment of mission motivation. Relief work became an increasingly important medium of mission activity, and the fields of linguistics and anthropology emerged as useful missionary tools.

Identifying with the people among whom they worked became an important value and strategy for missionaries in the postcolonial era. Along with indigenization, Joe found this approach, which contemporary missiologists labeled "identification," to be key for the future of Mennonite mission endeavors.[135] Developing deep relationships with Indian colleagues had been important for the Grabers during their two terms of service in India, but Joe was keenly aware of how missionaries there had been in a social class apart from most of the members of their churches. In the new day, he believed, missionaries needed to relate more intimately with the people and integrate themselves much more into the cultural and social structures of the societies in which they worked.

Joe was convinced that for both practical and ideological reasons, this was a strategy that Mennonite missionaries needed to appropriate, especially when working among those who were materially poor. He noted, "The question that is most pertinent nowadays among the world's poor people is, 'Is the church on our side, or is she an instrument of exploitation, imperialism, and oppression?'"[136] The answer was clear: Of course, the gospel was a message for the poor, and their welfare was of utmost concern. But more importantly, the church and its missionaries needed to prove that this was the case. For Joe, the best way to do that was for missionaries to identify as closely as possible with the people with whom they worked, building empathy, and adopting living standards that would not set them apart.[137] They should travel lightly and live simply, taking the minimum of North American material goods with them and using national goods instead. Furthermore, Western superiority, taken for granted by many for so long, no longer provided Western missionaries with credibility in the eyes of those whom they served.[138] Humility and the posture of a servant was a more appropriate approach for the new day. The missionary had to be willing to make sacrifices and lower his or her living standard if necessary in order to identify with those among whom he or she was sent to minister.[139]

When MBMC decided to initiate mission work in Japan in 1949, Joe saw an opportunity for a fresh start, unencumbered by a history of paternalistic approaches and structures that the colonial context had engendered in India. He and MBMC's first missionaries to Japan eschewed the mission-station model, spreading their work in different towns where they sought to build meaningful relationships with their Japanese contacts and friends instead of finding fellowship primarily among themselves. Joe encouraged them to "lose themselves among the people."[140] Missionaries used public transportation instead of buying vehicles and, when the postwar housing shortage forced them to build their own houses, Joe encouraged living arrangements that were simple and in line with what was typical in the communities where they lived, even when their accommodations would be much smaller than what North American standards would have dictated.[141]

He was pleased by Mennonite missionaries' efforts in Japan. He noted, however, that because the climate in Japan was moderate and public transportation available, it was easier to implement these standards of identification there than it was in India, where the heat was often severe and public transportation inadequate.[142] While the cultural differences that missionaries faced in Japan were as significant as those of other MBMC ministry sites, many of the people among

Joe on a visit to missionaries in Nakashibetsu, Japan, January 1954.
MCUSA ARCHIVES

whom they worked were literate and some had an educational level comparable to that of the missionaries.[143] This, Joe remarked, facilitated missionary relationships with the local people to a degree less easily attained in places where illiteracy was high and the educational level of the population was low. Identification was a helpful value and goal, but its practical implications varied across the different MBMC mission fields.

Beyond identification, Joe was convinced of the need for indigenization processes both in established mission fields and in new endeavors. However, the move to transfer mission structures to the Indian church provided the greatest challenge that he faced in his first decade as MBMC's chief executive officer. As a missionary in India, he had participated in negotiations about the process of ceding missionary control to Indian hands. Now from Elkhart he oversaw the implementation of a new power-sharing arrangement that integrated Indian representatives into missionary structures. Since collaboration between missionaries and Indians eventually faltered under this new organization, Joe then led a process of amalgamation that united both church and mission structures under the authority of the Indian church.

During the Grabers' ministry in India, they had been part of unsuccessful attempts to share missionary responsibility and authority with indigenous leaders. An evangelization committee made up of an equal number of Indians and North American missionaries had worked for six years before the Indian church conference concluded that it was unproductive and dissolved it.[144] Later, when Joe was secretary of the American Mennonite Mission in the 1930s, missionaries offered to transfer primary schools and the management of scholarships to the church.[145] The church asked instead to appoint representatives to AMM's governing committees.[146] Joe and his colleagues refused, citing the institutional separation of the church and mission agency, the latter having the purpose to move on to unevangelized areas to start new churches.[147] After becoming MBMC secretary, however, Joe changed his mind and supported a new structure, an experimental constitution that established the India Mennonite Mission (IMM) in 1946, which included Indian representatives on mission agency governing committees, as the Indian church had requested.[148]

Conscious of the social ramifications of political independence for India, Joe understood that a foreign mission agency working without close Indian collaboration would lose credibility in the new socio-political context. He argued for immediate processes of indigenization, writing to missionaries in India, "I am still entirely convinced that the matter of Indianization is as inevitable as the dawn and that if anyone thinks that they can go on in the future as we went on in the past they are in serious disillusionment."[149] Without a way toward full and equal cooperation, the best educated and most talented leaders would simply become disheartened and leave the church, a possibility that Joe sought to avoid. Dispelling any doubt about his views, he wrote the MBMC missionaries, "In my mind losing missionaries would not be nearly as serious for the Indian Church if [sic] losing the best leadership, and your best leadership will not stay with you if you do not succeed in finding a way in which they can work happily and fruitfully with us at the common problem."[150]

Building mutuality was to be a sine qua non of the new day. This approach was consistent with that of other Protestant mission leaders who, searching for innovative ways of working in the postcolonial period, suggested "partners in obedience" as a paradigm for how Western churches and mission agencies might work with churches that they had created.[151] The IMM exemplified partnership and seemed to be a path forward in the new day.

Joe faced a crisis in 1949, however, when the IMM partnership broke down after both Indians and North American missionaries expressed frustration with the new structure. Indians argued that although they held seats on governance committees, missionaries had maintained their hegemonic position in the mission structures.[152] They were not equal partners. The missionaries too were unhappy.[153] They noted that the Indian members of IMM committees were typically employed by mission institutions. Their presence on the committees meant they were sometimes helping to set policy and decide salary scales for the positions that they held. Their committee membership also gave them authority over their supervisors at the schools or hospitals that employed them, creating a conflict of interest. Missionaries reported that factions in the church maneuvered to control decisions and accrue benefits through Indian IMM members.

Amid deep frustration on both sides, MBMC rescinded the experimental constitution in September 1949 at the request of the missionaries, thus dissolving the IMM and returning to the former American Mennonite Mission structure.[154] The Indian church reacted strongly, arguing that MBMC had not consulted it before rescinding the experimental constitution and that, while it had not been perfect, it was better than a return to the former structure.[155] Formal collaboration between the Indian church and AMM ceased, although the mission institutions continued to function, and individuals maintained relationships and collaboration with members of the opposing side.

Faced with this situation at its annual meeting in June 1950, MBMC mandated the amalgamation of its mission agency structure in India and the Indian church. Indian leaders had asked for this move, and Joe considered it to be the correct way forward.[156] The maintenance of a foreign-controlled agency separate from the church was not a legitimate way of working in the new day, and the shared structure of the IMM had proven unworkable. The remaining option was to simply unite all church and mission structures under the authority of the Indian church. MBMC suggested a unification commission made up of missionaries and Indian church leaders that would write a new constitution and guide the process of amalgamation.[157] The missionary reaction was mixed, with some missionaries agreeing to amalgamation and others agreeing in principle but raising questions about its feasibility.[158] Still others disagreed with amalgamation entirely, believing that the church was not ready for the responsibility it entailed. The church appointed its representatives to the unification committee, but the missionaries dragged their feet and did not appoint theirs.

The situation required Joe's intervention. He traveled to India in December 1950 and spent three months advocating for amalgamation and setting up the unification commission, with both Indian and missionary members, that would guide the transition process.[159] Over the next year he communicated regularly with the missionaries and Indian leaders, urging everyone's wholehearted support of the transfer and making the argument that the new day in missions required it despite missionary doubts.[160] On July 1, 1952, the American Mennonite Mission in India ceased to exist, and the church took over responsibility for its varied ministries.[161] MBMC missionaries worked within the

Joe ordaining Sonu Milop Singh (seated) to the office of deacon at Rajnandgaon, India, in February 1954. MCUSA ARCHIVES

new structure, under the authority of the church. Some missionaries found their place within the new setup while others retired at their next furlough, unable to accept the change. In the long term, Joe's insistence on complete Indianization proved prophetic, and missionaries in India took pride in MBMC's early example as they helped other foreign mission agencies move in the same direction.

Joe's insistence on unification over the objections of those missionaries who disagreed is notable. Such use of his institutional authority as the chief executive of MBMC was rare, as Joe's strong communication and relational skills typically allowed him to find a common ground of agreement when conflict surfaced. The urgency of finding a credible way forward, though, pushed him to act decisively in this case. His insistence demonstrates how important indigenization was in Joe's missiological approach as he sought adequate practice and theory for the new day.

Beyond India, Joe pushed for indigenization as general mission policy, in established work and in new initiatives. After over thirty years of work in Argentina, MBMC urged the missionary team to transfer pastoral responsibilities and administrative control of the church to

Joe, standing, meeting with the MBMC Argentina missionary council in Argentina in January 1952.
MCUSA ARCHIVES

indigenous leaders.[162] Missionaries were to focus on new unreached fields. As in India, it was not until Joe visited in early 1952 that missionaries understood the urgency with which he was asking them to act. Joe noted that with both missionaries and national leaders entrenched in old habits, he needed to "stir the eagle's nest" during that visit.[163]

Although his strategy was simply to explain the indigenous church policy that MBMC had approved nearly two years earlier and for which he had been advocating for some time, missionaries spoke of his instructions as revolutionary and used them in their ongoing discernment in the years that followed.[164] After having worked so long within traditional mission structures, the idea of a more immediate transfer to indigenous hands, of eschewing the mission-station approach in favor of spreading missionaries out among the population, and of decreasing the importance of institutions provided a jolt to the system and gave missionaries a new way to envision their work.

As missionaries started work in new places around the world, Joe urged them to encourage indigenization from the very beginning, thus affirming the postcolonial value of empowering local leadership and avoiding the thorny process of subsequently transferring authority and ownership of churches and mission institutions from missionaries to local leaders. He wanted MBMC to learn from its experience in India and do better in other places.[165] Joe was pleased with the quality of the first believers that resulted from efforts in Japan and hoped they would provide early leadership for an indigenous church, one adapted to the cultural and economic pattern of the country.[166] He encouraged missionaries there to avoid weakening the church with foreign aid and contrasted institution-building with spreading missionaries around so they could deepen relationships with those among whom they ministered, the latter being his preference. In Europe the missionaries he supervised collaborated with local leaders at the outset of their mission initiatives and relied on their support, guidance, and direction.[167]

If Joe's vision for the church's mission engagement provided a clear expansionist focus, decisions about where to start mission endeavors and what motivated those endeavors were more complex in the new day. When the Mennonite Church established its work in India at the beginning of the twentieth century, the choice of the location was primarily a function of missionary interest among church leaders and the constituency and of finding a region that was not yet being evangelized by another mission agency. The dire needs associated with famines in India at the end of the nineteenth century and the growing desire for missionary initiatives motivated the establishment of mission activity in the Dhamtari region, which was not being actively evangelized by another missionary group. The goals were clear: to turn people to Christianity and build an indigenous church.

Constituency support, the existence of unevangelized areas, and the desire to birth new churches continued to be factors during Joe's tenure as mission leader, but the new day brought new complications. Europe, for example, was the cradle of Christendom and a historic missionary-sending region, but in the postwar years North Americans also directed mission efforts toward European countries. Moreover, while worldwide travel increased access to lands around the world, newly independent countries sometimes denied visas, cutting off access to places where missionaries had previously worked.

Joe forged ahead, reformulating mission goals and strategy for the new postwar context. He was constantly attentive to new opportunities and consulted with advisors at home and abroad. Later, after he retired, Joe reflected that even after one had weighed all the factors involved in establishing new mission outreach there were always unknowns. One simply had to move ahead, relying on the Holy Spirit.[168]

Finding unevangelized fields was one of Joe's priorities as he sought to expand overseas work.[169] Japan was an early opportunity. The official United States policy for the postwar occupation government was to promote freedom of religion and cease governmental support for Shintoism.[170] Supreme Commander Douglas MacArthur went further, however, not only abolishing Shintoism as the state religion but actively promoting a rapid increase of US missionary work in the country.

North American mission leaders were quick to respond, anticipating a spiritual vacuum that might provide a fertile ground for evangelization. For a mission agency in expansionist mode, it was an obvious opening. It was also an opportunity to offer the gospel message of reconciliation to a people that had suffered under the militarism of recent Japanese society and from extensive bombing by American military forces.[171] Among the constituency there were calls to work in the country and young people ready to serve there as missionaries. At its annual meeting in June 1949, MBMC resolved to "open a Gospel witness in Japan at the earliest opportunity."[172] During Joe's first visit to the country, resident missionaries and local Christians identified the island of Hokkaido as having few church communities.[173] Opportunities for evangelism seemed great and the possibilities of a positive response good. Joe favored rural communities since in Japan there was already a significant missionary presence in urban centers and because he thought that rural areas provided better opportunities for establishing strong indigenous churches. He noted that Mennonites were traditionally a rural people, after all.[174]

Brazil provided another inviting field. Unlike Japan, the church was large and growing there. However, with a large population and new communities being formed in the southwest region of the country, there seemed to be sizeable areas that were mostly unevangelized.[175] MBMC approved opening work there at its 1952 annual meeting and sent its first missionaries two years later.

Not every exploratory trip that Joe made to new fields led to opening MBMC mission work. He visited the Philippines, Korea, and Taiwan, but MBMC did not send missionaries to those places.[176] When Mennonite Central Committee executive secretary Orie Miller inquired about opening work in Korea, Joe replied that although many among the constituency favored initiating work there, the country was already well covered with mission and church activity. Adding another denomination to the mix would be more detrimental than helpful.[177] Joe was impressed with the vitality of the Korean church and considered it the result of the most successful missionary endeavor that he had ever seen.[178] Similarly, Taiwan and the Philippines were potential areas of MBMC expansion, but Joe found them relatively well served by other mission agencies and churches.[179] He observed, however, that there might be a way for a Mennonite presence to contribute its unique witness to the larger Christian community, even in regions with an established Christian presence.

Indeed, post–World War II Europe was one context where Joe and his MBMC colleagues developed a vision for missionary work in an area that was not a traditional missionary-receiving region. The India experience had left Joe convinced that new situations called for new mission approaches, and Europe presented vastly different challenges and opportunities than those he and his colleagues had faced in India and Argentina. Mennonites provided assistance in Europe after the war, rebuilding homes and villages that had been destroyed and distributing relief supplies that helped keep people alive.[180] MBMC's Mennonite Relief Committee assisted the families of political prisoners and rebuilt houses in Belgium.[181] Mennonite Central Committee channeled relief support to England during the war, and provided relief assistance and cared for disadvantaged children in France.[182] With less need for aid as Europe got back on its feet, Joe argued that Mennonites could not just pick up and leave people after having established themselves there.[183] Transitioning to a missionary presence was one way to continue relationships, focusing now on supporting local Christians and developing new communities of faith.

Joe's reason for initiating new mission activity in Europe is notable, since in general he argued that "starting a mission with relief work is a poor way of starting a mission."[184] It was better to initiate new mission work in places where there was not a history of such assistance. In India the focus on material aid in the early work around Dhamtari appeared to have created dependency. It seemed better, therefore, to focus on establishing an indigenous church and allowing material assistance to be part of the subsequent witness. Joe was not rigid, however, in the way he put his missiological commitments into practice. In this case, the value of maintaining relationships and collaboration that relief workers had developed during the war and immediately afterward trumped the preference for not starting mission work with material assistance.

Another argument for starting mission work in European countries grew from the attention to Anabaptist history among North American

Mennonites during the mid-twentieth century. Mennonite historians John Horsch and his son-in-law Harold S. Bender did much to highlight the importance of the Anabaptist beginnings in Europe for the church's theological identity. Early Anabaptists had been persecuted and banished from some regions. Bender became an influential leader in the church and thought that the postwar period was an opportunity for Anabaptists to return to those places.[185] MBMC leaders likewise felt a responsibility for "a positive, evangelistic testimony" in Europe, the continent from which their ancestors had come.[186] Joe supported the desire to introduce an Anabaptist influence into regions where the tradition seemed to have disappeared.

In London to discern the vision and strategy for work there, Joe went to a square where two Anabaptists had been martyred, and he wrote about it in the *Gospel Herald* for the church back home:

> As I stood today on the spot where my forebears laid down their lives in glad witness to the truth and reality of the Gospel as understood and practiced by the church I love and hold dear, I determined anew to bring encouragement and challenge to our brotherhood to close the gap across the centuries and take again to this generation of English people the witness their blind ancestors so violently stamped out. . . . Let us pray that the Mennonite witness may come back to London.[187]

Joe also found the emerging post-Christian character of Europe to be a strong motivation for establishing mission work there. Europe had been the birthplace of the modern missionary movement but seemed to be increasingly turning its back on Christian belief and practice. Mennonite relief workers in Belgium reported dissatisfaction with the Roman Catholic Church, the most important Christian tradition in the country.[188] Joe noted that MBMC's investigation in England found that participation in churches had decreased to between 1 and 5 percent of the population, motivating questions about the future of the Christian movement there.[189] France too was a mission field.[190] Joe was convinced that Mennonites had something to offer in these contexts. He supervised the first wave of MBMC's missionaries to Europe and encouraged them to move into the new European context with openness. They reflected on their work and articulated ways that the Mennonite faith tradition could strengthen the European church and provide a helpful witness alongside a Christendom tradition that was on the decline.[191]

Mission objectives in each of the European countries grew out of their respective realities. In Belgium missionaries continued some relief activities that they inherited from the Mennonite Relief Committee, worked to provide a Mennonite perspective to other Christian traditions, and sought to establish a Mennonite church.[192] The approach was similar in England, except that the establishment of a Mennonite church was not included in the original plan, the Free Church tradition being already represented there.[193] In the end a Mennonite church did emerge in London.[194]

In France Joe's primary concern was that missionaries address mission needs that were not yet being met and work in close collaboration with the French Mennonite Church.[195] That many North American Mennonites had ancestors who came from France reinforced the desire to work with their French counterparts.[196] Joe advised missionaries to work in collaboration with a local mission council, which had representatives from the French Mennonites, that would guide their ministries and tie them closely with the French church.[197] This was consistent with indigenous church principles and produced positive results compared to the work of other missionaries in France. In general, North American missionaries' efforts in France after World War II saw limited success due to cultural conflicts that plagued their relationships with their French evangelical counterparts.[198] Many French Protestants did not consider their country a mission field and did not welcome missionaries from across the Atlantic. MBMC's decision to collaborate with the French Mennonites reduced such difficulties, and its mission efforts were productive, combining evangelism with social work and cooperation with a range of groups and agencies.

While French Mennonites were comparatively friendly to the idea of working with their North American counterparts, they had some reservations as well. Past experiences led them to question whether they could count on their American cousins in the long run. During the interwar period MBMC had provided financial assistance to an itinerant French minister who worked to connect and revive congregations whose vitality had declined.[199] Miscommunication and misunderstandings between the MBMC and the French church left the worker with less support than the church had expected.[200] Tightening its belt during the depression years, MBMC stopped the support altogether in May 1932.[201] A few months earlier Joe, Minnie, and Ronald had stopped in France on the way home for furlough to visit some of Joe's relatives. Later, after Joe remarked to the MBMC treasurer that members of the French church he had met were doing well financially, word filtered to the French that MBMC had stopped the support because of Joe's comments.[202] In the years after World War II, French leaders, some of whom were Joe's distant relatives, remembered unfulfilled expectations and asked if they could trust that MBMC would keep the commitments it made.[203] Joe was chagrined, feeling that his relationship with the church had been unfairly compromised. The task of building trust was part of the missionary challenge and took time, even with fellow Mennonites.

Although Joe and his MBMC colleagues had some success at developing innovative mission approaches for Europe, they encountered challenges. Many European Christians resented their countries being identified as missionary-receiving countries. The English missionary magazine *World Dominion* published an editorial entitled "On Being Evangelized" after MBMC missionary Quintus Leatherman visited its office, asking for advice about starting work among young people in the neighborhood.[204] The *World Dominion* editor described a feeling of resentment at the thought of foreigners coming to England to do what the English should do for themselves. Anxious to explain MBMC's intent and cultivate good relations with local Christians, Joe wrote to the editor in his insightful and careful manner, explaining that Mennonite values of love and service had motivated the placement of a Mennonite Service Unit in England during World War II.[205] He explained that MBMC now wanted to contribute on the spiritual level and hoped that its work would strengthen Christian witness in the country. He noted that Mennonite missionaries sought fellowship and cooperation with other churches. Cultivating warm and helpful relationships with local Christians was always important for Joe, and he understood the importance of those relationships for MBMC's mission work. His letter earned a gracious response from the previously perturbed editor.[206]

The place of relief in the new day

The growing Mennonite relief activity in the postwar period presented opportunities and challenges for Joe and MBMC's missionary vocation. The Mennonite Relief Committee (MRC) and Mennonite Central Committee provided material aid and logistical support that saved lives and rebuilt communities in postwar China, Europe, Japan, and Korea. Assistance also flowed to places like Puerto Rico that had been ravaged by natural disasters. This was an important and growing aspect of the Mennonite Church's witness as it became less isolationist during the first half of the twentieth century. MCC and MRC leaders like Harold Bender and Orie Miller, and relief workers, provided material assistance out of a sense of Christian discipleship and suggested that their work prepared the way for focusing more explicitly on the spiritual aspects of the missionary task.[207] Joe's expansionist vision and MBMC's *Plan of Advance* meant that he was willing to consider opportunities to establish missionary work in those regions where Mennonites had responded to human needs with material and logistical assistance. In ways unique to each situation, MBMC initiated missionary activity that drew on relationships and infrastructure that relief workers had established in Belgium, England, and France.

Joe saw relief work to be emergency assistance for the short term, meeting material needs to help people and communities recover from war or natural disasters.[208] After such assistance was no longer needed, it was better to maintain a Mennonite presence than to abandon the relationships that relief workers had started.[209] Joe was convinced, however, that following in the footsteps of relief workers was not the best way to expand mission work into new regions. It was better to start with a focus on evangelism and the establishment of the church, providing relief assistance as an integrated part of missionary witness as the need arose.[210]

Moreover, Joe thought that a focus on material assistance was problematic within the missionary movement as a whole. Amid the many postwar needs around the world there was a temptation to concentrate primarily on relief and reconstruction. While he agreed that Christian ministry included material concerns, he reminded the church, "This physical need is not the deepest of [human] need. The famine of the Word of God; the moral breakdown; the frustration and hopelessness of the world's millions spells their real need."[211] Looking back over the first half of the twentieth century, he noted that in China much energy and financial assistance had gone to creating and maintaining benevolent mission institutions, but when the Chinese government curtailed foreign mission activity, it considered those schools and healthcare institutions to be Western impositions and liquidated them early in its anti-Western campaign.[212] Joe argued that the missionary witness of sincere and self-sacrificing Christian living was less susceptible to being misunderstood and provided a better base for long-term success than did a strong focus on programs of material and physical assistance.

Instead of following relief assistance with traditional mission work, Joe promoted a vision in which relief work was integrated into the larger mission purpose of Christian witness and the establishment of the indigenous church. He suggested that it was better to have long-term missionaries provide relief assistance than to send short-term personnel who focused primarily on material aid.[213] The former, he felt, increased the likelihood that such assistance would be integrated into the mission efforts of the church and enhance Christian witness. He made this point in reference both to the Mennonite Service Units that MBMC promoted among young people in North America and the larger context of Mennonite international relief work. Service intended to meet human needs should be integrated with the larger missionary vision and work of the church.[214] He called for a "balanced witness," seeking to avoid a focus on either "belief" or "service" in a way that diminished any aspect of the total witness of the church.[215] He pointed to the incarnational witness of Jesus as the model and theological precedent for his vision. Loving and serving God could not be separated from loving and serving one's fellow human beings.[216] Writing for *Gospel Herald* readers in August 1951, he asserted, "We dare not stop short of a full proclamation of the Christian Evangel if we would make our service and relief, our deeds of love and kindness, have a truly Christian significance."[217] As such, Joe articulated values that other mission theorists and practitioners would call "holistic" or "integral" mission, an approach that refused to separate the material from the spiritual in Christian ministry.[218]

As he established new mission outreach and supervised MBMC missionaries, Joe sought to encourage holistic missionary witness and avoid the pitfalls of separating spiritual and material ministries. Where there were mission institutions such as hospitals or schools, he urged missionaries to find ways to integrate their purpose into the missionary vision and witness of the church.[219] When the Japanese island of Hokkaido suffered an earthquake in the spring of 1952, Joe wrote to the missionaries there to encourage them to respond with relief assistance.[220] He wanted missionaries to be ready to provide emergency aid quickly when the need arose. The MRC kept resources available to respond on short notice. In Puerto Rico MBMC's mission work followed MCC medical and social service programs that had started in 1943 and continued later through the MRC. Finding that there was little coordination between missionaries and relief workers and that they were sometimes even at cross-purposes with one another, Joe intervened to help establish a set of policies and procedures that required them to establish a coordinated approach.[221]

Defining the purpose of the Mennonite Service Units that were drawing a growing number of Mennonite young people, Joe insisted that their service initiatives be combined with missionary concerns such as evangelism. He wrote to Milo Kaufman, president of Hesston College and member of MBMC's missions committee, that he was not interested in service units that did service work without gospel ministry.[222]

Anthropology and linguistics: Tools for identification and indigenization

Joe found the disciplines of anthropology and linguistics to be important tools as he led MBMC's expansionist mission engagement in the 1950s. Missionaries developed a growing interest in anthropology over the first half of the twentieth century.[223] Edwin Smith, a Primitive Methodist missionary and anthropologist who served as the president of the Royal Anthropological Institute of Great Britain and Ireland, was an early voice for the use of the discipline for better missiological understanding of indigenous religious and cultural systems.[224] Ethnology, more commonly included in anthropology now, became part of the curriculum at the Kennedy School of Missions at Hartford Seminary in the second decade of the twentieth century, and in 1937 Wheaton College, a leading evangelical college, introduced anthropology as a major.[225] *The Christian Mission in a Non-Christian World*, Hendrik Kraemer's landmark work written for the 1938 International Missionary Council conference in Madras, India, urged missionaries to make use of anthropological research.[226]

MBMC missionaries eventually made this anthropological turn as well, thanks in large part to Joe's influence. In 1951 MBMC initiated a discussion with Goshen Biblical Seminary and the Eastern Mennonite Board of Missions and Charities about how to provide anthropological and linguistic training for Mennonite missionaries. They organized a conference on the theme, out of which arose a plan for missionary training in those disciplines.[227] Joe and other MBMC missionaries subsequently pursued studies in linguistics and anthropology at the Kennedy School of Missions, and Joe taught mission courses at Goshen Biblical Seminary.[228] He provided literature such as copies of Eugene Nida's *Customs and Cultures* to MBMC missionaries and encouraged them to use it to understand better the cultural dimensions of their interaction with local contexts.[229]

MBMC's work in the Chaco region of Argentina reinforced Joe's appreciation of anthropology for mission purposes. The work there at first followed the traditional mission-station approach of providing the population, the Toba people in this case, with the opportunity to better themselves spiritually and materially.[230] As had happened with Joe and Minnie and their colleagues in India in the 1930s, missionaries in the Chaco became increasingly frustrated with traditional mission approaches and began looking for new strategies in the face of the challenges they encountered. While many Toba seemed interested in the Bible study that the missionaries provided, the number willing to join the mission church was small.[231] Another complication was that the Argentine government was threatening to place limits on non–Roman Catholic missionary work to the point where the expansion of a traditional mission field no longer seemed possible.[232] Joe visited Argentina in early 1952 and reminded the missionaries of MBMC's priority of indigenization.[233] It seemed clear that the mission-station approach, which depended on missionary leadership and resources, was not making progress in that direction. Missionaries also came to realize that they needed additional cultural and linguistic understanding to meaningfully engage the Toba people.[234] In late 1953 they started a reassessment of their strategy.[235] They resolved to learn the Toba language instead of relying on the lingua franca of Spanish and to find ways to encourage indigenization.

The consultancy visit of William and Marie Reyburn of the American Bible Society demonstrated the potency of the tools of anthropology and linguistics for Joe's missiological commitments and MBMC's subsequent mission practice. Eugene Nida had recommended the Reyburns in response to the missionaries' request for assistance in the Chaco, and they spent six months preparing the missionaries for ongoing study of Toba culture, outlining the beginnings of a Toba grammar, and establishing a method for language study.[236] William used a "participant observer" strategy, living among the Toba to gather data.[237] His research found that many of the Toba had already accepted the Christian gospel, but it was a Spirit-focused form that seemed more like Pentecostalism than the North American Mennonite expression of the faith that the missionaries had been offering.[238]

Anthropological and linguistic analysis provided new understanding of the Toba people and seemed to offer the tools with which missionaries might seek new ways of working with this Christian movement. The missionaries adopted a posture of sympathy toward Toba culture and hoped to assist the Toba church to realize its own goals.[239] They decided that their role should be to identify with the Toba, participate in the Toba church, assist the church in interpreting Christian faith in light of Toba life, and work within the framework of the Toba's existing piety. They abandoned the idea of a central mission station as the hub of mission activity, choosing instead to itinerate among Toba communities to teach, minister, and render the Scriptures into the Toba language.[240] In the story of Mennonite missions, this was an early acknowledgment that legitimate mission strategy might focus not only on non-Christian peoples, but also on nascent forms of non-Western Christianity that were very different from North American Mennonite faith expressions but were authentically Christian nonetheless.

Joe was pleased with the novel approach that was developing in the Argentine Chaco and recognized right away that it had implications beyond its immediate setting. Thanks to the increased appreciation for local contexts and cultures that anthropological and linguistic insights had facilitated, mission strategy had moved from a traditional mission-station approach to one that sought to serve an indigenous Christian movement from within that movement's religious and social understandings. Missionaries were assisting the emergence of an indigenous church, one deeply rooted in the local culture and led by local leaders from the very beginning of its existence. In his report about the new strategy to MBMC's executive committee, Joe noted that this approach would be indicative of future mission policy in other fields.[241]

Joe had Reyburn's report published as *The Toba Indians of the Argentine Chaco: An Interpretive Report* and included it in the missiological literature that he sent to MBMC missionaries around the world.[242] The Reyburn report and the changes it wrought were significant beyond the world of Mennonite missions. They became important in the historiography of native religious expressions in the Argentine Chaco as the point of departure for the analysis of indigenous Christianity in the region.[243]

For Joe and MBMC, the Chaco experience provided a new approach to mission, one that encouraged identification and indigenization and seemed tailor-made for the new day. Amalgamating church and mission structures in postcolonial India, testing new strategies in Japan, and adapting to a post-Christian context in Europe were all indicative of an openness to new ways of working. Such openness was also relevant to mission work at home, as Joe sought to have every congregation think of itself as a mission outpost.

FIVE

"Every Church a Mission Outpost"

Expanding Mission Horizons at Home

"**IF OUR GROUP** cannot go to China, India, Africa, South America, or Puerto Rico, that does not leave us with nothing to do. . . . If we cannot go to the nations, we can at least begin at our back door," wrote Ellis Gerber of Kidron (Ohio) Mennonite Church in 1949.[1]

Seven years earlier the Kidron church had rented a hotel room in Dillonvale, some eighty miles distant, to hold weekly Sunday school meetings for children.[2] Dillonvale was a small mining town populated by Polish, Italian, Hungarian, and Bohemian immigrants. With its fourteen bars, apparent prevalence of broken families, and evident unchurched population, it seemed an appropriate mission field for Kidron congregants who were looking for ways to participate directly in mission work. The afternoon Sunday school eventually expanded to include Sunday evening services, and with the purchase of a building in 1944, the Dillonvale Mission church came into being. When transportation to the mission outpost became a challenge, Kidron Mennonite bought a new car, which logged 33,000 miles over the next two and a half years. Although the Dillonvale congregation was never large, it was an active mission site until the late 1950s. One of its members caught the missionary vision and served in a Pennsylvania children's home.

Kidron Mennonite Church's initiative at Dillonvale was not unique. Across North America, energy for mission outreach increased among Mennonite Church congregations during the early decades of the twentieth century. An expanding international footprint had its mirror image at home as mission activists established Sunday schools, vacation Bible schools, mission outposts, charitable institutions, and nascent congregations.[3] These developments made the timing of Joe's appointment as the first full-time and remunerated executive secretary of Mennonite Board of Missions and Charities in 1944 especially propitious.[4]

The Mennonite Church was on the verge of change and expansion in 1944. That was the same year Paul Erb took over the editorship of the *Gospel Herald* from Daniel Kauffman, who had shepherded the publication from its inception in 1908 and had been the primary architect of the Mennonite Church's denominational structure. It was also the year that Harold S. Bender published *The Anabaptist Vision* and Guy F. Hershberger published *War, Peace, and Nonresistance*, foundational works for formulating Anabaptist and Mennonite theological identity in North America during the decades to follow. And it was the same year the Mennonite Church authorized the creation of Mennonite Mutual Aid, which has since evolved into the financial services agency and credit union called Everence. During the postwar period Mennonites built and solidified many other institutional structures.

Along with the opportunity to increase the Mennonite Church's international mission outreach, Joe's leadership of MBMC thrust him into an influential position at a time of growth in North America. MBMC's footprint and influence increased significantly over the two decades after 1944. Conference mission committees and congregations looked to MBMC for advice and support, especially when their needs or visions outstripped local resources. When Joe became executive secretary, the treasurer and his personal secretary were the only other staff, but the number of MBMC employees grew dramatically during subsequent years. The office at 1711 Prairie Street in Elkhart became a beehive of activity amid all the new departments and additional personnel. Ernest Bennett became treasurer in 1948, and he and Joe were the principal architects of a growing institutional structure meant to embody and motivate mission engagement. With Joe's significant gifts as a communicator, he became MBMC's primary visionary and advocate across the Mennonite Church.

From "a mission outpost for every congregation" to "every church a mission outpost"

Among North American Mennonite congregations and conferences there had been a growing movement of local mission activity. Within his Mennonite Church constituency, Joe was able to reinforce, augment, and to a certain extent channel that energy. Sectors of the church had broken with the more seclusive tendencies of the Mennonite tradition by the beginning of the century, and Sunday schools, revival meetings, and young people's meetings had cultivated energy for outreach among the generations that came of age in the 1920s and 1930s.[5] Conferences formed mission boards, and Mennonites became increasingly familiar with urban areas, sometimes making their homes there. Urban contexts provided mission fields relatively close to congregations that now were more likely to engage in outreach than they had been in previous decades. Mennonite university students participated in the Young People's Christian Association and the Student Volunteer Movement, hotbeds of Protestant mission impulses.

During the first half of the century the number of new local mission initiatives in the Mennonite Church roughly doubled every ten years, reaching approximately 180 during the fifth decade.[6] These included a variety of activities meant to start new church communities: Sunday schools, vacation Bible schools, charitable or service projects, preaching points, and evangelistic initiatives.[7]

Joe was quick to notice the importance of this growing mission activity at the local level and sought to encourage and increase it. One of the ways he did that was by formulating and propagating the slogan "every church a mission outpost," although its earliest form was "a mission outpost for every congregation."[8] Joe had highlighted the idea during furlough in 1933 when he reported on an invitation to speak at a Sunday school that young people from the Franconia Conference had started in an unchurched area.[9] Although disappointed that conference bishops opposed such outreach activities, he was convinced that most Mennonite congregations were not far from unevangelized populations and should initiate these kinds of outposts.

Later, in his March 1945 paper at the Conference on Mennonite Community Life (sponsored by the Mennonite Church's Committee on Industrial Relations), Joe used the slogan and suggested that the idea was a way to create new congregations, to provide young people opportunities to become involved in the church, and to discover and train new church workers.[10] While some presenters at the conference expressed alarm at the effects of urbanization on Mennonite life and faithfulness, a common anxiety among church leaders at the time, Joe was adamant that Mennonites needed to have outposts even in the city.[11] He argued that spiritual vitality did not depend on rural culture and declared, "Urbanization is going on. We cannot stop it. We can, we must have Mennonite Churches in our cities."[12]

He repeated the "mission outpost for every congregation" idea a few months later at MBMC's annual meeting, and it became an often repeated slogan as he advocated across the church for more mission activity at the congregational level.[13] Starting in 1945 a promotional folder entitled *A Mission Outpost for Every Congregation* was among the resources that MBMC provided to its constituency.[14]

The mantra caught the imagination of large sections of the Mennonite Church and propelled many of its members into action. Church leaders, congregations, and conferences appropriated and promoted the slogan, and it motivated a dramatic increase in local outreach and even the exploration of international mission opportunities. The *Ohio Mission Evangel*, the periodical of the Ohio Mennonite Conference's mission board, adopted the slogan as its masthead in 1948, and the mission board of the Iowa-Nebraska Mennonite Conference also used the slogan in the masthead of its periodical, *Missionary Challenge*.[15]

The idea of a mission station as a base from which to minister in the surrounding community had become common in foreign missions. While the mission station paradigm was falling out of favor in the postwar period, its application on the domestic level encouraged Mennonites to consider their congregations to be mission stations that would radiate mission in every direction.[16] In 1953 the Mennonite Church's General Conference made the opening of more congregational mission outposts one of its priority goals.[17] Many such outposts became congregations in their own right.[18] In 1955 Levi C. Hartzler, MBMC secretary for publicity and church relations, noted as much when he wrote, "Some years ago the slogan, 'A Mission Outpost for Every Congregation,' struck fire in our churches. Of the 312 home missions listed in the 1955 *Mennonite Yearbook*, 43 per cent stem from this effort to evangelize near the home base."[19]

By the early 1950s Joe sought to change the slogan from "a mission outpost for every congregation" to "every congregation a mission outpost." His concern was that despite enthusiasm for creating outposts, Mennonites often did not want to make room for "outsiders," people who were not already steeped in the Mennonite tradition and heritage, in their congregations.[20] Zealous for the purity of the church and fearful their heritage might be endangered, they too often built fences to protect themselves.

Joe wrote in the *Gospel Herald*,

> If we build fences around our faith and practice in order to preserve them, we must make sure that there are gates on all sides and that they swing inward. What a travesty on the meaning of a New Testament church to have it made up of a group of self-satisfied and self-righteous people, loud and zealous in their profession of wholehearted Christian living and hesitating to allow their neighbors of a different cultural pattern to come in! Surely there is something wrong.[21]

By mid-century many congregations had established outposts, but they often seemed to prefer that their outposts be some distance away from the home base.[22] It was safer to establish an outpost ten, twenty, or fifty miles away so that one's own congregation could be protected from the influences that might accompany newcomers from a different cultural or religious background.

Joe considered such an approach misguided and sought to convince congregations that their mission obligation was also to their immediate context and not only to something "out there somewhere."[23] Mennonites needed to reach out to people in their proximity, even if it meant facing the challenges that diversity might bring to a church still very much defined by a traditional European Mennonite heritage. Joe sensed resistance among congregations that seemed to want to be involved in mission activity without welcoming those who were different from themselves. The slogan "every congregation a mission outpost" thus seemed to better capture the immediacy of congregations' missionary task than did "a mission outpost for every congregation."[24] Other Mennonite Church outlets followed Joe's lead in adopting the new slogan. The *Ohio Evangel,* for example, did so in 1952 before modifying it again in 1961 to "every congregation active in her mission."[25]

Like Joe's promotion of the new day in missions, the "every congregation a mission outpost" slogan demonstrated his capacity as a mission leader and visionary. In his writing, speaking, and correspondence he repeatedly insisted that the postcolonial context required new, more equitable ways of working. Others in the church picked up on the *new day* moniker and it became a way of signaling the necessity of change in mission engagement in an evolving world. Joe used "every congregation a mission outpost" in a similar way. There had been growing mission activity in local congregations and conferences for some time when he became executive secretary, but energy was still waiting to be released and channeled. With Joe's leadership MBMC made the slogan a key part of its promotion of local mission activity. Individuals, congregations, and conferences across the church appropriated it and the vision for which it stood, significantly increasing the Mennonite Church's footprint.

Evolving mission institutions on the home field

Given that Joe's missionary experience in India led him to critique the way missionary-created institutions had contributed to colonial habits of paternalism and inhibited, in measure, the development of an indigenous church, it is perhaps ironic that he spent significant amounts of time and energy overseeing MBMC's program of charitable institutions during his first decade as executive secretary. Perhaps in North America it was not evident to him that institutions encouraged dependency or overshadowed the church in the same way he believed they did in India.

Joe inherited oversight of numerous MBMC-connected institutions, and there were plans for more. In La Junta, Colorado, a combined sanitorium, hospital, and school of nursing had been part of the church's mission program for decades, and when Joe became executive secretary plans were in the works to open a hospital with an attached nursing school in Elkhart, Indiana.[26] In Ohio, Illinois, and Kansas MBMC owned, operated, or contributed to two homes for care of the elderly and two homes for children in need. Congregations, conferences, and individuals supported these ministries, but they also relied on MBMC in varying degrees to appoint workers, provide oversight, and supplement financial support when necessary. Over Joe's tenure as executive secretary, these institutions and those that would be added evolved, and became the responsibility of their own boards of directors and social service specialists, but initially Joe spent significant time seeing to their oversight.

Hospitals were an integral part of MBMC's mission approach during the middle decades of the twentieth century, both as a healthcare ministry and to train Mennonite nurses. Healing was part of Jesus' ministry, and the curative purpose of hospitals seemed to provide missionaries a way to follow in his footsteps.[27] The provision of nursing training was also an important concern. Given gender stereotypes of the day, Mennonite young women who wanted to enter a profession had limited options. Teaching and nursing were the two most evident. Since the church would not ordain women to the ministry, nursing was one way that women with a missionary call could exercise their vocation.[28]

For Joe, who sought to encourage young people to dedicate themselves to the church's growing mission activity, nursing was an obvious way for young women to contribute. He championed the cause of nursing schools where Mennonites could train in a context where their faith and commitment to Christian service would develop alongside their nursing skills.[29] Too many Mennonite young women, he thought, were receiving nursing training in schools where negative influences hindered their spiritual development and reduced the likelihood that they would be a positive witness for the church.

The Elkhart community needed better hospital services, and the Mennonite Church needed another hospital where more Mennonite nurses could be trained.[30] Joe was MBMC's primary advocate and fundraiser for the proposed solution, a new Elkhart hospital and nursing training program.[31] If the church found it important to start Mennonite schools and colleges to instill its values in its young people, he argued, then it also needed to provide Mennonite nursing schools to do the same. The plan called for one hundred and twenty-five beds, the minimum number required for a training hospital.[32] MBMC was tasked with building and administering the hospital, with Goshen College and the Mennonite Board of Education responsible for developing and administering the training program.[33]

In the end, the building of the Elkhart hospital became a community project instead of an MBMC venture, but the provision of nursing training and hospital ministry continued. MBMC raised nearly $300,000 for the Elkhart initiative, going so far as to raise funds by developing a section of Elkhart close to its office, and building houses there for sale.[34] The community of Elkhart eventually moved in another direction with their hospital plans, and the bulk of the funds were redesignated for Mennonite nursing schools at La Junta and Goshen College.[35] Goshen College moved forward with its nursing training program, and MBMC changed tactics.

Providing hospital services and training nurses was still a priority, though, as there was an increasing demand for nurses and hospital care.[36] Instead of building and owning hospitals as it had in La Junta, however, MBMC entered into agreements to manage and staff hospitals that were owned by the communities in which they were located.[37] Mennonites could exercise their mission vocation by serving in those hospitals without building and owning the infrastructure. MBMC eventually managed hospitals in Lebanon, Oregon; Greensburg, Kansas; Rocky Ford, Colorado; and Glenwood Springs, Colorado. In its international work MBMC workers managed hospitals in India, Puerto Rico, and Nigeria and served in additional healthcare institutions.[38]

Nursing training continued to be a priority. Mennonite nurses, who typically met at the annual MBMC meetings, organized themselves into the Mennonite Nurses' Association in 1942.[39] Mennonite

Church physicians and medical students followed suit and organized the Mennonite Medical Association in 1944.[40] Both associations subsequently met alongside the annual MBMC meetings.[41] The regulatory structures that governed nursing training required that the program in La Junta be transferred to the Mennonite Board of Education in 1949.[42] This became the pattern as time progressed, and hospitals and other charitable institutions came under state and federal regulation. Ownership and oversight eventually passed to local boards or other local institutions.

After the decision not to build a hospital in Elkhart, Joe spent much less time attending to the various MBMC hospital ministries but still oversaw the child welfare institutions until the appointment of a secretary for hospitals and charitable homes in 1953. There were two children's homes, in West Liberty, Ohio, and Kansas City, Kansas, when Joe became executive secretary in 1944. The Mennonite Youth Village in White Pigeon, Michigan, was established in 1950. The homes had started as orphanages, but needs changed as public welfare departments and regulatory structures evolved to care for children in North America.[43] State and county institutions and systems now existed to care for and protect most orphans, but there was still an unmet need to provide temporary foster care and support for underprivileged children, as well as for their families.[44] In 1949 Joe initiated the reorganization of MBMC's ministry for underprivileged children with the establishment of a child welfare committee.[45]

Joe's vision for the new child welfare focus included adapting MBMC's work to changing social needs, professionalizing its approach, and encouraging young Mennonites to consider social service professions. While fewer orphans might need assistance, Joe suggested that there were delinquent children or, increasingly, children whose parents were divorced, often creating the need for assistance for those children and their families.[46] He envisioned meeting such needs through summer camps, through an MBMC-employed social worker, via services to unwed mothers, or by providing foster care or adoption placement in Mennonite homes when necessary.[47] Those working in child welfare needed to be trained social service workers and should follow the practices recommended by specialists in the field, he thought. Joe consulted a specialist to provide a bibliography of sources and a study outline to help orient those working with children. He advised the child welfare committee to make this material available to workers and parents.[48]

Joe also urged young people to consider training for a vocation in the social services. He argued that just as Mennonites found opportunities for service and witness in the professions of teaching, nursing, or medicine, so they could find fruitful vocations as social workers. Openings for such employment in state and county agencies were numerous, and their work would bring Christian service-minded social workers face to face with children in great need. Joe spoke about such opportunities during visits to Mennonite colleges, and MBMC produced and distributed a pamphlet entitled *You and Christian Love in Social Service* to encourage young people to choose social service professions as a vocation.[49] MBMC and its child welfare committee followed Joe's lead, modifying their approach and encouraging young people to pursue those kinds of careers.

In an address at a conference organized for Mennonite child welfare workers, later published in the *Gospel Herald*, Joe outlined a theological and missiological case for social service vocations.[50] He argued that sin was at the root of the problems that plagued underprivileged children. Broken homes, abandoned children, and delinquency were ultimately the social consequences of people living without God, without hope. Without some understanding of this dynamic, social service programs would remain at a superficial level, failing to address the root cause of the problem. Mennonite faith commitments, Joe argued, recognized the importance of addressing both the underlying spiritual needs of people as well as their social needs. This view contrasted with a faith posture that sought only personal salvation and satisfaction, with the fundamentalist focus on orthodoxy without concern for social practice, and with the modernistic view that did not recognize the spiritual foundation of human life. Social service vocations were a form of Christian witness. He wrote, "To bring the healing balm of the love of Christ, incarnated in the life and service of a Christian social worker, into the haunts of sin and misery stands as one of the great challenges to our faith today."[51]

His work with MBMC's charitable institutions like hospitals and children's homes demonstrated Joe's flexible approach to mission institutions. In India he had provided leadership at Dhamtari Academy and understood the valuable witness of MBMC's schools, clinics, and hospitals. He critiqued them, however, when they seemed to reinforce the colonial system by placing missionaries in positions of authority over their Indian counterparts or when their maintenance seemed to draw energy, resources, and personnel that might have otherwise reinforced the development of the church. He helped the Mennonite Church in India devolve ownership and control of the institutions it had inherited from MBMC to autonomous boards of directors.[52] Church members still worked in them, but the church no longer controlled them. Back in North America, Joe worked hard to advance the Elkhart hospital project, but once its development was no longer feasible, he articulated a vision of Mennonites serving in, and sometimes managing, hospitals that MBMC did not own. He was supportive of MBMC's children's homes, appointing staff to serve in them and providing oversight, but when the traditional orphanage model was no longer viable, he advised them to adapt. He outlined new ways to meet the needs of disadvantaged children and encouraged young people to pursue vocations in social services, for which there were opportunities beyond MBMC's children's homes.

For Joe, brick and mortar institutions could be an essential part of mission efforts. Mission-minded Mennonites needed to adapt to changing circumstances, however, and modify their approaches and institutional structures to fit the realities they faced.

Race relations

As he encouraged local mission activity with the "every congregation a mission outpost" slogan, one way Joe manifested his concern that congregations be more open to integrating people who were not of traditional European Mennonite backgrounds was by addressing the barriers of race. By the 1920s, the International Missionary Council was highlighting race relations as a core challenge for Christian missions, and the use of race as a divisive means of classification was a live topic among Protestant missionaries during the following decades.[53] Although entangled in colonial structures that assumed white privilege, missionaries believed their work was helping to end segregation by resisting the caste system in India, and they viewed the move toward segregation by Christian politicians in South Africa as detrimental to

Christian witness. Mennonite missionaries too argued against what they understood to be race prejudice.[54] Informed by his experiences in India, Joe had long been among their number.[55]

Issues of race became more important for Mennonites during the first decade of Joe's tenure as MBMC executive secretary. Some church leaders warned that racial prejudice was present and growing among Mennonites and encouraged the faithful to make more room for African Americans in congregations and church schools, but those who preferred a segregated church resisted.[56]

Joe was among those in favor of integration within the church and throughout society. In his editorials in the *Gospel Herald*, he argued that Mennonites needed to address the issues of racism and white supremacy, writing that it was time for the church to declare where it stood on the issue.[57] In 1949 he suggested a church conference on race. Two years later the church's Committee on Economic and Social Relations sponsored a study conference on Christian community relations, which issued a statement that included a call against racial discrimination.[58] Another conference, held at Goshen College in 1955, produced a statement condemning racial prejudice and discrimination and calling for integration; the Mennonite Church formally adopted it four months later.[59]

Joe was convinced that segregation could not be justified and should not be tolerated, and he warned MBMC's foreign missionaries against attitudes of superiority based on race or nationality.[60] He lamented that the church was slow to remove segregation and discrimination when it should have been pointing the way forward.[61] Joe made his argument on both theological and practical grounds. He used biblical references to argue that God did not discriminate and that all humans came from the same ancestor.[62] The same blood flowed through the veins of all, regardless of skin color.

Joe did not offer systemic analyses of race. In that respect he was like many other Mennonite leaders of the time. He saw racial prejudice as primarily a spiritual problem, and he believed that personal relationships and Christian fellowship across barriers of race and color would diminish it.[63] When Christians participated in discrimination, the integrity of their witness to the gospel diminished.[64] Discrimination was not only wrong, Joe argued, but the hypocrisy endemic to it also decreased the likelihood of missionary success. He highlighted the cases of public figures such as social reformer Mohandas K. Gandhi and jazz musician Dizzy Gillespie, suggesting that they rejected Christianity as a faith option for themselves because of the discrimination they had experienced in churches in South Africa and in the United States.

Joe's concerns about race prompted concrete actions as a mission administrator. Under his leadership MBMC and the Mennonite Commission for Christian Education and Young People's Work published a mission study guide entitled *The Christian and Race* in 1947; it promptly sold out.[65] Focused on both adults and youth, the guide did not offer a systematic analysis of racism. However, it did recommend resources that challenged the idea of racial superiority, suggested that participants identify racial prejudices in their communities, equated racism in North America to the caste system in India, and sought to dispel resistance to interracial marriages.[66]

When rumors arose that MBMC was planning to dismiss women missionaries in Puerto Rico who were considering marrying Puerto Rican men, Joe intervened to clarify that such was not the case. He assured the women that their standing with MBMC would not be affected by their marriage to someone of a different race or nationality.[67] While Joe defended mission workers who were considering marrying people of another race, his advocacy was tempered by concern that some Mennonites were against such marriages. He warned that resistance from some in the constituency might negatively affect the ministry or even the marriages of interracial couples.[68] Such warnings must have made his advocacy seem wanting to the young people involved and their advocates.

Joe was less equivocal when it came to segregation in MBMC's mission congregations. In 1952, he learned from African American Mennonite pastor James Lark that after some white members of the Chicago Home Mission congregation objected to the presence of African Americans in their church, the church council had decided to transport Black Sunday school students to a neighboring Black church each week.[69] The Home Mission council's fear of segregationist backlash increased after a nearby Methodist church was vandalized, apparently because of its integrationist practices.

This was not the first time MBMC had encountered resistance in Chicago when it came to integration. MBMC had started mission outreach among Mexicans in the vicinity of their Chicago mission in the early 1930s. White parishioners of the mission, however, did not want to worship with Mexican immigrants and pressured the missionaries to discontinue the Mexican work.[70] Fearing the loss of white members, missionaries moved the initiative to a different neighborhood.

When James Lark raised the alarm about the busing plan, Joe responded decisively, arguing that such segregation was not acceptable and urging the council to invite the children back and make them feel welcome.[71] The integrity of the Mennonite Church and its missionary witness took precedence over the possible loss of white attenders. Of the African American population, Joe wrote to the superintendent of the Chicago Home Mission,

> We dare not exclude their children from our Sunday School nor the parents from our church services [emphasis in original]. To do so lines us on the side of prejudice and vested privilege. A New Testament mission dare not be on that side. If we represent our Lord and His Gospel truly we shall always find ourselves out in front on these issues where it is dangerous, and not safely behind a solid front of prejudice. I know this is not your personal evaluation and that is why I make bold to point out the implications so frankly.[72]

Joe made it clear that the choice was between prejudicial attitudes and the principles of the gospel. If a church suffered vandalism because of its move toward integration, such an experience would not be unusual in the history of the church, he noted.[73] The Chicago Home Mission was just that, a mission, and it was meant to serve the entire community, not any one group. The move to make every congregation a mission outpost meant that everyone should be welcome, segregationist resistance notwithstanding.

Certainly, Joe's insistence about the situation in Chicago did not resolve the problem of racial prejudice for MBMC or the Mennonite Church, which were only then beginning to address the issue. Neither is there evidence that Joe's advocacy for integration extended to participation in the civil rights movement that was gaining strength in the

Joe, second from right, gathered to initiate the building of the Bethel Mennonite Church meeting place in Chicago, Illinois.
MCUSA ARCHIVES

postwar decades. While others might pick up that mantle, his vocational focus was his church's mission initiatives. The struggle to disentangle the church and its mission agency from prejudicial attitudes and practices would continue over the following decades. As an MBMC senior executive, its primary visionary, and an influential church leader, Joe had the administrative and moral authority to be direct and categorical when he thought it necessary, and his advocacy had an impact in his areas of influence.

A mission visionary as administrator

During the early years of Joe's tenure in executive leadership, the coordination of almost all of MBMC's work, other than the accounting tasks of the treasurer, fell on Joe's shoulders. MBMC expected him to be the primary voice of the institution among its constituency, promote its work, provide aid and direction to its missionaries, develop new mission fields, and increase efficiency.[74] The administration of a growing institution was one of the greatest challenges of his career.

New opportunities and MBMC's expanding domestic and international reach created administrative duties that took up an increasing portion of Joe's time and energy. An early focus was the proposed hospital/nursing school in Elkhart, for which Joe initially led the planning committee and its fundraising activities.[75] Eventually Ernest Bennett came on board to coordinate that effort, but Joe continued as chair of the board of the La Junta School of Nursing in Colorado. Soon after becoming executive secretary, Joe also took over the role of secretary of mission education and, under a joint appointment with the Mennonite Church's Commission for Christian Education and Young People's Work, added secretary of Christian education for the denomination to his responsibilities.[76]

A growing tide of relief activity among Mennonites in the mid-1940s led to the provision of short-term service opportunities for young people, at first organized as part of the Civilian Public Service network and Mennonite Central Committee.[77] When MBMC responded to the desire for service opportunities with its own Mennonite Service Units, Joe became director of the program.[78] The growth in relief activities involved appointing workers in collaboration with other agencies, such as MCC, and required negotiating and following new lines of administration and accountability.[79] Adding to Joe's responsibilities, MBMC in 1946 took over its first rural mission in the United States at Culp, Arkansas, a mission that had been an initiative of the Missouri-Kansas Mennonite Conference.[80] In 1953 MBMC added the Black Mountain Mennonite Mission in Arizona and Camp Rehoboth in Illinois.

The reach of Joe's administrative responsibilities thus extended well beyond MBMC's home office in Elkhart. He oversaw MBMC's relationship with local mission initiatives of Mennonite Church congregations and conferences in North America. These outposts and institutions often looked to him to resolve difficulties and help establish new governance structures as they grew and evolved.[81] Joe was also MBMC's primary representative for other churchwide committees and institutions, such as the Mennonite Church's Committee on Coordination of Church Program.[82]

Meanwhile, of course, he supervised MBMC's international missionaries, a role that increased as their number grew with the expansion into new fields and areas of service. Missionaries relied on him as their primary source of advice, news of the home church, and encouragement.[83] Writing to missionaries in Japan, Joe observed, "It seems my whole life is rushing around the office and house and getting ready to leave. The amount of travel I do is almost pathetic. . . . Somehow these administrative details of our far-flung mission program need constant looking after and [there] does not seem to be any substitute for visiting and for making the personal contact."[84]

Joe's administrative approach included encouraging teamwork and relying on his strong relational skills. Ernest Bennett worked closely with him and later became executive secretary when Joe took on the dual roles of general secretary and secretary for foreign missions. Ernest credited Joe with creating an atmosphere of teamwork in which it was more important to use one's skills and gifts for the shared mission vision than to establish and follow firm administrative lines of authority.[85] For Joe, institutional policy was less vital than supporting MBMC's missionaries and their work. He prioritized the needs of missionaries and his coworkers and was quick to defend them when others criticized their theology or mission methods.[86] Missionaries he supervised remembered his ability to correct people without causing offence, his willingness to apologize and change his mind when he had erred, and his skill at resolving conflicts.[87] He was tactful and courteous, even when he disagreed with others.[88]

John Mosemann, left, was a former missionary and president of MBMC 1948–71. Ernest Bennett, right, took over the administrative tasks at MBMC, working in tandem with Joe, center, who focused on propagating the mission vision and expanding international work. MCUSA ARCHIVES

Joe was quick to delegate responsibility, a characteristic that became a necessity as MBMC grew. He could not do everything, and he worked to cede responsibility to others. When his secretary, Gladys Widmer, informed him that she was planning to leave her position, he wrote to his sister Esther, asking if she would consider coming to work with him. He explained, "I have hundreds of details in a dozen or two areas to look after and to keep tab of besides the creative planning and writing that I ought to be doing. I would be glad to turn over responsibility for as many of these areas and for as many of these projects and as rapidly as you felt able to take them."[89] Esther accepted and, although her title was secretary, she played the role of Joe's executive assistant for the rest of his career, taking care of many of the details of his job so that he could dedicate himself as much as possible to public speaking, writing, and visiting missionaries and new fields abroad.

Joe entrusted coworkers with the authority to make decisions that responded to the contexts in which they worked. He encouraged his staff at MBMC's Elkhart headquarters to take the initiative, telling them that as long as their batting average was 95 percent, they should move ahead with ideas without consulting him.[90] He did not micromanage.

Joe with Tille Yoder, left, and his sister Esther, right, at MBMC offices. Esther became his secretary and served as an executive assistant to Joe during the 1950s and '60s. MCUSA ARCHIVES

One of Joe's responsibilities was the oversight and staffing of MBMC's charitable institutions.[91] Over time he worked to transfer the administrative charge for those ministries to local boards as much as possible.[92]

Joe expected overseas missionaries to make decisions that were appropriate for the cultures and situations in which they worked.[93] Minnie thought he might have achieved more if he had been a bit more like Orie Miller, an administrator for another agency and one of Joe's frequent collaborators, who had a reputation among missionaries of arriving to visit them with strong, predefined decisions about strategies and approaches that he expected them to follow.[94]

Issuing directives was not Joe's approach. The exception was his insistence on indigenization; missionaries were to transfer authority for decisions about mission activity to local people as soon as possible. His practice of placing decision-making authority on local actors was consistent with indigenization theory and with a strand of Mennonite tradition that he valued. He often referenced with approval his family's Amish Mennonite tradition, in which congregations met in conferences but retained the authority to make their own decisions about their faith practices.

Perhaps Minnie had a point when she suggested Joe might have accomplished more if he had been more ambitious about implementing his ideas in MBMC's many fields of activity. Still, his primary focus was on casting a vision, communicating it effectively, and motivating people to action. At that he was successful. It was rare that Joe involved himself in the details of MBMC missionaries' day-to-day decision-making and ministry. He provided the vision and was available when they called on him for advice. His tendency to delegate, his belief that mission approaches should be tailored to each specific context, and the sheer impossibility of managing all of MBMC's many initiatives meant that missionaries had much freedom to decide how they could or should actualize Joe's vision. Closer management of missionaries' work would have taken time and energy away from his busy schedule of visits and speaking assignments, which he seemed to prefer, and would have reduced the number of people who heard his vision and were motivated to action.

If his strong relational skills and willingness to delegate responsibility gained him the respect of his coworkers, Joe and those with whom he worked agreed that the administration of MBMC's growing institutional structure was not his forte. His true calling and gifts were as a mission visionary, advocate, and counselor, not as an administrator.[95] He often chose to leave the administrative details to others, sometimes even nodding off to sleep in meetings that focused on such matters.[96] His letters to missionaries rarely discussed policy, but rather addressed the importance of indigenization, of humility, and of working in harmony with others.[97]

Joe's lack of attention to lines of authority in institutional structures sometimes got him into trouble when he initiated activity without going through proper channels. Traveling in South America in early 1952, he wrote a letter to Paul Erb, editor of the *Gospel Herald*, but did not clear his ideas beforehand with either the *Herald*'s mission editor or the Mennonite Publishing House's publishing agent. When the letter arrived on Esther's desk to be typed and forwarded to Erb, she intervened and wrote back to Joe, "Your letter to Minnie yesterday came with the one you wrote to Paul Erb. It was quite clear to both Minnie and me that you were approaching this problem backwards. You will remember last year's experience. . . . You went to Erb and left out Ford and also Metzler. After all Metzler is House manager. I checked this through with Bennett and he also felt that you will run into an awful snag by going to Erb first."[98] Joe seemed to accept such advice, even to invite it. Esther caught nuances that Joe did not and saw to many of the details that he found hard to manage.

The role of executive secretary was taxing, and Joe felt the strain of the seemingly all-encompassing job, especially during the early years of his tenure. Family members remembered him taking a teaspoon of bicarbonate soda with water to calm what he considered to be stress-related stomach discomfort before retiring in the evening.[99] He took additional measures to relieve the stress, such as limiting the hours he worked each day, at least when he was home in Elkhart. When Esther started working for him, he told her that they were not going to get ulcers from their work. They would start at the appointed time in the morning and close at the appointed time. If they did not get all the work done, it could wait for later. Joe had a passion for gardening and would go straight to the garden after work. He found that it relieved stress and said that it was what he did instead of playing golf.

Joe had a well-developed sense of humor, which helped him maintain a healthy approach to life despite the pressures of his job.[100] From an early age he had been the clown of the family, and fellow missionaries in India remembered his humor as something that helped them through difficult times. He was always up for something silly.[101] Later, when he became their supervisor, Joe said that missionaries did not laugh enough and thus did things to get them to laugh more. He loved to tell jokes and stories, although Minnie thought he told too many stories. He had a limited repertoire and tended to repeat the same ones, but people would laugh anyway, responding to the joy he radiated when telling them.

The rapidly increasing work motivated MBMC to add personnel and create new departments as necessary, thus providing some relief for Joe. At the board's annual meeting in 1948, the executive committee formulated a proposal for the creation of committees or secretariates for the different mission domains, such as urban, rural, foreign, child welfare, hospitals, and relief and voluntary service.[102]

With the growth of the voluntary service program and the work of the Mennonite Relief Committee, the board followed through with the appointment of a secretary for service and relief later that year.[103] After MBMC decided not to pursue the hospital effort in Elkhart and turned

MBMC executive committee, November 1959. Left to right: Earl Buckwalter, J. B. Martin, Joe, John Mosemann, H. Ernest Bennett, Norman Derstine, Jacob Clemens. MCUSA ARCHIVES

over its nurses' training program to the Mennonite Board of Education, Joe was relieved of that focus too.[104] Ernest Bennett took over many of the administrative responsibilities. The creation of a department of publicity and church relations with its own full-time director in 1952 helped Joe in his efforts to keep the missionary vision on the church's front burner.[105]

During all but the first four years of Joe's tenure in executive leadership, John Mosemann served as president of the board and oversaw the evolution of the institution. He was a pastor in Goshen, Indiana, and he and his wife Ruth (Histand) had served as missionaries in eastern Africa. He was the son of Bishop John Mosemann, one of the protectionist bishops who had barred Joe from speaking in Lancaster Conference churches in Pennsylvania during Joe and Minnie's first furlough.

A revision of MBMC's bylaws in 1953 formalized the expanded institutional structure. It increased specialization across the array of mission activities, organized thereafter into divisions: foreign missions, home missions, radio evangelism, finance, publicity, hospitals and charitable homes, and service and relief, the last four of which had appointed secretaries.[106] Advisory committees helped guide the specialized areas of urban evangelism, child welfare, and investments. Joe still wielded considerable influence across the MBMC apparatus, but once the board appointed a secretary for home missions in the spring of 1955 and the rate of institutional growth slowed, he was able to concentrate on international mission work and promoting his missionary vision on the home front.[107]

Dorsa Mishler came onboard in 1956 to be secretary of personnel. Dorsa, Ernest Bennett, and Joe made a formidable trio for over a decade, with Dorsa managing the personnel details of MBMC's growing corps of workers, Ernest keeping the institution running smoothly, and Joe as the public face of the work, overseeing a growing international footprint and communicating a stimulating missionary vision across the North American constituency. These were areas for which he had a passionate commitment.

Communicating the vision

MBMC's evolving engagements and institutional structures soon required more sophisticated ways of communicating with, educating, and motivating the constituency. In 1947 Joe negotiated more space for mission news in the church's weekly *Gospel Herald*. The *Herald* agreed to include an enlarged weekly mission section, appoint a mission editor to oversee it, and increase MBMC's oversight of mission coverage.[108] Recognizing that radio technology was becoming an important missionary tool, Joe led the effort to use it in MBMC's work and helped integrate *The Mennonite Hour*, a broadcast from Harrisonburg, Virginia, into its web of endeavors.[109]

A gifted communicator, Joe had exercised his speaking and writing skills since his early days at Hesston College. He had worked hard to improve his oratory skills while a student at Princeton, giving attention to refining his preaching and public speaking. Much of the preaching in the Mennonite Church was of poor quality, Joe thought, and he worked to improve his own public speaking as well as impress upon others the importance of good preaching.[110]

As executive secretary he maintained a full public speaking schedule across North America. This was in addition to his already heavy international travel schedule and thus further increased Joe's time away from home. It seemed like he was always either coming or going. Composing the family's Christmas letter to send to friends and colleagues in 1947, he noted that he had been in Pennsylvania for two days the previous week and that he would be in Chicago for the upcoming weekend. He did not finish the letter, however, before having to depart. Minnie completed it for him, writing:

> Brief case in one hand, hat in the other, an open door, a few "last suggestions"—Joe leaves and I turn to the latest delegated task—which happens to be in this case wishing you the Season's Greetings. He has intimated Christmas is almost here but didn't actually say as I do now, Joe, Ronald and Eleanor joining me, A JOYOUS CHRISTMAS TO YOU, FRIENDS, ONE AND ALL.[111]

By all accounts Joe was an engaging and persuasive speaker. He was able to capture and focus his audience's attention and motivate people to action.[112] People remembered how he used facial expressions and body language to help communicate and that his compassion and concern for the church and its missionary commitments were evident. He "always warmed up an audience," and typically drew a crowd when visiting churches.[113] Although he used notes, Joe did not normally write out his

Joe speaking at the MBMC annual meeting in Milford, Nebraska. MCUSA ARCHIVES

sermons or presentations beforehand. He knew how to read an audience and would adjust accordingly, formulating a sermon right up until it was time for him to preach. Living with Joe's habit of such last-minute preparations made Minnie nervous, but it seemed to work for him.[114]

Joe preferred preaching and other public speaking assignments to writing, but he accepted writing assignments to reach a wider swath of the Mennonite Church.[115] As with his sermon prep, Joe generally waited until the last minute to meet his writing deadlines.[116] He would say that a deadline was "so near that it stinks."[117] Then he would sit at his desk and start writing, not stopping until he had finished. In his editorials and articles Joe addressed the crucial missiological issues of the day, but in a way that readers of all strata could understand. Joe's writing appeared most often in the Mennonite Church's *Gospel Herald* but also in its *Youth's Christian Companion* and *Christian Monitor*. During his career he published nearly seven hundred articles, both mission editorials and longer more substantial pieces. A handful were journal articles and chapters of edited books.[118] A series of his lectures was published as *The Church Apostolic* in 1960.[119]

Joe's public engagements, like most public meetings and events in the Mennonite Church, were typically listed in the *Gospel Herald*. Notices of his engagements included revival meetings, sermons at congregations and conference gatherings, mission conferences or rallies, evangelistic meetings, funeral services, wedding ceremonies, young peoples' meetings, college student gatherings, and Bible conferences.

During his tenure of executive leadership with MBMC, Joe arguably had the highest visibility of any figure within the Mennonite Church. On average, his name appeared in the *Gospel Herald* 127 times per year from 1948 to 1954.[120] By comparison, the name of Orie O. Miller, Joe's contemporary and frequent colleague in interagency Mennonite collaboration, appeared an average of 29 times per year during the same period. Orie was a primary architect and visionary in the development of Mennonite Central Committee and its international expansion, and was arguably the most important instigator of North American Mennonite institutions over the middle decades of the twentieth century. He excelled, however, in the boardroom and not, as Joe did, as a public speaker and motivator across a broad swath of the church. Harold S. Bender, also a contemporary and perhaps the most influential Mennonite scholar in the shaping of Mennonite and Anabaptist identity during the same period, averaged 56 mentions per year. Harold spoke frequently in congregations and at church events but focused on influencing the church's leadership, primarily at Goshen College and Seminary and through his scholarly writing.

In contrast to these other mid-twentieth century leaders, Joe focused on the people in the pew (although he also taught mission classes part-time at Goshen Seminary). His public speaking and writing were in a popular style that had broad appeal. He was the most prolific mission visionary and commentator of his day across all the North American Mennonite and Anabaptist groups.

Minnie too developed a ministry of public speaking and mission advocacy in North America after the Grabers' return from India. Although not officially on the staff at the home office in Elkhart, she was a constant presence and contributor at MBMC. She sometimes filled in for Joe at speaking assignments or other events when he was traveling.[121] While he was in the Philippines in November 1949, she took his place at Crumstown Mennonite Church in North Liberty, Indiana, where she talked to the congregation about MBMC's India work. Joe counted on Minnie as a confidante and counselor, whether in relation to responsibilities at the office or in his supervision of missionaries overseas.[122] He relied on her editorial advice when writing articles and reports for the *Gospel Herald*.[123]

The two worked on MBMC projects together and sometimes also traveled together, sharing speaking assignments at congregational visits and mission conferences. MBMC produced mission study materials for congregations and supporters to use as educational and motivational resources. As MBMC started work in China, Joe wrote a booklet, *We Enter China*, for the study packet explaining the initiative, and Minnie prepared the accompanying guide and supporting materials.[124] She taught mission study classes, even preparing curry for a class at Pleasant View Mennonite Church in Goshen, Indiana, to give participants a "taste" of India.[125] At missionary rallies and conferences at Mennonite churches in the United States and Canada, Joe and Minnie shared the stage with other Mennonite mission leaders such as African American pastor James Lark, MBMC colleagues George and Fanny Lapp, Indian church leader Pyarelal Malagar, and Mennonite Central Committee director C. J. Rempel.[126] In addition to speaking about missions, organizers often also asked Minnie to speak to the children, certainly because she was the female part of the Joe and Minnie partnership.[127] She obliged requests to work with children, although it was not her preference and she did not consider it to be her gift.[128]

Minnie was a gifted writer and contributed articles in the church press. In a short anecdotal piece in the *Gospel Herald*'s "Family Circle" section, she urged family members to practice the same courtesy among themselves that they used with strangers.[129] A "good morning" greeting was not a banal formality. Rather, it assured those with whom readers shared their lives of their good will, their gratitude for others, and their gratitude to God for a new day. In some of her writings, Minnie gave readers a view into the lives of the Indians with whom she and Joe had worked, conveying both the otherness and shared humanity of vastly different peoples and contexts.[130] She sometimes made comparisons with North America. In one article she remembered the well-earned dignity of grandmother figures in the church in which she grew up, and she reflected on the simple but profound faith of grandmothers she encountered in India.[131] In another the juxtaposition was between, on the one hand, toddlers, their antics, and their minders in a North American Mennonite worship service and, on the other hand, an Indian mother and her toddler bowing in reverence at a shrine.[132] In both articles the faith of people in those vastly different places was evident, but the faith of those on the Indian side was somehow more profound.

Minnie's writing often championed the church's mission activity. She encouraged readers to make use of the mission study class materials that MBMC produced and promoted the work of the Women's Missionary Sewing Circle Organization (WMSCO).[133] She called on women to participate, to stay abreast of its activities, and to adapt to the changing circumstances of Mennonite women. After being elected president of the WMSCO in 1950, her focus was largely on organizing and promoting its work in support of the church's mission programs.[134] As Joe noted to a colleague July 13, 1951, the work kept her quite busy. The day before, she had spent the morning at a church in Shipshewana, Indiana, attended a WMSCO meeting in the afternoon, and in the evening spoke at a farewell gathering for missionaries leaving to work in the Upper Peninsula of Michigan.[135] She arrived home after eleven o'clock that night, very tired.

MBMC's annual meetings became one of the ways that Joe and his colleagues promoted mission engagement across the Mennonite Church. The meetings were multiday conferences that drew large crowds of participants from all over the United States and Canada eager to hear about the work that many of them supported with their donations and followed via reports in the pages of *Gospel Herald*.[136] There were plenary worship services, sermons, and reports, as well as seminars and the buzz of networking and social interaction among leaders and lay people with a common commitment to furthering mission work at the local, national, and international levels.

After Joe took on the role of executive secretary, annual meetings were generally focused on a particular theme, and starting in 1950 the events were reported as the annual meeting and "related conferences" of MBMC, in recognition of the wide range of interests represented.[137] Concurrent gatherings of the Mennonite Nurses' Association, Mennonite Medical Association, Mennonite Youth Fellowship, WMSCO, voluntary service leaders, and other interest groups became part of the four-to-five-day event, which spanned a summer weekend and also included missionary-training activities. The meetings drew increasingly large crowds and eventually required venues such as college campuses or large churches with supplemental space provided by the revival-size tents set up beside them.

MBMC held the meetings in a different Mennonite community each year to encourage wider swaths of the church to catch the missionary vision. As such more people had an opportunity to host or attend a meeting and be inspired to support and join the church's growing mission footprint in North American and overseas. The hosting community marshaled its resources to feed and house those who attended from afar. On Sunday morning MBMC leaders and missionaries fanned out across the Mennonite congregations in the vicinity to serve as visiting preachers, Sunday school teachers, and storytellers, reinforcing the missionary spirit of the faithful.

Early in his tenure Joe invited conference and local missions to prepare posterboard displays that highlighted their ministries for exhibition at the MBMC meeting as well as at the smaller and more administration-focused Mennonite Church General Conference gathering.[138] The displays at the MBMC meetings became more numerous and detailed over the years, eventually requiring more space and including exhibits of other institutions such as Mennonite Central Committee, Mennonite Publishing House, and the Mennonite colleges.[139] Those attending the meetings had a wide range of gatherings, sermons, reports, and displays from which to draw inspiration. One of the highlights each year was the commissioning of overseas missionaries, those leaving for the first time as well as those returning to foreign fields after a furlough.

After each annual meeting Joe typically wrote a letter to MBMC's missionaries describing the gathering and reporting on new initiatives and new personnel appointments.[140] Frequently he shared his conviction and delight that the MBMC annual meetings were the most popular and best-attended gatherings of the Mennonite Church.[141] This was an unspoken comparison to the meetings of the Mennonite Church's General Conference, where debate and the business of denominational church structures seemed to lack the unifying inspirational focus of MBMC's missionary vision.

Growing energy for mission activity at home and expanding foreign work supplied momentum that Joe sought to channel by advocating for mission partnership on a global scale during his second decade of executive leadership at MBMC.

SIX

Partnership

Collaborative Mission Engagement with the Global Church

JOE HAD not expected to travel to Africa in the spring of 1959, so his visit to a fledgling Mennonite church in Nigeria was hurriedly planned. A few months earlier Mennonite Board of Missions and Charities missionaries in Ghana had sent word that they were contemplating a visit to a group of congregations in Nigeria that, on their own initiative, wanted to become Mennonite.[1] Joe was ever on the lookout for ways to expand MBMC's witness and continued to believe that the Mennonite faith had something of value to offer to the world. He was surprised but pleased with this new opportunity. He admitted to being "somewhat bewildered," however, at the pace of events with the group, which turned out to be quite large.[2] After three visits missionaries reported three thousand church members in several dozen congregations.[3] In India Joe and his colleagues had worked hard for nearly six decades to build a church with half that many members.

The new Nigerian church would, in one fell swoop, be the largest of any of the churches in MBMC's international work. While some missionaries in India had experienced mass movements into their churches, such a thing had never happened in MBMC churches.

Perhaps it would now in Nigeria. A visit to the church seemed wise to decide how to proceed.[4]

The visit came at a time of significant transition to postcolonial structures and norms in Nigerian society, and churches were part of the process. The official shift from colonial rule to Nigerian independence would take place in October 1960, but preparations were already well underway. The formal address that church leaders presented to Joe on his arrival shows that they identified with the move toward new post-colonial relationship patterns. They sought assistance but expected more mutuality than they had experienced previously with colonial authorities and foreign missionaries.

Their address communicated as much:

> As you must very well have known, we are at present struggling to take our stand among the nations of the world as an independent country. Naturally, we must be beset with difficulties. At this transitional period of ours, [during] which you come to meet us, we have to advise you not to look on us as you look on the people of America or England, but to look on us from the perspective of a child beginning to trod about the house. It will therefore be difficult for you folks to live and work in our midst, if you will not be able to appreciate our efforts and difficulties, and be prepared to stand firm by us and support us in every way possible, to retain our independence on a balance as we have already marched to its threshold. Furthermore we have to make it clear to you all that we are a peaceful people and that we always welcome and love our strangers, but that we do not tolerate, and shall employ every means possible to stamp out, any traces of colour discrimination within our community.[5]

The invitation from Nigeria demonstrates aspects of a partnership paradigm that became Joe's preferred reference point for mission theory and practice during his second decade of executive leadership at MBMC. This North American missionary engagement in Nigeria started at the initiative of Nigerian Christians, and they had already identified their priorities before Joe's visit.[6] This contrasted with the traditional paradigm in which the initiative rested primarily with

Western missionaries, as had been the case with early MBMC work in India and Argentina.

Whether with respect to taking the initiative or setting priorities, partnership meant that decision-making power should be shared between North American Mennonites and their counterparts in other lands. Attention to local contexts was becoming ever more important, and mission work was no longer the sole responsibility of North Americans. There was to be one church and one mission. MBMC missionaries and their interlocuters around the world were part of the global church and were to participate together and equitably in Christ's mission.

By the mid-1950s Joe had articulated and shared widely his conviction that the postcolonial era required new thinking and practice. During his final decade at MBMC, he embraced a partnership model to meet that need.

Appropriating the partnership paradigm

Into the twentieth century, as churches that grew out of the Protestant missionary movement were gaining strength, partnership emerged as a preferred approach. As early as 1928, the International Missionary Council (IMC) suggested partnership as the way that the "younger" and "older" churches should relate.[7] During the following decades, many mission-receiving nations moved toward shedding colonial chains, churches in those nations sought self-governance, and mission theorists anticipated that mission practice would need to change in the new day.[8] The partnership paradigm gained prominence in the decade after World War II with the IMC's statement "Partners in Obedience," approved during its 1947 meeting in Whitby, Ontario.[9] The meeting highlighted a sense of unity, mutuality, and common vision among participants from forty countries.[10]

The IMC envisioned that churches from traditionally mission-sending nations and churches started by missionaries would work together to realize common mission initiatives. This was, in measure, a reversal of indigenous church theory in which mission was to come to an end with the establishment of an independent church.[11] The desire for strong indigenous churches remained, but the goal was no longer autonomous churches that Western missionaries would leave in their wake as they moved on to unevangelized fields. Instead, mission activity was to result in partner churches, which would assume their role in the missionary task in collaboration with the missionary-sending churches that had founded them.

Joe's ideas along these lines grew from nearly four decades of mission experience. They were not his alone but corresponded with wider Protestant missiological discernment.[12] Joe kept up on what others were thinking and writing and taught mission-related courses at Goshen Biblical Seminary.[13] In his writing and public speaking he articulated a strong case for partnership.

As with his promotion of the new day in missions and the "every church a mission outpost" rallying cry, Joe's advocacy of partnership resonated with colleagues and the mission-minded constituency of the Mennonite Church. His last address to the annual MBMC meeting before handing most of his responsibilities over to his successor, Wilbert R. Shenk, in 1965 was entitled "Partners in World Mission," which was also the theme of that year's meeting.[14] The address was reprinted in *Being God's Missionary Community: Reflections on Mennonite Missions 1945–1975*, an edited volume in honor of Joe and Minnie published by Mennonite Board of Missions in 1975.[15] His articulation of the partnership paradigm was a fitting crown to Joe's missiological career. It brought together concerns that had arisen over the span of decades of experience and reflection.

For Joe, partnership pushed mission theory and practice beyond the indigenous church focus that had played such an important role for him and his colleagues.[16] Indigeneity had been an evident goal during the age when political control was vested in colonial powers, and the missionary was too often the religious counterpart to the colonial administrator.[17] Prioritizing the emergence of indigenous or independent churches highlighted autonomy and was a move away from the paternalism and dependency of the colonial age.[18] Yet the intent was not to sever relations between mission agencies and indigenous churches. Joe insisted that in the postcolonial era the goal was not just to birth new churches but also to establish equitable and ongoing collaboration with those churches. Key values of indigeneity continued, such as the placement of religious and administrative authority with the local or national churches and the development of local leaders and resources.

Joe and Minnie entertain friends from India living in Elkhart, Thomas Koshy, his wife, (name unknown), and their daughter Chrissie, 1963.
MCUSA ARCHIVES

The change in focus, however, was significant. Two decades earlier Joe had argued that MBMC missionaries and the Mennonite Church in India had distinct and separate functions.[19] The church was primarily to attend to its own needs, while the missionaries were to focus on evangelization and founding new churches. In contrast, the partnership paradigm prioritized collaboration instead of separating responsibilities between foreign missionaries and local Christians.

The partnership era also meant that Western missionaries needed to work even harder to overcome lingering attitudes of superiority. Joe suggested that North American Christians and missionaries they sent had too often identified people in missionary-receiving lands pejoratively, as heathen and benighted people inferior to Western Christians. While he believed that the Christ whom missionaries shared was uniquely "the way, the truth, and the life" and able to meet the spiritual needs of humankind, he also believed such a conviction needed to be held "in deep humility and with profound love."[20] In his address to the Mennonite World Conference in Karlsruhe, Germany, in 1957, he noted, "We are only becoming more aware of the incongruity between the Gospel of Christ and a spirit of arrogance and superiority."[21] His vision of the church's mission endeavors had no place for such a spirit. Instead, Joe believed that missionaries should value and identify with the people among whom they ministered. Real communication with another person was not possible, he suggested profoundly, unless the missionary understood the person so deeply that the missionary was tempted into the other's faith or belief structure.[22]

A focus on "one church and one mission" was an important theme in Joe's vision of partnership. Throughout the post–World War II period there were calls for ecumenical collaboration in missions and a growing consensus that mission belonged to and originated from God.[23] Missionaries and the churches that sent them could no longer claim ownership of churches they founded. Mission literature often referred to Western churches that sent missionaries as the "mother," "older," and "sending" churches, while the churches they founded were the "daughter," "younger," and "receiving" churches. During the last decade of his career, Joe criticized such terminology, arguing that it implied that missionary-founded churches were colonies of the missionary-sending churches.[24] There was a tendency to keep those churches in a state of perpetual adolescence, implying they were somehow inferior or not mature enough to assume their missionary responsibility.

Only one identifying characteristic was necessary for being a church, he argued, irrespective of its origin: that it be under the lordship of Jesus Christ. This was the same challenge for churches everywhere, whether they were missionary-sending or missionary-receiving churches. Under the lordship of Jesus Christ there was just one church, and it extended around the world.

There was also just one mission. "Mission is only and always Christ's mission," Joe wrote in the *Gospel Herald*.[25] MBMC's outreach, in fact all human mission initiatives, constituted specific contributions to this larger mission. Missionary-founded churches were part of the body of Christ, full-fledged churches that shared in the responsibility to participate in Christ's mission. Mission was equally the responsibility of all, Joe contended. Western Christians' assumption that it was their burden to evangelize the world was naïve and exposed their pride and self-centeredness.[26] The responsibility did not rest solely on their shoulders but was to be shared by the worldwide community of churches.[27]

Just as Christ was Lord of all, so mission was the responsibility of all. As such, mission activity was about creating a global community of churches that collaborated to further God's mission in the world. Joe urged both North American missionaries and the emerging Mennonite churches with which they worked to move forward in partnership. Christians from around the world needed each other and should learn from each other what it meant to be Christian.[28]

As the Mennonite Church in India came of age in the early 1950s and took ownership of ministries that had been under the direction of missionaries, Joe spent an extended visit in India helping the process along. By then he was convinced that partnership had become "a self-evident necessity."[29] He made that point clear to MBMC missionaries on his trip. Some of them resisted the move, but he encouraged them to collaborate wholeheartedly with Indian leadership. At his urging the missionaries pledged to embody the spirit of "Partners in Obedience" in their relationships with the church.[30] Joe invited the Mennonite Church in India to participate in MBMC work in Nepal and urged it to initiate and lead mission activity with which North American missionaries could collaborate.[31] Similarly, he was excited when leaders of the Mennonite church in Argentina informed him that they wanted to participate in mission work in Spain and pledged support for the church's outreach activities.[32]

Partnership, however, was hard. North American missionaries sometimes found it easier to implement mission projects on their own, without involving the local church.[33] Joe warned that such practices risked doing more harm than good. At the same time, MBMC missionaries admitted that sometimes it was easier, and perhaps seemed more efficient, to work under the indigenous church paradigm, which assumed that missionaries would move on to other fields once a church was established.[34] It was easier to maintain separate work than to negotiate when they disagreed with local church leaders. For Joe, however, partnership was worth the effort. It was better for North American missionaries and local church leaders to meet the challenge of finding ways to collaborate, even when they disagreed, than to work separately.

While there were theological, missiological, and historical reasons for Joe's appropriation of the partnership paradigm, his missionary experience and the deep relationships he formed with collaborators around

Teatime at the Mennonite Church in India 1964 Conference in Dhamtari, India.
MCUSA ARCHIVES

the world were no less important. He and Minnie had established meaningful friendships with Indian coworkers during their two terms in India. Joe maintained communication and relationship with them and other local church leaders from countries where MBMC worked. To him it was self-evident that ongoing relationships and collaborative mission engagement were the appropriate follow-up to founding new churches. He quoted with approval D. T. Niles, a Ceylonese church leader and a president of the World Council of Churches, who had declared to Western mission agencies, "If you want to go home when we have achieved a responsible existence of our own, you should never have come."[35]

Joe argued that encouraging missionary-founded churches to take responsibility for themselves did not mean abandoning them.[36] He no longer agreed with the adage that missionaries should work themselves out of a job. Instead, the roles they played and their relationships with local Christians were to undergo radical change. They were to become a partner in the work of the church instead of the instigator or person in charge.

As an agency MBMC chose partnership as its primary mission paradigm and sought ways to integrate its partner churches into the worldwide Mennonite community. At its annual meeting in 1965, it identified partnership with emerging churches around the world as key to sound missionary strategy.[37] MBMC resolved to accept them as equals in faith and life, to listen to their testimonies of grace, to learn from them, and to share in their activities. MBMC and the Mennonite Church arranged for regular visit exchanges between the

North American and overseas churches.[38] The General Conference Secretary of the Mennonite Church took on the leadership role in these exchanges to emphasize their church-to-church nature instead of a mission agency-to-church relationship.[39]

A discussion ensued about the best structure for including overseas churches. At first the North American Mennonite Church invited them to appoint members to its governance boards, assuming that they would become conferences within the North American structure. Eventually, however, they became members of the wider Mennonite World Conference and not conferences of the North American church.

Shifting vocational roles and family responsibilities

During his last decade of executive leadership, Joe maintained an intense schedule even as his responsibilities shifted with MBMC's growing institutional structures and new personnel coming onboard to take over areas of the work. After the appointment of a secretary for charitable institutions in 1953 and a secretary for home missions and evangelism in 1955, he was no longer responsible for rural missions, city missions, or charitable institutions in North America. His role in MBMC focused primarily on the development and promotion of mission philosophy and on the administration of the overseas program, which required long trips around the world.[40] Nevertheless, Joe continued a heavy program of travel and speaking in North America, wrote regular mission editorials for the *Gospel Herald*, served as bishop of several urban mission congregations, and represented MBMC at conference gatherings.[41]

A section of a letter he wrote to son Ronald on a Friday morning in October 1956 provides a glimpse of the nature of his schedule:

> I was in New York on Wednesday and got home yesterday afternoon and so had just a little time at the office besides doing some work around the flower beds at home and supper at Boyd Nelsons. This forenoon I am cleaning up a bit of office work and want to do a little work at home and get to the District Mission Board Meeting at Nappanee this afternoon where I am to give the final speech tonight on "The Challenge of Evangelism." That speech has not yet taken form in my mind so I will need to be working on that.

> Saturday is more or less open as I can remember now but Sunday morning I preach at Roselawn, speak in the afternoon at a Sunday School conference of some kind at Prairie Street and leave about 6:00 o'clock in the evening from Ft. Wayne for a week of work in Lancaster, Hartford, and Stony Point, Massachusetts. This ties me up a little bit tight.[42]

When Goshen Biblical Seminary wanted to incorporate mission studies classes into its curriculum, it turned to Joe. In 1955 MBMC released him to work half-time at the seminary, where his role was to organize a department of missions and teach mission courses.[43] To reinforce his credentials for this new role, Joe enrolled in a master's degree program at the Kennedy School of Missions at the Hartford Theological Seminary in Hartford, Connecticut. He started studies there in the winter/spring semester of 1956, intending to complete the course work in one year. When Minnie fell ill and required surgery, however, he postponed his second semester for a year so she could fully recuperate before continuing.[44] During their time in Hartford, Joe and Minnie resided on the seminary campus, and for Joe these periods were a respite from his habitual intense travel and speaking assignments.[45] He enjoyed the opportunity to study and took classes on a variety of subjects such as Latin American history and culture, Islam, Eastern approaches to Christianity, Indian thought and the Bible, and communism. Starting in 1957 Joe taught courses at Goshen Seminary on missions, missionary methods, Islam and Christianity, and Latin American missions.[46]

The plan was for other personnel to pick up some of Joe's responsibilities for overseas work, freeing up time for the seminary role.[47] MBMC struggled, however, to find someone to help Joe.[48] With his new role and MBMC's growing international footprint, he was as busy as ever. After a semester of teaching or an overseas trip, he often found himself at his desk responding to stacks of built-up correspondence, apologizing to those to whom he was writing for his delayed replies.

Such a heavy workload left little time for Joe to complete the thesis that was to follow his coursework at the Kennedy School of Missions. He first proposed to write about a Mennonite concept of the world mission of the church but later switched to a historical focus that sought to explain the development of missions in the Mennonite Church from 1865 to 1910.[49] With Minnie's help he located and read through the diaries of the nineteenth-century Mennonite leader John F. Funk, Funk's *Herald of Truth* magazine, and the extant documentation of the Sunday school conference movement in the Mennonite Church. Here he was convinced that he had found the beginnings of the missionary spirit that he had inherited and expanded after taking on MBMC executive leadership.[50]

During the same period that he was working on the thesis, Joe delivered the Conrad Grebel Lectures to Mennonite audiences around North America. His lectures offered a synthesis of his philosophy of missions, which the Mennonite Church's Herald Press published as *The Church Apostolic.*[51] With his heavy workload, however, he was not able to complete his thesis and did not acquire the degree from Hartford.[52]

Given his domestic and international travel, Joe continued to be away from home for extended periods. In December 1960 when he was in Nigeria, Minnie wrote describing Christmas in Elkhart with Ronald and Eleanor and their families. She added, "You would have

Joe and Minnie, with sister-in-law Mina Graber on the left, visited Joe's mother's childhood home in Switzerland in 1959 on the way to MBMC work in India and Japan. They found the artesian fountain that she had told Joe and his siblings about. MCUSA ARCHIVES

enjoyed this so much. I hope future trips can be planned with family functions in mind too. Easter, Thanksgiving, and Christmas were spent in other countries or communities this past year."[53]

Since both Ronald and Eleanor were by then adults, Joe and Minnie traveled together sometimes, which decreased the time they spent apart. One trip that lasted from November to April and took them through Europe, Israel, India, Nepal, and Japan allowed them to visit with relatives in France and old acquaintances in India alongside Joe's MBMC responsibilities.[54] They did the same in North America, combining travel for speaking assignments or to visit MBMC mission projects with vacation time to see sights like the Grand Canyon, visit friends, or even do some fishing.[55]

In addition to traveling with Joe, Minnie maintained her own ministry of mission activity during their second decade in Elkhart. She had been elected president of the Mennonite Church's Women's Missionary Sewing Circle Organization in 1950 and continued in that role until 1959.[56] She oversaw the writing of a new constitution and a change in name to Women's Missionary and Service Auxiliary, an adjustment meant to emphasize the totality of the many different women's concerns and contributions, beyond sewing, to the mission

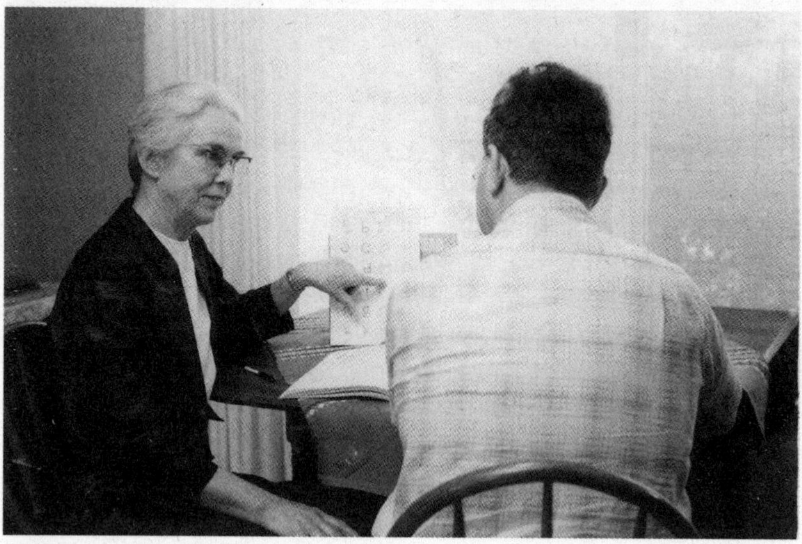

Minnie taught English in an adult literacy program in Elkhart. MCUSA ARCHIVES

of the church.[57] Minnie also taught literacy in a local program that a group of women had started for adults.[58] Most of the students had come to Elkhart from Southern regions where schooling was not adequate and now wanted to improve their reading and writing skills. If Joe maintained an intense schedule, Minnie too filled her time with mission-related activity.

Ronald and Eleanor had busy family lives and careers of their own. Ronald graduated from medical school in June 1956 and entered a one-year residency program in Little Rock, Arkansas.[59] Contemplating what vocational path to take after Little Rock, he consulted with Joe about options to work as a physician with MBMC or Mennonite Central Committee in places like Vietnam, Ghana, Newfoundland, or the Philippines.[60] In the end Ronald, Esther Rose, and their two daughters moved to the Pribilof Islands in the Bering Sea off the coast of Alaska, where he worked for two years at a Public Health Service hospital.[61] This fulfilled his United States Selective Service System requirements in lieu of military service. The sparsely populated islands are roughly two hundred miles from the Alaska coast, and mail service was limited to five deliveries per year. Letters were infrequent. Ronald built an amateur radio set, so when atmospheric conditions were conducive, Joe and Minnie enjoyed their weekly appointment to talk to Ronald and Esther Rose via the amateur radio of a friend who lived close by.[62]

After two years in the Pribilof Islands, Ronald entered a five-year program to specialize in surgery in Chicago, close enough to Elkhart that the family could visit periodically for birthdays, other special occasions, or for the grandchildren to attend summer Bible school in Elkhart.[63] Ronald and Esther Rose subsequently moved the family to Puerto Rico, where he became head of the surgery department at MBMC's hospital in Aibonito.[64] Joe and Minnie visited them for nearly two months in 1966–67.[65] By this time Ronald's family had grown to eight, so they enjoyed spending time with their six grandchildren, and Joe was able to do MBMC-related work and correspondence from there.

After studying music at Goshen College, Eleanor continued to pursue her interest in music and also started a family. She completed a master's degree in music at the University of Michigan and in 1958 married Richard Nase, who was also a musician.[66] Joe was pleased to have the privilege of officiating at their wedding. Over the next year Richard completed studies in music at Goshen College, and in the fall of 1959, Eleanor became a faculty member there, teaching piano.[67] Their daughter Joy Ellen was born in December 1959.[68] The plan was for the Nases to live with Joe and Minnie over the next school year, Eleanor teaching half-time at Goshen College and Richard studying music at the University of Michigan and coming back to Elkhart on weekends.[69] Tragically Richard was diagnosed with leukemia in November 1960.[70] Treatment brought remission, and he regained his strength by the following summer. The cancer recurred, however, and he died on Christmas Eve 1961.[71] In another blow, Joy was diagnosed with cancer the following April, and despite treatment she too passed away in August 1963.[72]

Joe and Minnie had sacrificed much, including family time and holidays together, for the good of the church's mission endeavors, but this was a time to make room for family priorities alongside the many MBMC responsibilities. Joe cut short a visit to mission work in Nigeria, Ghana, and Argentina to return to Elkhart when Richard's condition seemed critical in January 1961, and cut short a trip to Virginia the following December when his health deteriorated again.[73] Eleanor, Minnie, and Joe maintained a presence by Richard's bedside in the weeks leading up to his death. Similarly, when granddaughter Joy received radiation and chemotherapy treatments during her illness, Joe and Minnie found that their grandparenting responsibilities increased as the situation required their assistance and attention.[74]

Eleanor subsequently taught music at Goshen College. In 1965 she married Alan Kreider, a graduate student at Harvard University. After three years of study and research in England Alan completed his PhD, and they both joined the faculty at Goshen College. Appointed by Mennonite Board of Missions in 1974, they then served for twenty-six years as missionaries in England in ministries of teaching and Anabaptist presence.

A church-centric approach

Writing to missionary S. Paul Miller about MBMC's approach in India, Joe noted, "It is an age when the Church must increase and the Mission decrease."[75] Joe often repeated that phrase during the partnership era.

He meant that the establishment and well-being of the churches that missionaries created needed to have a place of priority in the plans and activities of missionaries and mission agencies.[76]

Proponents of indigenous-church theory had long pointed out that Western missionaries and their mission organizations had come to overshadow the church in many places in which they worked.[77] Joe agreed, and critiqued Mennonite mission engagement, arguing that MBMC had been fairly successful at establishing missions but less so at establishing churches.[78] Institutions such as mission hospitals or schools provided gainful employment for Christian professionals and commanded financial resources that often dwarfed what churches could muster. This created the impression that the missionaries' work and their institutions were more important than the church. Institutions attracted the attention, energy, and commitment of church members and others, sometimes seeming to compete with the church. The devolution of missionary institutions to churches when missionary agencies ceded control also burdened the church with tasks that did not properly belong to it, Joe thought.

Joe recognized how managing schools, hospitals, or other institutions took time and energy away from the life of the church and its witness in society.[79] The focus should be on establishing and reinforcing churches, "microcosms of the divine community," imperfect though they might be, which would be a continuing witness that institutions could not match.[80] Joe was willing to help create and support institutions, but he came to believe that they were legitimate only inasmuch as they contributed in some meaningful way to the church and its witness.[81] Where there were legacy mission institutions, he worked to put them in the hands of autonomous boards of directors, thus freeing the church for its true purpose.[82]

Prioritizing the church was about more than mission strategy for Joe, however. It was also important to him because it was part of the Mennonite Church's Anabaptist tradition. Some Protestant missionaries considered preaching the gospel and saving souls to be their primary purpose. Joe was adamant that such an approach was insufficient for Mennonites.[83] Missionaries also needed to focus on building up a Christian community, which was a much more difficult and longer process than simply focusing on preaching and converting people to the faith. Mission objectives were not met unless a living church was established that consisted of a group of believers who modeled their life together on the New Testament witness. The Christian faith was not to be lived individually but in community. Mennonite missionaries had always understood this to be part of the heritage they shared, Joe believed, but he noted that it was not until after World War II that they were careful to articulate this value clearly.

The postwar years were a period of theological formulation for Mennonites, who delved into the Anabaptist tradition to help articulate a faith identity for the twentieth century. Harold S. Bender's 1944 *Anabaptist Vision* had stressed the importance of the gathered faith community, and such an emphasis likely helped Joe and his colleagues formulate their church-centric approach. Joe advised MBMC missionaries against losing themselves in tasks that would not contribute toward building congregations in the Anabaptist tradition.[84] During the partnership epoch there were times when such an approach needed to be modified for specific contexts. These were, however, exceptions to the rule. The establishment of Mennonite churches was a priority, and Joe believed that the Anabaptist tradition that they embodied would be a faithful witness and positive contribution in the societies of which they were a part.[85]

New strategies for the partnership era

Working in partnership meant finding new strategies that were appropriate for evolving contexts and shifting relationship patterns around the world. Joe maintained an expansionist outlook, believing that the Mennonite Church should focus a significant part of its ministry on the world outside of the Mennonite fold.

Establishing and enlarging churches continued to be a primary goal, but the need to respond appropriately to local contexts tempered that priority as Joe and his colleagues sought to move beyond traditional paradigms. In Israel, for example, missionaries arrived during a period when Christian leaders were reevaluating their approach to the Jewish faith tradition and adapting to the reality of the existence of the state of Israel. In Algeria missionaries established work in an Islamic context where founding Christian communities of faith in the traditional way was not an option. In the Argentine Chaco and Nigeria

MBMC reoriented its focus from establishing Mennonite churches to empowering indigenous Christian communities to develop their own Christian identities. This period also saw an increase in lay participation in Mennonite mission activity as teachers, medical professionals, and other technical experts served alongside long-term missionaries around the world. For Joe this was a way to meet new needs and increase mission involvement by the North American church.

Joe recruited and sent MBMC's first missionaries to Israel in 1953, but the constituency's desire for ministry among Jewish people and eventually in the new state of Israel started at least a decade earlier. In 1942 the annual meeting resolved to open mission work among Jews, and subsequent articles in the *Gospel Herald* oriented the church in that direction.[86] Joe added his encouragement, while reminding Mennonites of the challenges that Jewish refugee migration, the stain of anti-Semitism, and the theological questions of mission to the Jews represented for those attempting such outreach.[87]

Concrete steps followed. In 1950 the Ontario Board of Missions appointed a worker to Jewish evangelism in Toronto, and in 1955 MBMC established ministry among the Jewish community in New York City, focusing on hospitality, visitation, and making personal contacts in the community.[88] During the same period Mennonite Central Committee was working in Jordan, and Orie O. Miller, who held executive positions at both MCC and Eastern Mennonite Board of Missions and Charities, was eager to see Mennonite presence in the region continue with mission work in Israel. Members of the Virginia Mennonite Board of Missions agreed, and in 1952 MBMC joined the initiative.[89] It was a joint effort with the Virginia and Eastern boards, but since its administrative home was MBMC, Joe held primary oversight.[90] He and Mennonite missionaries to Israel were aware that the initiative faced challenges in a society that resisted missionary activity and that founding a Mennonite church would not likely be possible.[91] They moved forward in faith, however, trusting that some kind of missionary witness would be feasible.[92]

If missionaries had once assumed that mission activity among Jewish communities was analogous to work among other peoples, World War II had profoundly changed the dynamic. The extermination of millions of Jews during the war had heightened awareness of

Christian complicity in anti-Semitism and in the persecution of Jewish communities, during the war and in previous centuries. Protestant mission theorists of the time called on Christians to recognize anti-Semitism in their own ranks.[93]

The change was such that some Christian leaders, including renowned theologian Reinhold Niebuhr, argued that Christian witness was so tainted that Jews were more likely to find God from within their own tradition; they thus contended that missionaries should not invite Jewish persons to join or form their own Christian communities.[94] Not everyone agreed with Niebuhr, but most did come to believe that mission activity among Jewish communities was unique. The priority, they suggested, should entail recognizing the common Jewish and Christian heritage, rejecting anti-Jewish propaganda, reducing ignorance and caricatures between people of the two faiths, and showing love and building trust where centuries of prejudice discredited Christian witness.[95] Joe was one of the representatives of the National Council of Churches' Division of Foreign Missions on the IMC's Committee on the Christian Approach to the Jews, so he was conversant with this discourse.[96]

Within the context of this larger conversation, Joe and MBMC missionaries in Israel faced their own particular challenges that required rethinking their aspirations for missionary witness. The most practical impediment was the inability of missionaries to get visas to live and work in the country. They were able to get temporary visitor or student visas and so enrolled in courses to study Hebrew and Jewish tradition, but government opposition to Christian missionary activity meant that it would not issue them long-term visas.[97] The missionaries lived a somewhat uncertain existence, extending their short-term visas when they could, but having to leave and attempt reentry when officials denied renewal. MBMC typically sought to establish itself as a legal entity in the countries where it sent missionaries in order to provide a justification for missionary visas. In Israel the government rejected such applications due to a policy of recognizing only those Christian mission agencies that existed in the region before the birth of the state of Israel.[98] In some cases MBMC missionaries collaborated with initiatives that the government already recognized, thus opening the door for them to receive visas. It was clear, however, that in the face of strong opposition in Israeli society and refusal on the part of government officials, the traditional missionary role of founding a Mennonite church was not an option.

Joe and the missionaries he supervised formulated an approach that seemed appropriate for maintaining a Mennonite mission in the Israeli context. The establishment of an indigenous church was a priority for Joe throughout his career, but he set that priority aside in this case.[99] He encouraged MBMC's Israel missionaries to take the time necessary to understand this unique context and find creative witness opportunities. They established friendships, initiated conversations about faith with those who so desired, studied the Bible with interested individuals, contributed to a variety of local ministries, and sought ways to improve relationships between Jews and Christians.[100] Joe described the mission posture in Israel as one of Christian presence meant to demonstrate redemptive living and self-giving love, which would be required over the long term to decrease prejudice and mistrust between Jews and Christians.[101] He considered this to be a faithful missionary witness given the history of mistreatment of the Jews at the hands of Christians and the resulting mistrust and suspicion.

As MBMC was sending its first missionaries to Israel, an opportunity came to expand its witness into North Africa. André Trocmé, a Reformed Church pastor in France and co-secretary, along with his wife Magda, of the International Fellowship of Reconciliation (IFOR), shared Mennonites' pacifist convictions. He proposed that IFOR and Mennonites collaborate in a "work camp" model of missionary activity among North Africans, including North Africans living in France.[102] Algeria was a French colony with a relatively large settler population. At the time of Trocmé's offer, it was on the verge of violent anticolonial struggle that led to independence in 1962.

Despite such complicating factors, Trocmé's idea landed in fertile soil at MBMC where, after some deliberation, Algeria seemed to be the most promising place to start.[103] French Mennonites had already been looking for a mission opportunity in Africa, so work in Algeria presented a way for MBMC to partner with them in a new field.[104] In addition, Algeria was a majority Islamic nation and a "new frontier" for North American Mennonites.[105] Earlier Mennonite missionary encounters with Muslims in Java, India, and eastern Africa had not resulted in any particularly Mennonite approach to their faith.

Joe developed a strong interest in Islam and its relationship with Christianity. He advocated respectful dialogue and patience, sharing the Christian message with Muslims but avoiding labeling it as a heathen religion.[106] At Hartford Seminary he studied under Kenneth Cragg, an Islamicist who urged a deeply respectful posture toward Islamic worship and practice.[107] Joe chaired the conference on Islam at the Mennonite World Conference meetings in Kitchener, Ontario, in 1962 and taught courses at Goshen Seminary on Islam and Christianity. Algeria was a context for MBMC to focus specifically on the particularities and implications of ministry among Islamic communities and to try to develop respectful approaches.

Like the work in Israel, MBMC's expansion into Algeria did not follow a traditional mission paradigm of preaching, evangelization, and founding new churches. Joe and his colleagues were convinced that a history of Christian violence toward Islam and an association of colonial rule with Christian faith in the minds of many Muslims had tainted the credibility of Christian witness.[108] Previous missionaries had done enough ineffective preaching, and it was time for a new approach, one that focused on Christian service and personal relationships over the long term that would build bridges of understanding with Muslim coworkers. Joe was insistent, however, that the focus on acts of Christian service should not eclipse what he referred to as a direct mission witness, the goal of which was to establish the church of Jesus Christ.[109]

Another concern in Algeria was the material aid that service projects typically provided. Joe had long understood that such assistance risked complicating missionary witness and wanted to avoid creating dependency and attitudes of superiority. By having personnel work alongside local partners in humility, MBMC sought to avoid repeating such mistakes and to integrate Christian service with the establishment of the church through direct missionary witness.[110] Both were part of mission work and needed to happen, but neither was to be done alone, and neither was to be done for the sake of the other. Instead of playing the role of wealthy foreign benefactors, missionaries did physical labor alongside their Algerian counterparts, treated the sick, and in some cases lived with local families.

As with the case of Israel, Joe described MBMC's mission posture in Algeria as one of Christian presence. The missionaries in Algeria were to embody the presence of Christ.[111] Christ-like living and service would be the most effective way to work. The goal was still to establish the church of Jesus Christ, but Joe realized that was not likely to happen soon or in any traditional sense. Given the religious and political context, he suggested that the church might have to meet in secret, that it might remain small and inconspicuous, that it might not have a clearly defined organization, but that it might well have a strong witness of good works. It would take a long-term commitment, new mission strategies might be needed, and the outcome was unclear, but the Algeria initiative represented an important mission witness nonetheless. Joe assumed an oversight role in this collaborative endeavor with the French Mennonite Mission, with assistance from MCC.[112]

Three decades of work in Algeria started somewhat precipitously when an earthquake shook the northern region of the country in September 1954. The needs after the earthquake preempted initial plans, and a group of volunteers, including several MCC workers previously assigned to Europe, arrived in 1955 to assist with rebuilding efforts.[113] The group helped build houses in the village of Flatters, but work was slow due to war between rebels and the colonial government. A Swiss Mennonite nurse joined the group in 1956, adding a healthcare component to the initiative, and MBMC appointed the first North American missionaries the following year. The group eventually left Flatters for Algiers because of the war and, contrary to plans, was not able to return after it ended.[114] Relief work among refugees and encouraging the emergence of a church were among the priorities in Algiers, where missionaries led Bible classes, participated in educational efforts, and provided nursing services.[115]

After the war ended with Algeria gaining independence in 1962, MCC contributed significant material assistance and personnel in the years that followed. The last North America Mennonite workers departed in 1978.[116] Missionaries participated in an initiative to form a church in the late 1960s, but in the end the government would not allow it. Joe and MBMC's approach of Christian presence in Algeria failed in that objective, but it was a creative mission strategy in a society with significant resistance to Christian witness.

Mission engagement during the age of partnership took yet another turn in the Argentine Chaco and southeastern Nigeria for Joe and MBMC. Already in the early 1950s missionaries in the Chaco had appropriated the tools of linguistics and anthropology to identify more closely with the Toba people and to develop an approach meant to encourage local leadership and local ownership of Christian thought and practice.[117] A significant portion of the Toba population had chosen to identify with an indigenous form of Christianity that missionaries described as Pentecostal-like in its expressions. Joe's encouragement to focus on indigenization and the MBMC missionaries' commitment to a culturally appropriate form of Toba Christianity led them to set aside their initial strategy of forming congregations that copied the polity and theology of North American Mennonites. Instead, they sought to identify with the Toba, become as much as possible members of the Toba church, assist the church in interpreting Christian faith in light of Toba life, and work within the frame of the Toba's existing piety. MBMC workers developed a ministry of itinerant teaching, helped the Toba church become the first aboriginal church to gain official recognition from the government, and worked to document and formalize Toba language grammar, eventually helping to publish a Toba version of the Bible.[118] Joe was pleased with the new approach, which was a partnership with the Toba church, even if it did not result in new Mennonite churches.[119] His appropriation of the partnership paradigm allowed for mission collaboration beyond the frontiers of the Mennonite church and with new local expressions of the faith.

Joe recruited and sent missionaries to southeastern Nigeria in 1959, five years after missionaries in the Argentine Chaco had changed their mission strategy to empower the indigenous Christian movement

Joe with Edwin and Irene Weaver, whom he recruited to serve in Nigeria starting in 1959.
MCUSA ARCHIVES

among the Toba. The year before, MBMC missionaries in Ghana had initiated work with a group of churches that wanted to join the Mennonite fold. By the time the first resident missionaries arrived in Nigeria, the Mennonite church was already a reality, and missionaries expected to continue the process of accepting new congregations into the church.

Just as the Chaco missionaries changed their approach in response to the situation they encountered on the ground, so the context of southeastern Nigeria motivated MBMC's missionaries to reassess traditional missionary practice and stop adding congregations to the new church. The value of peacemaking and the priority of indigenization were two of the primary reasons why they did so. Missionaries found deep resentment and competition between two streams of the Christian movement in the region, the churches founded by Western missionaries and independent churches made up of people who had left the missionary-founded churches.[120] The independent churches, the group from which the new Mennonite congregations had come, accused the missionary-founded churches of being controlling and colonialist.[121] The churches with connections to Western missions accused the independents of sub-Christian standards. The resentment and competition were such that schism was rampant with religious confusion the result.

Fearing that adding yet another denominational identity to the mix might simply increase resentment and competition, missionary Edwin Weaver wrote back to MBMC, "Must we now add to the confusion?"[122] While both Joe and the missionaries in Nigeria considered the formation of new Mennonite congregations to be a helpful mission strategy, the heavily conflictual situation they found in southeastern Nigeria seemed to tarnish Christian witness, suggesting that the ecumenical principle of cultivating positive interchurch relations should become the primary missionary imperative in that context.[123] Missionaries worked to strengthen the existing group of Mennonite congregations. However, contrary to the original plan, they did not encourage a large influx of new Mennonites into the fold.

The priority of encouraging local Christian identity also caused Joe and the missionaries in Nigeria to reconsider their missionary posture. The independent churches that had left the missionary-founded churches seemed to have already attained a significant level of indigeneity.[124] They were largely self-sufficient and had developed Christian faith and practice for their context. Some independent church leaders were publishing their reflections for wider distribution.[125] MBMC missionaries in Nigeria believed that such local theologizing was necessary.[126] Joe agreed that indigenous agency was crucial in the development of local expressions of Christian belief.[127] With churches that seemed to be well on their way to being authentic indigenous churches, a mission approach that sought to help them reinforce their own efforts to build Christian identity instead of advocating that they adopt Mennonite faith and practice from North America seemed to make sense.

In consultation with Joe, missionaries developed an approach that sought reconciliation between independent African churches and churches that Western missionaries had founded. They also sought to strengthen the independent churches through initiatives of theological education. When the Nigerian government refused to issue visas to the missionaries, Joe encouraged them to partner with the Church of Scotland Mission (CSM) and the Nigerian Presbyterian Church it had founded.[128] Missionaries received their visas under the umbrella of the CSM in exchange for MBMC's commitment to provide personnel to manage and serve at a Presbyterian hospital in the region.[129] This provided credibility with Western mission churches. MBMC missionaries also worked with the independents, establishing the United Independent Churches Fellowship as a medium through which to develop relationships with them and encourage them toward better communication with, and understanding of, missionary-founded churches.[130]

Mennonite missionaries formed the Inter-Church Study Group, a quarterly meeting of missionaries and missionary-founded church leaders that focused on building better understanding of the independents.[131] With time some independent church leaders attended the study group, and it became a place where they could interpret their churches to missionaries and other church leaders.[132] Missionaries also formed the United Churches Bible College and coordinated scholarships from the World Council of Churches' Theological Education Fund for independent church leaders to receive theological training.[133] Creating space for reconciliation and providing training opportunities for African independent leaders became the primary mission approach.

Under Joe's leadership mission engagement within the partnership paradigm was flexible and able to respond creatively to the new post colonial context in which indigenous forms of Christianity were gaining strength. The value of indigenization meant that missionaries took seriously the theological assumptions of indigenous Christian movements and the priorities they articulated. Equipping their leaders so that they could formulate and share more widely their understandings of the faith and working for reconciliation between different streams of the worldwide Christian movement became mission priorities in Argentina and Nigeria. Forming Mennonite communities of faith where they did not exist remained of primary importance for Joe, but he was also convinced that the changing realities of the period demanded new approaches. He was ever seeking new forms of mission activity to meet the challenges of the new day. In Nigeria and Argentina such openness allowed Mennonite missionaries to partner with indigenous Christians to create space for them within the larger Christian movement, even if they did not identify as Mennonite.

During the last decade of his career, Joe also advocated for more involvement by lay people in the church's missionary endeavors and oversaw the creation of programs to help that happen at MBMC. In the era of partnership, mission activity was not just for long-term missionaries who chose it as their life's vocation. Joe thought that the whole church should mobilize for its mission commitments, both by providing financial support and by direct participation in mission programs. Once again, this was not an idea unique to Joe but was a topic in the larger Protestant missionary movement of the day.

With the increasing intensity of globalization over the twentieth century, Western Christians were traversing the world like never before, thus presenting new possibilities for international mission work. In the decades after World War II there was growing recognition of the important role of lay people in the history of the spread of Christianity and in the development of modern mission activity.[134] At its 1952 meeting at Willingen, Germany, the International Missionary Council challenged churches to consider the strategic importance of the global mobility of lay people. It raised the possibility of new forms of missionary witness in which Christians around the world would serve as lay missionaries. They might earn their living working in business, industry, or government institutions and provide services that were not traditional missionary roles. Since doors were closing to professional missionaries in some countries and financial shortfalls were forcing missionary societies to curtail programs, the focus on lay people in mission seemed timely. During the decade following the Willingen meeting, numerous organizations established programs to provide lay people opportunities in foreign mission service. At its third assembly at New Delhi, the World Council of Churches established a Secretariat for Lay Service Abroad in response to increasing interest on the part of young people.[135]

Twentieth-century Mennonites were no strangers to the concept of Christian service by lay people. In the wake of World War I, Mennonites had participated in American Friends Service Committee work camps in Europe and eventually organized their own programs.[136] Mennonites served in Turkey and Lebanon during the interwar years with the Near East Relief initiative and were heavily involved in the Civilian Public Service programs during World War II. After the war numerous Mennonite denominations and conferences as well as Mennonite Central Committee developed programs to provide lay people with Christian service opportunities.

Still, Joe was convinced that there was yet undeveloped potential for mission work among the lay people of the church. He articulated a vision of Mennonite professionals taking overseas posts in their fields of expertise, concurrently becoming "non-professional" missionaries who would contribute missionally through jobs related to human welfare or in their spare time.[137] There seemed to be an abundance of opportunities in newly independent countries that were ramping up their educational, health, and other services.

MBMC formalized the concept in its Overseas Missions Associates (OMA) program.[138] OMAs typically served for one term of two or three years and received their salaries from the institutions or projects in which they worked. Assignments were normally in the fields of education, medicine, research, or agriculture. Joe touted the OMA program as a "new dimension" in missions, arguing that it provided a way to expand mission initiatives at a time when funds were tight, even suggesting that the use of such lay missionaries in large numbers would be "the missionary method of the future."[139] It was a way for Christian lay people to use their vocational skills to advance mission objectives alongside their long-term missionary colleagues, thus embodying the important connection between word and deed.

MBMC also appointed lay people through its Overseas Voluntary Service program. It was similar to the OMA program in that it allowed lay people to participate without becoming long-term missionaries.[140] It was different in that participants usually were young people, had no professional training, lived and worked as part of a unit, and received a modest living stipend instead of regular remuneration.

The overseas programs for lay people provided the Mennonite Church constituency with mission opportunities and increased MBMC's footprint, but they did not prove the wave of the future in quite the way Joe had hoped. Government and private agencies around the world sometimes did not recognize credentials from North America or had policies that prioritized local hires.[141] When delays arose because of visa complications, improper credentials, or other difficulties, prospective workers often chose to serve under another North American agency, of which there were a growing number, that placed personnel in overseas posts.[142] Nevertheless, these lay missionaries did increase MBMC's impact in important ways, often serving alongside long-term missionaries in agriculture, administration, or healthcare roles. For example, of the fifty-four missionaries who served in southeastern Nigeria between 1960 and 1967, when they were forced to evacuate because of the Nigerian Civil War, twenty-four were Mission Associates and eight were Overseas Volunteers.[143]

Mennonite ecumenism during the partnership era

Joe maintained constructive relationships in the wider Christian community, especially through mission-related contacts and the institutions that facilitated ecumenical mission collaboration, internationally and domestically. He found such collaboration helpful since the challenges that other mission agencies and their missionaries encountered were often like those that he and MBMC missionaries faced. He read books written by a wide range of mission practitioners and theorists and sought advice from officials in the Foreign Missions Conference of North America or the Division of Foreign Missions of the National Council of Churches. He had to be careful, however, since parts of the Mennonite Church constituency were suspicious of such collaboration, fearing its influence on Mennonite faith. Joe collaborated widely, but he and his colleagues took care not to involve MBMC in commitments or formal relationships with ecumenical structures that their fellow Mennonites found suspect.

During Joe and Minnie's service in India, relationships with missionaries from other traditions had offered them and their colleagues an orientation to missiological thought and experience that the church back home was unprepared to provide, and ecumenical collaboration likewise allowed their work to benefit from projects that MBMC could not afford to implement on its own. The International Missionary Council sponsored reflection on relevant missiological issues such as indigenization, Eastern religions, and educational strategy in the Indian context.[144] Joe and his colleagues participated in the ecumenical Mid-India Representative Christian Council, an affiliate of the National Christian Council (NCC) of India.[145] Mennonite missionaries played leading roles on some of the Mid-India Council's committees and participated in a number of interdenominational institutions that provided theological education, literature development, and health services.[146]

Joe realized that issues arising out of the Indian church context that the ecumenical movement sought to address would eventually arise among Indian Mennonites as well. After the 1938 Conference on World Mission and Evangelism in Madras, India, he looked forward to the day when the conference's focus on the priority of the church, in contrast to the mission agency, would be realized among Indian Mennonites. At the same time, Joe thought that the conference's emphasis on church union would likely create more problems than solutions for the Indian church.[147] The ecumenical movement provided insight and resources for Joe and MBMC, but Joe was not convinced that initiatives of church union were either practical or helpful.

Voices within MBMC's constituency raised alarm at ecumenical tendencies among its missionaries. Likely, those critics did not fully understand the practical importance of ecumenical relationships and collaboration between missionaries of different denominations on international mission fields. Three years after Joe and Minnie arrived for their first term in India, the Virginia conference suggested that missionaries should neither fellowship with other missions nor cooperate with them more than was the practice of the home church.[148] A year later Lancaster Conference bishops expressed similar sentiments.[149]

In response, in 1934 MBMC instructed Joe and his fellow missionaries to "discontinue organic relations with the NCC and affiliated organizations."[150] Under Joe's leadership the missionaries embarked on a period of reflection and responded with their own policy.[151] They decided to allow for collaboration with the NCC that did not contribute to the church union movement, that steered clear of social programs that might become a substitute for Christianity, that did not inhibit promulgating distinctive Mennonite principles, and that did not involve missionaries in prominent positions in the NCC.[152] Ecumenical relationships continued among the missionaries, albeit more discreetly and with less involvement in NCC leadership roles.[153]

With time the home church became more comfortable with some kinds of interdenominational collaboration, so Joe and his colleagues had more freedom. During his time in executive leadership back in North America, he sat on the Foreign Mission Conference's India Committee and on the International Missionary Council's Committee on the Christian Approach to the Jews. MBMC declined to become a member of the Missionary Education Movement but decided to use its materials when they proved helpful.[154] Presented with the option of joining the Evangelical Foreign Missions Conference in 1946, MBMC shelved the decision but sent representatives to its annual meeting.[155] Three years later it authorized one of its officers to attend the annual meeting if it was "convenient."[156] When the Foreign Mission Conference of North America became the Division of Foreign Missions under the National Council of Churches, MBMC became a consultative agency instead of a charter member, and Joe designated its financial contributions to projects with which MBMC sympathized.[157]

During Joe's tenure at MBMC, he and his colleagues participated in and used the resources from the wider missionary movement but were careful not to give up the ability to set their own course or to move too far ahead of a constituency that valued a certain differentiation from wider North American Protestantism and was theologically more conservative than most denominations within the National Council of Churches.

Even as he found collaboration with other denominations helpful, Joe was not in favor of church union initiatives that grew out of the ecumenical movement. In India several church unions had brought together different denominations into new church bodies. Church union advocates argued that the divisions in Protestantism were a scandal and a detriment to the witness of the church. Others demurred, arguing that the existence of different denominations allowed for greater spiritual vitality and stimulated mission activity. Joe agreed with the latter position.[158] While he recognized that the lack of unity threatened the integrity of the church's witness, he did not think that organizational unity was necessarily the best solution.[159] There were other ways to achieve unity. He compared denominations within the world Christian movement to families in a community. They should live together peacefully and fruitfully, stressing points of accord. He encouraged MBMC missionaries to work harmoniously with national councils and other denominations but thought that sometimes national councils overplayed their authority, creating divisions with their intransigence even as they sought to build unified structures at the national or regional levels. "They tie the thing together at the top and actually split things at the bottom," he wrote of such dynamics.[160] Ecumenical collaboration was a good thing, but one had to allow for the diverse contributions of different Christian traditions. Joe argued that strong Mennonite churches that represented the best of the Mennonite tradition would be an encouragement and help to other churches and to regional or national councils.

Collaboration with other mission agencies in the Mennonite/Anabaptist tradition was its own ecumenical task. Within the Mennonite Church some conferences created their own mission agencies that sent missionaries domestically and internationally. While he might have focused on how such a dynamic created competition for MBMC, Joe chose to highlight the positive implications, noting that conference mission initiatives motivated interest and financial giving for missions that MBMC likely would not have generated on its own.[161] They added to the total Mennonite mission footprint even if they did so outside of MBMC structures. Joe sought ways to collaborate with conference mission agencies and lend support to their work. Under his leadership MBMC partnered with the Virginia Mennonite Board of Missions and Charities in mission work in Sicily and Israel, and it also cooperated closely with Lancaster Conference's Eastern Mennonite Board of Missions and Charities.[162] Joe also sought opportunities for mission collaboration with other Mennonite/Anabaptist denominations. He helped establish collaborative ministries in Japan and Uruguay.[163] Such collaboration was not always successful, but it was important enough to Joe that he continued to search for ways to bring Mennonite ecumenical initiatives to fruition.

The growing footprint of Mennonite Central Committee's international reach presented Joe with his biggest challenge of interagency collaboration within the larger North American Mennonite/Anabaptist movement. Early in Mennonite mission history, MBMC missionaries had provided relief and other material assistance as part of their ministries. During the middle half of the twentieth century, MCC expanded as a response to the need for large-scale relief efforts, especially given widespread destruction during World War II. Joe and his colleagues expected that emergency relief would become gradually less necessary after the war and that MCC activity would decrease proportionally. Mission agencies would then regain their place as the primary medium through which Mennonites would participate in a wide range of ministries, including relief assistance. In 1947 MBMC recommended that MCC cease expansion of relief and service projects and, along with the Mennonite Church, expressed a preference for integrating voluntary service work into its own programs.[164] By then, however, MCC was on an expansionist trajectory that showed no signs of abating.[165] It was an institutional reality that Mennonite mission agencies would have to accommodate.

While Joe consistently collaborated across agencies, including with MCC, he objected to some of MCC's policies and approaches. He disagreed with MCC's expectation that Mennonite mission activity should follow MCC relief work.[166] MCC secretary Orie Miller was an avid proponent of this idea and sought ways to facilitate it.[167] Pointing to MBMC's experience in India and Puerto Rico, Joe believed that relief initiatives too often sowed the seeds of dependency, thus making it harder for an authentically indigenous church to emerge from mission efforts.[168] He was open to following in MCC's footsteps when there were specific reasons for doing so but thought such should be the exception rather than the rule. Missionary initiatives had a better chance of resulting in the emergence of indigenous partner churches if missionaries laid their own foundations for their work.

In conversations with other mission board and MCC leaders, Joe also argued against compartmentalizing relief activity from other missionary endeavors, which he feared MCC's approach risked doing. Christian witness was enhanced when the administration of relief activity was integrated with that of the broader mission engagement, he thought.[169] Separating relief and other mission initiatives into different organizations was tantamount to separating faith from life, secular from sacred, word from deed, or service to humankind from service to God. Mennonites, he thought, should resist such separation and seek to convey a more integrated Christian witness. There were situations, Joe noted, when Mennonites might need to provide relief or material aid on its own or through different structures, but they should be the exception. Joe feared that the creation of organizations such as MCC for relief, service, and material aid made separation the norm, and for him this was detrimental to Mennonite witness.

Furthermore, Joe argued that providing assistance through material aid or service activities was an incomplete Christian witness if there was no explanation of how such assistance was an expression of Christian love. The deed needed the word to explain its meaning and purpose just as the word needed the deed to demonstrate and clarify its meaning.[170] Mennonites too easily assumed that providing Christian service was a self-evident expression of Christian witness.

Joe drew on his experience in India to make his point. He argued that in Hinduism the meaning of service to another human being was different than the Christian conception of service. According to Joe, the assumption was that the person serving or assisting another did so out of self-interest, so that God would reward him or her. Those who were on the receiving end assumed this to be the case, so that they would understand Christian service or assistance to be rendered out of such self-interest. They did not understand it to be an expression of the love of God or the love of the Christian service worker or missionary. Serving in the name of Christ without some sort of further explanation, argued Joe, risked communicating a self-benefiting motive for service or material relief, which was the opposite of the intended message of Christian service.

Given the reality of separate agencies, however, Joe thought it was imperative that MCC and Mennonite mission organizations find ways to integrate their work as much as possible, and he worked to help that happen. Joe and MCC secretary Orie O. Miller maintained a close working relationship, visiting and advising each other's workers around the world and finding ways for MCC and MBMC to share personnel and collaborate.[171] They consulted with each other about where to establish new overseas initiatives and sought to avoid misunderstandings between their respective institutions.[172] Orie had a forceful personality, and MBMC missionaries sometimes called on Joe to intervene when Orie implemented program or projects they considered ill-advised or outside of MCC's mandate.[173] Joe was willing to confront Orie on such occasions, and the two of them found ways to adjust plans and programs to address the concerns of MBMC and its missionaries. Joe and his colleagues found Orie's overseas trips to be most profitable if they assigned Orie specific tasks for MBMC. That approach helped avoid Orie's unilateral initiatives that sometimes created difficulties or countered MBMC's vision or policy.[174]

Orie and other MCC leaders were aware of Joe's concerns about MCC's approach and sought ways to accommodate him and the various North American Mennonite mission agencies in deliberations about MCC programs. MCC convened a meeting of its executive committee with mission board officials in 1951 to seek their counsel. Joe was a member of the ad hoc committee that formulated the shared commitments that the meeting produced.[175] Seven years later MCC executive secretary William Snyder convened another meeting in the same spirit, seeking to address concerns of Mennonite mission boards about MCC policy and work.[176] The initiative resulted in regular meetings of the mission board secretaries, among themselves as well as with MCC, to address differences and ways to collaborate. Joe put his influence behind the move and convened and chaired the first meeting of what would become the Council of Mission Board Secretaries and eventually the Council of International Anabaptist Ministries, which instituted yearly meetings at which MCC and the mission boards would seek opportunities for cooperation and manage the tensions that arose from their differing approaches.[177] Reflecting on his relationship with Joe three decades later, Snyder remembered him as a critic of MCC but

A meeting of the Council of Mission Board Secretaries in September 1966. Front row left to right: Joe, Henry N. Hostetter, H. Ernest Bennett, Paul N. Kraybill, and Reuben Short. Standing left to right: Ira Stern, Malcolm Wenger, Marion W. Kliewer, J. H. Epp, Verney Unruh, Andrew Shelly, and H. R. Wiens. MCUSA ARCHIVES

also as someone who could bring people together despite their different opinions. He noted, "We could always talk to MBM when Graber was there. He kept an open door and an open heart and an open mind."[178]

Challenging ethnocentrism in the Mennonite Church

During his second decade of executive leadership at MBMC, Joe continued to challenge the Mennonite Church to become a more diverse faith community. He had long urged congregations to integrate people who were not of European, and especially Swiss-German, ethnic identities into their churches.[179] The desire to protect the church from the world or from impurity by maintaining cultural uniformity was misguided, he thought. Allowing the church to become a cultural enclave was inconsistent with the Anabaptist principle of the church as a voluntary association of committed Christians who gathered together because of their faith commitment and not because of ethnic heritage or territorial boundaries.[180]

By the end of his career Joe was employing the term "ethnocentrism."[181] Previous generations of missionaries had assumed that the West was the center of the universe and that its technology, civilization, way of life, outlook, and religion were superior to that of the rest of the world. This was completely misguided, he thought, and had become an embarrassment. Joe suggested that the Mennonite Church suffered from ethnocentrism and needed to rid itself of such an attitude. It needed to open itself to diverse peoples and allow itself to be changed in the process.[182]

Becoming a more diverse church was not only a matter of faithfulness, he argued; the health of the Mennonite Church depended on it. He believed that the only way for the church to maintain a vigorous faith was to welcome new members from different cultural strains and other strata of society and allow them to add their new life and vigor.[183] Without such new life the church would be plagued with ill health and senility. He likened the possibility to the embalming process in that a church might be preserved but with a weak or even dead faith. By discerning together, Mennonites of many different ethnicities, races, and nationalities could comprehend better how to be devoted followers of Christ.[184] The church was meant to be a fellowship of diverse peoples who would be a blessing to each other.[185]

In addition to advocating for a more inclusive Mennonite Church, Joe sought to understand why it seemed difficult for Mennonites in North America to integrate people of diverse ethnic heritages. He was instrumental in instituting a study in the early 1950s to discover whether people of non-Mennonite background were joining Mennonite churches, why they did or did not join, and the extent of membership loss in Mennonite churches.[186] The study became a doctoral dissertation by John A. Hostetler, and it found that one reason people not of Mennonite heritage declined to remain in the church was their feeling of not being accepted by the other members.[187] They felt like outsiders and found it impossible to become part of the social fabric of the church. This corresponded with Joe's suspicions. Close-knit Mennonite communities felt like, and sometimes were, a family affair, and that had its strengths, Joe admitted. Yet while he understood that church communities that maintained long-held traditions felt comfortable and safe for many Mennonites, Joe argued that maintaining traditions to the exclusion of diversity was not a faithful embodiment of the gospel.[188]

Joe thought that Mennonite markers of separation from the world such as plain dress needed to be rethought to make the church more truly reflect a faithful and welcoming Christian witness. During the early decades of the twentieth century influential voices in the church urged Mennonites to enforce dress codes that would reflect simplicity and modesty, reject new fashions, and institute a sense of uniformity and separation from the world.[189] For ordained Mennonite Church leaders, who were men, this meant wearing a plain coat, a distinctive style of suit coat that lacked lapels and buttoned to the throat. As college students Joe and Minnie had not been convinced of the value of enforcing standards of plain attire, but they chose to show deference to the church by accommodating themselves to such practice. For Joe the exception was as a student at Princeton Seminary, where he decided that in that context the plain coat would have been conspicuous, the

Left: Portrait of Joe, taken by a professional photographer who approached Joe as he traveled and asked to take his photo. MCUSA ARCHIVES PROVIDED BY ROBERTA YODER.

Right: Joe was relieved when he no longer felt obligated to wear the plain suitcoat. MCUSA ARCHIVES

opposite of simple attire.[190] He worried that Mennonites who visited him might notice and raise objections, but that did not happen. By the 1950s practices were changing, with some church leaders shedding the plain coat or even wearing ties. Joe did not voice public opposition to standards of attire but continued to wear the plain coat and encouraged missionaries on furlough to do the same, since many Mennonites in the eastern conferences of the United States considered it essential.[191]

Despite his loyalty to church traditions, Joe thought that the church needed to find more meaningful ways to express its rejection of worldliness and its nonconformity, ways that did not create a sense of exclusiveness and isolate the church. Otherwise, its witness to the world would be inhibited and people of non-Mennonite heritage would not understand Mennonites' interpretation of the gospel.[192] He thus applauded changing attitudes about attire. In 1960, when the Indiana-Michigan Conference, his home conference, scheduled a vote that would remove the requirement that church leaders wear the plain coat, he was careful to arrange his schedule to attend and vote for the measure.[193] Revoking less meaningful markers such as the plain coat would put the church's teaching of nonconformity, modesty, and "unworldliness" in attire on more solid footing, he believed.

Joe was troubled that too often Mennonites seemed to have been unable to make others feel at home or at ease among them. The fact that after over fifty years of mission activity, Mennonites had not been able to absorb enough people of non-Mennonite backgrounds to break the habit of identifying some surnames as "Mennonite," and others as not, indicated a missionary failure in his mind.[194] Joe seemed at a loss to know what more to do to effect change. The task was bigger than Joe and the mission vision that he developed. His skill at casting and communicating a vision notwithstanding, the challenge of becoming more ethnically diverse continued for MBMC and the Mennonite Church in the decades that followed his career.

Joe appropriated the partnership paradigm to promote new thinking and practice and to move mission engagement beyond colonial habits. It was a way to prioritize collaboration with churches around the world and counter North American attitudes of superiority, all in the service of his vision of a global community of churches collaborating to further God's mission in the world. Despite MBMC's attempt to hire staff to relieve Joe of some of his responsibilities, his second decade of executive leadership was as busy as the first, with new teaching responsibilities and overseas missionaries to visit.

Joe continued to give priority to the establishment of churches in the Mennonite/Anabaptist tradition but also encouraged missionaries to try novel approaches that responded to evolving contexts around the world. In places like Israel, Algeria, Argentina, and Nigeria, MBMC missionaries developed creative approaches when a traditional focus on establishing new churches was not possible or did not seem like the most faithful option. The decade was also one of collaboration with North American partners, navigating joint initiatives for which negotiations about values, priorities, and turf were necessary. Finally, during the last decade of his career as an administrator and missiologist, Joe was adamant that the Mennonite Church needed to broaden its scope to include people who were not of European heritage, and he sought to understand why there was not more progress in that direction. Joe's missionary vision had evolved over forty-two years of mission engagement, and the partnership paradigm allowed him to refine and articulate it in a compelling way.

Conclusion
A Bridge to Global Anabaptism

AS JOE NEARED retirement age and looked forward to stepping down, finding someone to assist him and eventually take over became an urgent task. In 1965 MBMC hired Wilbert R. Shenk, who became overseas assistant to Joe and would replace him when he retired two years later.[1] Shenk assumed oversight responsibility for work in Africa, Asia, and Europe, and Joe kept working with the missionaries and church partners in Latin America.[2] In 1967 Joe retired, forty-two years after he and Minnie left for their first assignment in India and twenty-three years after he became MBMC's first full-time executive secretary.

The Mennonite Church's mission engagement and mission structures had expanded significantly during Joe's tenure. When Joe became executive secretary in 1944, MBMC did international work in two countries, India and Argentina. When he left that role in 1967, it reported work in fourteen countries with 243 missionaries, thanks in large part to his expansionist vision (To be sure, not all of those initiatives resulted in established churches or institutions).[3] The treasurer and a secretary were the only other office staff when Joe moved to Elkhart. By the time he retired fifty-one people worked out of the main office there, and numerous others filled administrative positions from other locations. In 1944 MBMC reported twenty-two workers

Joe with two Indian colleagues during his six-month MCC relief assignment in India after retiring from MBMC in 1967.
MCUSA ARCHIVES

in charitable institutions in North America.[4] By 1967 there were over eight hundred.

Upon retirement, Joe still had opportunities for continuing vocational commitments. Indeed, almost immediately, Mennonite Central Committee called Joe to a six-month term in India for famine relief, which he completed from August 1967 to January 1968.[5] He and other MCC personnel oversaw emergency food assistance and a program through which participants received foodstuffs in exchange for their labor at projects like building roads, digging wells, and creating ponds. Toward the end of his time in India, he waited expectantly for word from London, where Eleanor and Alan were awaiting the birth of another grandchild.[6] He finally heard that Andrew Joseph had arrived and was pleased to be able to spend three days with him and his parents on the way back to Elkhart.[7]

Eastern Mennonite College invited Joe to be a visiting missions professor during the 1968–69 school year, an assignment that was extended for an additional year.[8] He and Minnie spent the two years living at the college, where Joe enjoyed reading up on recent mission trends, teaching, counseling students, and advocating for Mennonite mission engagement in the world. They socialized with friends and former colleagues who lived close by. Ezra Bender, who had been an MBMC colleague, first as treasurer then as health and welfare secretary, and his wife Gertrude lived next door.[9] Joe and Minnie frequently visited them to watch shows that Joe liked, since they did not have a television. Back in Elkhart, Joe continued preaching and speaking in various venues, occasionally contributing to MBMC programs, and enjoying visits from grandchildren from time to time.[10]

Although Joe and Minnie were still quite active, their life slowed considerably in retirement. Writing to Minnie as she was returning to their Elkhart home where a garden and lawn that had been unattended for a time awaited, Joe reminded her from his MCC assignment in India, "Do not try to do everything at once, but just keep pecking away at it slowly."[11] They decided to henceforth travel together more often and seemed to mostly succeed in doing so. They were happy not to have "maddening deadlines," as had been the case during their travels in the past.[12] While kept as busy as they cared to be with church activities and visits with Ron and Eleanor's families, retirement was a welcome respite from earlier demands on their time and energy. Joe still

Joe with international students at Eastern Mennonite College, where he was a visiting missions professor during the 1968–69 and 1969–70 school years. MCUSA ARCHIVES

Seventy-fifth birthday celebration. Left to right: Joe and Minnie, Verna (Joe's sister) and Willard Smith, Nelline and Sam King, former missionary colleagues in India. MCUSA ARCHIVES

had a voice in the church, however. In what was one of his last public speaking events, if not the last, at Prairie Street Mennonite Church in April 1976, Joe called on Mennonites to rid themselves of ethnocentric ideas and self-righteous arrogance in mission endeavors.[13]

In June of 1976, Joes suffered a stroke. It left him with difficulty verbalizing what he wanted to say, and he was not able to tell stories and preach as before, a significant trial for someone who had dedicated time and effort early in his career to improve his public speaking and who subsequently had much success as an orator.[14] Even at the age of seventy-six he worked hard to rebuild his vocabulary, making remarkable progress. He continued to attend Prairie Street Mennonite Church and participate in discussions there and wrote to everyone who sent him letters.

Joe died on January 25, 1978, at Goshen General Hospital in Indiana, where he had been a patient since suffering another stroke nineteen days earlier. The announcement of Joe's passing in the *Gospel Herald* shared the page with a similar announcement about James Lark, the Mennonite Church's first African American bishop, who died two weeks before Joe.[15] Their contributions to mission leadership spanned

Gardening was a favorite pastime for Joe. He said that he gardened instead of golfing, here experimenting with bags to protect the fruit. MCUSA ARCHIVES

the same period. MBMC had called James and his wife Rowena to mission work in Chicago in 1944, the same year that it called Joe to become executive secretary.

Joe died as one of the worst blizzards on record hit northern Indiana and paralyzed travel. Funeral services were disrupted because of the storm. A family service was held on January 28 at the funeral home, but the public memorial service took place on February 11 at Prairie Street Mennonite Church. As someone who was known for his sense of humor and who made a habit of studying the weather, Joe likely would have made some sort of joke about the effect of the storm on the funeral services.

Joe traveled widely and maintained relationships with people far and wide during his lifetime, and after his death, telephone calls, telegrams, and letters flowed in to northern Indiana from across North America and around the world. For those who followed the Mennonite Church's mission work, the names of the places from which the messages came sounded familiar. In addition to Mennonite communities in North America, they came from places like Curitiba, Brazil; Buenos Aries, Argentina; Asuncion, Paraguay; Montevideo, Uruguay; Dhamtari, Indore, Ranchi, Yeotmal, New Delhi, and Prayagraj, India; Furano, Sapporo, and Obihiro, Japan; Aibonito and San Juan, Puerto Rico; and Ramat Gan, Israel.[16]

The messages of condolences expressed deep appreciation for Joe's friendship, his warm spirituality, and his devotion to the church and its mission activity. Former colleagues, missionaries whom he had supervised, and church leaders from around the world remembered his concern for innovative approaches, his zeal to inspire the church to increase mission engagement, his insistence that North American missionaries cede decision-making responsibility to local leaders, and his mastery of the Hindi language.[17] The Mennonite Church in India closed its schools for a period in memory of him, and the church held memorial services at the Mennonite High School and the Mennonite Hospital in Dhamtari.[18]

"Mr. Missions of the Mennonite Church"

The warm and heartfelt messages that came after Joe's passing suggest that he left a legacy of fruitful relationships in his wake. Clarifying the legacy of any individual and the reasons for it is a complicated affair. As humans we each exist in a social context that provides both opportunities and limitations. There is an interdependent relationship between the ensemble of skills, priorities, and commitments that we bring and the particularities of the world that we seek to influence. Individuals and groups interact with social, cultural, and religious forces to effect change and shape the world. Joe brought significant capacities to his work as a missionary and leader, and he interacted in important ways with his times and with the Mennonite Church in particular.

More than any other person, Joe embodied the Mennonite Church's growing ownership of the mission paradigm. With his missionary service in India, executive leadership of the Mennonite Board of Missions and Charities, and seemingly tireless advocacy for mission activity across the church, he became the go-to person for mission affairs. People knew him as "Mr. Missions of the Mennonite Church."[19] If Joe was at a church event, one could count on hearing an inspiring message about the imperative of mission for the church. His renown and the respect with which many held his leadership was such that there were instances of Mennonite parents naming their children so they would have the same initials as Joe.[20] Roy and Florence Kreider, missionaries to Israel, named their first son Jerold David for that reason, as did the parents of historian and long-time Goshen College professor John D. Roth, when he was born in Aibonito, Puerto Rico, where they were serving with MBMC.

Joe increased Mennonite engagement in the world through the mission paradigm. During a period when Mennonites were becoming less isolationist, mission initiatives gave them a way to engage the world and seek to change it, even as they sought to stay true to their faith heritage and religious values. Soon after taking the reins of executive leadership, Joe initiated a program of international expansion that required the church to provide moral and financial support for steadily increasing programs and institutional structures. Expansion also required laborers ready to make multi-year commitments to overseas work and home communities willing to support them. As architect of the expansionist vision and as MBMC's primary mission advocate and orator, Joe motivated the church to support international work and inspired young people to serve in a growing number of countries around the world.

Similarly, his articulation and promotion of the "every congregation a mission outpost" slogan motivated individuals, congregations, and conferences to initiate local mission activity that resulted in a significant number of new North American Mennonite congregations. Amid the shifting dynamics of religious identity and the evolution of Christian denominations, not all those congregations remained in the Mennonite Church or even continued to exist into the twenty-first century. Nevertheless, the mid-twentieth-century expansion and the focus on the local congregation as a primary mission focal point had a significant and durable impact on the church.

Minnie and Joe were partners in their dedication to the church and its mission endeavors. The nature of their time in ministry, however, meant that Joe was assigned institutional leadership positions that were not open to women. Minnie's contribution as a missionary in India, in leadership of the Women's Missionary and Service Auxiliary back in North America, and in ministries in Elkhart, Indiana, was significant. She also filled in for Joe when he had more things scheduled than he could do on his own. They collaborated on speaking assignments and relied on each other for counsel. Neither the ministry of Joe nor that of Minnie would have had the impact that it did without the support of the other. In a biography about Joe, it is important to recognize that the impact of his work depended also on her support.

Institutional legacy

Joe left a durable legacy at the Mennonite Board of Missions and Charities (renamed the Mennonite Board of Missions, or MBM, in 1971), the Mennonite Church's mission agency. The vision and priorities that he championed guided the institution and its church's mission approaches after his retirement.

Under Joe's leadership MBMC adapted its approach to the different contexts in which it worked. Missionaries established priorities and strategies for the particularities of Japan, European countries, the Argentine Chaco, Israel, Algeria, and West Africa. For Joe, mission approaches, like theology, had to be contextualized. He found the missiological critiques that Donald McGavran, a friend and colleague from his time in India, developed in favor of church-growth theory to be helpful and shared McGavran's zeal for seeing churches grow. Joe warned, however, against what he understood to be a tendency for the church-growth school of missiology to develop general theory from a few missionary experiences where rapid growth had occurred.[21] The complexities of different places and cultures required the development of mission priorities and approaches tailored to their particular situations, he thought. During the last decades of the twentieth century, MBM followed Joe's lead, prioritizing contextualization rather than other theories or strategies, thus effectively choosing one of the main streams of late twentieth century missiological focus over others.[22]

Wilbert R. Shenk, Joe's successor at MBMC, continued many of the priorities that Joe had established. Shenk described MBM's posture in the face of changing realities as one of flexibility, an inductive approach, a dialogical method, a multilateral stance, and a grassroots orientation.[23] MBM continued to champion the value of indigenization and innovation through its commitment to take local contexts seriously and explore new mission methods. Shenk's career as a mission administrator, and to a certain extent as a scholar of missiology, built on the foundation that Joe had established. Shenk continued to advocate for the church's mission commitments, to encourage critical reflection on mission practice, to focus on the importance of understanding culture, to promote the agency of indigenous actors in international mission activity, to encourage ecumenical missiological consultation, and to promote postcolonial approaches that would move mission activity toward mutuality and equity within multilateral partnerships.

Mission Insight, a pamphlet series published by MBM from 1999 to 2001, demonstrated that Joe's legacy continued to provide a framework for the agency's work through the end of the century. Notable themes in the series were congregations as centers of mission; innovative mission strategies; ecumenical collaboration; holistic approaches; identification, presence, and accompaniment as mission methods; trading colonial habits for mutual partnerships; expanding into new places and new ministries; focusing on relationship and reciprocity with the other; understanding local cultures; affirming indigenous spirituality and theology; and welcoming persons who are not ethnic Mennonites into the church.

Given the persistence of neocolonial assumptions and habits, it would be wrong to assume that Joe's ideas were easily or fully implemented across the breadth of MBMC's global initiatives during his tenure or even in the following decades. His vision and his ability to propagate it, however, significantly impacted MBMC's theory and practice. Certainly a denominational mission agency and its work are more than the result of any one individual's vision and labor. Still, Joe's contribution to the mission activity of the Mennonite Church, its mission values and strategies, and the development of its mission agency were arguably more important than that of any other single individual. Joe's impact on the church and its mission was significant and long-lasting.

Theology

Joe's missiological commitments were rooted in deeply held theological understandings. Instead of articulating them as a systematic theology, however, he typically expressed them in his speaking and writing about mission theory and practice. Joe's theology was consistent with the Anabaptist vision articulated by Harold S. Bender and prioritized by Mennonite leaders in the post–World War II decades. He affirmed the commitment to discipleship, the importance of the church as a faith community, and the integral place of peace (often still characterized as nonresistance at the time) for Mennonite faith.

Of those, the priority of the church and theological reflection about the church were perhaps the most prevalent among the many themes he developed.[24] For Joe the Christian faith was not to be lived individually but in community. The church was Christ's body on earth and the channel or instrument through which Christ was working out his redemptive and reconciling purposes, God's mission in the world.[25] Without that sense of mission vocation, the church was not the true church. Joe often quoted theologian Emil Brunner: "The Church exists by mission, just as a fire exists by burning."[26] Local churches were meant to be "microcosms of the divine community," and they were the present, although imperfect, beginnings of the eternally and fully consummated reign of God that would one day emerge.[27]

A clear focus for Joe was that the church was universal. Since the gospel was for everyone, the church was to be multicultural, multiethnic, and global, rooted in diverse contexts. Under the lordship of Jesus Christ there was just one church, and it extended around the world.[28] When he shared an overview of the gospel, Joe typically added this universalist priority to the traditional Christian summary: God created the world, creation showed that all humans belonged to one family, humans rebelled against God, in love God promised and sent the Redeemer, God would forgive the repentant sinner, and the assurance of redemption was the glorious gospel for the whole world.[29] For Joe the whole of the biblical story showed this intention. The selection of Israel as the people of God was ultimately to draw the Gentiles into the family of God, and the emergence of ethnically and socially diverse Christian communities as recorded in the New Testament demonstrated God's will for the emergence of a new humanity in a worldwide church.[30] Joe identified several functions of the church, such as worship, nurture, faith, fellowship, and witness. Until congregations understood that they were part of the redemptive and global mission of the church, however, they had not yet grasped their own nature and role.[31]

A universal focus meant that the church had to be willing to change as it became rooted in diverse contexts. Establishing a church in a culture different from one's own entailed calling into question belief and practice that was culturally specific.[32] This was the price for being seriously engaged in mission, Joe thought. The mission task was to plant the church in the different cultures of the world and permit the Holy Spirit to give life and direct how that life would be expressed in ways that were culturally meaningful and relevant, even if the faith expressions and patterns that emerged were different from time-honored North American Mennonite traditions.

Joe emphasized discipleship as well. Christians were people who identified themselves with Christ and joined him in his world-focused mission of bringing those estranged by sin, an inextricable human reality, back into reconciliation with himself.[33] The lordship of Christ, discipleship, and mission were inextricably linked.[34] If Christ was Lord, then the disciple had to follow Christ's example and command, having been sent into the world to carry out the Father's mission.[35] Following Christ was necessary to truly understand the Christian faith and required the disciple to participate in Christ's work to save the world.[36] It was not too strong, wrote Joe, to say that one could not be saved without identifying with Christ in his saving ministry. Faith was never simply intellectual or abstract; belief and obedience could not be separated.[37] The reality of faith was found in the life that resulted from it and not in the clarification of an idea.

Disciples participated in offering the world a salvation that was holistic. Joe argued that to speak of saving souls was inadequate, because the whole person was to be redeemed.[38] Christ's miracle of regeneration made all things new, including habits, ambitions, desires, and occupations. It was meant to create a new community of transformed people whose relationships were governed by love. There was no way to love God except by loving people.[39] Declaring one's love for God was mere noise if it was not proven by deeds of self-giving love, and loving "one of the least of these" was the best indicator that one loved Christ. The gospel needed to be communicated by both word and deed; it was for the soul as well as for the body.[40] It presented Christ's way of peace in a war-weary world.[41]

Joe's spirituality held together a strong conviction of theological truth with a generous and open approach to the world and the unknown. He attributed his spiritual grounding to his childhood homelife and the influence of Indian friends.[42] He remembered his childhood home as a place where standards of Christian conduct were high, where love and charity prevailed, and where it was an honor to serve the church. Joe considered his and Minnie's time as missionaries in India to have been a period of spiritual maturation. He credited

Indian friends for helping them learn piety, faith, devotion, and how to pray. For Joe, theological conviction and Christian spirituality emerged from a deep sense of gratitude to God and a deep sense of living in connection with the living and glorious Christ.[43] The appropriate posture of a Christian engaging the world in mission was a spirituality of gratitude for God's love.[44]

While he was convinced of the truth and imperative of the Christian gospel, Joe argued that such truth needed to be held "in deep humility and with profound love."[45] The gospel was incongruous with a spirit of arrogance and superiority. Opening a class on Christian mission after retiring from MBMC, Joe told his students that unless they understood others so deeply that they were tempted into those persons' faiths or beliefs, they would not be able to communicate with them.[46] Joe's son-in-law, Alan Kreider, remembered being amazed at the way Joe demonstrated both certainty and humility in his Christian faith.

Integrated and ecumenical approaches

Joe thought mission activity should address the whole range of human needs and concerns. He often spoke of the need to witness in both word and deed. By this he meant that MBMC missionaries should be involved in ministries of preaching, teaching, and establishing new churches as well as in ministries meant to improve the general well-being of people.

Missionaries needed to be just as ready to provide material relief when needed as they were to share the gospel in their preaching and other witness activities. Creating new communities of faith, providing medical or social services, or decreasing poverty through economic empowerment were all part of the mission task. Ministering to the physical and social needs of people was necessary to embody the gospel message.

Explaining the faith motivations of Christian efforts to provide such assistance was equally essential. Joe conceded that there were situations in which there was an imperative to prioritize a particular aspect of mission activity, but an integrated approach had more integrity, he thought. As he led the expansion of MBMC's work in the decades after World War II, Joe oversaw missionaries and programs that addressed a wide range of human needs and concerns and encouraged the church to keep word and deed together in its endeavors.

Given his involvement in the wider Protestant mission movement and his commitment to collaboration among Mennonite mission agencies, including Mennonite Central Committee, Joe clearly valued ecumenical relationships that extended beyond MBMC and the Mennonite Church. He was a member of the International Missionary Council's Committee on the Christian Approach to the Jews and collaborated with the Division of Foreign Missions of the National Council of Churches of Christ, sometimes participating in its Southern Asia meetings. His reading list included a range of books and other publications, such as the *International Review of Missions*, which kept him up to date on missiological issues and from which he gleaned useful ideas as he formulated mission philosophy and strategy.

Joe was selective, rejecting, for example, the ecumenical movement's focus on church union initiatives. With Joe's leadership MBMC used discretion in its associations with the wider Protestant mission movement, appropriating helpful ideas but rejecting those that did not fit with its values and heritage or those that were at significant variance with its constituency's values. His approach contrasted with wholesale borrowing from evangelical Protestantism for which scholars have critiqued pre–World War II Mennonite Church missionaries.[47]

Within the Mennonite/Anabaptist community, Joe worked to increase collaborative efforts and led interagency mission initiatives. He was a leader in the establishment of the Council of Mission Board Secretaries, which became the Council of International Anabaptist Ministries, a network that seeks to maintain productive and positive working relationships among North American Mennonite/Anabaptist agencies involved in international ministries.

Postcolonial mission engagement

Early in their time in India, Joe and Minnie raised questions about the way colonialism influenced mission work, and after taking on executive leadership at MBMC, Joe became an early proponent of postcolonial mission approaches. Joe and Minnie came to regret the stratification in the Indian Christian community, which placed missionaries in positions of authority over their Indian counterparts and reinforced colonial hegemony. They developed deep friendships with

Indian colleagues and sought ways to improve relationships between Mennonite missionaries and Indian Christians.

Once he assumed executive leadership at MBMC, Joe made a strong argument that mission approaches had too often been embedded in colonial ways of thinking and working. It was time for a new day in mission engagement. He advocated for indigenization, ceding decision-making authority for the churches and institutions that missionaries created to local Christians and empowering them to adopt doctrine and practice that was faithful for their contexts. He developed a plan to invest the Mennonite Church in India with ownership and control of all church and mission programs and institutions and followed through with its implementation, over the objection of some of the MBMC missionaries whom he supervised. Missionaries later lauded his decision, recognizing that Joe had anticipated the significance of the end of the colonial era sooner than many of his contemporaries and that their work and the Indian church had benefited as a result. He encouraged missionaries to identify with the people whom they sought to serve, living and working as much as possible in the same social strata and upholding the value of indigenization from the very beginning of their mission initiatives. In his appropriation of the partnership paradigm, Joe envisioned Christians of diverse heritages and places collaborating equitably to advance the church's mission in the world.

With the benefit of hindsight, one might argue that Joe underestimated the tenacity of colonial influences during the postcolonial decades or that he was less successful at implementing his vision than he was at communicating it. He articulated a compelling vision of increasing equity and mutuality with partners around the world and was able to move MBMC in that direction. In the wider sweep of history, however, the optimism that accompanied the fall of colonialism after World War II was tempered by ongoing colonial habits that seemed bent on replacing local social frameworks with foreign impositions. Assumptions of superiority continued to plague Western actors on the international stage, including missionaries.

Scholars use the term neocolonialism to describe how colonial assumptions, structures, and mentalities are a continuing reality, even in the third decade of the twenty-first century. This situation suggests the necessity of decolonization, a focus on acknowledging the reality of neocolonialism and actively seeking to dismantle it. Joe's advocacy of a new day in mission engagement at the midpoint of the twentieth century can seem naïve in the face of ongoing critiques of neocolonialism or of instances of Mennonite or Anabaptist mission activity that perpetuate neocolonial habits. With time it became clear that the changes he proposed would be a long-term challenge, and he consistently called for new attitudes that would counter colonial mentalities.

If creating new, more mutual and equitable mission paradigms was a bigger task than he at first imagined, Joe nevertheless left a legacy of a postcolonial missionary vision and an ongoing commitment to its realization in the face of stubborn colonial attitudes and habits. He modeled a tenacious commitment to equity and mutuality across time and differing contexts, setting a precedent that helped move MBMC and Mennonite Church mission commitments toward a postcolonial mindset.

Global Anabaptism

Through the inclusion of people from cultures around the world and by urging the North American church to welcome people of non-European heritage into their congregations, Joe sought to increase the breadth of the Mennonite Church and encourage the emergence of a global Anabaptist church. The framework of world Christianity is one way to understand his vision and work. World Christianity is a way of recognizing that the global Christian movement is made up of an increasingly complex diversity of cultural and ethnic identities and Christian doctrines and practices. Despite such diversity, Christians around the world share a religious identity and are connected through webs of historical links, ecclesial networks, and personal relationships.

Joe's vision and work were consistent with such a global understanding of the Christian movement. As the architect of the Mennonite Church's post–World War II global expansion, he was instrumental in widening the ethnic and cultural mix in the global Anabaptist movement. His insistence on indigenization promoted doctrine and practice that responded to the realities of the diverse contexts in which new Anabaptist church communities were emerging. As a proponent of the use of linguistic and anthropological methods and theory to meet the challenge of working and communicating across cultures, Joe encouraged mission workers to give significant weight to the religious assumptions of the diverse peoples among whom they labored. His advocacy of the partnership paradigm sought to strengthen the web of connections among the worldwide community of churches with a view to advancing the global church's mission activity. In North America, Joe called on Mennonites of European descent to welcome people of other ethnic heritages into the church and to be willing to change for that to happen. He viewed such inclusion as a faithful and positive step forward and found it troubling when the church did not seem to be making progress in that direction.

The global Anabaptist movement in the twenty-first century is the result of a complex array of influences and the contributions of innumerable people, primarily from persons not of European descent. Nonetheless, Joe's work for a more ethnically and culturally diverse church, at home and around the world, and his attempts to increase collaborative mission initiatives between MBMC and international partners made a significant contribution to the emergence of the global Anabaptist movement.

That movement has experienced considerable expansion and demographic change over the last twelve decades, changes that reflect those within the larger Christian movement. When Joe was a youngster at the beginning of the twentieth century, over 80 percent of Christians lived in Europe and North America.[48] A century later less than 40 percent did, and the majority of adherents to the faith lived in Africa, Asia, and Latin America. This shift also happened among Anabaptists, most significantly in the decades after Joe died. Mennonite World Conference estimated that between 1978 and 2024 the number of Anabaptists increased from around 613,000 to 2.13 million, with most of the growth taking place in Africa, Asia, and Latin America.[49] Anabaptists in those three continents accounted for 33 percent of the global Anabaptist communion in 1978, but their percentage doubled to 66 percent by 2024. This increase happened not under the tutelage of North American or European missionaries but as the result of the mission engagement within those fast-growing churches.

Joe would have been pleased with such expansion, its indigenous nature, and the growing ethnic and cultural breadth embodied in the demographic shift to new regions of the world. The new reality pushes members of twenty-first-century Anabaptist communities to make room for diverse expressions of the faith that will enrich a movement that can no longer be solely defined by its European and North American heritages. Such change makes the reassessment and reformulation of Anabaptist identity an imperative as the newer members seek faithful doctrine and practice for their contexts and add their contributions to the shared identity of a global and dynamic movement.

If Joe was a tireless proponent of increasing the ethnic and cultural diversity of the Mennonite Church, he did not propose a blueprint for how to develop and maintain a common religious identity in a more diverse church. Mission activity was how the church could fulfill its mandate to welcome people of diverse heritages. Joe's method included witnessing in word and deed, creating new congregations, and inviting those not of ethnic Mennonite background into existing congregations. He was open to new strategies and innovative approaches that went beyond traditional missionary practice to help that happen. To accommodate new peoples and traditions into the church, moreover, required an openness to change. Mission success depended on the church being willing to adapt, Joe argued. How to cultivate a common faith identity that accommodated diverse heritages in a more diverse church, however, was a step beyond Joe's focus during his career.

Nor did he articulate a systematic critique of structural racism and inequity as factors in the church's success or failure to become more diverse. He was aware of the social and political context of his day and could converse about it, but vocationally he focused on the church and its mission activity. In a church that was still very homogeneous in its ethnic and cultural makeup, Joe's primary focus was on becoming more welcoming and inclusive. He called North American Mennonites to greater humility and advocated for the partnership paradigm, but he did not attempt to outline more specific strategies for how to live faithfully in diverse church communities. Perhaps there were not enough instances of multiethnic congregations for such a focus to be a priority. Perhaps he was at a loss about how to proceed. In the first decades of the twenty-first century, however, building common religious identity has become an important challenge for both the global Anabaptist movement and its increasingly heterogeneous regional streams around the world.

Nearly a half century after his passing, Joe's legacy continues to reverberate. He spent significant time and energy urging a church that was suspicious of the world outside its rather withdrawn religious communities to proactively engage that world via the mission paradigm. Today many members of the Anabaptist movement participate in the world beyond their church without many, if any, second thoughts. Yet in the minds of some, the mission paradigm is largely discredited because of associations with colonialism. In such a context, advocacy for mission engagement that is holistic, cultivates faith communities of diverse ethnic and cultural identities, and builds networks of partnership on a global scale presents a challenge, just as it did in Joe's day.

Joe's missiological commitments emerged from an early zeal to share the gospel of Jesus Christ with the world and culminated in the vision of a global community of indigenous churches participating together in Christ's holistic mission. Nurtured by deep fellowship with Indian colleagues, Joe came to prioritize relational over institutional mission approaches. Troubled by colonialism's impact on mission engagement, he championed the development of indigenous churches rooted in their own cultures, in equitable relationship with each other, and witnessing in word and deed. Such was his vision of a global church and its holistic gospel, the remedy for a fallen world.

Today, service work and sharing the gospel message often seem to be separate initiatives implemented by different people, suggesting that Joe's call for integrated mission activity remains as relevant as ever. The goal of encouraging and sustaining intercultural faith communities also continues. How to live faithfully and fruitfully with the diversity of religious expressions and expectations that interculturality implies is a question that is perhaps even more pertinent now than it was in the middle decades of the twentieth century. Inequalities, especially those of wealth and opportunity, plague international relationships today as they did when North Atlantic powers were colonial overlords of large swaths of the world.

The challenge of developing equitable partnerships within the global Anabaptist movement is as real this century as it was during the previous one. Building and maintaining equitable relationships requires intentionality and goodwill—the same approach that J. D. Graber modeled in his mission work and leadership of MBMC, whether the setting was central India or northern Indiana. The missiological values Joe advanced have enduring significance.

Notes on Sources / Bibliographical Essay

How One Tells the Story

THE STORIES we tell are always from a particular perspective, and the historical representation of Joe's vision and work and the Mennonite Church's mission engagement during the twentieth century is no exception. It has been primarily insiders, members of the church, and in many cases mission practitioners or theorists who have told the story of the church's increasing involvement in mission activity during this period.[1] Early accounts in denominational publications outlined the church's growing missionary spirit, described initiatives that exemplified that spirit, sought to increase mission commitment among the faithful, and sometimes described the religious, social, and geographic contexts in which missionaries labored.[2]

During the last half of the twentieth century scholars trained in the fields of history and mission studies brought a more critical eye to the story. John A. Lapp's *The Mennonite Church in India, 1897–1962* grew out of his PhD dissertation. He described the background to the India work, the long struggle from mission activity to the emergence of an Indian church, and factors such as missionary paternalism that made the devolution of the work to Indian hands difficult.

Theron Schlabach's research on Mennonite Church mission activity from the 1860s to 1944 produced several publications, most importantly the magisterial *Gospel Versus Gospel: Mission and the Mennonite Church, 1863–1944*.[3] Schlabach looked back on the period through the lens of Anabaptist/Mennonite faith commitments that coalesced around Harold S. Bender's Anabaptist vision during the post–World War II decades.[4] He critiqued Mennonites' appropriation of mission theory and practice from the evangelical Protestant mission movement because, he argued, it failed to embody Jesus' holistic vision of shalom, which he saw in the historic Mennonite commitment to peace. Schlabach admitted that the whole of the Mennonite Church, not only the missionaries it produced, had borrowed from its Protestant siblings; but since his work was one of mission history, it was Mennonite mission engagement upon which the burden of his critique rested.

Wilbert R. Shenk's *By Faith They Went Out: Mennonite Missions 1850–1999* is not just about the Mennonite Church but about the mission work of the ensemble of North American Anabaptist/Mennonite groups. He shared Schlabach's assessment of a seemingly uncritical appropriation of Protestant mission approaches among Mennonites but helpfully unpacked the reasons for such borrowing and found value in some of it.[5] It was, after all, the influence of the mission-oriented Pietism and evangelical Protestantism that prodded Mennonites toward mission activity in the first place, helping to challenge their enclave mentality and providing much of the impetus for the twentieth-century emergence of a global Anabaptist/Mennonite faith community.

More than the aforementioned studies of Mennonite Church mission work, this study is informed by the framework of world Christianity to understand the Christian movement and Joe's vision and work. The world Christianity framework highlights the cultural and linguistic diversity within the world Christian movement and the vast array of shifting networks that birthed and nurture it.[6] It provides a way to make sense of the shift in the demographic weight of the faith to the Global South and of the way distinct local expressions of belief and practice exist alongside the common religious identity of a world religion. It also brings to the forefront Joe's insistence that missionaries make use of disciplines such as anthropology and linguistics to understand local contexts and that missionaries value indigenous, locally generated expressions of the faith. The world Christianity framework highlights his concern that North American Mennonite churches make room for people of cultures and backgrounds other than that of the dominant European heritage that typified those churches. Joe articulated a vision of MBMC's global expansion and partnership that sought to cross boundaries of geography and identity to create and sustain collaborative engagement with the world. He wanted to create networks that would generate shared Anabaptist/Mennonite witness and identity.

The world Christianity framework highlights the importance of context for Christian faith. It underlines the impact of Joe's missionary experience in India and of his time as mission executive in North America on the vision he developed. It recognizes the impact of Protestant mission theory and practice and the influence of his own faith tradition on Joe's thinking. Joe drew on his own experience, the discourse of the wider Protestant missionary movement, and his Mennonite heritage to formulate vision and strategy that was attractive to mid-twentieth-century Mennonites and provided a way to increase their engagement in the world via the mission paradigm.

This account of Joe's life and work suggests that a world Christianity framework provides a fruitful approach for the study of Anabaptist mission history and of Anabaptist history in general. It is an appropriate approach for understanding the emergence of a global Anabaptist movement.

A word about sources

Sources for this history come primarily from the Mennonite Church USA Archives in Elkhart, Indiana. This archival material includes official minutes and reports from MBMC (later MBM); correspondence between Joe and colleagues, friends, and family; sermon notes; and recorded interviews with Joe, Minnie, and their coworkers and family. Missionary reports to the MBMC home office and the MBMC yearly reports, published in book form for distribution throughout the constituency, provide a chronological record in large strokes of the institution's evolution, the issues Joe and his colleagues faced, and his evolving vision, first as a missionary and then as executive secretary.

Joe's correspondence with missionaries, other Mennonite leaders, and contacts in the wider Protestant mission community are more useful for understanding the details and nuances of his experience, reflections, and vision. Starting from 1947 the MBMC material is well organized and increasingly voluminous.

The archives also contain numerous relevant recordings. Material from the mission-history project directed by Theron Schlabach in the 1970s contains four hours and forty-five minutes of interviews with Joe in which he reflected on his work and the mission engagement of the Mennonite Church over his lifetime.[7] Wilbert R. Shenk organized a J. D. and Minnie Graber oral history project (1986–88), which gathered many hours of interviews with Minnie, other family members, colleagues, and friends.[8] This material is a rich source of information about Joe's life and ministry.

Published material provides an indispensable window into Joe's advocacy for mission activity in the Mennonite Church and for tracing the development of his thinking. The *Gospel Herald*, the church's weekly periodical, was the primary vehicle through which MBMC communicated and inspired the church's mission commitments.[9] Joe wrote over 630 editorials and articles in the *Herald* from 1925 to 1971 that show how his thinking developed over more than four decades. The *International Review of Mission*, earlier the *International Review of Missions*, was the primary Protestant mission study journal from its inception in 1912 through the middle decades of the twentieth century. Joe read the journal, and MBMC provided subscriptions to the members of its executive committee. The ideas and issues in its pages often found their way into Joe's reflections. He shared ideas that he read in books and journals, and sometimes the actual books and articles, with missionaries he supervised. Such correspondence and published material show how Joe approached the missiological issues of the day as he sought new methods and frameworks for Mennonite mission activity in the postcolonial era.

Notes

Introduction

1 J. D. Graber, "A Witnessing People," sermon, Prairie Street Mennonite Church, April 4, 1976, Elkhart, IN, IV-18-12, Box 3, Tape 1, commentary edited into the recording after Graber's prayer at the end of the sermon. MCUSA Archives. Unless otherwise noted, all archival sources are from the Mennonite Church USA Archives – Elkhart. Elkhart, IN.

2 J. D. Graber, *100 Years: Prairie Street Mennonite Church*, 1, 11, 16–17, 21–22.

3 Lederach, "History of the Young People's," 217.

4 Lapp, *Mennonite Church in India*, 38–39.

5 J. D. Graber, "A Witnessing People."

6 J. D. Graber, "A Witnessing People."

7 J. D. Graber, "Why I Am a Christian," December 3, 1925, *Gospel Herald*; J. D. Graber, "A Witnessing People."

8 J. D. Graber, "Why I Am a Christian," December 3, 1925, *Gospel Herald*; J. D. Graber, "Why I Am a Christian," tract, November 15, 1925, IV-18-03, Reports —Missionaries, undated.

9 J. D. Graber, "A Witnessing People."

10 J. D. Graber, "A Witnessing People."

11 See Robert, "Christianity in the Wider World," 525–80; Robert, *Christian Mission.*

12 Casas, *A Short Account.*

13 Walls, "American Dimension," 5.

14 Sanneh, *Translating the Message.*

15 Schlesinger, "The Missionary Enterprise," 336–73; Comaroff and Comaroff, *Of Revelation and Revolution*, vol. 1 and 2.

16 Johnson and Ross, *Atlas of Global Christianity*, 8–9.

17 Cabrita and Maxwell, "Introduction: Relocating World Christianity," 1–44; Hanciles, "World Christianity Interrupted"; Robert, "World Christianity as a Revitalization"; Frederiks and Nagy, *World Christianity: Methodological Considerations*, 1–39.

18 Kasdorf, "Anabaptist Approach to Mission," 51–69; Schäufele, "Missionary Vision and Activity," 70–87; Shenk, *By Faith They Went*, 15–27.

19 Zijpp, "From Anabaptist Missionary Congregation," 119–36.
20 Littell, "Anabaptist Theology of Mission," 13–23; Shenk, *By Faith They Went*, 29.
21 MacMaster, *Land, Piety, Peoplehood*, 50–58, 109–10.
22 MacMaster, *Land, Piety, Peoplehood*, 165–69.
23 MacMaster, *Land, Piety, Peoplehood*, 177–82; Schlabach, *Peace, Faith, Nation*, 95–105.
24 Hutchison, "Moral Equivalent for Imperialism," 91–124; Schlabach, *Peace, Faith, Nation*, 105; Juhnke, *Vision, Doctrine, War*, 36.
25 Schlabach, *Peace, Faith, Nation*, 127–29.
26 Coffman, *His Name Was John*.
27 Lapp, *Mennonite Church in India*, 17–18; Schlabach, *Peace, Faith, Nation*, 299–300; Schlabach, *Gospel Versus Gospel*, 38–40.
28 Schlabach, *Gospel Versus Gospel*, 65, 92; J. S. Hartzler, "Report of Committee on Consolidation of Mission Boards," (Rittman, OH: Mennonite Board of Missions and Charities, May 19, 1906), IV-06-02, Box 2, Minute Book, 1 May 1906—May 1913.
29 Lambert, *Around the Globe*.
30 Lambert, *Around the Globe*, 6, 80–82; Lapp, *Mennonite Church in India*, 27–34; Schlabach, *Gospel Versus Gospel*, 78–79; Juhnke, *Vision, Doctrine, War*, 144–45.
31 Lambert and Kolb, *India, the Horror-Stricken Empire*.
32 Lapp, *Mennonite Church in India*, 40.
33 Schlabach, "The Humble Become."
34 Hartzler, "Missions Section in Retrospect."
35 Nasaw, "Historians and Biography."
36 Presler, "Mission Is Ministry."

Chapter 1

1 Esther Graber et al., interview by John M. Bender, March 16, 1987, IV-18-12, Box 3, Tape 9; Vernon Gerig et al., interview by John M. Bender, August 26, 1987, IV-18-12, Box 3, Tape 10; Chris L. Graber, *Looking Back*.
2 Irene Weaver, Ruth Koppenhaver, John Koppenhaver, and Milo Kauffman, interview by John Bender, October 10, 1987, IV-18-12, Box 3, Tape 15.
3 Esther Graber et al., interview; S. C. Yoder, "Certificate of Missionary Appointment for Joseph Graber," July 21, 1925, HM1-503, Box 9, folder 11, Certificates of Missionary Appointments, July 21, 1925; electronic mail from Eleanor Kreider, December 9, 2022.
4 Gingerich, *Mennonites in Iowa*, 304. Juhnke, *Vision, Doctrine, War*, 211–29.
5 J. D. Graber to Daniel Graber, January 27, 1921, HM1-503, Box 15, folder 5, Letters to-from Family, 1922–24.
6 Delbert L. Gratz, "Graber (Greber, Grayber, Gräber) Family," in *Global Anabaptist Mennonite Encyclopedia Online*, accessed May 16, 2020, https://gameo.org/index.php?title=Graber_(Greber,_Grayber,_Gr%C3%A4ber)_family; Kauffman, *Mennonite Cyclopedic Dictionary*, 135.
7 Foster, *Indians of Iowa*.
8 Esther Graber et al., interview.
9 "Obituary of Fanny Graber," *Gospel Herald*.
10 Gingerich, *Mennonites in Iowa*, 93–112; McCarley, "Reconnaissance Level Historical," 16–28.

11 Kauffman, *Mennonite Cyclopedic Dictionary*, 135–36; Gingerich, *Mennonites in Iowa*, 112.
12 Gingerich, *Mennonites in Iowa*, 303; Max Haines, "United Orphanage and Mission Society, The," in *Global Anabaptist Mennonite Encyclopedia Online*, accessed March 9, 2025, https://gameo.org/index.php?title=United_Orphanage_and_Mission_Society,_The; Lapp, *Mennonite Church in India*, 18, 36.
13 Gingerich, *Mennonites in Iowa*, 305; Gerig et al., interview.
14 J. D. Graber, interview by John S. Miller, August 18, 1972, HM6–81, Box 1, Tape 3; Minnie Graber, interview by J. Nelson Kraybill, January 20, 1980, IV-18-12, Box 3, Tape 4; Esther Graber et al., interview; "Obituary of Daniel Graber," *Gospel Herald*; Schlabach, *Gospel Versus Gospel*, 88, 107–8.
15 Showalter, "Mr. Missions," *Gospel Herald*.
16 J. D. Graber, "Always a Christian."
17 Showalter, "Mr. Missions," *Gospel Herald*.
18 Esther Graber et al., interview.
19 "Obituary of Daniel Graber," *Gospel Herald*; Esther Graber et al., interview.
20 J. D. Graber, "Always a Christian."
21 Esther Graber et al., interview.
22 Minnie Graber, interview by Mary Mishler, n.d., HM1-503, Box 12, Cassette Tape of Courtship Stories.
23 Esther Graber et al., interview.
24 Gerig et al., interview.
25 J. D. Graber, interview, August 18, 1972.
26 Sharp, *School on the Prairie*, 53–57.
27 T. M. Erb to Daniel Graber, March 20, 1909, HM1-503, Box 9, folder 5, Family-Related Miscellaneous Materials; The Executive Committee of Hesston Mennonite School to Brother or Sister, Form Letter, February 1, 1909, HM1-503, Box 9, folder 5, Family-Related Miscellaneous Materials.
28 Shank, Eash, and Kauffman, "Missouri-Iowa Conference Report," *Gospel Herald*.
29 Toews, *Mennonites in American Society*, 64–76.
30 Kauffman, *Manual of Bible Doctrines*; Kauffman, *Bible Doctrine*; Kauffman, *Doctrines of the Bible*.
31 Toews, *Mennonites in American Society*, 64–76; Juhnke, *Vision, Doctrine, War*, 257–60.
32 Miller, *Culture for Service*, 53–122.
33 Miller, *Culture for Service*, 65.
34 The Executive Committee of Hesston Mennonite School to Brother or Sister, February 1, 1909.
35 Sharp, *School on the Prairie*, 99–100, 102–3, 126, 146–47, 158–59, 166–67.
36 Lawrence Burkholder et al., interview by John M. Bender, September 1, 1987, IV-18-12, Box 3, Tape 14; Esther Graber et al., interview.
37 Irene Weaver et al., interview; Miller, *Pillar of Cloud*, 89.
38 J. D. Graber to Daniel Graber, November 26, 1923 and J. D. Graber to Daniel Graber, January 3, 1922, HM1-503, Box 15, folder 5, Letters to-from Family, 1922–24.
39 Sharp, *School on the Prairie*, 90–91.
40 J. D. Graber to Minnie Swartzendruber, May 8, 1923, HM1-503, Box 13, folder 6, Letters—JD to Minnie, January–July 1923; Miller, *Pillar of Cloud*, 90–91; Walter E.

Oswald, "Hesston College Journal (Periodical)," in *Global Anabaptist Mennonite Encyclopedia Online*, accessed March 3, 2025, https://gameo.org/index.php?title=Hesston_College_Journal_(Periodical); Sharp, *School on the Prairie*, 156.

41 Umble, *Goshen College*, 123.

42 Minnie Graber, interview, January 20, 1980.

43 Gingerich, *Mennonites in Iowa*, 333–34; "Obituary of Sarah Knepp Swartzendruber," *Gospel Herald*.

44 Minnie Graber, interview by J. Nelson Kraybill, January 6, 1980, IV-18-12, Box 3, Tape 3.

45 Gingerich, *Mennonites in Iowa*, 334–36.

46 Juhnke, *Vision, Doctrine, War*, 189–96.

47 "Obituary of Elias Swartzendruber," *Gospel Herald*.

48 Minnie Graber, interview by Mary Mishler.

49 Minnie Graber, interview, January 6, 1980.

50 "Obituary of Elias Swartzendruber"; Gingerich, *Mennonites in Iowa*, 335.

51 Minnie Graber, interview, January 6, 1980; Minnie Graber, interview, January 20, 1980.

52 Minnie Swartzendruber to J. D. Graber, April 29, 1924, HM1-503, Box 15, folder 1.

53 Minnie Graber, interview by Mary Mishler.

54 Minnie Graber, interview, January 20, 1980; Minnie Graber, interview by Mary Mishler.

55 Minnie Graber, interview, January 20, 1980.

56 Minnie Swartzendruber to J. D. Graber, May 1921, HM1-503, Box 13, folder 1, Letters—Minnie and J. D., 1921.

57 Minnie Swartzendruber to J. D. Graber, April 28, 1921, HM1-503, Box 13, folder 1, Letters—Minnie and J. D., 1921.

58 Minnie Swartzendruber to J. D. Graber, April 28, 1924, HM1-503, Box 15, folder 1; Minnie Graber, interview, January 6, 1980.

59 Minnie Graber, interview, January 20, 1980.

60 Minnie Graber, interview by Mary Mishler.

61 Communication from Eleanor Kreider, July 2020.

62 Minnie Graber, interview, January 20, 1980.

63 Minnie Graber, interview, January 20, 1980.

64 J. D. Graber to Minnie Swartzendruber, June 6, 1922, HM1-503, Box 13, folder 2, Letters—JD to Minnie, 1922.

65 Minnie Graber, interview, January 20, 1980; Minnie Swartzendruber to J. D. Graber, June 2, 1923, HM1-503, Box 13, folder 4, Letters—Minnie to JD, 1923.

66 Minnie Graber, interview by Mary Mishler.

67 Homan, "Orie Benjamin Gerig," 755–57.

68 Gerig, "Mennonite Young People's Conference," *Gospel Herald*; Meyer, "Origin of the Young People's."

69 J. D. Graber to Daniel Graber, September 17, 1920, HM1-503, Box 15, folder 5, Letters to-from Family, 1922–24.

70 Homan, "Orie Benjamin Gerig," 751, 755–57.

71 J. D. Graber to Daniel Graber, September 17, 1920.

72 Homan, "Orie Benjamin Gerig," 759–63.

73 Orie B. Gerig to J. D. Graber, March 31, 1921, HM1-503, Box 1, folder 16,

Corres.—O. Ben Gerig, 1921.

74 J. D. Graber to Orie B. Gerig, April 7, 1921, HM1-503, Box 1, folder 16, Corres.—O. Ben Gerig, 1921.

75 Orie B. Gerig to J. D. Graber, April 9, 1921, J. D. Graber to Orie B. Gerig, April 13, 1921, and Orie B. Gerig to J. D. Graber, April 1921, HM1-503, Box 1, folder 16, Corres.—O. Ben Gerig, 1921.

76 Miller, *Culture for Service*, 62.

77 Sharp, *School on the Prairie*, 103, 126, 147, 158–59, 166–67.

78 Smith, *Trail to Santa Fe*, 48.

79 Smith, *Trail to Santa Fe*, 171; Miller, *Culture for Service*, 147.

80 J. D. Graber to Minnie Swartzendruber, July 1, 1922, HM1-503, Box 13, folder 3, Letters—Minnie to JD, 1922.

81 J. D. Graber, "Why I Am a Christian," December 3, 1925, *Gospel Herald*; J. D. Graber, "Why I Am a Christian," November 15, 1925, *Gospel Herald*.

82 Smith, *Trail to Santa Fe*, 180–183, 202; Smith, "William Jennings Bryan and the Social Gospel"; Smith, *William Jennings Bryan Christian Reformer*; Smith, *Social and Religious Thought*.

83 Schlabach, *War, Peace, and Social Conscience*, 125.

84 Schlabach, *War, Peace, and Social Conscience*, 125.

85 Schlabach, *War, Peace, and Social Conscience*, 125.

86 J. D. Graber to Minnie Swartzendruber, June 6, 1922, HM1-503, Box 13, folder 2, Letters—JD to Minnie, 1922.

87 Miller, *Culture for Service*, 77.

88 Minnie Swartzendruber to J. D. Graber, November 1924, HM1-503, Box 15, folder 2, Letters—Minnie to JD, August–December 1924.

89 Minnie Swartzendruber to J. D. Graber, May 1921, HM1-503, Box 13, folder 1, Letters—Minnie and J. D., 1921.

90 J. D. Graber to Minnie Swartzendruber, July 1, 1922; Minnie Swartzendruber to J. D. Graber, January 27, 1923, HM1-503, Box 13, folder 4, Letters—Minnie to JD, 1923.

91 Minnie Graber, interview, January 20, 1980.

92 J. D. Graber, "Always a Christian."

93 J. D. Graber to Minnie Swartzendruber, July 1, 1922.

94 J. D. Graber, "Always a Christian."

95 Minnie Graber, interview by Mary Mishler; J. D. Graber to Daniel Graber, May 1, 1922 and J. D. Graber to Daniel Graber, April 8, 1924, HM1-503, Box 15, folder 5, Letters to-from Family, 1922–24.

96 S. C. Yoder to J. D. Graber, May 1, 1923, HM1-503, Box 15, folder 6, Miscellaneous Correspondence, 1921–26.

97 Sharp, *School on the Prairie*, 164.

98 Miller, *Culture for Service*, 125–28.

99 S. C. Yoder to J. D. Graber, May 1, 1923.

100 Daniel Graber to J. D. Graber, May 8, 1922, HM1-503, Box 15, folder 5, Letters to-from Family, 1922–24.

101 Minnie Graber, interview, January 20, 1980.

102 Sharp, *School on the Prairie*, 92, 114, 116, 125, 129, 143–44, 150–52, 171, 175–76.

103 Smith, *Trail to Santa Fe*, 131.

104 J. D. Graber to Minnie Swartzendruber, June 2, 1923, HM1-503, Box 13, folder 6, Letters—JD to Minnie, January–July 1923; J. D. Graber to Minnie Swartzendruber, June 3, 1924, HM1-503, Box 14, folder 4, Letters—JD to Minnie June–November 1924; Minnie Graber, interview, January 20, 1980.
105 J. D. Graber to Minnie Swartzendruber, June 2, 1923.
106 J. D. Graber to Minnie Swartzendruber, June 3, 1924.
107 Litwiller, "Call to Mission," *Gospel Herald.*
108 Minnie Swartzendruber to J. D. Graber, June 2, 1924, HM1-503, Box 15, folders 1; J. D. Graber to Minnie Swartzendruber, June 3, 1924.
109 Showalter, "Mr. Missions," *Gospel Herald.*
110 Minnie Swartzendruber to J. D. Graber, June 2, 1924.
111 S. C. Yoder to J. D. Graber, June 17, 1924, HM1-503, Box 14, folder 4, Letters—JD to Minnie, June–November 1924.
112 An India Missionary to J. D. Graber, April 1, 1925, HM1-503, Box 12, folder 2, Miscellaneous Correspondence.
113 Minnie Graber, interview, January 20, 1980.

Chapter 2

1 Compare J. D. Graber, "Why I Am a Christian," December 3, 1925, *Gospel Herald* and J. D. Graber, "Why I Am a Christian," April 19, 1934, *Gospel Herald.* See 1 Peter 3:15.
2 "Report of Twenty-Sixth Annual Meeting," *Gospel Herald,* 390; J. D. Graber, "Call from India," *Gospel Herald.*
3 Graber, "Call from India."
4 J. D. and Minnie Graber to Folks at Home, December 4, 1925, HM1-503, Box 10, folder 1, First Term in India (1925–31); J. D. and Minnie Graber, Ada Hartzler, and Minnie Kanagy, "New York to Port Said," *Gospel Herald.*
5 J. D. Graber to Folks at Home, December 26, 1925, HM1-503, Box 10, folder 1, First Term in India (1925–31).
6 J. D. Graber to Martha Stoltzfus and Chris Swartzendruber, December 17, 1925, HM1-503, Box 10, folder 1, First Term in India (1925–31).
7 J. D. and Minnie Graber to Folks at Home, December 4, 1925.
8 J. D. Graber to Martha Stoltzfus and Chris Swartzendruber, December 17, 1925; J. D. and Minnie Graber to Uncle and Aunt, December 23, 1925, HM1-503, Box 1, folder 17, Correspondence India—1925.
9 Esther Graber et al., interview.
10 E.g., J. D. Graber to Daniel Graber, January 3, 1922, HM1-503, Box 15, folder 5, Letters to-from Family, 1922–24.
11 J. D. and Minnie Graber to Folks at Home, December 4, 1925.
12 J. D. Graber to Dear Ones at Home, January 9, 1926, HM1-503, Box 10, folder 1, First Term in India (1925–31).
13 John E. Lapp, interview by Alice W. Lapp, January 30, 1988, IV-18-12, Box 3, Tape 2; Esther Graber et al., interview.
14 J. D. Graber to Dear Ones at Home, January 9, 1926.
15 Burkholder et al., interview.
16 Burkholder et al., interview
17 Fanny Lapp to Ones at Home, July 19, 1926, HM1-143, Box 1, folder 2, Corr.—1925.

18 Lapp, *Mennonite Church in India,* 69.

19 J. D. Graber, "Our India Letter," *Gospel Herald*; Minnie Graber to Dear Ones at Home, September 19, 1926, HM1-503, Box 10, folder 1, First Term in India (1925–31).

20 J. D. Graber to Vernon Reiff, January 13, 1927, IV-7-01, Box 5, folder 6, Graber, J. D., 1928–30.

21 J. D. Graber to Henry and Lela, December 2, 1926, HM1-503, Box 10, folder 1, First Term in India (1925–31).

22 Minnie Graber to Home Folks, December 16, 1926, HM1-503, Box 10, folder 1, First Term in India (1925–31).

23 J. D. Graber to Vernon Reiff, July 28, 1927, IV-7-01, Box 5, folder 6, Graber, J. D., 1928–30.

24 Ezra C. Bender, interview by John M. Bender, January 1, 1988, IV-18-12, Tape 17; Irene Weaver et al., interview.

25 Lapp, *Mennonite Church in India,* 27–40; Lambert and Kolb, *India, the Horror-Stricken Empire*.

26 Hartzler, "Report of Committee on Consolidation."

27 Lapp, *Mennonite Church in India,* 40–48, 101–3, 117, 136, 165.

28 Grundmann, *Sent to Heal!*; Grundmann, "Role of Medical Missions"; Jackson, "Missions and Lepers."

29 Lapp, *Mennonite Church in India,* 65–66; "Mission Directory 1926," *Gospel Herald.*

30 Minnie Graber to Ones at Home, February 14, 1927, HM1-503, Box 10, folder 1, First Term in India (1925–31).

31 Minnie Graber to Dear Ones at Home, September 19, 1926.

32 J. D. Graber to Uncle Joe and Aunt Katie, July 20, 1927, HM1-503, Box 1, folder 17, Correspondence India—1925.

33 J. D. Graber to Henry and Lela, December 2, 1926.

34 E.g., Afigbo, "Missions, the State and Education"; Lapp, *Mennonite Church in India,* 121–22.

35 J. D. Graber to Vernon Reiff, January 13, 1927.

36 Tucker, "Role of Bible Women."

37 Troyer, "The Work of the Bible Women," *Gospel Herald.*

38 Minnie Graber to Dear Ones at Home, September 19, 1926; J. D. Graber to Henry and Lela, December 2, 1926.

39 J. D. Graber to Vernon Reiff, March 20, 1928, IV-7-01, Box 5, folder 6, Graber, J. D., 1928–30.

40 Minnie Graber to Ones at Home, February 14, 1927; Minnie Graber, interview by J. Nelson Kraybill, January 21, 1980, IV-18-12, Box 3, Tape 5.

41 J. D. Graber to Vernon Reiff, January 13, 1927.

42 J. D. Graber to Vernon Reiff, March 24, 1927, IV-7-01, Box 5, folder 6, Graber, J. D., 1928–30.

43 Minnie Graber to Mother and Father, March 10, 1927 and Minnie Graber to Father and Mother, February 1928, HM1-503, Box 10, folder 1, First Term in India (1925–31).

44 Lapp, *Mennonite Church in India,* 112–13.

45 J. D. Graber to Home Folks, November 15, 1928, HM1-503, Box 10, folder 1, First Term in India (1925–31).

46 "Report of the Twenty-Third Annual Meeting," *Gospel Herald*, 400; J. D. Graber, Hostetler, and Kaufman, "Report of Auditing Committee," *Gospel Herald.*
47 J. D. Graber, "Report of Christian Work"; Lapp, *Mennonite Church in India,* 95.
48 J. D. Graber to Home Folk, July 24, 1930, HM1-503, Box 10, folder 1, First Term in India (1925–31).
49 Lapp, *Mennonite Church in India,* 159.
50 Minnie Graber to Folks at Home, December 1, 1927, HM1-503, Box 10, folder 1, First Term in India (1925–31).
51 J. D. Graber, "My Work," *Gospel Herald.*
52 Minnie Graber to Father and Mother, November 29, 1928, HM1-503, Box 10, folder 1, First Term in India (1925–31).
53 J. D. Graber and Minnie Graber, "Shantipur Leper Home," *Gospel Herald* 22, 134–35; J. D. Graber, "Shantipur," *Gospel Herald.*
54 Minnie Graber to Father and Mother, January 23, 1929, HM1-503, Box 10, folder 1, First Term in India (1925–31); J. D. Graber to Home Folks, November 15, 1928; Minnie Graber to Folks at Home, July 13, 1929, HM1-503, Box 10, folder 1, First Term in India (1925–31); Fannie Lapp to Family, August 26, 1931, HM1-143, Box 1, folder 5, Corr. November, 1930–31.
55 J. D. Graber and Minnie Graber, "Shantipur Leper Home," *Gospel Herald* 22, 134.
56 J. D. Graber, "Shantipur Leper Home," *Gospel Herald* 24, 206.
57 J. D. Graber and Minnie Graber, "Shantipur Leper Home" *Gospel Herald* 22, 134–5; J. D. Graber to Vernon Reiff, July 12, 1929, IV-7-01, Box 5, folder 6, Graber, J. D., 1928–30; J. D. Graber, "Teaching Christ," *Gospel Herald*; J. D. Graber, "Conversion of Ganpat," *Gospel Herald.*
58 Keay, *India: A History*, chapter 17.
59 Newbigin, *Unfinished Agenda*, 39–42.
60 Minnie Graber, interview, January 21, 1980; J. D. Graber to Minnie Graber, October 29, 1932, and J. D. Graber to Minnie Graber, November 9, 1932, HM1-503, Box 10, folder 4, 2nd Term in India (1932–41).
61 McGavran, "Missionaries and Indigenous Standards of Living."
62 Minnie Graber to Ones at Home, February 14, 1927; Minnie Graber, interview, January 21, 1980.
63 J. D. Graber, "Call from India," *Gospel Herald*; J. D. Graber to Minnie Graber, October 19, 1932, HM1-503, Box 10, folder 4, 2nd Term in India (1932–41).
64 Graber, "Call from India."
65 E.g., Andrews, "Missions in India."
66 Azariah, "Problem of Co-Operation."
67 Harper, *In the Shadow*.
68 Robert, "Cross-Cultural Friendship"; Fleming, "Facing World Friction Points"; Paton, "Indian Mission of Fellowship."
69 Keay, *India: A History*, chapter 18.
70 J. D. Graber, "India Letter," *Gospel Herald* 23, 501; George Lapp to Family, August 5, 1931, HM1-143, Box 1, folder 5, Corr. November, 1930–31; J. D. Graber, "India Letter," *Gospel Herald* 23, 580–81; Minnie Graber, "India: Thirty-First Annual Report," *Gospel Herald*, 193.
71 J. D. Graber, "India Letter," *Gospel Herald* 23, 776–77; Kniss, "Swaraj," *Gospel Herald*; Friesen, "Is Our Evangelistic Work Effective?," *Gospel Herald*; Kniss and Kniss, "Swaraj Andolan in the Villages," *Gospel Herald.*

72 J. D. Graber, "India: Thirtieth Annual Report," *Gospel Herald.*

73 J. D. Graber, "India Letter," *Gospel Herald*, 23, 580–81.

74 J. D. Graber, "Call from India," *Gospel Herald.*

75 Minnie Graber, "India: Thirty-First Annual Report."

76 Minnie Graber, interview, January 21, 1980.

77 J. D. Graber to S. C. Yoder, June 17, 1932, IV-7-01, Box 5, folder 7, Graber, J. D. 1931–34. The Biblical Seminary in New York was more recently known as New York Theological Seminary.

78 Edwin Weaver to S. C. Yoder, June 5, 1931 and S. C. Yoder to Edwin Weaver, June 9, 1931, IV-7-01, Box 20, folder 14 Weaver, Edwin I., 1928-1943; Schlabach, *Gospel Versus Gospel*, 142.

79 Registrar to S. C. Yoder, June 30, 1932, IV-7-01, Box 5, folder 7, Graber, J. D., 1931–34.

80 J. D. Graber to S. C. Yoder, July 28, 1932, IV-7-01, Box 5, folder 7, Graber, J. D., 1931–34.

81 Minnie S. Graber, interview by J. Nelson Kraybill, January 22, 1980, IV-18-12, Box 3, Tape 6.

82 Yoder, "Mission Board and Finances," *Gospel Herald.*

83 J. D. Graber to Minnie Graber, September 30, 1932, J. D. Graber to Minnie Graber, October 2, 1932, J. D. Graber to Minnie Graber, October 5, 1932, J. D. Graber to Minnie Graber, October 13, 1932, and J. D. Graber to Minnie Graber, October 19, 1932, HM1-503, Box 10, folder 4, 2nd Term in India (1932–41).

84 HM1-503, Box 10, folder 4, 2nd Term in India (1932–41).

85 Communication from Eleanor Kreider, January 24, 1921; Adams, "Homiletical Innovations."

86 J. D. Graber to Minnie Graber, November 3, 1932, HM1-503, Box 10, folder 4, 2nd Term in India (1932–41).

87 J. D. Graber to Minnie Graber, December 5, 1932, HM1-503, Box 10, folder 4, 2nd Term in India (1932–41).

88 J. D. Graber to Minnie Graber, October 5, 1932; J. D. Graber to Minnie Graber, November 3, 1932.

89 J. D. Graber to Minnie Graber, October 29, 1932.

90 Ruth, *Maintaining the Right Fellowship*, 417–18, 453–54, 471.

91 J. D. Graber to Minnie Graber, November 3, 1932; J. D. Graber to Minnie Graber, November 17, 1932, HM1-503, Box 10, folder 4, 2nd Term in India (1932–41).

92 J. D. Graber to Minnie Graber, November 21, 1932, HM1-503, Box 10, folder 4, 2nd Term in India (1932–41).

93 Ruth, *Maintaining the Right Fellowship*, 433; Hostetler, "Defensive Structuring and Codification," 434–35; J. D. Graber to Minnie Graber, March 27, 1933, HM1-503, Box 15, folder 7, Princeton Letters, 1933.

94 J. D. Graber to Minnie Graber, December 5, 1932; J. D. Graber to Minnie Graber, March 13, 1933, HM1-503, Box 15, folder 7, Princeton Letters, 1933; J. D. Graber to Vernon E. Reiff, March 14, 1933, IV-7-01, Box 5, folder 7, Graber, J. D., 1931–34; J. D. Graber to Minnie Graber," March 27, 1933; Minnie Graber, interview, January 22, 1980, Tape 6.

95 Ruth, *Maintaining the Right Fellowship*, 463; Hostetler, "Defensive Structuring and Codification," 441–42.

96 J. D. Graber to Minnie Graber, March 27, 1933; Ruth, *Maintaining the Right Fellowship*, 483–86; J. D. Graber to Vernon E. Reiff, April 3, 1933, IV-7-01, Box 5, folder 7, Graber, J. D., 1931–34.
97 J. D. Graber to Minnie Graber, March 27, 1933.
98 J. D. Graber to Minnie Graber, March 27, 1933.
99 J. D. Graber to Vernon E. Reiff, April 3, 1933.
100 Lapp, *Mennonite Church in India,* 62; "Proceedings of the Mennonite Board of Missions and Charities, 1930," May 3, 1930, IV-06-02, Box 2, Minutes 1927–33; Yates, *Christian Mission*, 82–86; Patterson, "Loss of a Protestant."
101 "Proceedings of the Mennonite Board of Missions and Charities, 1930"; Schlabach, *Gospel Versus Gospel*, 144.
102 Kniss, "The Bible in India," *Gospel Herald*; Esch, "Modernism in India," *Gospel Herald*; Kaufman, "What About the Next Generation?," *Gospel Herald*; Lapp, "What Shall the Answer Be?," *Gospel Herald.*
103 George J. Lapp, "Report of Meeting Held at East Chestnut Street Mennonite Church, July 22, 1929," IV-7-01, Box 10, Lapp, George J., 1921–45.
104 J. D. Graber to Minnie Graber, September 30, 1932; J. D. Graber to Minnie Graber, October 2, 1932; J. D. Graber to Minnie Graber, November 17, 1932.
105 J. D. Graber to S. C. Yoder, January 31, 1933, IV-7-01, Box 5, folder 7, Graber, J. D., 1931–34.
106 Musser, "Correspondence: New Holland," *Gospel Herald*; John H. Mosemann to J. D. Graber, February 3, 1933, HM1-503, Box 15, folder 7, Princeton Letters, 1933.
107 J. D. Graber to S. C. Yoder, March 22, 1934, and J. D. Graber to Vernon Reiff, March 23, 1934, IV-7-01, Box 5, folder 7, Graber, J. D., 1931–34.
108 Yoder, "Mission Board and Finances," *Gospel Herald*; Fahs, "Protestant Benevolent Giving."
109 "Report of the Twenty-Seventh Annual Meeting," *Gospel Herald.*
110 "Report of the Twenty-Second Annual Meeting," *Gospel Herald.*
111 Yoder, "Mission Board and Finances."
112 "Report of the Twenty-Fifth Annual Meeting," *Gospel Herald.*
113 Reiff, "Twenty-Eighth Annual Financial Report," *Gospel Herald.*
114 "Report of the Twenty-Fifth Annual Meeting," *Gospel Herald.*
115 Yoder, "Closing the Year," *Gospel Herald.*
116 Yoder, "Statement from the Mission Board," *Gospel Herald.*
117 Reiff, "Funds for Our General Mission Board," *Gospel Herald.*
118 "Notes from Our Mission," *Gospel Herald*; Reiff, "India Support Reductions, 1933," *Gospel Herald.*
119 S. C. Yoder to Edwin Weaver, June 9, 1931, IV-7-01, Box 20, folder 14, Weaver, Edwin I., 1928-43; Yoder, "Mission Board and Finances."
120 Yoder, "Our Home Coming Missionaries," *Gospel Herald*; "Minutes of the Executive Committee of the Mennonite Board of Missions and Charities," March 19, 1934, IV-06–02, Box 3, Minutes 1933–39.
121 Yoder, "Statement from the Mission Board"; Reiff, "Funds for Our General Mission Board"; Reiff, "Special Needs for Missions," *Gospel Herald*; Reiff, "Board's Finance Problem," *Gospel Herald*; "Special Foreign Missionary Needs," *Gospel Herald*; Yoder, "Closing the Year."
122 "An Income That Does Not Shrink," appearing nine times, labeled No. 1 to No.

9, December 17, 1931, to February 18, 1932, *Gospel Herald.*

123 Vernon Reiff to Mary Good, January 29, 1933, IV-7-01, Box 5, folder 3, Good, Mary, 1919–34; Reiff, "India Support Reductions, 1933"; "Minutes of the Executive Committee of the Mennonite Board of Missions and Charities," October 9, 1933, IV-06–02, Box 3, Minutes 1933–39.

124 Yoder, "Mission Board and Finances"; Yoder, "Closing the Year"; "Minutes of the Executive Committee of the Mennonite Board of Missions and Charities," March 19, 1934.

125 Vernon Reiff to J. D. Graber, February 13, 1933, HM1-503, Box 15, folder 7, Princeton Letters 1933; J. D. Graber to Vernon E. Reiff, October 2, 1933, IV-7-01, Box 5, folder 7, Graber, J. D., 1931–34.

126 J. D. Graber to Minnie Graber, January 7, 1933, HM1-503, Box 10, folder 4, 2nd Term in India (1932–41).

127 J. D. Graber to Minnie Graber, October 29, 1932 and J. D. Graber to Minnie Graber, November 9, 1932, HM1-503, Box 10, folder 4, 2nd Term in India (1932–41).

128 J. D. Graber to Minnie Graber, December 7, 1932, HM1-503, Box 15, folder 7, Princeton Letters 1933.

129 Yoder, "Mission Board and Finances."

130 "Meeting of the Executive and Mission Committees," February 13, 1934, IV-06-02, Box 3, Minutes 1933–1939; Yoder, "Plans for the Return of Missionaries," *Gospel Herald.*

131 S. C. Yoder to J. D. Graber, February 16, 1934, IV-7-01, Box 5, folder 7, Graber, J. D., 1931–34.

Chapter 3

1 J. D. Graber to Home Folk, August 13, 1936, HM1-503, Box 10, folder 4, 2nd Term in India (1932–41).

2 Lapp, *Mennonite Church in India,* 134.

3 Sharvananda, *Taittiriya-Upanishad,* 43.

4 Minnie Graber, interview, January 21, 1980.

5 J. D. Graber to Home Folk, August 13, 1936.

6 Weaver, *Irene Weaver, Reminiscing,* 9, 18–20; Personal communication from Eleanor Kreider, September 13, 2020.

7 Personal communication from Eleanor Kreider, November 11, 2020; Lapp, *Mennonite Church in India,* 131.

8 Personal communication from Eleanor Kreider, November 11, 2020.

9 J. D. Graber to Fellow Missionaries on Furlough, February 15, 1939, Box 12, folder 2, Miscellaneous Correspondence; J. D. Graber to S. C. Yoder, February 23, 1939 and J. D. Graber to S. C. Yoder, January 30, 1940, IV-07-01, Box 8, folder 1, India Mission—Sec. J. D. Graber, 1937–41; Burkholder et al., interview.

10 Minnie Graber, interview, January 21, 1980.

11 "Minutes of the Annual Business Meeting of the American Mennonite Mission," November 9, 1937, IV-17-1 folder AMM India Bus Mtg Minutes, 1933–39.

12 "Minutes of the Annual Meeting of the American Mennonite Mission," November 17, 1936, IV-17-1, folder AMM India Bus Mtg Minutes, 1933–39; "Report of the Thirty-First Annual Meeting," *Gospel Herald*; "Minutes of the Annual Business Meeting of the American Mennonite Mission," November 15, 1938,

IV-17-1, folder AMM India Bus Mtg Minutes, 1933–39; "Report of the Thirty-Third Annual Meeting," *Gospel Herald*; Minnie Graber, interview, January 22, 1980, Tape 6.

13 Lapp, *Mennonite Church in India,* 66.

14 Minnie Graber to Ones at Home, February 14, 1927, HM1-503, Box 10, folder 1, First Term in India (1925–31).

15 J. D. Graber to Fellow Missionaries on Furlough, February 15, 1939.

16 J. D. Graber to S. C. Yoder, January 10, 1940, IV-17-004, Box 2, folder 9, Corres 1940–44 J. D., Graber.

17 Minnie Graber, interview, January 21, 1980; J. D. Graber to Minnie Graber, January 7, 1933, HM1-503, Box 10, folder 4, 2nd Term in India (1932–41).

18 "Thirty-Ninth Annual Report," *Gospel Herald.*

19 Minnie Graber, interview, January 22, 1980, Tapes 6 and 7.

20 Shenk, "Henry Venn's Legacy"; Shenk, "Rufus Anderson and Henry Venn"; Shenk, *Henry Venn: Missionary Statesman.*

21 Keay, *India: A History*, chapters 18–19; Metcalf and Metcalf, *Concise History of Modern India*, 167–202.

22 Dube, "Issues of Christianity," 99–100.

23 Dube, "Paternalism and Freedom."

24 Philip, "Indigenous Church: An Indian View"; International Missionary Council, *Relation Between the Younger and the Older Churches*, 165–74; Beaver, "History of Mission Strategy," B58–72.

25 Lapp, *Christian Church and Rural India*, 4; Lapp, *Mennonite Church in India,* 97, 145, 195, 173; Shenk, *By Faith They Went,* 73.

26 Lapp, *Mennonite Church in India,* 160–63, 168, 170; "India Mennonite Conference," n.d., IV-18-10, Box 2, India—Church-Mission Relations, 1947–51.

27 Lapp, *Mennonite Church in India,* 174–76.

28 Kauffman, "Report of the Indian Mission in Twenty-Sixth Annual Report of the MBMC," May 22, 1932, IV-06-02, Box 2, Minutes 1927–33; Schlabach, *Gospel Versus Gospel*, 209; Belawa, "India Mennonite Church Report - 1939."

29 J. D. Graber, "Field Reports of Missions, India."

30 J. D. Graber to S. C. Yoder, March 30, 1938, IV-07-01, Box 8, folder 1, India Mission—Sec. J. D. Graber, 1937–41; Minnie Graber, interview, January 22, 1980, Tape 6.

31 J. D. Graber to J. N. Kaufman, January 19, 1939, HM1-503, Box 12, folder 2, Miscellaneous Correspondence.

32 J. D. Graber to S. C. Yoder, March 30, 1938; J. D. Graber to S. C. Yoder, August 24, 1939, IV-07-01, Box 8, folder 1, India Mission—Sec. J. D. Graber, 1937–41; J. D. Graber, "Why the A. M. Mission Should Turn Over Church Buildings to the Church Conference," August 24, 1939, IV-17-04, Box 2, folder 7, Corres 1939, J. D. Graber.

33 J. D. Graber, "Transfer of India Church Properties."

34 "Minutes of the Annual Business Meeting of the American Mennonite Mission," November 15, 1938; J. D. Graber to J. N. Kaufman, January 19, 1939.

35 J. D. Graber to S. C. Yoder, January 7, 1939, IV-07-01, Box 8, folder 1, India Mission—Sec. J. D. Graber, 1937–41; "India Mennonite Church Conference Report," *Gospel Herald.*

36 S. C. Yoder to J. D. Graber, June 28, 1938, IV-17-004, Box 2, folder 6, Corres

1937–38, J. D. Graber; J. D. Graber to S. C. Yoder, August 25, 1938, and S. C. Yoder to J. D. Graber, June 28, 1939, IV-07-01, Box 8, folder 1, India Mission—Sec. J. D. Graber, 1937–41; S. C. Yoder to J. D. Graber, August 31, 1939, and S. C. Yoder to J. D. Graber, October 25, 1939, IV-17-004, Box 2, folder 7, Corres 1939, J. D. Graber; S. C. Yoder to J. D. Graber, May 13, 1940, and S. C. Yoder, "Certified Copy of Authorization to Transfer Title of India Church Properties to India Mennonite Church Conference," February 20, 1941, IV-07-01, Box 8, folder 1, India Mission—Sec. J. D. Graber, 1937–41.

37 J. D. Graber to Emil W. Menzel, July 18, 1960, IV-18-13-02, Box 9, Menzel, Emil—Ex Sec Asia Near East Comm Div For Missions; personal communication with Wilbert R. Shenk, Joe's successor at MBMC, December 28, 2020. Property laws in India were archaic and subject to legal challenges that could take many years to resolve.

38 "Minutes of the Annual Meeting of the American Mennonite Mission," November 14, 1939, IV-17-1, folder AMM India Bus Mtg Minutes, 1933–39; J. D. Graber to S. C. Yoder, January 30, 1940; "Thirty-Fourth Annual Report of the Mennonite Board of Missions and Charities," May 5, 1940, 17, IV-06-03, Box 4, Annual Meetings Annual Reports, 1939–46.

39 J. D. Graber to S. C. Yoder, January 7, 1939.

40 J. D. Graber to S. C. Yoder, January 30, 1940; "Thirty-Fourth Annual Report of the Mennonite Board of Missions and Charities," 17.

41 J. D. Graber to S. C. Yoder, January 30, 1940.

42 J. D. Graber to Minnie Graber, February 16, 1947, HM1-503, Box 11, folder 2, Letters J. D. to Minnie, 1930–70; J. D. Graber, "Organization of the India Mission"; "Constitution of the India Mennonite Mission," 1946, IV-18-13-02, Box 5, India—Church—Mission Relation, 1959.

43 Personal communication from Eleanor Kreider, November 11, 2020.

44 Minnie Graber to Folks at Home, July 29, 1934, HM1-503, Box 10, folder 4, 2nd Term in India (1932–41).

45 Lapp, *Mennonite Church in India,* 131.

46 J. D. Graber, "India Mission News," *Gospel Herald* 31; J. D. Graber, "India Mission Page," *Gospel Herald.*

47 J. D. Graber, "The Strength and Weakness of Our Mennonite Heritage as Reflected in Our Mission and Church Work," 1940, HM1-503, Box 4, folder 76, Manuscripts.

48 J. D. Graber, "Sundarganj," *Gospel Herald*; J. D. Graber, "India Mission News," *Gospel Herald* 28; J. D. Graber, "In and About Dhamtari," *Gospel Herald*; J. D. Graber to D. D. Miller, April 1, 1937, IV-7-01, Box 5, folder 8, Graber, J. D., 1935–41.

49 Lapp, *Mennonite Church in India,* 118.

50 J. D. Graber to D. D. Miller, December 12, 1934, IV-7-01, Box 5, folder 7, Graber, J. D., 1931–34; J. D. Graber to Home Folk, September 5, 1935, HM1-503, Box 10, folder 4, 2nd Term in India (1932–41); J. D. Graber, "Teaching Scripture," *Gospel Herald*; J. D. Graber, "Reports on Teaching Evangelism," *Gospel Herald.*

51 Personal communication from Eleanor Kreider, January 24, 2021.

52 Lapp, *Mennonite Church in India,* 75, 89, 232.

53 J. D. Graber to Ones at Home, February 24, 1937, HM1-503, Box 10, folder 4,

2nd Term in India (1932–41); personal communication with Eleanor Kreider, November 11, 2020.

54 Personal correspondence from Eleanor Kreider, November 11, 2020.

55 Menzel, *A Missionary's Leisure*; J. D. Graber to Emil W. Menzel, November 24, 1958, IV-18-13-02, Box 9, Menzel, Emil—Ex Sec Asia Near East Comm Div For Missions.

56 J. D. Graber to Ronald Graber, September 6, 1937, HM1-503, Box 10, folder 4, 2nd Term in India (1932–41).

57 Minnie Graber, interview, January 22, 1980, Tape 7; Lapp, *Mennonite Church in India,* 76.

58 Metcalf and Metcalf, *A Concise History of Modern India*, 111.

59 Minnie Graber, "Let It Alone," *Gospel Herald*; Personal communication with Eleanor Kreider, November 11, 2020.

60 Hostetler and Hostetler, "Riding Third Class," *Gospel Herald.*

61 Troyer, "India Letter," *Gospel Herald*; J. D. Graber to Ones at Home, February 24, 1937 and J. D. Graber to Ones at Home, June 29, 1939, HM1-503, Box 10, folder 4, 2nd Term in India (1932–41); J. D. Graber to S. C. Yoder, April 12, 1941, IV-07-01, Box 8, folder 1, India Mission—Sec. J. D. Graber, 1937–41.

62 "India Mission Page: News," *Gospel Herald*; J. D. Graber to Ronald Graber, September 6, 1937; Minnie Graber, interview, January 22, 1980, Tape 7.

63 Minnie Graber, interview, January 21, 1980; Minnie Graber to Mother, January 23, 1936, HM1-503, Box 10, folder 4, 2nd Term in India (1932–41).

64 "Obituary of Fanny Graber"; communication with Eleanor Graber, January 26, 2021.

65 Latourette, *History of Christianity: Volume I*, 351, 386.

66 Oldham, "A Missionary Survey," 28–41; Donohugh, "Caste Movements"; International Missionary Council, *World Mission of the Church*; Pickett, *Christian Mass Movements.*

67 "Survey of the Year 1936," 33; Harper, *In the Shadow*, 307–13.

68 J. D. Graber to D. D. Miller, February 6, 1936, IV-7-01, Box 5, folder 8, Graber, J. D., 1935–41.

69 "Thirty-First Annual Report of the Mennonite Board of Missions and Charities," June 13, 1937, 129, IV-06-03, Box 4, Annual Meetings Annual Reports, 1933–38.

70 Lapp, *Mennonite Church in India,* 118–19.

71 Minnie Graber, "Minnie's Diary for Her Mother," 1930s, opposite 12 to opposite 16, HM1-503, Box 15.

72 Minnie Graber, "Minnie's Diary for Her Mother," opposite 15.

73 "To What Purpose Is This Waste?," *Gospel Herald.*

74 Minnie Graber, "Minnie's Diary for Her Mother," opposite 15.

75 J. D. Graber to The Mennonite Board of Missions and Charities, March 30, 1938, IV-17-004, Box 2, folder 6, Corres 1937–38 J. D. Graber; J. D. Graber, "Reports from Foreign Missions and the Mexican Border Work, India"; Hostetler, "Soul Winning Methods That Have Proved Successful in India"; Brunk, "Reports from Foreign Missions, India."

76 "Thirty-Sixth Annual Report of the American Mennonite Mission," *Gospel Herald*; Dube, *Untouchable Pasts*, 1, 11–12, 17, 32, 80, 85–86, 149–52; Dube, "Paternalism and Freedom"; McGavran, "My Pilgrimage in Mission."

77 A. C. Brunk, "A Caste Wide Survey of Our Mission Field," *Gospel Herald*; Brunk, "Reports from Foreign Missions, India."

78 Hostetler, "Soul Winning Methods That Have Proved Successful in India."

79 J. W. Pickett, D. A. McGavran, and G. H. Singh, *Christian Missions in Mid India* (The Mission Press, 1938), 2.

80 Pickett, McGavran, and Singh, *Christian Missions in Mid India*, 1–4.

81 Pickett, McGavran, and Singh, *Christian Missions in Mid India*, 24–33.

82 Beaver, "The History of Mission Strategy."

83 J. D. Graber to Home Folk, January 28, 1937, HM1-503, Box 10, folder 4, 2nd Term in India (1932–41).

84 S. C. Yoder to J. D. Graber, June 28, 1938 and J. D. Graber to S. C. Yoder, December 1, 1938, IV-17-004, Box 2, folder 6, Corres 1937–38 J. D. Graber; J. D. Graber to S. C. Yoder, August 24, 1939, and "The New Field Situation in the American Mennonite Mission," August 1939, IV-07-01, Box 8, folder 1, India Mission—Sec. J. D. Graber, 1937–41; J. D. Graber to S. C. Yoder, January 18, 1940, IV-17-004, Box 2, folder 9, Corres 1940–44, J. D. Graber.

85 Ward, "Towards a Theology of Missions"; Hoffman, "Development of Mission Theology"; Bassham, "Mission Theology."

86 Sharp, *School on the Prairie*, 171; J. D. and Minnie Graber to Folks at Home, December 4, 1925, HM1-503, Box 10, folder 1, First Term in India (1925–31); J. D. Graber to Till, June 8, 1927, HM1-503, Box 10, folder 7, Miscellaneous Correspondence (1920–70s); J. D. Graber to Minnie Graber, September 30, 1932, HM1-503, Box 10, folder 4, 2nd Term in India (1932–41).

87 J. D. Graber, "Evangelism in Its Biblical Setting," *Gospel Herald*; J. D. Graber, "The Power of the Gospel," *Gospel Herald*.

88 J. D. Graber, "Why I Am a Christian," April 19, 1934, *Gospel Herald*.

89 J. D. Graber, "Evangelism in Its Biblical Setting"; J. D. Graber, "The Road to Certainty," *Gospel Herald*; J. D. Graber, "Training in Christian Experience," *Gospel Herald*; J. D. Graber, "Power of the Gospel to Make Men Preach," *Gospel Herald*.

90 J. D. Graber, "Evangelism in Its Biblical Setting."

91 J. D. Graber, "Evangelism in Its Biblical Setting."

92 J. D. Graber, "Without Shedding of Blood," *Gospel Herald*; J. D. Graber, "Teaching Scripture," *Gospel Herald*; J. D. Graber, "Bazar Preaching," *Gospel Herald*; J. D. Graber, "The Cross of Christ," *Gospel Herald*; "Redeeming Heathen Words," *Gospel Herald*.

93 J. D. Graber, "Preaching the Gospel," *Gospel Herald*; J. D. Graber, "I Am the Truth," *Gospel Herald*; Race, *Christians and Religious Pluralism*.

94 J. D. Graber, "Preaching the Gospel"; Farquhar, *The Crown of Hinduism*.

95 Pickett, *Christian Mass Movements*, 45, 330–60.

96 Pickett, McGavran, and Singh, *Christian Missions in Mid India*, 3–4, 24–33; J. D. Graber to Home Folk, January 28, 1937; J. D. Graber to S. C. Yoder, August 24, 1939.

97 Pickett, McGavran, and Singh, *Christian Missions in Mid India*, 3.

98 J. D. Graber to Eugene R. Braum, February 12, 1964, IV-18-13-02, Box 8, folder 25, McGavran, Donald, 1956–64; Shenk, ed., *Challenge of Church Growth*.

99 J. D. Graber, "Call from India," *Gospel Herald*.

100 Hartley, "Mission: Agnes C. L. Donohugh"; Kraemer, *Christian Message*, 341–43.

101 I am indebted to Wilbert R. Shenk for suggesting the helpful term *incubator* here. It describes well this period of missiological reassessment within the larger Protestant mission movement in general and for Joe in particular.

Chapter 4

1 J. D. Graber, "Missions Editorial: Shall We Expand?," *Gospel Herald.*

2 J. D. Graber, "The Church at Work"; J. D. Graber to Glen Graber, September 28, 1951, IV-18-10, Box 2, folder 33 G; J. D. Graber, "Report on Trip to Latin America."

3 Harold Eshleman to Members of the General Board, May 5, 1952, IV-18-10, Box 3, folder 14, Israel Evangelism Committee, 1952–55.

4 Wilbert Shenk described this dynamic as Mennonites having discovered "a new sense of responsibility for the world." Shenk, *By Faith They Went*, 85.

5 Church Missionary Society, *The Church Missionary Atlas*; Dennis, Beach, and Fahs, *World Atlas of Christian Missions*; Snead and Christian and Missionary Alliance, *Missionary Atlas.*

6 J. D. Graber, "Sermon Notes—The Church's Mission Program—A Gospel Crusade," March 9, 1950, HM1-503, Box 1, folder 29, Sermon Notes, 1950, a sermon Joe preached at least six times, once a few weeks before the December 1951 meeting. Pierard, "Pax Americana," 166–69.

7 J. D. Graber, "Radio Sermon—Making Non-Resistance Live," 1950, HM1-503, Box 4, folder 49, Manuscripts; J. D. Graber, "Nonresistance and Mission," presented at the MCC Peace Section Conference at Winona Lake, IN, 1950.

8 J. D. Graber to John H. Mosemann, January 21, 1952, IV-18-10, Box 4, folder 39, Mosemann, John H., Confidential, 1951–54; "Minutes of the Mission Council," January 28, 1952, IV-18-10, Box 1, folder 18, Argentina Mennonite Mission Council, 1951–55.

9 "Quarterly Notes"; "Quarterly Notes IMC October 1940."

10 S. C. Yoder to J. G. Graber, November 19, 1940, IV-07-01, Box 8, folder 1, India Mission—Sec. J. D. Graber, 1937–41.

11 "Field Notes," *Gospel Herald* 34, 1024.

12 Minnie Graber, interview, January 22, 1980, Tape 7.

13 "Report of the Thirty-Sixth Annual Meeting of the Mennonite Board of Missions and Charities," *Gospel Herald.*

14 Lapp, "With the Bible Women."

15 "Field Notes," *Gospel Herald* 34, 1024.

16 Howard Donovan, "American Consulate in Bombay to Americans in India," April 21, 1942, HM1-503, Box 10, folder 6, Mission Work Related Correspondence; C. F. Barnard to American President Lines Limited Passenger, May 19, 1942, HM1-503, Box 12, folder 2, Miscellaneous Correspondence; Yoder, "Our India Missionaries," *Gospel Herald.*

17 "Report of the Thirty-Sixth Annual Meeting of the Mennonite Board of Missions and Charities," 323; Vinson and Casey, "S.S. Brazil, Timeline (1928–1964)." With the Grabers were Sarah Lapp and the families of Edwin and Irene Weaver, George and Ida Beare, and Lloy and Elizabeth Kniss.

18 C. F. Barnard to American President Lines Limited Passenger, May 19, 1942; Bill Vinson and Ginger Quering Casey, "Moore-McCormack Lines, S.S. Brazil, Timeline (1928–1964)"; Charles, *Troopships of World War II*, 161; Personal communi-

cation from Eleanor Kreider, January 24, 2021; Weaver, *Irene Weaver, Reminiscing,* 11–14.

19 Weaver, *Irene Weaver, Reminiscing,* 11–14; Minnie Graber, interview, January 22, 1980, Tape 7.

20 "Field Notes," *Gospel Herald* 35, 360.

21 Minnie Graber, interview by J. Nelson Kraybill, January 24, 1980, IV-18-12, Box 3, Tape 8; J. D. Graber to S. C. Yoder, December 4, 1942, IV-7-01, Box 5, folder 9, Graber, J. D., 1942–43.

22 "Field Notes," *Gospel Herald* 36, 120; "Special Meetings," *Gospel Herald*; S. C. Yoder to J. D. Graber, April 20, 1943, IV-7-01, Box 5, folder 9, Graber, J. D., 1942–43.

23 Hartzler, "News Notes from Our Church Schools," *Gospel Herald*; J. D. Graber, "Training in Christian Experience," *Gospel Herald.*

24 A. J. Metzler to J. D. Graber, April 29, 1943, HM1-503, Box 10, folder 7, Miscellaneous Correspondence (1920–70s); C. F. Yake to J. D. Graber, June 2, 1943, HM1-503, Box 10, folder 6, Mission Work Related Correspondence.

25 S. C. Yoder to J. D. Graber, May 27, 1943 and Harold S. Bender to J. D. Graber, July 7, 1943, HM1-503, Box 1, folder 21, Corr. India-China Relief, 1943–44.

26 Shenk, *By Faith They Went,* 71–73; Mumaw, "Editorial," *Gospel Herald*; "Report of the Thirty-Fifth Annual Meeting of the Mennonite Board of Missions and Charities," *Gospel Herald*, 229; "China, a Challenge," *Gospel Herald*; Mumaw, "For China," *Gospel Herald.*

27 Orie O. Miller to Samuel J. Goering and Joseph D. Graber, June 24, 1943 and Orie O. Miller to Samuel J. Goering and J. D. Graber, July 7, 1943, HM1-503, Box 1, folder 21, Corr. India-China Relief, 1943–44.

28 "Report and Recommendation from the Relief Committee to the Executive Committee Concerning Mennonite Service Units," February 12, 1943, IV-06-02, Box 3, Minutes 1939–44.

29 J. D. Graber to Minnie Graber, July 27, 1943, HM1-503, Box 11, folder 2, Letters J. D. to Minnie, 1930–70, undated; Hallman, "Dona Juana Passes On," *Gospel Herald.*

30 J. D. Graber to J. S. Yoder, December 1943, HM1-503, Box 10, folder 7, Miscellaneous Correspondence (1920–70s); Owen, "Air Transport in World War II."

31 J. D. Graber to Minnie, Ronald, and Eleanor Graber, November 13, 1943, HM1-503, Box 11, folder 7, Letters J. D. to Family, 1930–70.

32 J. D. Graber to Minnie, Ronald, and Eleanor Graber, January 25, 1944, HM1-503, Box 11, folder 7, Letters J. D. to Family, 1930–70.

33 Sam Goering and J. D. Graber to Orie O. Miller, December 13, 1943, HM1-503, Box 1, folder 21, Corr. India-China Relief, 1943–44; Sinclaire, "Survey of the Year 1943," 18; Horst, "Mennonite Relief Work in China," *Gospel Herald*; J. D. Graber, "China, a Need and a Problem," *Gospel Herald.*

34 J. D. Graber to S. C. Yoder, February 13, 1944, HM1-503, Box 1, folder 20, Correspondence, China Trip, 1943–44.

35 J. D. Graber and S. J. Goering to Orie O. Miller, November 13, 1943, HM1-503, Box 1, folder 21, Corr. India-China Relief, 1943–44.

36 J. D. Graber to Minnie, Ronald, and Eleanor Graber, January 25, 1944; Sam to J. D. Graber, February 7, 1944, HM1-503, Box 1, folder 18, Correspondence, Miscellaneous, 1942–58; "Relief Notes," *Gospel Herald.*

37 Willard H. Smith, "Yoder, Sanford Calvin (1879–1975)," in *Global Anabaptist Mennonite Encyclopedia Online*, accessed November 4, 2020, https://gameo.org/index.php?title=Yoder,_Sanford_Calvin_(1879–1975); Sharp, *My Calling to Fulfill*, 194.

38 "Report of the Thirty-Eighth Annual Meeting of the Mennonite Board of Missions and Charities," June 1944, 59–61, 85, 132–33, IV-06-3, Box 4, Annual Meetings Annual Reports, 1939–46, Annual Reports 1944.

39 "Report of the Thirty-Eighth Annual Meeting," 6.

40 "Report of the Thirtieth Annual Meeting," *Gospel Herald*; "Report of the Thirty-Second Annual Meeting," *Gospel Herald*; S. C. Yoder to J. D. Graber, June 28, 1939, IV-07-01, Box 8, folder 1, India Mission—Sec. J. D. Graber, 1937–41.

41 Minnie Graber, interview, January 24, 1980; Bender, interview.

42 Harold S. Bender to J. D. Graber, February 19, 1944, HM1-503, Box 1, folder 20, Correspondence, China Trip, 1943–44.

43 "In the Vale of Kidron," *Gospel Herald*; "Minutes of the Thirty-Eighth Annual Meeting of the Mennonite Board of Missions and Charities," *Gospel Herald*.

44 Erb, *Studies in Mennonite City Missions*.

45 Yoder, *Days of My Years*, 139–42; Yoder, "Mission Problems," *Gospel Herald*; J. D. Graber, interview by John S. Miller, January 31, 1973, HM6-81, Box 1, Tape 27.

46 "Minutes of the Thirty-Ninth Annual Meeting," *Gospel Herald*; J. D. Graber, "Half Century of Missionary Progress."

47 Hostetler, *God Uses Ink*, 236–47, 250; Schlabach, *Gospel Versus Gospel*, 224–62; Toews, *Mennonites in American Society*, 191–94, 199–206. The Mennonite Publishing House's average annual production of new imprints doubled during the postwar years, its net worth doubled between 1945 and 1955, and its sales tripled.

48 Pierard, "Pax Americana."

49 J. D. Graber, interview, January 31, 1973; "Report of the Thirty-Eighth Annual Meeting," 38.

50 J. D. Graber, interview, January 31, 1973; Toews, *Mennonites in American Society*, 184–87; The same dynamic occurred among veterans of World War II. Pierard, "Pax Americana," 170–75.

51 J. D. Graber, interview, January 31, 1973.

52 "Minutes of the Thirty-Ninth Annual Meeting," *Gospel Herald*.

53 "Resolutions," 35; *Report of the Forty-First Annual Meeting*, 19, 40–41, 127–28, 166. The Plan of Advance foresaw an increase in the annual budget for mission work from $116,201 to $246,833, not including relief efforts. *"Look on the Fields" of the Mennonite Church* (Mennonite Board of Missions & Charities, 1948), HM1-503, Box 2, folder 37, Sermon Notebook; "Reports from the Annual Mission Board Meeting," *Gospel Herald*.

54 J. D. Graber, "Today in Missions," *Gospel Herald* 41, 90; J. D. Graber, "Today in Missions," *Gospel Herald* 41, 402.

55 J. D. Graber, "Why I Am a Christian," December 3, 1925, *Gospel Herald*.

56 J. D. Graber, "Power of the Gospel to Make Men Preach," *Gospel Herald*.

57 J. D. Graber, "Pastor and Missions," *Gospel Herald*; J. D. Graber, "Sermon Notes—The Church's Mission Program—A Gospel Crusade," HM1-503, Box 1, folder 29, Sermon Notes, 1950.

58 J. D. Graber, "Sermon Notes—World Traveler," March 27, 1950, HM1-503, Box 1, folder 29, Sermon Notes, 1950.

59 J. D. Graber, "Mennonite Youth Fellowship," *Gospel Herald.*

60 E.g., "Echoes from Mackinaw Dells," *Gospel Herald*; J. D. Graber, "The Plan of Advance"; J. D. Graber, "Why Not a Youth Missionary Project?"; J. D. Graber, "The Christian Sense of Mission."

61 J. D. Graber, "Mennonite Youth Fellowship," *Gospel Herald*; J. D. Graber, "The Present Missionary Task."

62 J. D. Graber, "Mennonite Youth Fellowship," *Gospel Herald.* Note, for example, the 1948 to 1953 MBMC annual meetings and their accompanying MYF and missionary training events. "Echoes from Shenandoah," *Gospel Herald.*

63 J. D. Graber, "Report of the Secretary," 1949; J. D. Graber, "The Present Missionary Task"; J. D. Graber, "Missions Editorial: Shall We Expand?," *Gospel Herald.*

64 "Resolutions, Our Mission Outreach."

65 Hartzler, "Missions Editorial: A Major Crisis in Financing Missions," *Gospel Herald*; Mosemann, "Special Missions Week," *Gospel Herald*; Kauffman, "Does 'Missions Week' Mean a New Era in Church Finance?," *Gospel Herald.*

66 J. D. Graber, "The Church at Work."

67 "Report of the Thirty-Eighth Annual Meeting," 85, 132–33; *Report of the Forty-Eighth Annual Meeting*, 214–15.

68 *Report of the Forty-Eighth Annual Meeting*, 24; "Report of the Thirty-Eighth Annual Meeting," 35.

69 Beaver, "Expansion of American Foreign Missionary Activities"; Pierard, "Pax Americana," 158–59; Shenk, *By Faith They Went,* 77–79.

70 Conversation with Eleanor Kreider, December 4, 2020.

71 Bender, interview.

72 J. D. Graber to S. N. Solomon, November 6, 1951, IV-18-10, Box 5, folder 32, Solomon, Stephen—Confidential, 1951; J. D. Graber to Esther Graber, February 9, 1954, HM1-503, Box 11, folder 7, Letters J. D. to Family, 1930–70; J. D. Graber to Ron, Esther, and Jamie Graber, February 27, 1954, HM1-503, Box 11, folder 8, Letters J. D. to Ron Graber, 1943, 1954, 1956.

73 J. D. Graber to Anne Graber, March 23, 1946, and J. D. Graber to Mrs. C. M. Stoltzfus, March 23, 1946, HM1-503, Box 10, folder 6, Mission Work Related Correspondence.

74 Esther Graber et al., interview; conversation with Eleanor Kreider, December 4, 2020.

75 Showalter, "Mr. Missions," *Gospel Herald.*

76 J. D. Graber to Ones at Home, December 21, 1946, and J. D. Graber to Minnie Graber, February 18, 1947, HM1-503, Box 11, folder 7, Letters J. D. to Family, 1930–70.

77 J. D. Graber to Minnie Graber, February 16, 1947, HM1-503, Box 11, folder 2, Letters J. D. to Minnie, 1930–70.

78 "Mennonite Board of Missions and Charities Minutes of Conjoint Meeting of Executive and Missions Committee," May 7, 1948, IV-06-02, Box 3, Minutes 1944–48, Exec Committee.

79 J. D. Graber to Minnie Graber, February 18, 1947.

80 J. D.Graber to Minnie Graber, December 6, 1950 and J. D. Graber to Minnie Graber, January 19, 1951, HM1-503, Box 11, folder 2, Letters J. D. to Minnie, 1930–70, undated.

81 Conversation with Eleanor Kreider, May 10, 2021.

82 J. D. Graber to Mr. and Mrs. H. S. Martin, December 30, 1964, IV-18-13-02, Box 6, folder 9, India—Mennonite Medical Board, 1963–64.
83 Smith, *Trail to Santa Fe,* 178, 202.
84 Minnie Graber to J. D. Graber, undated, probably November 1949, HM1-503, Box 11, folder 1, Letters—Minnie, to J. D. (1940s, '50s, '60s, undated); J. D. Graber to Friends, October 30, 1947, HM1-503, Box 11, folder 3, J. D. and Minnie Updates to Family, 1947, 1950–60, updates.
85 J. D. Graber to Friends, October 30, 1947; J. D. Graber to P. J. Malagar, September 12, 1951, IV-18-10, Box 3, Malagar, P. J., 1951–55.
86 J. D. Graber to J. W. Samida, November 1, 1952, IV-18-10, Box 5, folder 4, Samida, J. W., Confidential, 1951–55,
87 J. D. Graber to S. N. Solomon, January 6, 1953, IV-18-10 MBM, Box 5, folder 31, Solomon, Stephen N., 1951–55; J. D. Graber to Mario Snyder, October 22, 1954, IV-18-10, Box 1, folder 54, Chicago Mexican Mission, 1951–55.
88 J. D. Graber to A. K. Biswas, July 30, 1953, IV-18-10, Box 3, India—Secretary, 1951–55.
89 J. D. Graber to P. J. Malagar, July 13, 1951, IV-18-10, Box 3, Malagar, P. J., 1951–55.
90 Conversation with Eleanor Kreider, December 4, 2020.
91 J. D. Graber to J. W. Samida, March 4, 1953, IV-18-10, Box 5, Samida, J. W., Confidential, 1951–55.
92 Timeline of J. D. Graber's life in the author's possession.
93 Minnie Graber to J. D. Graber, November 1946, and Minnie and Eleanor Graber to J. D. Graber, no date but probably November 1949, HM1-503, Box 11, folder 1, Letters—Minnie, to J. D. (1940s, '50s, '60s, undated).
94 J. D. Graber to Eleanor Graber, December 3, 1950, HM1-503, Box 11, folder 7, Letters J. D. to Family, 1930–70.
95 J. D. Graber to Dear Ones at 1525, December 4, 1949, HM1-503, Box 11, folder 7, Letters J. D. to Family, 1930–70.
96 Esther Graber et al., interview.
97 Minnie and Eleanor Graber to J. D. Graber, no date but probably November 1949.
98 J. D. Graber to Minnie Graber, January 19, 1947, HM1-503, Box 11, folder 2, Letters J. D. to Minnie, 1930–70, undated; J. D. Graber to Minnie Graber, February 18, 1947; Minnie Graber to J. D. Graber, February 27, 1947, HM1-503, Box 11, folder 1, Letters—Minnie, to J. D. (1940s, '50s, '60s, undated).
99 Minnie Graber to J. D. Graber, December 11, 1946, HM1-503, Box 11, folder 1, Letters—Minnie, to J. D. (1940s, '50s, '60s, undated).
100 J. D. Graber to Minnie Graber, February 18, 1947; J. D. to Minnie Graber, December 6, 1950; J. D. Graber to Minnie Graber, December 12, 1953, HM1-503, Box 11, folder 2, Letters J. D. to Minnie, 1930–70, undated.
101 Esther Graber et al., interview.
102 J. D. Graber to Ones at Home, December 12, 1949, HM1-503, Box 11, folder 7, Letters J. D. to Family, 1930–70; J. D. Graber to Minnie Graber, January 1, 1950, HM1-503, Box 11, folder 2, Letters J. D. to Minnie, 1930–70, undated.
103 J. D. Graber to Minnie Graber, January 4, 1951, HM1-503, Box 11, folder 2, Letters J. D. to Minnie, 1930–70, undated; Showalter, *Mennonite Community Cookbook.*

104 Esther Graber et al., interview.
105 J. D. Graber to Dear Ones at 1525, December 4, 1949.
106 Minnie Graber to J. D. Graber, January 13, 1952, and Minnie Graber to J. D. Graber, January 15, 1952, HM1-503, Box 11, folder 1, Letters—Minnie, to J. D. (1940s, '50s, '60s, undated).
107 J. D. Graber to Minnie Graber, March 7, 1951, HM1-503, Box 11, folder 2, Letters J. D. to Minnie, 1930–70, undated.
108 E.g., J. D. Graber to Dear Ones at Home, December 28, 1949, HM1-503, Box 11, folder 7, Letters J. D. to Family, 1930–70; J. D. Graber to Minnie Graber, January 4, 1951.
109 J. D. Graber to Ones at Home, January 6, 1954, HM1-503, Box 11, folder 7, Letters J. D. to Family, 1930–70.
110 Minnie Graber to J. D. Graber, December 26, 1960, HM1-503, Box 11, folder 1, Letters—Minnie, to J. D. (1940s, '50s, '60s, undated).
111 J. D. Gaber to Ronald Graber, November 26, 1946 and J. D. Graber to Ronald Graber, December 14, 1949, HM1-503, Box 11, folder 7, Letters J. D. to Family, 1930–70.
112 Ronal Graber to J. D. Graber, February 12, 1951, HM1-503, Box 11, folder 13, Letters Miscellaneous Family Correspondence.
113 Eleanor Graber to J. D. Graber, January 21, 1951, HM1-503, Box 11, folder 13, Letters Miscellaneous Family Correspondence; Minnie and Eleanor Graber to J. D. Graber, no date but probably November 1949.
114 J. D. Graber to Eleanor Graber, December 3, 1950.
115 J. D. Graber to Eleanor Graber, December 3, 1950.
116 Esther Graber et al., interview.
117 Conversation with Eleanor Kreider, May 10, 2021.
118 J. D. Graber to Missionaries of the Mennonite Board of Missions and Charities, January 19, 1953, IV-18-10, Box 4, Planting the Church, 1953; J. D. Graber to Foreign Missionaries of the MBMC, October 14, 1954, IV-18-10, Box 4, folder 70, Puerto Rico, 1952–54; J. D. Graber to John Litwiller, December 17, 1954, IV-18-10, Box 3, Litwiller, John and Mary Ann, Confidential, 1951–55; J. D. Graber to Edwin Weaver, January 12, 1955, IV-18-10, Box 5, Weaver, Edwin and Irene, 1951–55.
119 "Minutes of the Executive Committee," December 8, 1945, IV-06-02, Box 3, Minutes 1944–48, Exec Committee; "Mennonite Board of Missions and Charities Minutes of the Executive Committee," December 6, 1948, "Mennonite Board of Missions and Charities Minutes of the Executive Committee," July 22, 1948, and "Mennonite Board of Missions and Charities Minutes of Executive Committee," June 27, 1949, IV-06-02, Box 3, Minutes Exec Committee, 1948–50.
120 Allen, *Missionary Methods*.
121 Latourette, "Suggestion Toward a Reorientation"; Latourette, "Need for Missions"; Rankin, "New and Old in Missions"; Thompson, "New Approach in a New Day"; Davis, "Mission Strategy in the New Age."
122 J. N. Kaufman, "President's Report 1944," *Gospel Herald*.
123 Edwin Weaver to J. D. Graber, April 26, 1954, IV-18-10, Box 5, Weaver, Edwin and Irene, 1951–55.
124 J. D. Graber to S. N. Solomon and G. H. Beare, June 21, 1950, IV-18-10,

Box 2, folder 97, India—Church-Mission Relations, 1947–52; J. D. Graber to G. H. Beare, Arnold Dietzel, E. I. Weaver, and J. G. Yoder, July 25, 1950, IV-18-10, Box 2, India—Church-Mission Relations, 1947–51.

125 J. D. Graber, "New Day in Missions I," *Gospel Herald.*

126 J. D. Graber, "New Day in Missions II," *Gospel Herald.*

127 J. D. Graber, "New Day in Missions III," *Gospel Herald.*

128 J. D. Graber, "New Day in Missions IV," *Gospel Herald.*

129 Harold S. Bender, a filler quotation at the bottom of a page, *Gospel Herald* 43, no. 43 (October 24, 1950): 1046.

130 J. D. Graber, "By the Way I," *Gospel Herald*; J. D. Graber, "By the Way II," *Gospel Herald.*

131 J. D. Graber to Ronald Graber, December 30, 1950, HM1-503, Box 11, folder 7, Letters J. D. to Family, 1930–70; J. D. Graber, "By the Way IX," *Gospel Herald.*

132 J. D. Graber to India Missionaries, April 6, 1951, IV-18-10, Box 3, India—Unification Commission 1950–53; J. D. Graber to Samida, May 4, 1951, IV-18-10, Box 5, folder 4, Samida, J. W., Confidential, 1951–55; J. D. Graber to S. N. Solomon, November 6, 1951, IV-18-10, Box 5, folder 32, Solomon, Stephen, Confidential, 1951.

133 J. D. Graber to Wilber Hostetler, June 16, 1951, IV-18-10, Box 3, India—Unification Commission, 1950–53; J. D. Graber to Edwin Weaver, July 13, 1951, IV-18-10, Box 5, Weaver, Edwin and Irene, 1951–55; J. D. Graber to D. A. Sonwani, July 15, 1952, IV-18-10, Box 5, Solomon, Stephen N., Confidential, 1951, and Sonwani, D. A., 1952–54; Albert and Lois Buckwalter to Joe and Selena Shank, August 24, 1952, HM1-097, Box 4, Correspondence with J. W. Shank, 1952–70; J. D. Graber to Ralph Buckwalter, October 21, 1953, IV-18-13-01, folder 7, Japan—Correspondence, 1952–53.

134 S. N. Solomon to J. D. Graber, September 12, 1951, IV-18-10, Box 5, Solomon, Stephen N., Confidential, 1951, and Sonwani, D. A., 1952–54; Albert and Lois Buckwalter to Joe and Selena Shank, August 24, 1952; "Japan Missionaries to J. D. Graber," July 20, 1953, IV-18-13-01, folder 7, Japan—Correspondence, 1952–53; Irene Weaver to Esther Graber, October 25, 1953, IV-18-10, Box 5, Weaver, Edwin and Irene, 1951–55; John Litwiller to J. D. Graber, November 10, 1954, IV-18-10, Box 3, Litwiller, John and Mary Ann, Confidential, 1951–55; Hollinger-Janzen, *"New Day in Mission" Irene Weaver Reflects.*

135 J. D. Graber to Orie O. Miller, January 14, 1954, IV-18-10, Box 4, folder 20, Miller, Orie O., 1951–55; Nida, "Identification, a Major Problem"; Reyburn, "Identification in the Missionary Task"; Bonk, *Theory and Practice of Missionary Identification.*

136 J. D. Graber, "Missionary in Today's World," *Gospel Herald.*

137 J. D. Graber to Foreign Missionaries of the Mennonite Board of Missions and Charities, November 5, 1953, IV-18-10, Box 4, folder 31, Missionary Orientation, 1953–55.

138 J. D. Graber to Noah Reber, June 29, 1953, IV-18-13-01, folder 5, Japan—Reber Car, 1953.

139 J. D. Graber, "The Missionary in Today's World."

140 J. D. Graber to Missionaries of MBMC in Japan, April 25, 1953, IV-18-13-01, folder 7, Japan—Correspondence, 1952–53; Hershberger, "Neo-Anabaptist

Approach to Missions."

141 J. D. Graber to Noah Reber, June 29, 1953; J. D. Graber to Ralph Buckwalter, March 30, 1954, IV-18-13-01, folder 6, Japan—Correspondence, 1954–55; J. D. Graber to Ralph Buckwalter, Don Raber, Carl Beck, Don McCammon, and Lee Kanagy, May 15, 1954, IV-18-13-01, folder 6, Japan—Correspondence, 1954–55.

142 J. D. Graber to Fannie Lapp, April 21, 1954, IV-18-10, Box 3, folder 40, Lapp George J. and Fannie, 1951–55.

143 J. D. Graber to Missionaries of MBMC in Japan, April 25, 1953.

144 J. N. Kauffman, "Progress Toward Self-Support in the Indian Church," in *Report of the Twenty-Fifth Annual Meeting of the Mennonite Board of Missions and Charities*, 140; J. D. Graber to S. C. Yoder, January 7, 1939, IV-07-01, Box 8, folder 1, India Mission—Sec. J. D. Graber, 1937–41.

145 "Minutes of the Annual Business Meeting of the American Mennonite Mission," November 15, 1938, IV-17–1, folder AMM India Bus Mtg Minutes, 1933–39.

146 J. D. Graber to S. C. Yoder, January 7, 1939.

147 J. D. Graber to S. C. Yoder, January 30, 1940, IV-07-01, Box 8, folder 1, India Mission—Sec. J. D. Graber, 1937–41.

148 J. D. Graber to Minnie Graber, February 16, 1947, HM1-503, Box 11, folder 2, Letters J. D. to Minnie, 1930–70; J. D. Graber, "Organization of the India Mission," *Gospel Herald.*

149 J. D. Graber to Jonathan Yoder, April 20, 1948, J. D. Graber to Edwin Weaver, February 4, 1948, and J. D. Graber, "Procedures in the India Mennonite Mission, a Line of Reasoning," February 4, 1948, IV-18-10, Box 2, folder 97, India—Church-Mission Relations, 1947–52.

150 J. D. Graber to Jonathan Yoder, April 20, 1948.

151 International Missionary Council, "Partners in Obedience."

152 Edwin Weaver to J. D. Graber, April 21, 1948, IV-18-10, Box 2, folder 97, India—Church-Mission Relations, 1947–52; John A. Lapp, *Mennonite Church in India,* 181–82.

153 Jonathan Yoder to J. D. Graber, March 26, 1948, and R. R. Smucker to E. E. Miller and J. D. Graber, May 9, 1949, IV-18-10, Box 2, folder 97, India—Church-Mission Relations, 1947–52.

154 "Mennonite Board of Missions and Charities Minutes of Executive Committee," September 9, 1949, IV-06-02, Box 3, Minutes Exec Committee, 1948–50.

155 "Address Presented by the India Mennonite Conference to the Fraternal Delegates from America," November 27, 1949, IV-18-10, Box 3, India—Unification Commission, 1950–53; Lapp, *Mennonite Church in India,* 181–82.

156 "Remarks on Indianization," March 1950, S. N. Solomon to The Mission Board, February 7, 1950, and S. N. Solomon to J. D. Graber, February 7, 1950, IV-18-10, Box 2, folder 97, India—Church-Mission Relations, 1947–52.

157 J. D. Graber, "Special Actions, India Mission-Church Relationship," in *Report of the Forty-Fourth Annual Meeting,* 82–83; J. D. Graber to S. N. Solomon and G. H. Beare, June 21, 1950, IV-18-10, Box 2, folder 97, India—Church-Mission Relations, 1947–52.

158 J. W. Samida to J. D. Graber, October 11, 1950, George Beare to J. D. Graber, October 30, 1950, and George Beare to J. D. Graber, October 31, 1950, IV-18-10, Box 2, folder 97, India—Church-Mission Relations, 1947–52; Edwin Weaver to

J. D. Graber, October 20, 1951, IV-18-10, Box 5, Weaver, Edwin and Irene, 1951–55; J. D. Graber to Minnie Graber, March 7, 1951, HM1-503, Box 11, folder 2, Letters J. D. to Minnie, 1930–70, undated.

159 "Annual Business Meeting of the American Mennonite Mission 1950," December 12, 1950, IV-18-10, Box 2, folder 93, India—Minutes Annual Meeting, 1950–51; J. D. Graber, "Report on Central Provinces, India Mission," June 7, 1951, 87–89, IV-06-3, Box 4, Change to workbooks, Annual Reports, 1951.

160 J. D. Graber to India Missionaries, April 6, 1951, IV-18-10, Box 3, India—Unification Commission, 1950–53; J. D. Graber to George Beare, April 11, 1951, IV-18-10, Box 3, India—Secretary, 1951–55; J. D. Graber to Edwin Weaver, May 4, 1951, IV-18-10, Box 5, Weaver, Edwin and Irene, 1951–55; J. D. Graber to Samida, May 4, 1951, and J. D. Graber to Mr. Samida, June 26, 1951, IV-18-10, Box 5, folder 4, Samida, J. W., Confidential, 1951–55; J. D. Graber to P. J. Malagar, September 12, 1951, IV-18-10, Box 3, Malagar, P. J., 1951–55.

161 Lapp, *Mennonite Church in India,* 188–89.

162 J. D. Graber, "Special Actions, Argentine Mission-Church Policy," in *Report of the Forty-Fourth Annual Meeting*, 1950, 84–85; "Minutes of the Mission Council," January 28, 1952, IV-18-10, Box 1, folder 18, Argentina Mennonite Mission Council, 1951–55.

163 J. D. Graber to John H. Mosemann, January 21, 1952, IV-18-10, Box 4, folder 39, Mosemann, John H., Confidential, 1951–54.

164 J. D. Graber to Minnie Graber, January 24, 1952, HM1-503, Box 11, folder 2, Letters J. D. to Minnie, 1930–70, undated; J. D. Graber, "The Kingdom to the South VI," *Gospel Herald*; Albert and Lois Buckwalter to Joe and Selena Shank, August 24, 1952, HM1-097, Box 4, Correspondence with J. W. Shank, 1952–70; J. Delbert Erb, "Minutes of the Missionary Fellowship," June 22, 1953, IV-18-10, Box 1, Argentina Mennonite Mission Council, 1951–55.

165 J. D. Graber, "New Day in Missions III," *Gospel Herald.*

166 J. D. Graber to Missionaries of MBMC in Japan, April 25, 1953; J. D. Graber to Ralph Buckwalter, September 18, 1954, IV-18-13-01, folder 6, Japan—Correspondence, 1954–55.

167 David and Wilma Shank to John Mosemann and J. D. Graber, March 8, 1951, and David Shank to J. D. Graber, October 8, 1954, IV-18-10, Box 5, folder 10, Shank, David and Wilma, 1951–55; J. D. Graber to John H. Yoder, August 27, 1954, IV-18-10, Box 5, Yoder, John Howard, 1951–55.

168 J. D. Graber, interview, January 31, 1973; J. D. Graber, interview by John S. Miller, February 13, 1973, HM6-81, Tape 30.

169 J. D. Graber, interview, January 31, 1973.

170 Wittner, "MacArthur and the Missionaries."

171 J. D. Graber, *We Enter Japan*, 5, 10–11; Hershberger, "Neo-Anabaptist Approach to Missions."

172 J. D. Graber, *We Enter Japan,* 11.

173 J. D. Graber to Dear Ones at Home, December 12, 1949, HM1-503, Box 11, folder 7, Letters J. D. to Family, 1930–70; J. D. Graber, "Report of Mission Investigation in Japan," *Gospel Herald*; J. D. Graber, "Report on Japan," IV-18-13-01, folder 2, Japan—General, 1951–55.

174 J. D. Graber, "Report of Mission Investigation in Japan."

175 J. D. Graber, "Kingdom to the South VII"; J. D. Graber, "Report on Trip to

Latin America"; *Report of the Forty-Sixth Annual Meeting*, 97; *Report of the Forty-Eighth Annual Meeting*, 130.

176 J. D., Graber to the Executive Committee of the Mennonite Central Committee, January 25, 1954, IV-07-03, Box 1, J. D. Graber—Reports.

177 Orie O. Miller to J. D. Graber, March 25, 1953, and J. D. Graber to Orie O. Miller, March 30, 1953, IV-18-10, Box 4, Mennonite Central Committee, 1951–55.

178 J. D. Graber to John Litwiller, December 17, 1954, IV-18-10, Box 3, Litwiller, John and Mary Ann, Confidential, 1951–55.

179 J. D. Graber to Glen Graber, September 28, 1951, and J. D. Graber to Glen D. Graber, July 15, 1952, IV-18-10, Box 2, folder 33 G; J. D. Graber, "Report of the Mission Investigation in the Philippine Islands," in *Report of the Forty-Fourth Annual Meeting*, 75–76.

180 Gingerich, "North American Mennonite Overseas Outreach."

181 "Minutes of the Forty-First Annual Meeting," *Gospel Herald*, 406; "Report of the Work in Belgium," *Gospel Herald*.

182 "Mennonite Relief Program in France," *Gospel Herald*.

183 J. D. Graber, interview, January 31, 1973.

184 J. D. Graber, interview, January 31, 1973.

185 J. D. Graber, interview, January 31, 1973.

186 Mosemann, "Report of the Belgian Mission Study Committee," *Gospel Herald*; Long, "Church's Responsibility in Belgium," *Gospel Herald*.

187 J. D. Graber, "By the Way II," *Gospel Herald*.

188 Mosemann, "Report of the Belgian Mission Study Committee"; Long, "Church's Responsibility in Belgium."

189 J. D. Graber, "Today in Missions," *Gospel Herald* 41, 618.

190 J. D. Graber, interview, January 31, 1973. Joe appears to refer to Godin and Daniel, *La France, Pays de Mission?*

191 Peachey, "Why Europe?," *Gospel Herald*; Shank, "Missionary Approach to a Dechristianized Society."

192 "Special Actions: Belgium Mennonite Center."

193 "Special Actions: London Mennonite Center."

194 Blough, "Mission Efforts in Europe," 239.

195 J. D. Graber to Dave Shank and Orley Swartzentruber, December 17, 1951, IV-18-10 MBM, Box 5, folder 10, Shank, David and Wilma, 1951–55.

196 J. D. Graber, interview, January 31, 1973.

197 J. D. Graber to Dave Shank and Orley Swartzendruber, January 29, 1953, IV-18-10, Box 5, folder 10, Shank, David and Wilma, 1951–55; John H. Yoder to J. D. Graber, August 23, 1954, IV-18-10, Box 5, Yoder, John Howard, 1951–55; J. D. Graber to John H. Yoder, August 27, 1954.

198 Koop, *American Evangelical Missionaries in France*, 24, 48–49, 99–91.

199 Yoder, *Days of My Years*, 150–52.

200 John Horsch to S. C. Yoder, December 17, 1926, Fritz Goldschmidt to Brother in Christ, January 1927, S. C. Yoder to Fritz Goldschmit, May 31, 1929, S. C. Yoder to Fritz Goldschmit, June 12, 1930, and Fritz Goldschmidt to MBMC, October 9, 1930, IV-7-01, Box 5, folder 2, Goldschmit, Fritz, 1926–31.

201 "Report of Twenty-Sixth Annual Meeting," *Gospel Herald*, 392.

202 J. D. Graber, interview, January 31, 1973.

203 David Shank to J. D. Graber, May 24, 1952, and David Shank and Orlie Swartzentruber, *Report and Recommendation Belgium* and *Report and Recommendation* France, May 24, 1952, IV-18-10, Box 2, folder 28, France, 1951; J. D. Graber to David Shank and Orley Swartzentruber, July 3, 1952, IV-18-10, Box 5, folder 10, Shank, David and Wilma, 1951–55.
204 Bingle, "On Being Evangelized"; J. D. Graber to Quintus Leatherman, April 28, 1953, IV-18-10, Box 3, London, England, 1951–55.
205 J. D. Graber to E. J. Bingle, April 28, 1953, IV-18-10, Box 3, London, England, 1951–55.
206 E. J. Bingle to J. D. Graber, May 8, 1953, IV-18-10, Box 3, London, England, 1951–55.
207 Long, "Church's Responsibility in Belgium"; Orio O. Miller to Paul Mininger, H. S. Bender, and J. D. Graber, March 15, 1952, and Orie O. Miller to J. D. Graber, Henry N. Hostetter, A. E. Janzen, John Thiessen, and Henry F. Garber, April 4, 1952, IV-18-10, Box 4, Mennonite Central Committee, 1951–55; "Program on Relief," *Gospel Herald*; Blough, "Mission Efforts in Europe," 236–37; Hershberger, "Historical Background," 238.
208 J. D. Graber to Minnie Graber, January 19, 1947, HM1-503, Box 11, folder 2, Letters J. D. to Minnie, 1930–70, undated.
209 J. D. Graber, interview, January 31, 1973.
210 J. D. Graber, interview, January 31, 1973; J. D. Graber, *We Enter China*, 13, 22; J. D. Graber, "Today in Missions," *Gospel Herald* 42, 378; J. D. Graber, "Missions Editorial: Proclaiming Doctrine," *Gospel Herald*.
211 J. D. Graber, "Panorama of World Need," *Gospel Herald*.
212 J. D. Graber, "Missions Editorial: Proclaiming Doctrine."
213 J. D. Graber to Minnie Graber, January 19, 1947; J. D. Graber to Levi Hartzler, January 11, 1951, IV-18-10, Box 4, folder 1, MRC General, 1951–52.
214 J. D. Graber to J. L. Horst, July 31, 1947, and J. D. Graber to Milo Kauffman, July 31, 1947, IV-07-02, Box 3, folder 18, Graber, J. D., 1943–49; J. D. Graber, "Missions Editorial: Why Not a Mission Restaurant?," *Gospel Herald*.
215 J. D. Graber, "Today in Missions," *Gospel Herald* 42, 378.
216 J. D. Graber, "Supreme Motive for Missionary Endeavor," *Gospel Herald*.
217 J. D. Graber, "Missions Editorial: Proclaiming Doctrine."
218 Padilla, "Wholistic Mission"; Jayakumar, "Work of God as Holistic Mission"; Kirkpatrick, "C. René Padilla and the Origins of Integral Mission."
219 J. D. Graber, "Missions Editorial: Why Not a Mission Restaurant?."
220 J. D. Graber to Ralph Buckwalter, March 22, 1952, IV-18-13-01, folder 7, Japan—Correspondence, 1952–53.
221 J. D. Graber to John Driver, October 23, 1952, IV-18-10, Box 4, folder 74, MRSC—La Plata, Puerto Rico, General Policies, 1951–54; J. D. Graber to Lester Hershey, May 20, 1953, IV-18-10, Box 5, folder 54, Ulrich Foundation, 1952–55; "Review of Objectives and Methods of Our Mission-Service Program," August 1953, and "General Policies of the Mennonite Church in Puerto Rico," August 1953, IV-18-10, Box 4, folder 72, Puerto Rico, Confidential, 1953–55.
222 J. D. Graber to J. L. Horst, July 31, 1947; J. D. Graber to Milo Kauffman, July 31, 1947.
223 Whiteman, "Anthropology and Mission." Articles having to do with culture and anthropological subjects start to appear in the *International Review of Mission* in

1915. Smith, *International Review of Mission: Index*, 117–19.

224 "Smith, Edwin Williams (1876–1957)," History of Missiology, Boston University, accessed April 4, 2015, http://www.bu.edu/missiology/missionary-biography/r-s/smith-edwin-williams-1876–1957/.

225 Hartley, "Apostle of Ethnology"; Howell, "Anthropology and the Making of Billy Graham."

226 Kraemer, *Christian Message*, 341–43.

227 Harold S. Bender to John H. Mosemann, March 29, 1951, Harold S. Bender, "Report to the Seminary on the Conference on Missionary Linguistics," April 21, 1951, Levi C. Hartzler, "Conference on Missionary Linguistics and Anthropology," April 21, 1951, Harold S. Bender to J. D. Graber, May 3, 1951, IV-18-10, Box 3, Linguistics and Anthropology, 1951–53.

228 J. D. Graber to the Dean, Kennedy School of Missions, July 16, 1955, IV-18-10, Box 1, Buckwalter, Albert and Lois, Confidential, 1951–55; J. D. Graber to Quintus Leatherman, January 21, 1956, IV-18-03-02, Box 4, Ghana, 1956; J. D. Graber to Albert Buckwalter, April 5, 1956, IV-18-03-02, Box 2, Argentine Chaco, 1956–60.

229 J. D. Graber to Edwin Weaver, January 12, 1955, IV-18-10, Box 5, Weaver, Edwin and Irene, 1951–55; J. D. Graber to Albert Buckwalter, January 20, 1955, IV-18-10, Box 1, Argentina Chaco, 1951–55.

230 Shank and Shank, "Mission to the South American Indians."

231 Reyburn, *Toba Indians*, 47, 77; "Chaco Mission Directory"; Nelson Litwiller to J. D. Graber, November 4, 1953, IV-18-10, Box 1, Argentina Field Secretary, 1951–55.

232 Peron and Ministers, "Translation—On the Appointing of a Commission by the Ministry of Foreign Affairs and Worship, Said Commission Is to Study the Location of Religious Missions, Decree No. 15498," August 20, 1953, IV-18-10, Box 1, Argentina Field Secretary, 1951–55; Ceriani Cernadas, "Misión, Nación y Religion," 83; Bianchi, *Historia de Las Religiones En La Argentina*, Kindle Edition location 3299–3342.

233 "Minutes of the Mission Council," January 28, 1952, IV-18-10, Box 1, folder 18, Argentina Mennonite Mission Council, 1951–55.

234 Albert Buckwalter, "Are We Adequately Meeting the Needs of the Indian Through the Spanish and Interpreters? Or Should the Mission Officially Take Steps to Put the Toba in Writing?," December 31, 1951, HM1-097, Box 9, Folder 4, unpublished manuscripts, 1951–65; J. D. Graber, "Report on Trip to Latin America"; "Minutes of the Chaco Mission Council," December 12, 1953, IV-18-10, Box 1, Argentina Chaco, 1951–55.

235 Nelson Litwiller to Albert Buckwalter and Wife and John Litwiller and Wife, October 22, 1953, IV-18-10, Box 1, Argentina Field Secretary, 1951–55; "Minutes of the Chaco Mission Council," December 12, 1953; Nelson Litwiller to J. D. Graber, December 31, 1953, IV-18-10, Box 1, Argentina Field Secretary, 1951–55;.

236 Nelson Litwiller to J. D. Graber, April 7, 1954, IV-18-10, Box 1, Argentina Field Secretary, 1951–55; Albert Buckwalter to J. D. Graber, May 1, 1954, IV-18-10, MBM Office of the Secretary, 1941–57, Box 1, Argentina Chaco, 1951–55.

237 Nelson Litwiller to J. D. Graber, May 17, 1954, IV-18-10, Box 1, Argentina Field Secretary, 1951–55.

238 Albert Buckwalter, "Minutes of the Chaco Mission Council," August 18, 1954, and Nelson Litwiller to J. D. Graber, August 26, 1954, IV-18-10, Box 1, Argentina Field Secretary, 1951–55.

239 Buckwalter, "Minutes of the Chaco Mission Council," August 18, 1954.

240 Nelson Litwiller to J. D. Graber, August 26, 1954; Buckwalter, "Conversion in the Chaco."

241 J. D. Graber to Members of the Executive Committee of the Mennonite Board of Missions and Charities, October 5, 1954, IV-18-10, Box 1, Argentina Field Secretary, 1951–55.

242 Reyburn, *Toba Indians*; J. D. Graber to Edwin Weaver, August 3, 1955, IV-18-10, Box 5, Weaver, Edwin and Irene, 1951–55; Edwin Weaver to J. D. Graber, September 29, 1955, IV-18-10, Box 5, Weaver, Edwin and Irene, Confidential, 1955.

243 Altman, "Dissolution of Nam Cum." Previously published as Altman, "Disolucíon de Nam Cum."

Chapter 5

1 Gerber, "What and Where of Dillonvale," *Gospel Herald.*

2 Gerber, "The What and Where," 646–47; Gerber, "Tenth Anniversary at Dillonvale."

3 Schlabach, *Gospel Versus Gospel*, 224–62; Hartzler, "Why a Mission Sunday School?," *Gospel Herald.*

4 As Guy F. Hershberger observed. See Schlabach, *War, Peace, and Social Conscience*, 508.

5 Schlabach, *Gospel Versus Gospel*, 224–62; Wenger, "Study of Rural Missions," 126–73.

6 Schlabach, *Gospel Versus Gospel, 225.*

7 Survey of the *Rural Evangel*, the periodical of the Indiana-Michigan Conference's mission board (later the *Gospel Evangel*), from the 1920s and 1930s.

8 J. D. Graber, "Utilizing Our Resources." Theron Schlabach suggested that the slogan "every congregation a mission outpost" was a motivating factor in Mennonite congregations by the 1930s, referencing Wenger's "Study of Rural Missions" to that effect. Wenger, however, refers to "outposts" but not the slogan as such. If the slogan had been used widely before Joe's tenure at MBMC, it would have been something more akin to the earlier version, "a mission outpost for every congregation," and not the later formulation that came into use in the 1950s. It is most likely that the slogan, in its earlier and later versions, and its use as a rallying cry originated with Joe after he took over the role of executive secretary. Wenger was simply using terms contemporary with the writing of his thesis to describe the increase in congregational mission activity earlier in the century. Schlabach, *Gospel Versus Gospel*, 230; Wenger, "Study of Rural Missions"; Linden N. Wenger to J. D. Graber, February 2, 1955, and J. D. Graber to Linden N. Wenger, February 4, 1955, IV-18-10, Box 5, folder 62 V, 1951–55.

9 J. D. Graber to Vernon E. Reiff, April 3, 1933, IV-7-01, Box 5, folder 7, Graber, J. D., 1931–34.

10 J. D. Graber, "Utilizing Our Resources."

11 Mumaw, "Current Forces Adversely Affecting"; Baker, "Effects of Urbanization"; Hershberger, "Maintaining the Mennonite Rural Community."

12 J. D. Graber, "Utilizing Our Resources."

13 "Minutes of the Thirty-Ninth Annual Meeting," *Gospel Herald*, 267; J. D. Graber, "Youth at Work," *Gospel Herald*; J. D. Graber, "Christian Strategy in Rural Missions," *Gospel Herald*; J. D. Graber, "Missionary Day, November 16," *Gospel Herald*; J. D. Graber, "Mennonite Youth Fellowship," *Gospel Herald*.
14 J. D. Graber, "Report of the Secretary of Missionary Education," 1946; J. D. Graber, "Mission Outpost of the Congregation," *Gospel Herald*.
15 Metzler, "Making Each Congregation a Center," *Gospel Herald*; "Mission Notes," *Gospel Herald*; Willard Roth et al., interview by John M. Bender, August 31, 1987, IV-18-12, Box 3, Tape 13; Ken Weaver et al., interview by John M. Bender, December 31, 1987, IV-18-12, Box 3, Tape 16; Blosser Yoder, *The Same Spirit*, 152.
16 Metzler, "Making Each Congregation a Center."
17 "Forward in 1953–55," June 1953, and Minutes of a Meeting of Committee on Coordination of Church Program, April 8, 1954, IV-18-10, Box 1, folder 65, Coordination Committee, 1951–55.
18 Schlabach, *Gospel Versus Gospel*, 228–29; Preheim, *In Pursuit of Faithfulness*, 182–83; "Our Growing Mission Program."
19 Hartzler, "Why a Mission Sunday School?"
20 J. D. Graber, "Mission Outpost of the Congregation."
21 J. D. Graber, "Mission Outpost of the Congregation."
22 J. D. Graber, "Missions Editorial: Out-Post or In-Branch," *Gospel Herald*.
23 J. D. Graber to Linden N. Wenger, February 4, 1955.
24 Linden N. Wenger to J. D. Graber, February 2, 1955; J. D. Graber to Linden N. Wenger, February 4, 1955.
25 *Ohio Mission Evangel* 2, no. 1 (March 1948); *Ohio Evangel* 7, no. 1 (January–February 1953): 4; *Ohio Evangel* 15, no. 5 (September–October 1961).
26 Erb, "Mennonite Church and Hospital Work"; "In the Vale of Kidron," *Gospel Herald*; J. D. Graber, "Our New Hospital and Nurses' Training School" *Gospel Herald*.
27 Dougall, "Reason for Medical Missions"; Erb, "Nursing Education in the Mennonite Church," *Gospel Herald*; J. D. Graber, "Our New Hospital and Nurses' Training School"; J. D. Graber, "The Church and Medicine," 1946, HM1-503, Box 4, folder 4, Manuscripts—The Church and Medicine; Erb, "New Frontiers in World Evangelism," *Gospel Herald*; Erb, "Rebirth in Missions," *Gospel Herald*.
28 Ressler, "Nursing as a Profession," *Gospel Herald*; Ressler, "Nursing as a Profession," *Gospel Herald*.
29 J. D. Graber, "Mennonite Hospital and Nursing School," *Gospel Herald*; J. D. Graber, "Mennonite Hospital and School of Nursing," *Gospel Herald* 38, 672; J. D. Graber, "Hospital Planning Committee," in *Report of the Fortieth Annual Meeting of the Mennonite Board of Missions and Charities* (Elkhart, IN: Mennonite Board of Missions and Charities, 1946), 30–32; Graber, "The Church and Medicine"; J. D. Graber, "A Christian Witness Through Hospital Service," *Christian Monitor* 38 (March 1946): 78, 96.
30 J. D. Graber, interview, February 13, 1973.
31 J. D. Graber, "Mennonite Hospital and School of Nursing," *Gospel Herald* 38, 768; J. D. Graber, "Mennonite Hospital and School of Nursing," *Gospel Herald* 38, 784; J. D. Graber to Anne Graber, March 23, 1946, HM1-503, Box 10, folder 6, Mission Work Related Correspondence.

32 J. D. Graber, "Mennonite Hospital and School of Nursing," *Gospel Herald* 38, 672.

33 J. D. Graber, "Mennonite Hospital and Nursing School"; Kreider, "Mennonite Hospital and School of Nursing," *Gospel Herald* 38, 688; J. D. Graber, "Hospital Committee," in *Report of the Thirty-Ninth Annual Meeting of the Mennonite Board of Missions and Charities*, 1945, 23.

34 "Minutes of the Forty-First Annual Meeting of the Mennonite Board of Missions," *Gospel Herald,* 409.

35 J. D. Graber, "Elkhart Hospital Developments," *Gospel Herald*; "Report of the Forty-Third Annual Meeting of the Mennonite Board of Missions and Charities," *Gospel Herald,* 683–84.

36 "Reports from the Annual Mission Board Meeting," *Gospel Herald,* 968; J. D. Graber, "Today in Missions," *Gospel Herald* 42, 430; J. D. Graber, "Today in Missions," *Gospel Herald* 42, 482; Dye, "Our Nursing Power Problem," *Gospel Herald*; "Annual Mission Board Report," *Gospel Herald,* 663.

37 J. D. Graber, interview, February 13, 1973; "Report of the Forty-Third Annual Meeting of the Mennonite Board of Missions and Charities," *Gospel Herald,* 679.

38 "Doctors Serving Overseas under the MBMC," May 1967, IV-18-13-03, Box 5, Mennonite Medical Association, 1966–69.

39 Zimmerman, "Organization of a Mennonite Nurses' Association," *Gospel Herald.*

40 "Field Notes," *Gospel Herald* 38, 296.

41 E.g., "Report of the Forty-Third Annual Meeting of the Mennonite Board of Missions and Charities," *Gospel Herald,* 675, as well as the reports of the other MBMC annual meetings of the period.

42 J. D. Graber, "Today in Missions," *Gospel Herald* 42, 506.

43 "Report of the Forty-Third Annual Meeting of the Mennonite Board of Missions and Charities," *Gospel Herald,* 678–79; "Reports from the Home Missions and Institutions," *Gospel Herald,* 673; "Statement Concerning Care of Children at the West Liberty Children's Home," April 1953, IV-18-10, Box 4, folder 6, Mennonite Children's Home General West Liberty, Ohio, 1951–55;. J. D. Graber, interview, February, 13, 1973.

44 "Annual Mission Board Report," *Gospel Herald,* 652.

45 "Mennonite Board of Missions and Charities Minutes of Executive Committee," May 17, 1949, IV-06-02, Box 3, Minutes Exec Committee, 1948–50; "Reorganization Plan for Child Welfare," May 17, 1949, IV-18-10, Box 4, folder 6, Mennonite Children's Home General West Liberty, Ohio, 1951–55.

46 "Reorganization Plan for Child Welfare"; J. D. Graber, "Social Implications of the Gospel: Child Welfare and Social Service as a Christian Challenge," *Gospel Herald.*

47 "MBMC Meeting of the Child Welfare Committee," May 8, 1953, and "Child Welfare by Mennonite Families, Communities and Institutions," May 8, 1953, IV-18-10, Box 1, folder 55, Child Welfare, 1951–55.

48 "Minutes of Committee on Child Welfare," May 10, 1951; J. D. Graber to C. Richard Yoder, September 4, 1953, and C. Richard Yoder, "Bibliography on Child Development," August 1953, IV-18-10, Box 1, folder 55, Child Welfare, 1951–55.

49 "Minutes of Committee on Child Welfare"; Stoltzfus, "Report of the Child Welfare Committee," *Gospel Herald*; "MBMC Meeting of the Child Welfare Committee."

50 J. D. Graber, "Social Implications of the Gospel: Child Welfare and Social Service as a Christian Challenge"; see also J. D. Graber, *Church Apostolic*, 82–83.

51 J. D. Graber, "The Social Implications of the Gospel: Child Welfare and Social Service as a Christian Challenge."

52 J. D. Graber to Ernest Bennett and John H. Yoder, January 29, 1960, IV-18-13-02, Box 1, Administrative Travel—JD Graber, 1959–60.

53 Robert, "Cooperation, Christian Fellowship, and Transnational Networking," 20–27; see Andrews, "India and Segregation"; Scott, "Christian Churches and the Colour Bar"; G. B. A. Gerdener, "Crux of the Racial Situation in South Africa"; Mokitimi, "Apartheid and the Christian Spirit"; Goodall, "Dilemma of Race Relations."

54 Burkhart, "Our World Missionary Outlook," *Gospel Herald*; Lapp, "My Colored Brother," *Gospel Herald.*

55 J. D. Graber, "Call from India," *Gospel Herald.*

56 Horst, "Mennonites and the Race Question," *Gospel Herald*; Gingerich, "The Color Line," *Gospel Herald*; Lind, "Biblical Principles Governing Race Relations," *Gospel Herald* 47; Shenk, "God Deals with Race Prejudice," *Gospel Herald*; Miller Shearer, "A Pure Fellowship," 40–49.

57 J. D. Graber, "Today in Missions," *Gospel Herald* 41, 966; J. D. Graber, "Today in Missions," *Gospel Herald* 42, 554; J. D. Graber, "Today in Missions," *Gospel Herald* 42, 602.

58 "Editorial: Sharpening the Conscience," *Gospel Herald*; "Statement of Concerns," *Gospel Herald.*

59 "Way of the Cross in Race Relations," *Gospel Herald*; "General Conference Day by Day," *Gospel Herald.*

60 J. D. Graber, "Today in Missions," *Gospel Herald* 41, 966; J. D. Graber to Foreign Missionaries of MBMC, February 21, 1950, IV-18-13-01, folder 11, Troyer, G. D.—Correspondence, 1946–50.

61 J. D. Graber, "Half Century of Missionary Progress."

62 Acts 10:34–37; Acts 17:26; J. D. Graber, "Today in Missions," *Gospel Herald* 42, 554.

63 J. D. Graber to S. C. Yoder, January 30, 1940, IV-07-01, Box 8, folder 1, India Mission—Sec. J. D. Graber, 1937–41; J. D. Graber, "Annual Business Meeting of the American Mennonite Mission," *Gospel Herald*; J. D. Graber, "Today in Missions," *Gospel Herald* 41, 966.

64 J. D. Graber, "Today in Missions," *Gospel Herald* 41, 474; J. D. Graber, "Today in Missions," *Gospel Herald* 42, 602; J. D. Graber to J. I. Byler, March 3, 1952, IV-18-10, Box 1, folder 52, Chicago Home Mission, 1952–55.

65 J. D. Graber, "Mennonite Commission for Christian Education and Young People's Work, Report of the Secretary for Missionary Education," HM1-503, Box 7, folder 28; Erb, *The Christian and Race.*

66 E.g., Henry Smith Leiper, *Blind Spots: Experiments in the Self-Cure of Race Prejudice*, 2nd ed. (Friendship Press, 1944); Ethel Alpenfels, *Sense and Nonsense About Race*, Study and Action Pamphlets on Race Relations (Friendship Press, 1946).

67 J. D. Graber to G. D. Troyer, August 22, 1949, IV-18-13-01 MBM Overseas Ministries Division 1947–55, folder 11, Troyer, G. D.—Correspondence, 1946–50.

68 J. D. Graber to Vern Miller, April 5, 1954, Vern Miller to D. J. Mishler, May 21,

1954, and J. D. Graber to Vern Miller, August 5, 1954, IV-18-10 MBM Office of the Secretary 1941–57, Box 1, folder 61, Cleveland, Ohio, Mennonite Mission,1951–55.

69 James H. Lark to J. D. Graber, February 13, 1952, IV-18-13-02 MBM Overseas Ministries Division 1956–1965, Box 3, folder 49, Chicago Bethel Mission, 1956–57; Le Roy Bechler to J. D. Graber, February 29, 1952, IV-18-10 MBM Office of the Secretary 1941–57, Box 5, folder 3, Saginaw, Michigan, 1951–55; J. I. Byler to J. D. Graber, March 6, 1952, IV-18-10 MBM Office of the Secretary, 1941–57, Box 1, folder 52, Chicago Home Mission, 1952–55.

70 Felipe Hinojosa, "Making Noise Among the 'Quiet in the Land': Mexican American and Puerto Rican Ethno-Religious Identity in the Mennonite Church, 1932–1982" (PhD diss., University of Houston, 2009), 25–29.

71 J. D. Graber to J. I. Byler, March 3, 1952; J. D. Graber to Leroy Bechler, March 4, 1952, IV-18-10 MBM Office of the Secretary 1941–57, Box 5, folder 3, Saginaw, Michigan, 1951–55.

72 J. D. Graber to J. I. Byler, March 3, 1952.

73 J. D. Graber to J. I. Byler, March 3, 1952.

74 Kauffman, "A Full-Time Secretary," *Gospel Herald*.

75 "Minutes of the Thirty-Eighth Annual Meeting of the Mennonite Board of Missions and Charities," *Gospel Herald*, 279; Erb, "Leaves from Oak Grove," *Gospel Herald*, 228; Mosemann, "Annual Mission Board Meeting at Maple Grove," *Gospel Herald*, 274.

76 "Field Notes," *Gospel Herald* 37, 416; "Field Notes," *Gospel Herald* 37, 632.

77 Toews, *Mennonites in American Society*, 168–69, 241–42.

78 "Mennonite Board of Missions and Charities Minutes of Conjoint Executive and Relief Committees," December 6, 1945, and "Mennonite Board of Missions and Charities Minutes of Conjoint Executive, Missions, and Relief Committees," April 18, 1947, IV-06-02, Box 3, Minutes 1944–48, Exec Committee.

79 J. D. Graber, "India Report on M. R. C. Relief Activities," April 16, 1947, IV-06-02, Box 1, Minutes, Report, Corr., 1923–62.

80 Mosemann, "Annual Mission Board Meeting at Maple Grove," 274.

81 J. D. Graber to John L. Horst and Paul Mininger, March 31, 1952, and Paul Mininger, John L. Horst, and J. D. Graber, "Progress Report on Canton, Ohio, Church-Mission Situation," April 21, 1952, IV-18-10, Box 1, folder 49, Canton Congregation—Confidential, 1951–52; J. D. Graber to Ezra Beachy, April 23, 1953, IV-18-10, Box 2, folder 7, Detroit Mission, 1951–55; J. D. Graber to Harold Zehr, April 15, 1953, and J. D. Graber to James Lark, Robert Stoltzfus, Boyd Nelson, Gordon Strichter, Clifford A. Hartman Howard Kauffman, and Edwin Stalter, September 3, 1953, IV-18-10, Box 2, folder 77, Hopkins Park Illinois, 1953–55.

82 John Mumaw to Harry Diener, Paul Lederach, John Mosemann, A. J. Metzler, J. D. Graber, and Nelson Kauffman, February 2, 1952, IV-18-10, Box 1, folder 65, Coordination Committee, 1951–55.

83 E.g., J. D. Graber to Foreign Missionaries of MBMC, February 21, 1950, IV-18-13-01, folder 11, Troyer, G. D.—Correspondence, 1946–50; J. D. Graber to Mr. and Mrs. Dave Shank and Mr. and Mrs. Orley Swartzentruber, December 1, 1951, IV-18-10, Box 5, folder 10, Shank, David and Wilma, 1951–55; J. D. Graber to Edwin Weaver, January 25, 1955, IV-18-10, Box 5, Weaver, Edwin and Irene, 1951–55.

84 J. D. Graber to Ralph Buckwalter, May 21, 1952, IV-18-13-01 MBM Overseas Ministries Division 1947–55, folder 7, Japan—Correspondence, 1952–53.
85 Burkholder et al., interview.
86 Minnie Graber, interview, January 24, 1980; Lapp, interview.
87 Burkholder et al., interview; Irene Weaver et al., interview.
88 William T. Snyder, interview by Alice W. Lapp, February 1, 1988, IV-18-12, Box 3, Tape 2.
89 J. D. Graber to Esther Graber, July 13, 1949, HM1-503, Box 10, folder 6, Mission Work Related Correspondence.
90 Esther Graber et al., interview.
91 "Meeting of the Executive and Missions Committees," June 11–12, 1953, IV-18-10, Box 1, folder 12, Annual Meeting, 1953; J. D. Graber to Superintendents of City Missions and Superintendents of Charitable Institutions, September 10, 1953, IV-18-10, Box 2, folder 23, Executive Committee, 1953–55.
92 J. D. Graber to Willard Liechty and Menno M. Troyer, April 19, 1952, IV-18-10, Box 1, folder 55, Child Welfare, 1951–55; J. D. Graber to Gordon Stichter, June 4, 1953, IV-18-10, Box 2, folder 77, Hopkins Park Illinois, 1953–55; J. D. Graber, "Mennonite Board of Missions and Charities," 1954, HM1-503, Box 4, folder 51, Manuscripts.
93 Minnie Graber, interview, January 24, 1980.
94 Ken Weaver et al., interview.
95 Roth et al., interview; Bender, interview.
96 Burkholder et al., interview; Bender, interview.
97 E.g., J. D. Graber to Foreign Missionaries of MBMC, February 21, 1950.
98 Esther Graber to J. D. Graber, February 1, 1952, IV-18-10, Box 2, folder 58, Graber, J. D., Trip to Latin America, 1951–52, Confidential.
99 Esther Graber et al., interview.
100 Roth et al., interview; Burkholder et al., interview.
101 Irene Weaver et al., interview.
102 "Mennonite Board of Missions and Charities Minutes of Conjoint Meeting of the Executive and Missions Committees," June 12, 1948, IV-06-02, Box 3, Minutes 1944–48, Exec Committee; "Report of the Forty-Third Annual Meeting of the Mennonite Board of Missions and Charities," *Gospel Herald*, 676.
103 "Reports from the Annual Mission Board Meeting," *Gospel Herald*.
104 "Report of the Forty-Third Annual Meeting of the Mennonite Board of Missions and Charities," 683–84.
105 J. D. Graber, "Report of the Secretary," June 12, 1952, 16–17, IV-06-3, Box 4, Change to workbooks, Annual Reports 1952.
106 J. D. Graber, "Mennonite Board of Missions and Charities," 1954, HM1-503, Box 4, folder 51, Manuscripts.
107 J. D. Graber to Missionaries of the MBMC in Continental USA, April 14, 1955, IV-18-10, Box 5, folder 56, Urban Evangelism Committee, 1951–55.
108 *Report of the Forty-First Annual Meeting*, 46.
109 Ken Weaver et al., interview; Stoneman, "Preparing the Soil for Global Revival"; Stoneman, "Radio: Missions: Station ELWA; Pellman, *Mennonite Broadcasts*, 18–21; "Mennonite Board of Missions and Charities Minutes of the Executive Committee," June 10–11, 1953, IV-18-10, Box 1, Annual Meeting 1953; "Special Actions and Resolutions," in *Report of the Forty-Seventh Annual Meeting*.

110 J. D. Graber to Minnie Graber, December 5, 1932, HM1-503, Box 10, folder 4, 2nd Term in India (1932–41); J. D. Graber, "Under Constraint to Preach—Sermon Preached at the Franconia Mennonite Board of Missions and Charities," May 4, 1943, HM1-503, Box 1, folder 27, Sermon Notes, 1941–45; J. D. Graber, "Power of the Gospel to Make Men Preach," *Gospel Herald.*

111 J. D. and Minnie Graber to Friends, October 30, 1947, HM1-503, Box 11, folder 3, J. D. and Minnie Updates to Family, 1947, 1950–60.

112 Lapp, interview; Snyder, interview; Gerig et al., interview; Guy F. Hershberger and Russel Krabill, interview by John M. Bender, August 31, 1987, IV-18-12, Box 3, Tape 11; Ken Weaver et al., interview; Bender, interview.

113 Snyder, interview.

114 Ken Weaver et al., interview.

115 Roth et al., interview.

116 Snyder, interview.

117 Roth et al., interview.

118 If one counts papers given at conferences or meetings and then printed as part of the proceedings, there are seven hundred and one published pieces.

119 J. D. Graber, *The Church Apostolic: A Discussion of Modern Missions* (Herald Press, 1960).

120 Search of digital copies of the *Gospel Herald.*

121 E.g., Minnie and Eleanor Graber to J. D. Graber, no date but probably November 1949, HM1-503, Box 11, folder 1, Letters—Minnie to J. D. (1940s, '50s, '60s, undated).

122 J. D. Graber to Family, December 7, 1946, HM1-503, Box 11, folder 7, Letters J. D. to Family, 1930–70.

123 J. D. Graber to Minnie Graber, December 6, 1950, HM1-503, Box 11, folder 2, Letters J. D. to Minnie, 1930–70, undated.

124 J. D. and Minnie Graber to Friends, October 30, 1947; J. D. Graber, *We Enter China.*

125 Minnie Graber to J. D. Graber, December 11, 1946, and Minnie Graber to J. D. Graber, February 27, 1947, HM1-503, Box 11, folder 1, Letters—Minnie to J. D., (1940s, '50s, '60s, undated).

126 E.g., Esther Graber to J. D. Graber, February 1, 1952, IV-18-10, Box 2, folder 58, Graber, J. D., Trip to Latin America, 1951–52, Confidential.

127 E.g., Minnie and Eleanor Graber to J. D. Graber, no date but probably November 1949.

128 Minnie Graber, interview, January 24, 1980.

129 Minnie Graber, "Good Morning," *Gospel Herald.*

130 Minnie Graber, "Let It Alone," *Gospel Herald.*

131 Minnie Graber, "With Us Are Both the Grayhaired and the Aged," *Gospel Herald.*

132 Minnie Graber, "Concerning Crackers and Other Things," *Gospel Herald* 36.

133 E.g., Mrs. J. D. Graber, "Hundred Things Concerning One Subject"; Mrs. J. D. Graber, "Twenty Women," *Gospel Herald*; Minnie Graber, "Women's Work—United or Divided?," *Gospel Herald.*

134 Showalter, "Women's Missionary Sewing Circle Meet," *Gospel Herald*; E.g., J. D. Graber to P. J. Malagar, July 13, 1951, IV-18-10, Box 3, Malagar, P. J., 1951–55; Minnie Graber, "Women's Activities," *Gospel Herald* 44, 766; "Women's Activities," *Gospel Herald* 45, 1210; "Women's Activities," *Gospel Herald* 47,18–19.

135 J. D. Graber to P. J. Malagar, July 13, 1951.

136 MBMC printed and distributed the proceedings of these annual gatherings. A complete set is archived at the Mennonite Church USA Archives. See IV-06-3, Box 4. Except for the more mundane minutes and financial reports, the proceedings, reports, and sermons were typically printed as articles in the *Gospel Herald* over the months that followed the annual gathering.

137 "Minutes of the Forty-First Annual Meeting of the Mennonite Board of Missions," *Gospel Herald* 40, 402; See the list on the inside cover of Wilbert R. Shenk, ed., *Being God's Missionary Community; Forty-Fourth Annual Meeting and Related Conferences of the Mennonite Board of Missions and Charities.*

138 J. D. Graber, "Notice to Superintendents," *Gospel Herald*; "City and Rural Missions," *Gospel Herald*; J. D. Graber, "City Mission Display," *Gospel Herald.*

139 "Mission News," *Gospel Herald* 43, 600; "Echoes from Shenandoah," *Gospel Herald*; J. D. Graber to Missionaries of the MBMC, June 16, 1955, IV-18-10, Box 1, Annual Meeting, 1955.

140 J. D. Graber to Foreign Missionaries of the MBMC, June 14, 1951, IV-18-10, Box 1, folder 10, Annual Meeting, 1951; J. D. Graber to Missionaries on the Foreign Fields, June 25, 1952, IV-18-10, Box 1, Annual Meeting, 1952; J. D. Graber to Missionaries of the MBMC, June 19, 1953, IV-18-10, Box 1, Annual Meeting, 1953; J. D. Graber to Missionaries of MBMC in Fields Outside the United States, June 25, 1954, IV-18-10, Box 1, folder 13, Annual Meeting, 1954; J. D. Graber to Missionaries of the MBMC, June 16, 1955.

141 J. D. Graber to Foreign Missionaries of the MBMC, June 14, 1951; J. D. Graber to S. N. Solomon, May 13, 1952, IV-18-10, Box 5, folder 31, Solomon, Stephen N., 1951–55; J. D. Graber to Missionaries on the Foreign Fields, June 25, 1952.

Chapter 6

1 S. J. Hostetler to J. D. Graber, October 10, 1958, and S. J. Hostetler to J. D. Graber, November 1, 1958, IV-18-13-02, Box 4, Ghana, 1958.

2 J. D. Graber to S. J. Hostetler, October 18, 1958, and J. D. Graber to S. J. Hostetler, December 17, 1958, IV-18-13-02, Box 4, Ghana, 1958.

3 Matthew Ekereke to John R. Mumaw, Orie O. Miller, and S. J. Hostetler, December 3, 1958, HM1-563, Box 3, folder 21, Nigeria Church, 1958–60; S. J. Hostetler to J. D. Graber, December 19, 1958, IV-18-13-02, Box 10, folder 24, Nigeria, 1956–59.

4 J. D. Graber to S. J. Hostetler, December 31, 1958, IV-18-13-02, Box 4, Ghana, 1958; J. D. Graber to Dave Shank, March 10, 1959, IV-18-13-02, Box 2, folder 67, Belgium, 1959.

5 P. E. Udo et al., "Welcome Address Presented by the People of Ibiono to Bishop J. D. Graber," March 29, 1959, IV-18-13-02, Box 10, Nigeria, 1956–59.

6 Udo et al., "Welcome Address Presented by the People of Ibiono to Bishop J. D. Graber."

7 International Missionary Council, *Relation Between the Younger and the Older Churches*, 173, 209–10.

8 Latourette, "Need for Missions"; Rankin, "New and Old in Missions."

9 International Missionary Council, "Partners in Obedience."

10 International Missionary Council, *Witness of a Revolutionary Church*; Latourette and Hogg, *Tomorrow Is Here.*

11 Ilogu, "The Biblical Idea of Partnership"; Hesselink, "Future of the Christian World Mission."

12 E.g., International Missionary Council, *Witness of a Revolutionary Church*; Latourette and Hogg, *Tomorrow Is Here*; Warren, *Partnership: The Study of an Idea*.

13 See documentation of Joe's book reviews, which represent a range of missionary topics, and of the various mission-related courses he taught at Goshen Seminary. HM1-503, Box 6, Folders 2, 4, 5, and Box 8.

14 J. D. Graber, "Partners in World Mission."

15 Shenk, *Being God's Missionary Community*. Mennonite Board of Missions and Charities became Mennonite Board of Missions in 1971.

16 Critique of the indigenous church focus was not uncommon during this period. E.g., Beyerhaus and Lefever, *Responsible Church and the Foreign Mission*.

17 J. D. Graber, "Missions Today: Beyond Independence," *Gospel Herald*.

18 J. D. Graber, "Partners in World Mission."

19 J. D. Graber to S. C. Yoder, January 30, 1940, IV-07-01, Box 8, folder 1, India Mission—Sec. J. D. Graber, 1937–41; J. D. Graber, "Annual Business Meeting of the American Mennonite Mission," *Gospel Herald*.

20 J. D. Graber, "What Is Today the Task?"

21 J. D. Graber, "What Is Today the Task?"

22 Esther Graber et al., interview.

23 Hogg, *One World, One Mission*; Levai, "Christian World Mission at This Hour"; Flett, "Tributaries to the IMC Willingen Conference, 1952."

24 J. D. Graber, "Partners in World Mission"; J. D. Graber, "One Church, One Mission," *Gospel Herald*; J. D. Graber, "Missions Today: Mission Churches," *Gospel Herald*.

25 J. D. Graber, "One Church, One Mission."

26 J. D. Graber, "Race Relations in World Evangelism."

27 J. D. Graber, "Partners in World Mission."

28 J. D. Graber, "Race Relations in World Evangelism."

29 J. D. Graber, "New Day in Missions II," *Gospel Herald*; J. D. Graber to Minnie Graber, February 23, 1951, HM1-503, Box 11, folder 2, Letters J. D. to Minnie, 1930–70, undated.

30 "From the Annual Business Meeting of the American Mennonite Mission, Dhamtari, India, December 12–16, 1950," IV-18-10, Box 3, India—Unification Commission, 1950–53.

31 J. D. Graber to E. P Bachan, May 23, 1957, IV-18-13-02, Box 6, folder 16, India Secretary, 1956–58; J. D. Graber to P. J. Malagar, March 24, 1965, IV-18-13-02, Box 8, folder 18, Malagar, P. J., 1960–65; J. D. Graber to Joseph Bhelwa, May 5, 1965, IV-18-13-02, Box 6, folder 13, India—Secretary, 1965.

32 Raúl O. García to J. D. Graber, March 20, 1965, IV-18-13-02, Box 2, folder 28, Argentina—Central, 1965; J. D. Graber, "Missions Today: Vision in Argentina," *Gospel Herald*.

33 J. D. Graber, "Missions Today: Partnership," *Gospel Herald*.

34 Joe Richards to J. D. Graber, October 27, 1962, IV-18-13-02, Box 7, folder 6, Japan—Correspondence, 1962.

35 J. D. Graber, "Partners in World Mission."

36 J. D. Graber, "Missions Today: Beyond Independence," *Gospel Herald*.

37 *Partners in World Mission 1965*, 76, 218–19.

38 *Partners in World Mission 1965*, 77–79; Benner, "Six-Day Partnership," *Gospel Herald*.

39 J. D. Graber, "Partners in World Mission," 250.

40 Mosemann, "Announcement," *Gospel Herald*; Peachey, "Case of the New Board Member Part II," *Gospel Herald*.

41 J. D. Graber to James Kratz, April 12, 1963, IV-18-13-02, Box 2, folder 29, Argentina Chaco, 1961–65; J. D. Graber to Donald King, January 12, 1957, IV-18-13-02, Box 4, folder 67, Graber, J. D., Appointments, 1957; J. D. Graber to Nelson Kauffman, July 27, 1962, and J. D. Graber to Chester K. Lehman, July 13, 1959, IV-18-13-02, Box 4, folder 69, Graber, J. D., Appointments, 1954–65.

42 J. D. Graber to Ronald D. Graber, October 26, 1956, HM1-503, Box 11, folder 8, Letters J. D. to Ron Graber, 1943, 1954, 1956.

43 J. D. Graber to Missionaries of the MBMC, June 16, 1955, IV-18-10, Box 1, Annual Meeting, 1955; "Our Schools: Goshen College," *Gospel Herald*; Paul Mininger, "Notice of Appointment to the Goshen College Faculty and Administrative Staff," July 1, 1957, HM1-503, Box 10, folder 8, Miscellaneous Letters (mold damage).

44 J. D. Graber to Robert Parsons, September 14, 1956, IV-18-13-02, Box 5, folder 17, Hartford Plans 1956–1963; J. D. Graber to Ernest Miller, September 26, 1956, IV-18-13-02, Box 6, folder 24, India—Woodstock School, 1956–61.

45 J. D. and Minnie Graber to Mr. and Mrs. C. L. Graber, February 13, 1956, IV-07-03, Box 1, J. D. Graber and C. L. Graber Correspondence, 1951–61; J. D. Graber to Rhoda Ressler, January 30, 1958, IV-18-13-02, Box 7, folder 12, Japan—Correspondence, 1957–63.

46 Documentation from courses that Joe taught are found in HM1-503, Box 8.

47 J. D. Graber to Pierre Widmer, July 16, 1958, IV-18-13-02, Box 4, folder 69, Graber, J. D., Appointments, 1954–65.

48 J. D. Graber to Paul Swarr, January 2, 1964, IV-18-13-02, Box 6, folder 41, Israel Evangelism Committee, 1963–64.

49 J. D. Graber to Paul Mininger, February 12, 1957, IV-18-13-02 MBM, Box 3, 58 Conrad Grebel Lectures; J. D. Graber to J. Maurice Hohlfeld, January 17, 1962, IV-18-13-02, Box 5, folder 13 H, 1952–65. Theron F. Schlabach later did extensive study of the roots of Mennonite mission engagement during this period. See Schlabach, *New Rhythm for Mennonites*; Schlabach, "Reveille for Die Stillen Im Lande; Schlabach, *Gospel Versus Gospel*.

50 J. D. Graber to P. J. Malagar, November 10, 1960, IV-18-13-02, Box 8, folder 18, Malagar, P. J., 1960–65.

51 J. D. Graber to Paul Mininger, February 12, 1957; Paul Mininger to J. D. Graber, June 9, 1958, IV-18-13-02, Box 3, 58 Conrad Grebel Lectures; J. D. Graber, *Church Apostolic*.

52 J. D. Graber to J. Maurice Hohlfeld, January 17, 1962; J. Maurice Hohlfeld to J. D. Graber, October 2, 1962, and J. D. Graber to J. Maurice Hohlfeld, April 26, 1963, IV-18-13-02, Box 5, folder 17, Hartford Plans, 1956–63.

53 Minnie Graber to J. D. Graber, December 26, 1960, HM1-503, Box 11, folder 1, Letters—Minnie, to J. D. (1940s, '50s, '60s, undated).

54 J. D. and Minnie Graber to Ed and Irene Weaver, November 28, 1959, HM1-696, Box 2, folder 3, J. D. Graber, 1958–61; Esther Graber to J. B. Martin, April 20, 1960, IV-18-13-02, Box 4, folder 64, Graber, J. D., Appointments, 1960.

55 J. D. Graber to Ernest E. Miller, October 14, 1963, IV-18-13-02, Box 5, folder 60, India—Educational Committee—Confidential, 1963–64.
56 Rich, *Mennonite Women*, 207.
57 Communication from Eleanor Kreider, October 6, 2020; Melvin Gingerich and Barbara K. Reber, "Women's Missionary and Service Commission (Mennonite Church)," in *Global Anabaptist Mennonite Encyclopedia Online*, accessed March 28, 2024, https://gameo.org/index.php?title=Women%27s_Missionary_and_Service_Commission_(Mennonite_Church).
58 J. D. Graber to Dr. and Mrs. H. S. Martin, December 30, 1964, IV-18-13–02, Box 6, folder 9, India—Mennonite Medical Board, 1963–64.
59 J. D. Graber to P. J. Malagar, June 4, 1956, IV-18-13-02, Box 8, folder 19, Malagar, P. J., 1956–59.
60 J. D. Graber to Ronald D. Graber, October 26, 1956.
61 J. D. Graber to P. J. Malagar, July 2, 1957, IV-18-13-02, Box 8, folder 19, Malagar, P. J., 1956–59.
62 J. D. Graber to P. J. Malagar, December 24, 1958, IV-18-13-02, Box 8, folder 19, Malagar, P. J., 1956–59; J. D. Graber to J. Robert Eshleman, January 14, 1959, IV-18-13-02, Box 4, folder 1 E, 1958–62.
63 J. D. Graber to Peter W. Bhelwa, December 3, 1960, IV-18-13-02, Box 3, folder 8, Bhelwa, Peter, 1959–62; J. D. Graber to Quintus Leatherman, July 8, 1960, IV-18-13-02, Box 8, folder 7, London, England, 1956–60; J. D. Graber to Albert Buckwalter, June 12, 1965, IV-18-13-02, Box 3, folder 37, Buckwalter, Albert, 1956–65.
64 "15th Annual Meeting," *Gospel Herald*.
65 J. D. Graber to Peter W. Bhelwa, February 10, 1967, IV-18-13-02, Box 3, folder 8, Bhelwa, Peter, 1959–62.
66 J. D. Graber to Weyburn Groff, March 15, 1958, IV-18-13-02, Box 6, folder 31, India—Yeotmal Seminary, 1958; J. D. Graber to Pierre Widmer, July 16, 1958.
67 "Field Notes," *Gospel Herald* 52, 468.
68 "Obituaries," *Gospel Herald* 56, 767.
69 J. D. Graber to Quintus Leatherman, September 20, 1960, IV-18-13-02, Box 8, folder 7, London, England, 1956–60.
70 "Mission News," *Gospel Herald* 54, 91.
71 "Obituary of Richard Nase," *Gospel Herald* 55, 47.
72 J. D. Graber to Paul L. Conrad, April 16, 1963, IV-18-13-02, Box 6, folder 11, India—Medical Board Confidential, 1963–64; "Obituary of Joy Ellen Nase," *Gospel Herald* 56, 767.
73 J. D. Graber to S. Paul Miller, February 10, 1961, IV-18-13-02, Box 5, folder 48, India—American Mennonite Association, 1961–62; J. D. Graber to Ralph Buckwalter, January 15, 1962, Box 7, folder 6, Japan—Correspondence, 1962.
74 J. D. Graber to Paul L. Conrad, April 16, 1963.
75 J. D. Graber to S. Paul Miller, November 2, 1961, IV-18-13-02, Box 5, folder 48, India—American Mennonite Association, 1961–62.
76 J. D. Graber, "Report of the Secretary," 1956.
77 Allen, *Missionary Methods*; Lamott, *Revolution in Missions*; Soltau, *Missions at the Crossroads*.
78 J. D. Graber to J. Frederick Erb, June 3, 1955, IV-18-10, Box 2, folder 7, Detroit Mission, 1951–55.

79 J. D. Graber to P. J. Malagar, July 7, 1960, IV-18-03-02, Box 9, Mennonite World Conference, 1962.
80 J. D. Graber, "The Church in the World."
81 J. D. Graber, "What Is Today the Task?"
82 J. D. Graber to E. P. Bachan, November 3, 1961, IV-18-13-02, Box 6, folder 14, India—Secretary, 1961–64.
83 J. D. Graber, "Building the Mission Church," 1960, HM1-503, Box 3, folder 24, Manuscripts—Building the Mission Church; J. D. Graber, interview, August 18, 1972; J. D. Graber, interview, January 31, 1973.
84 E.g., J. D. Graber to Richard Burkholder, August 30, 1955, IV-18-13-01, folder 1, Brazil Secretary; "Brazil Mennonite Mission Council," Meeting Minutes, November 15, 1955, IV-18-13-01, Brazil Secretary, 1951–55.
85 J. D. Graber, "Anabaptism Expressed in Missions and Social Service."
86 "A Week in Ontario," *Gospel Herald* 35, 273; Miller, "Power of the Gospel Among the Jews," *Gospel Herald*; Brunk, "Opportunities in Jewish Mission Work," *Gospel Herald.*
87 J. D. Graber, "Today in Missions," *Gospel Herald* 42, 186.
88 Esther Graber to J. D. Graber, January 5, 1951, IV-18-10, Box 2, folder 59, Graber, J. D., Trip Europe and Far East, 1950–51; Nelson Kauffman, "Report of Investigation on Jewish Mission Work in New York," May 12, 1955, IV-18-10, Box 3, folder 14, Israel Evangelism Committee, 1952–55; "Meeting of the Executive Committee," June 10, 1955, IV-18-10, Box 2, Executive Committee, 1953–55.
89 J. D. Graber to Orie O. Miller, May 7, 1952, IV-18-10, Box 4, folder 13, Mennonite World Conference, 1952; "Meeting of the Executive and Missions Committees," June 17, 1952, IV-18-10, Box 1, Annual Meeting, 1952; J. D. Graber to Orie O. Miller and Harold Eshleman, June 26, 1952, IV-18-10, Box 3, folder 14, Israel Evangelism Committee, 1952–55; Orie O. Miller to J. D. Graber, A. E. Janzen, and John Thiessen, November 20, 1952, IV-18-10, Box 4, folder 14, Mennonites in Buenos Aires, 1951–55; Orie O. Miller to J. D. Graber, December 19, 1952, IV-18-10 MBM, Box 3, folder 13, Israel, 1952–55.
90 Ira J. Buckwalter to Harry N. Frank, June 18, 1953, IV-18-10, Box 3, folder 13, Israel, 1952–55.
91 Roy Kreider to J. D. Graber, July 17, 1953, IV-18-10, Box 3, folder 13, Israel, 1952–55; "A Survey of the Year 1953"; Ken Weaver et al., interview; Kreider, *Land of Revelation*, 44–45.
92 "Special Committees and Reports," 1953.
93 Harold Floreen to The American Committee on the Christian Approach to the Jews, August 29, 1955, IV-18-10, Box 3, folder 13, Israel, 1952–55; Hedenquist, "'Dialogue' Between the Christians and Jews."
94 Stevens, "Christian Approach to the Jew."
95 Hedenquist, "Christian Approach to the Jews"; Ellison, "Christian Approach to the Jews"; Marshal, "World Council of Churches and the Theology of Christian-Jewish Relations."
96 Luther A. Gotwald to J. D. Graber, May 5, 1955, IV-18-10, Box 3, folder 13, Israel, 1952–55; Harold Floreen to J. D. Graber, July 24, 1956, IV-18-13-02, Box 6, folder 38, International Missionary Council, 1956–60.

97 Roy Kreider to J. D. Graber, October 11, 1954, Roy Kreider to J. D. Graber, May 30, 1955, and Roy Kreider to J. D. Graber, November 11, 1955, IV-18-10, Box 3, folder 13, Israel, 1952–55; J. D. Graber, "Memorandum on Mission Work in Israel," November 2, 1954, IV-18-10, Box 3, folder 14, Israel Evangelism Committee, 1952–55; Roy Kreider to J. D. Graber, February 4, 1957, and Roy Kreider to J. D. Graber, February 25, 1957, IV-18-13-02, Box 6, folder 44, Israel Evangelism Committee, 1957–58.

98 J. D. Graber to Roy Krieder, November 2, 1954, and J. D. Graber to Roy Kreider, September 6, 1955, IV-18-10, Box 3, folder 13, Israel, 1952–55; J. D. Graber to Department of Immigration The State of Israel, November 2, 1954, IV-18-10 MBM, Box 3, folder 14, Israel Evangelism Committee, 1952–55; J. D. Graber, "Israel: Striving for a Foothold in Israel"; Kreider, *Land of Revelation*, 103.

99 J. D. Graber, "Holy Spirit and Missions," *Gospel Herald*, 654.

100 Wilbert R. Shenk, "Administrative Visit to Israel," November 10, 1965, and J. D. Graber, "Israel, Mennonite Board of Missions and Charities," 1965, IV-18-13-02, Box 6, folder 39, Israel, 1964–65; "Christian Community in Israel," *Gospel Herald*; Kreider, *Land of Revelation*, 206–12, 336–43.

101 J. D. Graber, "Missions Today: Who Crucified Jesus?," *Gospel Herald*; J. D. Graber, "Missions Today: Love as God Loved," *Gospel Herald*; J. D. Graber, "Israel, Mennonite Board of Missions and Charities."

102 André Trocmé to Friend (probably Guy Hershberger, see Orie O. Miller to J. D. Graber, December 8, 1953, IV-18-10, Box 5, folder 73, Yoder, John Howard, 1951–55), November 19, 1953, Boyd Nelson to André Trocmé and Orley Swartzentruber, May 1954, and Orie O. Miller to Orley Swartzentruber and André Trocmé, May 19, 1954, IV-18-10, Box 5, folder 50, Trocmé, André, Program, 1953–55; J. D. Graber to Orie O. Miller, January 14, 1954, IV-18-10, Box 4, folder 20, Miller, Orie O., 1951–55.

103 A. Orley Swartzentruber to J. D. Graber, June 14, 1954, IV-18-10, Box 5, folder 50, Trocmé, André, Program, 1953–55.

104 J. D. Graber to John H. Yoder, December 1, 1954, IV-18-10, Box 5, folder 50, Trocmé, André, Program, 1953–55; Yoder, "Our First Three Years in Algeria," *Gospel Herald*.

105 J. D. Graber to Wilbert Lind, February 27, 1958, IV-18-13-02, Box 2, folder 24, Annual Mission Board Meeting, 1958; Yoder, "Islam's Special Challenge to Christian Missions," *Gospel Herald*.

106 "Conference on Islam, Kitchener, Ontario, Canada," August 3–4, 1962, X-16, Box 1, folder 5, Minutes, 1962.

107 See Cragg, *Call of the Minaret*; Cragg, *Sandals at the Mosque*.

108 John H. Yoder, "Report on Investigation Trip to Algeria," May 30, 1955, IV-18-10, Box 1, folder 7, Algeria, 1955; Smeltzer, "Our Service Approach to Missions in Algeria," *Gospel Herald*; Yoder, "Islam's Special Challenge to Christian Missions"; J. D. Graber to Nelson Litwiller, December 19, 1956, IV-18-13-02, Box 2, folder 38, Argentina Field Secretary, 1956.

109 J. D. Graber to Orie O. Miller, June 1, 1954, and J. D. Graber to John H. Yoder, October 19, 1954, IV-18-10, Box 5, folder 50, Trocmé, André, Program, 1953–55; J. D. Graber to John H. Yoder, December 1, 1954; J. D. Graber, "Missions Today: By Word and by Deed in Algeria II," *Gospel Herald*.

110 Yoder, "Missions and Material Aid in Algeria," *Gospel Herald*; J. D. Graber,

"Missions Today: By Word and by Deed in Algeria," *Gospel Herald*; J. D. Graber, "Missions Today: By Word and by Deed in Algeria II," *Gospel Herald*.

111 J. D. Graber, "Missions Today: By Word and by Deed in Algeria II."

112 Orie O. Miller to Orley Swartzentruber and André Trocmé, May 19, 1954.

113 "Beginning a Mission-Service Project in Algeria," *Gospel Herald*; Yoder, "Our First Three Years in Algeria."

114 "Minutes of the European Mission Council," March 26, 1959, and John H. Yoder, "Housing Project for Algiers," November 1959, IV-18-13-02, Box 4, folder 17, European Mission Council, 1955–59, Yoder trip to Europe and N. Africa.

115 "Overseas Report on the Fields Israel, Ghana, Nigeria, and Algeria," 1964, IV-18-13-02, Box 1, folder 10, Algeria, January 1–May 31, 1964; J. D. Graber to Harold Weaver, December 7, 1964, IV-18-13-02, Box 1, folder 9, Algeria, June 1–December 31, 1964.

116 Hostetler, "Algeria."

117 Albert Buckwalter, "Minutes of the Chaco Mission Council," August 18, 1954, IV-18-10, Box 1, Argentina Field Secretary, 1951–55; Reyburn, *Toba Indians*; Litwiller, "Our New Responsibility: The Toba Church," *Gospel Herald*; Buckwalter, "Conversion in the Chaco, 1954."

118 Albert Buckwalter to the 16 Churches of the IEU, February 12, 1959, and Albert Buckwalter to Paulino Carlos Taboada, February 24, 1959, HM1-097, Box 4, Correspondence with "Toba Brethren," 1958–60; Ceriani Cernadas and Citro, "El movimiento del evangelioentre los Toba del Chaco argentino: Una revisión histórica y etnográfica"; Buckwalter, *Vocabulario Toba*.

119 J. D. Graber to Members of the Executive Committee of the Mennonite Board of Missions and Charities, October 5, 1954, IV-18-10, Box 1, Argentina Field Secretary, 1951–55.

120 Edwin and Irene Weaver to John H. Yoder, February 19, 1960, IV-18-13-02, Box 10, Nigeria, January–May 1960.

121 Matthew Ekereke et al., "Welcome Address from the People of Ibiono to Mr. and Mrs. Hostetler," February 15, 1959, HM1-563, Box 3, folder 21, Nigeria Church, 1958–60; Edwin and Irene Weaver to John H. Yoder, December 24, 1959, IV-18-13-02, Box 11, Nigeria—Edwin Weaver, 1959.

122 Edwin Weaver to John H. Yoder, December 9, 1959, IV-18-13-02, Box 11, Nigeria—Edwin Weaver, 1959.

123 Edwin Weaver to J. D. Graber, September 12, 1960, and J. D. Graber, "Report on Visit to Nigeria," December 31, 1960, IV-18-13-02, Box 10, Nigeria, June–December 1960.

124 Edwin and Irene Weaver to John H. Yoder, December 24, 1959.

125 Akam, *Fasting or the School of God*; E. J. Akam, "Are Pentecostal Manifestations Real and Scriptural?," n.d., HM1-696, Box 6, folder 4, I. U. Nsasak and D. U. Otong.

126 Edwin Weaver to S. J. Hostetler, January 1960, HM1-563, Box 3, folder 22, Nigeria Mission, Personal, 1959–60; Edwin Weaver to John H. Yoder, January 5, 1960, IV-18-13-02, Box 10, Nigeria, January–May 1960.

127 J. D. Graber to Overseas Representatives of the MBMC, July 5, 1956, IV-18-03-02, Box 4, Executive Committee, 1956–64; J. D. Graber to Edwin Weaver, October 22, 1954, IV-18-10, Box 5, Weaver, Edwin and Irene, 1951–55.

128 Edwin Weaver, "Notes for Telephone Conversation," May 6, 1960, HM1-696,

Box 4, folder 39, Yoder, John Howard, 1959–60; Weaver and Weaver, *The Uyo Story*, 36.

129 "Tentative Agreement Between the Presbyterian Church of Nigeria and MBMC," June 1960, HM1-696, Box 3, folder 37, Presbyterian Church, Nigeria, 1963–65.

130 Edwin Weaver to J. D. Graber, September 23, 1963, IV-18-13-02, Box 10, Nigeria, 1963; Edwin Weaver, "Files on the United Independent Churches Fellowship, Transcript," 1968, HM1-696, Box 4, folder 27, United Independent Churches Fellowship.

131 Edwin Weaver, "An Introductory Statement for a Special Study Committee," September 19, 1961, HM1-696, Box 3, folder 36, Presbyterian Church, Nigeria, 1960–62; Edwin Weaver to J. D. Graber, March 6, 1962, IV-18-13-02, Box 10, Nigeria, 1962; Edwin I. Weaver, "An Introduction to the Inter-Church Study Group," December 1967, HM1-696, Box 6, folder 10, John Howard Yoder.

132 Edwin Weaver, "Minutes of the Inter-Church Group Meeting," May 13, 1967, HM1-696, Box 2, folder 22, Inter-Church Study Group, Minutes, etc.; Edwin I. Weaver, "The Inter-Church Study Group," December 1967, HM1-696, Box 6, folder 9, Inter-Church Study Group on AICs in Uyo, Nigeria.

133 Edwin Weaver to David Roberts, March 6, 1963, HM1-696, Box 3, folder 35, P–R Miscellaneous; Edwin Weaver to J. D. Graber, February 1964, IV-18-13-02, Box 10, Nigeria, 1964; H. W. Gensichen to Edwin I. Weaver, December 5, 1963, HM1-696, Box 1, folder 42, Misc.; J. Walter Cason to Edwin Weaver, June 11, 1964, and Edwin Weaver to Walter Cason, January 1, 1965, IV-18-13-02, Box 11, Nigeria—Edwin Weaver, 1964–65.

134 Löffler, *The Layman Abroad*, 7–30.

135 Löffler, *The Layman Abroad*, 34, 40–51.

136 Toews, *Mennonites in American Society*, 120–22; Redekop, *The Pax Story*, 28–29.

137 J. D. Graber, "Today in Missions," *Gospel Herald* 41, 426; J. D. Graber, *Church Apostolic*, 119–21; J. D. Graber to Orie O. Miller, January 19, 1962, IV-18-13-02, Box 9, Miller, Orie O., 1956–65; J. D. Graber to Mike Thornberry, March 8, 1962, IV-18-13-02, Box 12, 1956–65; J. D. Graber, "Missions Today: Overseas Mission Associates," *Gospel Herald*.

138 "Overseas Mission Committee," January 23, 1962, IV-06-02, Box 4–5; J. D. Graber, "Missions Today: Overseas Mission Associates."

139 J. D. Graber to Mike Thornberry, March 8, 1962.

140 Harold S. Bender and Harold A. Penner, "Voluntary Service," in *Global Anabaptist Mennonite Encyclopedia Online*, 1989, accessed March 14, 2025, https://gameo.org/index.php?title=Voluntary_Service; Redekop, *The Pax Story*, 33; Toews, *Mennonites in American Society,* 197–99; "Proposed VS Program for Nigeria," October 1962, HM1-696, Box 4, folder 41, Yoder, John Howard, 1962.

141 Edwin Weaver to John H. Yoder, May 10, 1960, IV-18-13-02, Box 10, Nigeria January–May 1960; John H. Yoder to J. Winfield Fretz, March 27, 1961, IV-18-13-02, Box 11, Nigeria—Teachers for 1960–61; V. N. Muoneke to All Educational Secretaries and Principles of Voluntary Agency Schools, September 21, 1963, IV-18-13-02, Box 10, Nigeria—Lloyd Fisher, 1963.

142 John H. Yoder to U. Iso, October 17, 1960, HM1-696, Box 4, folder 39, Yoder, John Howard, 1959–60; Glen Miller to J. D. Graber, August 17, 1962, IV-18-13-02, Box 10, Nigeria, Glen R. Miller, 1962–63; John H. Yoder to Glenn Miller,

October 15, 1962, HM1-696, Box 3, folder 18, Miller, Glen.

143 Yoder, "Mennonite Missionaries and African Independent Churches," 615–21.

144 E.g., Gray, "New Relationship Between Church and Missionary"; International Missionary Council, *World Mission of the Church*, 24–26, 44–46; International Missionary Council, "The Indigenous Church."

145 Lapp, *Mennonite Church in India,* 96–97.

146 J. D. Graber to Edwin Weaver, September 13, 1951, and J. D. Graber to Edwin Weaver, April 4, 1952, IV-18-10, Box 5, Weaver, Edwin and Irene, 1951–55.

147 J. D. Graber, "Field Reports of Missions, India."

148 "Meeting of the Full Board," May 18, 1929, IV-06-02, MBM Exec Committee Documents and Mtg Minutes, 1906–71, Box 2, Minutes, 1927–33.

149 "Proceedings of the Mennonite Board of Missions and Charities, 1930," May 3, 1930, IV-06-02, Box 2, Minutes, 1927–33

150 "Committee on Affiliation"; Lapp, *Mennonite Church in India,* 98; Schlabach, *Gospel Versus Gospel*, 140–41.

151 J. D. Graber to S. C. Yoder, May 12, 1938, IV-07-01, Box 8, folder 1, India Mission—Sec. J. D. Graber, 1937–41.

152 "Minutes of the Annual Business Meeting of the American Mennonite Mission," November 9, 1937, IV-17-1, folder AMM India Bus Mtg Minutes, 1933–39.

153 Lapp, *Mennonite Church in India,* 98, 235.

154 "Mennonite Board of Missions and Charities Minutes of Executive Committee," March 18, 1948, IV-06-02, Box 3, Minutes, 1944–48, Exec Committee.

155 "Mennonite Board of Missions and Charities Minutes of Conjoint Meeting of Executive and Missions Committee," February 7, 1946, IV-06–02, Box 3, Minutes, 1944–48, Exec Committee.

156 "Mennonite Board of Missions and Charities Minutes of the Executive Committee," November 4, 1949, IV-06-02, Box 3, Minutes Exec Committee, 1948–50.

157 J. D. Graber to Fred Field Goodsell, October 1, 1952, and "Approved Appropriations for the Division of Foreign Missions for 1955," July 16, 1954, IV-18-10, Box 4, NCC—Division of Foreign Missions Budget, 1951–54; J. D. Graber to International Missionary Council, September 17, 1954, IV-18-10, Box 3, International Missionary Council, 1951–55.

158 J. D. Graber, "Missions Editorial: Ecumenicity," *Gospel Herald.*

159 J. D. Graber, "Missions Today: Unity and Mission," *Gospel Herald.*

160 J. D. Graber to Edwin and Irene Weaver, January 26, 1960, HM1-696, Box 2, folder 3, J. D. Graber, 1958–61.

161 J. D. Graber, interview, February 13, 1973.

162 J. D. Graber, "By the Way V," *Gospel Herald*; J. D. Graber to Orie O. Miller and Harold Eshleman, June 26, 1952, IV-18-10 MBM, Box 3, folder 14, Israel Evangelism Committee, 1952–55.

163 J. D. Graber to John Thiessen, A. E. Jansen, and Henry N. Hostetter, February 13, 1958, and J. D. Graber to John Thiessen, A. E. Janzen, and Henry H. Hostetter, March 7, 1958, IV-18-13-02, Box 7, folder 10, Japan—Correspondence, 1958; J. D. Graber to Henry A. Fast, July 30, 1955, IV-18-10, Box 4, folder 35, Montevideo Bible Seminary, 1955.

164 "Mennonite Board of Missions and Charities Minutes of Conjoint Executive, Missions, and Relief Committees," April 18, 1947, IV-06-02, Box 3, Minutes, 1944–48, Exec Committee; *Report of the Forty-First Annual Meeting*, 20–21;

Erb and Hostetler, *Mennonite General Conference Report*, 30–32; J. D. Graber to O. O. Miller and H. S. Bender, January 25, 1949, IV-07-02, Box 3, folder 18, Graber, J. D., 1943–49.

165 "MCC Contributions Last Year," *Gospel Herald*; Toews, *Mennonites in American Society*, 199.

166 J. D. Graber to Orie O. Miller, October 18, 1954, IV-18-10, Box 4, Orie O., 1954–55, Confidential; J. D. Graber, "To Proclaim or to Serve?"; J. D. Graber, interview, January 31, 1973.

167 Orio O. Miller to Paul Mininger, H. S. Bender, and J. D. Graber, March 15, 1952, and Orie O. Miller to J. D. Graber, March 25, 1953, IV-18-10, Box 4, Mennonite Central Committee, 1951–55; Snyder, interview.

168 J. D. Graber, "MCC Relief & Service Program and Mennonite Missions," Study Meeting on the Relationship of the MCC Relief and Service Program and Mennonite Missions, January 24, 1958, IV-18-13-02, Box 8, folder 52, MCC—Mission Board Relationship, 1957–60.

169 J. D. Graber, "MCC Relief & Service Program and Mennonite Missions"; J. D. Graber, "The Deed and the Declaration"; J. D. Graber, "Motivating for Mission"; J. D. Graber, *Church Apostolic*, 58–60, 66–67.

170 J. D. Graber, "Motivating for Mission."

171 Orie O. Miller to J. D. Graber, December 8, 1953, IV-18-10, Box 5, Yoder, John Howard, 1951–55; J. D. Graber to Orie O. Miller, January 14, 1954, IV-18-10, Box 4, folder 20, Miller, Orie O., 1951–55; J. D, Graber to the Executive Committee of the Mennonite Central Committee, January 25, 1954, IV-07-03, Box 1, J. D. Graber—Reports; J. D. Graber to Emma Richards, December 24, 1958, IV-18-13-02, Box 7, folder 10, Japan—Correspondence, 1958.

172 J. D. Graber to Members of the Executive Committee of the MBMC, May 29, 1957, IV-18-13-02, Box 4, folder 20, Executive Committee, 1956–64.

173 Don McCammon to J. D. Graber, June 30, 1953, IV-18-13-01, folder 3, Japan—Tokyo Center, Confidential, 1953; "Japan Missionaries to J. D. Graber," July 20, 1953, IV-18-13-01, folder 7, Japan—Correspondence, 1952–53; J. D. Graber to Orie O. Miller, October 18, 1954, IV-18-10 MBM, Box 3, folder 13, Israel, 1952–55; J. D. Graber to Edwin Weaver, October 22, 1954, IV-18-10, Box 5, Weaver, Edwin and Irene, 1951–55; J. D. Graber to E. C. Bender, April 23, 1957, and Orie O. Miller to J. D. Graber, May 22, 1957, IV-18-13-02, Box 4, folder 24, Foreign Literature Committee, 1956–58; Ken Weaver et al., interview.

174 J. D. Graber to Henry Weaver, November 29, 1955, IV-18-10, Box 5, Weaver, Henry D. Jr., Confidential.

175 "Joint Session MCC Executive Committee and Officials of Mennonite and Brethren in Christ Mission Boards," September 14, 1951, IV-18-10, Box 4, Mennonite Central Committee, 1951–55.

176 William T. Snyder to MCC Members, January 6, 1958, and "Minutes Study Meeting on the Relationship of the MCC Relief and Service Program and Mennonite Missions," January 24, 1958, IV-18-13-02, Box 8, folder 52, MCC—Mission Board Relationship, 1957–60; Weaver, "'Habit of Social Concern.'"

177 "Report of Meeting of Mennonite Mission Board Secretaries," May 15, 1958, IV-18-03-02, Box 8; Snyder, interview.

178 Snyder, interview.

179 J. D. Graber, "Pastor and Missions," *Gospel Herald*; J. D. Graber, "Today in Missions," *Gospel Herald* 42, 554; J. D. Graber, "Mission Outpost of the Congregation," *Gospel Herald*.
180 J. D. Graber, "Anabaptism Expressed in Missions and Social Service."
181 J. D. Graber, *Church Apostolic*, 111–112; J. D. Graber, "Missions Today: Be a Missionary and See the World," *Gospel Herald*; J. D. Graber, "A Witnessing People."
182 J. D. Graber, interview, February 13, 1973.
183 J. D. Graber, "Pastor and Missions," *Gospel Herald*.
184 J. D. Graber, "Race Relations in World Evangelism."
185 J. D. Graber, "General Secretary's Message," 1961; J. D. Graber, "Missions Today: The Whole Family," *Gospel Herald*.
186 J. D. Graber, "Mission Editorial: The Mennonite Outreach Study," *Gospel Herald*; Hostetler, *Sociology of Mennonite Evangelism*, ii.
187 Hostetler, "Sociology of Mennonite Evangelism"; Hostetler, *Sociology of Mennonite Evangelism*, 229–32, 245–46.
188 J. D. Graber, "Unto the Uttermost Part," *Gospel Herald*; J. D. Graber, "Missions Today: Integration and Mission," *Gospel Herald*.
189 Bixler, "Who Is to Blame for the Worldliness in Apparel in the Church," *Gospel Herald*; Delp, "Plain Clothing Among the Brethren," *Gospel Herald*; "Maintaining a Plain Church," *Gospel Herald*; "Maintaining a Plain Church: II. Why Maintain It," *Gospel Herald*; "Maintaining a Plain Church: III. How Maintain It?," *Gospel Herald*.
190 J. D. Graber to Minnie Graber, September 1932, HM1-503, Box 10, folder 5, Letters, undated; J. D. Graber to Minnie Graber, November 3, 1932, HM1-503, Box 10, folder 4, 2nd Term in India (1932–41); J. D. Graber to Minnie Graber, December 7, 1932, HM1-503, Box 15, folder 7, Princeton Letters, 1933.
191 Henry Weaver to J. D. Graber, August 2, 1955, IV-18-10 MBM, Box 5, folder 66, Weaver, Henry D. Jr., Confidential, 1955; J. D. Graber to Paul Vougtlin, October 5, 1955, IV-18-10, Box 5, folder 57 V, 1951–55; J. D. Graber to Albert Buckwalter, July 16, 1955, IV-18-10, Box 1, Buckwalter, Albert and Lois, Confidential, 1951–55.
192 J. D. Graber, *Church Apostolic*, 87–88.
193 J. D. Graber to S. Paul Miller, May 31, 1960, IV-18-13-02, Box 6, folder 17, India Secretary, Confidential, 1956–64.
194 J. D. Graber, "Missions Today: Integration and Mission."

Conclusion

1 "Shenk Appointed Overseas Assistant," *Gospel Herald*; J. D. Graber to John R. Mumaw, March 2, 1965, IV-18-13-02, Box 4, folder 61, Graber, J. D., Appointments, 1964–65.
2 J. D. Graber to MBMC Missionaries, May 26, 1965, IV-18-2, Box 1, Overseas Committee Correspondence, 1965–70.
3 *Becoming God's People Today 1967*, 17–43, 86. This yearly MBMC published report included Puerto Rico as one of the fourteen. Cuba and Alaska had previously been included in the list, but by 1967 there was no longer MBMC work there.
4 *Report of the Thirty-Eighth Annual Meeting*, 59–61.
5 William T. Snyder to J. D. Graber, June 5, 1967, IV-18-13-03, Box 3, Graber, J.

D.—Correspondence, 1967–69; J. D. to Jane, September 4, 1967, HM1-503, Box 11, folder 7, Letters J. D. to Family, 1930–70; J. D. Graber, "Government Evaluates Famine Relief," *Gospel Herald*; J. D. Graber to Family, February 12, 1968, HM1-503, Box 11, folder 3, J. D. and Minnie Updates to Family, 1947, 1950–60, update.

6 J. D. Graber to Minnie Graber, December 7, 1967, and December 10, 1967, HM1-503, Box 11, folder 2, Letters J. D. to Minnie, 1930–70, undated; J. D. Graber to Family, December 14, 1967, HM1-503, Box 11, folder 7, Letters J. D. to Family, 1930–70.

7 J. D. Graber to Minnie Graber, December 19, 1967, HM1-503, Box 11, folder 2, Letters J. D. to Minnie, 1930–70, undated.

8 Myron S. Augsburger to J. D. Graber, February 28, 1968, HM1-503, Box 1, folder 19, Correspondence, Miscellaneous, 1953–74; "Faculty Changes at Eastern Mennonite College," *Gospel Herald*; J. D. Graber to Wilbert R. Shenk, February 7, 1969, IV-18-13-03, Box 3, Graber, J. D.—Correspondence, 1967–69.

9 Bender, interview.

10 Wilbert R. Shenk to J. D. Graber, February 11, 1969, IV-18-13-03, Box 3, folder 21, Graber, J. D.—Correspondence, 1967–69.

11 J. D. Graber to Family, September 28, 1967, HM1-503, Box 11, folder 7, Letters, J. D. to Family, 1930–70.

12 J. D. Graber to Minnie Graber, December 7, 1967.

13 J. D. Graber, "A Witnessing People."

14 Russell Krabill, "Joseph Daniel Graber," January 1978, IV-18-12, Box 2, folder 7, Collected Documentation, 1943–78; Levi C. Hartzler, "Memorial Service Recognizes J. D. Graber's Contribution to Missions," February 1977, HM1-503, Box 1, folder 13, Artifacts—Memorial Service for J. D. G.; Tobianne Price to D. L. Minter, August 25, 1976, HM1-503, Box 12, folder 1, Personal—related miscellaneous; Bender, interview.

15 Roth, "J. D. Graber Leaves Mission Legacy," *Gospel Herald*; "James H. Lark Leaves Church Planting Legacy," *Gospel Herald*; Ruth, *Maintaining the Right Fellowship*, 485.

16 HM1-503, Box 1, folder 13, Artifacts—Memorial Service for J. D. G.

17 HM1-503, Box 1, folder 13, Artifacts—Memorial Service for J. D. G.; "Memories from Memorial Service for J. D. Graber Held at the Hospital in Dhamtari, M. P., India," 1978, IV-18-12, Box 2, folder 6, Memorial Service for J. D. Graber, 1978; E. P. Bachan to Minnie Graber, January 30, 1978, HM1-503, Box 1, folder 13, Artifacts—Memorial Service for J. D. G.

18 Elvina and Jehoash Harishchandra to Esther Graber, February 6, 1978, IV-18-12, Box 2, folder 6, Memorial Service for J. D. Graber, 1978; "Memories from Memorial Service for J. D. Graber Held at the Hospital in Dhamtari, M. P., India."

19 Showalter, "Mr. Missions," *Gospel Herald*; Burkholder et al., interview.

20 Ken Weaver et al., interview; personal email from John D. Roth, May 26, 2023.

21 J. D. Graber to Eugene R. Braum, February 12, 1964, IV-18-13-02, Box 8, McGavran, Donald, 1956–64.

22 For a critique of the church growth school from MBM leaders see Shenk, ed., *Challenge of Church Growth*; Robert, "Forty Years of the American Society of Missiology."

23 Shenk, "Mission Agency and African Independent Churches."

24 J. D. Graber, "Putting the Church in the Center."
25 J. D. Graber, *Church Apostolic*, viii, 2–3, 11; J. D. Graber, "General Secretary's Message," 1961; J. D. Graber, "A Witnessing People."
26 Brunner, *The Word and the World*, 108; Burkholder et al., interview.
27 J. D. Graber, "The Church in the World" (Seminary Commencement Address, Goshen, IN, 1960), Mennonite Historical Library; J. D. Graber, *Church Apostolic*, 8–12; J. D. Graber, "Theology of Missions," *Gospel Herald*.
28 J. D. Graber, "To All Lands and Peoples."
29 E.g., J. D. Graber, "God's Good News for All the World," Sermon Notes, Summer 1972, HM1-503, Box 2, folder 27, Sermon Notes data and clippings—Mission.
30 J. D. Graber, "General Secretary's Message," 1961; "Partners in World Mission"; J. D. Graber, "Missions Today: Your Job Is Too Small," *Gospel Herald*; J. D. Graber, "Mission in the Bible," *Gospel Herald*.
31 J. D. Graber, "Missions Today: My Congregation and Mission," *Gospel Herald*.
32 J. D. Graber, *Church Apostolic*, 33, 38–41; J. D. Graber, "Mennonite Distinctives, Speech given to Bapt/Menn Seminar, Japan," 1964, HM1-48, Box 181, The Church as Indigenous.
33 J. D. Graber, "Changeless Gospel in a Changing World"; J. D. Graber, *A Witnessing People*.
34 J. D. Graber, "Disciple in Mission," *Gospel Herald*.
35 John 20:19–23.
36 J. D. Graber, "Pursuing God," *Gospel Herald*.
37 J. D. Graber, "Live Your Faith - Goshen College Baccalaureate," May 31, 1964, IV-18-13-02, Box 7, folder 3, Japan—Correspondence, 1964.
38 J. D. Graber, "Missions Today: The Nature of Our Task," *Gospel Herald*.
39 J. D. Graber, "Missions Today: Love as God Loved," *Gospel Herald*.
40 J. D. Graber, "By Word and Deed"; J. D. Graber, "Motivating for Mission."
41 J. D. Graber, *Church Apostolic*, 115.
42 J. D. Graber, "Always a Christian."
43 J. D. Graber, "General Secretary's Message," 1963.
44 J. D. Graber, "A Witnessing People."
45 J. D. Graber, "What Is Today the Task?"
46 Esther Graber et al., interview.
47 E.g., Schlabach, *Gospel Versus Gospel*.
48 Johnston and Ross, *Atlas of Global Christianity*, 59.
49 Kanagy, Miller, and Roth, *Global Anabaptist Profile*, 5–6; "Membership, Map and Statistics," Mennonite World Conference, March 12, 2025, https://mwc-cmm.org/en/membership-map-and-statistics/.

Notes on Sources

1 For an exception to this rule, see Altman, "Dissolution of Nam Cum." Previously published as Altman, "Disolución de Nam Cum."
2 See Ressler, "God's Leading in Mission Work," *Gospel Herald*; Erb, "The Mennonite Church and Hospital Work"; Kauffman, *Mennonite History*, 116–21; Lehman, *Our Mission Work in India*.
3 Schlabach, *New Rhythm for Mennonites*; Schlabach, "The Humble Become"; Schlabach, *Gospel Versus Gospel*.

4 Bender, "Anabaptist Vision"; Schlabach, *Gospel Versus Gospel*, 15–16.
5 Schlabach, *Gospel Versus Gospel*, 15, 193–94; Shenk, *By Faith They Went;* Shenk, "Mennonites and the Evangelical Network."
6 Cabrita and Maxwell, "Introduction: Relocating World Christianity"; Hanciles, "World Christianity Interrupted."
7 HM6-81, Mennonite Board of Missions, Mission History Interview Project, Box 1, Tapes 3, 27, and 30.
8 IV-18-12, Mennonite Board of Missions, Overseas Missions Tapes.
9 Hartzler, "Missions Section in Retrospect"; J. D. Graber, "Missions Section or Missions Magazine?," *Gospel Herald*.

Bibliography

Collections at Mennonite Church USA Archives, Elkhart, IN.

American Mennonite Mission (Dhamtari, India) Annual Reports, Meeting Minutes, and Constitutions, 1902–1952. IV-17-001.

American Mennonite Mission (Dhamtari, India) Secretary's Correspondence and Subject Files, 1917–52. IV-17-004.

Buckwalter, Albert S., and Lois, Papers, 1949–2004. HM1-097.

Graber, J. D. (Joseph Daniel) and Minnie (Swartzendruber), Papers, 1920–78. HM1-503.

Hostetler, S. Jay (Sylvan Jay), and Ida Miller, Papers, 1927–77. HM1-563.

Lapp, George Jay, Papers, 1897–1951. HM1-143.

Mennonite Board of Missions Annual Meeting Minutes and Annual Reports, 1900–2000. IV-06-003.

Mennonite Board of Missions Executive Committee Governing Documents and Meeting Minutes, 1906–71. IV-06-02.

Mennonite Board of Missions Executive Office Correspondence, Part 1, 1900–45. IV-07-01.

Mennonite Board of Missions Executive Office Correspondence, Part 2, 1938–68. IV-07-02.

Mennonite Board of Missions Executive Office Secretary Records (J. D. Graber), 1951–61. IV-07-03.

Mennonite Board of Missions Mission History Interview Project, 1972–77. HM6-81.

Mennonite Board of Missions Office of the Secretary Overseas and Home Mission Correspondence, 1951–55. IV-18-10.

Mennonite Board of Missions Overseas Committee Official Records, IV-18-03.

Mennonite Board of Missions Overseas Ministries Division Data Files Part 1, 1947–55. IV-18-13-01.
Mennonite Board of Missions Overseas Ministries Division Data Files Part 2, 1956–65. IV-18-13-02.
Mennonite Board of Missions Overseas Ministries Division Data Files Part 3, 1966–69. IV-18-13-03.
Mennonite Board of Missions Overseas Mission Tapes. IV-18-12.
Weaver, Edwin and Irene, Records, 1910–2023. HM1-696.
Yoder, John Howard, Papers, 1944–2013. HM1-048.

Gospel Herald articles

"Annual Mission Board Report." 45, no. 27 (July 1, 1952): 649–63.
"Beginning a Mission-Service Project in Algeria." 48, no. 27 (July 5, 1955): 638–39.
Benner, Richard. "A Six-Day Partnership." 58, no. 27 (July 13, 1965): 598–600.
Bixler, Jacob K. "Who Is to Blame for the Worldliness in Apparel in the Church." 19, no. 41 (January 6, 1927): 850–51.
Brunk, A. C. "A Caste Wide Survey of Our Mission Field." 29, no. 14 (July 2, 1936): 312–313
Brunk, George R. "Opportunities in Jewish Mission Work." 41, no. 40 (October 5, 1948): 935.
Burkhart, I. E. "Our World Missionary Outlook Today." 25, no. 40 (January 5, 1933): 852–55.
"China, a Challenge." 34, no. 41 (January 8, 1942): 873.
"Christian Community in Israel." 59, no. 24 (June 21, 1966): 561.
"Church Correspondence." 43, no. 19 (May 9, 1950): 451.
"City and Rural Missions under District Boards." 41, no. 15 (April 13, 1948): 349.
Delp, Oscar. "Plain Clothing Among the Brethren." 20, no. 8 (June 16, 1927): 250–51.
Dye, W. J. "Our Nursing Power Problem." 42, no. 33 (August 16, 1949): 814–17.
"Echoes from Mackinaw Dells." 41, no. 26 (June 29, 1948): 601–2, 604–5.
"Echoes from Shenandoah." 46, no. 26 (June 23, 1953): 609–10, 629–30.
"Editorial: Sharpening the Conscience." 44, no. 33 (August 14, 1951): 779.
Erb, Allen H. "New Frontiers in World Evangelism: Hospital and School of Nursing." 39, no. 32 (November 5, 1946): 698–700.
———. "Nursing Education in the Mennonite Church." 36, no. 49 (March 2, 1944): 1026–1107, 1031.
———. "A Rebirth in Missions as Evidenced in Nursing." 41, no. 25 (June 22, 1948): 590–91.
Erb, Paul. "Leaves from Oak Grove." 39, no. 11 (June 11, 1946): 225, 228–29.
Esch, C. D. "Modernism in India." 21, no. 16 (July 19, 1928): 324–25.
"Faculty Changes at Eastern Mennonite College." 61, no. 35 (September 3, 1968): 800.
"Field Notes." 34, no. 48 (February 26, 1942): 1024.
"Field Notes." 35, no. 17 (July 23, 1942): 360.

"Field Notes." 36, no. 6 (May 6, 1943): 120.
"Field Notes." 37, no. 21 (August 25, 1944): 416.
"Field Notes." 37, no. 31 (November 3, 1944): 632.
"Field Notes." 38, no. 15 (July 13, 1945): 296.
"Field Notes." 42, no. 11 (March 15, 1949): 260.
"Field Notes," 52, no. 20 (May 19, 1959): 468.
"15th Annual Meeting." 59, no. 10 (March 15, 1966): 242–43.
Friesen, P. A. "Is Our Evangelistic Work Effective?" 24, no. 9 (May 28, 1931): 196.
"General Conference Day by Day." 48, no. 37 (September 13, 1955): 865–66, 885.
Gerber, Ellis. "The What and Where of Dillonvale." 42, no. 27 (July 5, 1949): 646–47.
Gerig, Orie B. "Mennonite Young People's Conference." 13, no. 3 (April 15, 1920): 61.
Gingerich, Melvin. "The Color Line." 42, no. 7 (February 15, 1949): 149.
Graber, J. D. "Annual Business Meeting of the American Mennonite Mission." 32, no. 49 (March 7, 1940): 1043.
———. "Bazar Preaching." 32, no. 14 (July 6, 1939): 293.
———. "By the Way I." 43, no. 49 (December 5, 1950): 1200–1201.
———. "By the Way II." 43, no. 50 (December 12, 1950): 1225.
———. "By the Way IX." 44, no. 6 (February 6, 1951): 136.
———. "By the Way V." 44, no. 1 (January 2, 1951): 17.
———. "The Call from India." 25, no. 22 (September 1, 1932): 468–69.
———. "China, a Need and a Problem." 37, no. 9 (June 2, 1944): 153–54.
———. "Christian Strategy in Rural Missions." 39, no. 42 (January 14, 1947): 929–30.
———. "City Mission Display." 42, no. 18 (May 3, 1949): 425.
———. "The Conversion of Ganpat." 22, no. 45 (February 6, 1930): 930–31.
———. "The Cross of Christ, the Power of God." 35, no. 38 (December 17, 1942): 824–25.
———. "The Disciple in Mission." 55, no. 2 (January 9, 1962): 36.
———. "Elkhart Hospital Developments." 41, no. 39 (September 28, 1948): 913.
———. "Evangelism in Its Biblical Setting as to Spirit and Method." 27, no. 1 (April 5, 1934): 24–26.
———. "Government Evaluates Famine Relief." 61, no. 2 (January 9, 1968): 42.
———. "The Holy Spirit and Missions." 52, no. 28 (July 21, 1959): 641–42, 646, 654.
———. "I Am the Truth." 36, no. 10 (June 3, 1943): 186–87.
———. "In and About Dhamtari." 31, no. 11 (June 16, 1938): 249.
———. "India Letter." 23, no. 23 (September 4, 1930): 501.
———. "India Letter." 23, no. 27 (October 2, 1930): 580–81.
———. "India Letter." 23, no. 36 (December 4, 1930): 776–77.
———. "India Mission News." 28, no. 8 (May 23, 1935): 187–88.
———. "India Mission News." 31, no. 22 (September 1, 1938): 492.

———. "India Mission Page." 32, no. 23 (September 7, 1939): 504.
———. "India: Thirtieth Annual Report of the American Mennonite Mission." 23, no. 16 (July 17, 1930): 353–54.
———. "The Kingdom to the South VI." 45, no. 9 (February 26, 1952): 210.
———. "The Kingdom to the South VII." 45, no. 10 (March 4, 1952): 234.
———. "Mennonite Hospital and Nursing School." 38, no. 27 (October 5, 1945): 523.
———. "Mennonite Hospital and School of Nursing." 38, no. 35 (November 30, 1945): 672.
———. "Mennonite Hospital and School of Nursing." 38, no. 40 (January 4, 1946): 768.
———. "Mennonite Hospital and School of Nursing." 38, no. 41 (January 11, 1946): 784.
———. "Mennonite Youth Fellowship and Our Advancing Mission Program." 41, no. 21 (May 25, 1948): 485.
———. "Mission Editorial: The Mennonite Outreach Study." 45, no. 17 (April 22, 1952): 402.
———. "Mission in the Bible." 64, no. 9 (March 2, 1971): 193.
———. "The Mission Outpost of the Congregation." 44, no. 1 (January 2, 1951): 14.
———. "Missionary Day, November 16," 40, no. 33 (November 11, 1947): 708.
———. "The Missionary in Today's World." 46, no. 23 (June 9, 1953): 550–51.
———. "Missions Editorial: Ecumenicity." 45, no. 40 (September 30, 1952): 970.
———. "Missions Editorial: Out-Post or In-Branch." 44, no. 49 (December 4, 1951): 1178.
———. "Missions Editorial: Proclaiming Doctrine vs. Doing Deeds." 44, no. 35 (August 28, 1951): 842.
———. "Missions Editorial: Shall We Expand?" 45, no. 1 (January 1, 1952): 18.
———. "Missions Editorial: Why Not a Mission Restaurant?" 44, no. 38 (September 18, 1951): 914.
———. "Missions Section or Missions Magazine?" 57, no. 5 (February 4, 1964): 102, 110.
———. "Missions Today: Be a Missionary and See the World." 60, no. 15 (April 18, 1967): 343.
———. "Missions Today: Beyond Independence." 59, no. 24 (June 21, 1966): 547.
———. "Missions Today: By Word and by Deed in Algeria." 58, no. 2 (January 12, 1965): 38–39.
———. "Missions Today: By Word and by Deed in Algeria II." 58, no. 3 (January 19, 1965): 62–63.
———. "Missions Today: Integration and Mission." 57, no. 17 (May 5, 1964): 382, 385.
———. "Missions Today: Love as God Loved." 54, no. 49 (December 19, 1961): 1089, 1092.

———. "Missions Today: Mission Churches." 59, no. 8 (March 1, 1966): 187.
———. "Missions Today: My Congregation and Mission." 53, no. 33 (August 23, 1960): 741.
———. "Missions Today: Overseas Mission Associates." 55, no. 14 (April 3, 1962): 318.
———. "Missions Today: Partnership." 58, no. 11 (March 23, 1965): 254.
———. "Missions Today: The Nature of Our Task." 54, no. 1 (January 3, 1961): 13.
———. "Missions Today: The Whole Family in Heaven and Earth." 56, no. 14 (April 9, 1963): 302.
———. "Missions Today: Unity and Mission." 55, no. 18 (May 1, 1962): 406.
———. "Missions Today: Vision in Argentina." 59, no. 18 (May 10, 1966): 420.
———. "Missions Today: Who Crucified Jesus?" 53, no. 1 (January 5, 1960): 13.
———. "Missions Today: Your Job Is Too Small." 60, no. 3 (January 17, 1967): 61.
———. "My Work During the Year." 21, no. 10 (June 7, 1928): 215–16.
———. "The New Day in Missions I." 43, no. 46 (November 14, 1950): 1113–14.
———. "The New Day in Missions II." 43, no. 47 (November 21, 1950): 1153.
———. "The New Day in Missions III." 43, no. 48 (November 28, 1950): 1174.
———. "The New Day in Missions IV." 43, no. 49 (December 5, 1950): 1198–99.
———. "Notice to Superintendents of City and Rural Missions and Church Institutions Under District Mission Boards." 40, no. 20 (August 12, 1947): 432.
———. "One Church, One Mission." 58, no. 26 (July 6, 1965): 574–75.
———. "Organization of the India Mission." 39, no. 47 (February 18, 1947): 1014.
———. "Our India Letter." 19, no. 30 (October 21, 1926): 629, 639–40.
———. "Our New Hospital and Nurses' Training School." 37, no. 39 (December 29, 1944): 792.
———. "A Panorama of World Need." 40, no. 7 (May 13, 1947): 153–54.
———. "The Pastor and Missions." 41, no. 22 (June 1, 1948): 518–19.
———. "The Power of the Gospel to Make Men Preach." 36, no. 28 (October 7, 1943): 579–80, 585.
———. "Preaching the Gospel to the Heathen." 33, no. 45 (February 6, 1941): 965–66.
———. "The Pursuing God." 57, no. 27 (July 14, 1964): 599–600.
———. "Report of Mission Investigation in Japan." 43, no. 28 (July 11, 1950): 696–97.
———. "Reports on Teaching Evangelism." 34, no. 23 (September 4, 1941): 494.
———. "The Road to Certainty." 35, no. 47 (February 18, 1943): 1021, 1024.
———. "Shantipur." 23, no. 16 (July 17, 1930): 362–63.

———. "Shantipur Leper Home." 24, no. 9 (May 28, 1931): 206–7.
———. "The Social Implications of the Gospel: Child Welfare and Social Service as a Christian Challenge." 44, no. 23 (June 5, 1951): 529–30.
———. "Sundarganj." 28, no. 5 (May 2, 1935): 116.
———. "The Supreme Motive for Missionary Endeavor." 41, no. 1 (January 6, 1948): 14–15.
———. "Teaching Christ to the Illiterate." 22, no. 28 (December 12, 1929): 757–58.
———. "Teaching Scripture to High School Seniors." 30, no. 25 (September 16, 1937): 533, 539–40.
———. "The Theology of Missions." 51, no. 35 (September 2, 1958): 821–22, 839.
———. "Today in Missions." 41, no. 4 (January 27, 1948): 90.
———. "Today in Missions." 41, no. 17 (April 27, 1948): 402.
———. "Today in Missions." 41, no. 18 (May 4, 1948): 426.
———. "Today in Missions." 41, no. 20 (May 18, 1948): 474.
———. "Today in Missions." 41, no. 26 (June 29, 1948): 618.
———. "Today in Missions." 41, no. 41 (October 12, 1948): 966.
———. "Today in Missions." 42, no. 8 (February 22, 1949): 186.
———. "Today in Missions." 42, no. 16 (April 19, 1949): 378.
———. "Today in Missions." 42, no. 18 (May 3, 1949): 430.
———. "Today in Missions." 42, no. 20 (May 17, 1949): 482.
———. "Today in Missions." 42, no. 21 (May 24, 1949): 506.
———. "Today in Missions." 42, no. 23 (June 7, 1949): 554.
———. "Today in Missions." 42, no. 25 (June 21, 1949): 602.
———. "Training in Christian Experience." 36, no. 14 (July 1, 1943): 282–83, 291.
———. "Unto the Uttermost Part." 50, no. 40 (October 1, 1957): 825–26.
———. "Why I Am a Christian." 18, no. 36 (December 3, 1925): 738–40.
———. "Why I Am a Christian." 27, no. 3 (April 19, 1934): 75–76.
———. "Without Shedding of Blood No Remission." 28, no. 36 (December 5, 1935): 772–73.
———. "Youth at Work in the Local Church." 38, no. 1 (April 6, 1945): 20.
Graber, J. D., and Minnie Graber. "Shantipur Leper Home." 22, no. 6 (May 9, 1929): 134–35.
Graber, J. D., Minnie Graber, Ada Hartzler, and Minnie Kanagy. "From New York to Port Said." 18, no. 43 (January 21, 1926): 869.
Graber, J. D., S. Jay Hostetler, and J. N. Kaufman. "Report of Auditing Committee." 23, no. 16 (July 17, 1930): 368.
Graber, Minnie. "Concerning Crackers and Other Things." 36, no. 42 (January 13, 1944): 890–91.
———. "Good Morning." 37, no. 45 (February 9, 1945): 902.
———. "India: Thirty-First Annual Report of the American Mennonite Mission." 24, no. 9 (May 28, 1931): 193–208.
———. "Let It Alone, It Is Blind." 37, no. 46 (February 16, 1945): 922–23.
———. "Twenty Women." 41, no. 12 (March 23, 1948): 280.
———. "With Us Are Both the Grayhaired and the Aged." 36, no. 41 (January 6, 1944): 858.

———. "Women's Activities." 44, no. 32 (August 7, 1951): 766.

———. "Women's Work—United or Divided?" 47, no. 4 (January 26, 1954): 86–87.

Hallman, William E. "Dona Juana Passes On." 36, no. 24 (September 9, 1943): 500.

Hartzler, Levi. C. "Missions Editorial: A Major Crisis in Financing Missions." 47, no. 40 (October 5, 1954): 953.

———. "Missions Section in Retrospect." 57, no. 5 (February 4, 1964): 100–102.

———. "News Notes From Our Church Schools." 35, no. 26 (September 24, 1942): 558.

———. "Why a Mission Sunday School?" 48, no. 20 (May 17, 1955): 473.

Horst, Irvin B. "Mennonites and the Race Question." 38, no. 14 (July 6, 1945): 284.

Horst, John L. "Mennonite Relief Work in China." 36, no. 49 (March 2, 1944): 1044, 1053.

Hostetler, Wilbur, and Velma Hostetler. "Riding Third Class." 38, no. 24 (September 14, 1945): 460.

"In the Vale of Kidron." 37, no. 11 (June 16, 1944): 201–3.

"An Income That Does Not Shrink No. 1." 24, no. 38 (December 17, 1931): 827.

"An Income That Does Not Shrink No. 2." 24, no. 39 (December 24, 1931): 843.

"An Income That Does Not Shrink No. 3." 24, no. 40 (December 31, 1931): 859.

"An Income That Does Not Shrink No. 4." 24, no. 41 (January 7, 1932): 875.

"An Income That Does Not Shrink No. 5." 24, no. 42 (January 14, 1932): 907.

"An Income That Does Not Shrink No. 6." 24, no. 43 (January 21, 1932): 922.

"An Income That Does Not Shrink No. 7." 24, no. 44 (January 28, 1932): 955.

"An Income That Does Not Shrink No. 8." 24, no. 45 (February 4, 1932): 971.

"An Income That Does Not Shrink No. 9." 24, no. 47 (February 18, 1932): 1019.

"India Mennonite Church Conference Report." 32, no. 6 (May 11, 1939): 142.

"India Mission Page: News." 28, no. 14 (July 4, 1935): 315.

"James H. Lark Leaves Church Planting Legacy." 71, no. 6 (February 7, 1978): 118.

Kauffman, Daniel. "A Full-Time Secretary." 32, no. 27 (October 5, 1939): 578.

Kaufman, J. N. "President's Report 1944." 37, no. 13 (July 7, 1944): 275–76.

———. "What About the Next Generation?" 21, no. 8 (August 2, 1928): 387–88.

Kauffman, Milo. "Does 'Missions Week' Mean a New Era in Church Finance?" 47, no. 49 (November 23, 1954): 1120.

Kniss, Lloy A. "The Bible in India." 20, no. 27 (October 6, 1927): 586–87.

———. "Swaraj." 23, no. 36 (December 4, 1930): 771.

Kniss, Lloy A., and Elizabeth Kniss. "Swaraj Andolan in the Villages." 24, no. 9 (May 28, 1931): 198–99.

Kreider, Carl. "Mennonite Hospital and School of Nursing." 38, no. 36 (December 7, 1945): 688.

Lapp, George J. "My Colored Brother." 40, no. 31 (October 28, 1947): 666.
———. "What Shall the Answer Be?" 21, no. 8 (August 2, 1928): 388.
Lapp, Sarah. "With the Bible Women." 35, no. 10 (June 4, 1942): 214.
Lind, Millard. "Biblical Principles Governing Race Relations in the Church." 47, no. 41 (October 12, 1954): 961–62, 981.
Litwiller, John T. N. "Our New Responsibility: The Toba Church." 48, no. 9 (March 1, 1955): 206–7.
Litwiller, Nelson. "The Call to Mission." 56, no. 42 (October 22, 1963): 941–42, 949.
Long, Warren. "The Church's Responsibility in Belgium." 41, no. 31 (August 3, 1948): 719.
"Maintaining a Plain Church." 21, no. 2 (April 12, 1928): 33–34.
"Maintaining a Plain Church: II. Why Maintain It?" 21, no. 3 (April 19, 1928): 49–50.
"Maintaining a Plain Church: III. How Maintain It?" 21, no. 4 (April 26, 1928): 81–82.
"MCC Contributions Last Year: Reports to Annual Meeting Show Refugee Aid, Relief Work Continues on Large Scale." 43, no. 16 (April 18, 1950): 377.
"The Mennonite Relief Program in France." 38, no. 29 (October 19, 1945): 556.
Metzler, A. J. "Making Each Congregation a Center of Living Evangelism." 40, no. 3 (April 15, 1947): 49–50, 61.
Miller, Martin Z. "The Power of the Gospel Among the Jews." 36, no. 49 (March 2, 1944): 1047–48.
"Minutes of the Forty-First Annual Meeting of the Mennonite Board of Missions and Charities." 40, no. 19 (August 5, 1947): 401–13.
"Minutes of the Thirty-Eighth Annual Meeting of the Mennonite Board of Missions and Charities." 37, no. 13 (July 7, 1944): 275–82.
"Minutes of the Thirty-Ninth Annual Meeting of the Mennonite Board of Missions and Charities." 38, no. 14 (July 6, 1945): 266–75.
"Mission Directory 1926." 19, no. 6 (May 6, 1926): 135.
"Mission News." 42, no. 18 (May 3, 1949): 425.
"Mission News." 43, no. 25 (June 20, 1950): 600.
"Mission News," 54, no. 4 (January 24, 1961): 91.
"Mission Notes." 42, no. 2 (January 11, 1949): 37.
Mosemann, John H. "Announcement." 52, no. 33 (August 25, 1959): 729.
———. "The Annual Mission Board Meeting at Maple Grove." 40, no. 13 (June 24, 1947): 273–74, 276.
———. "Report of the Belgian Mission Study Committee." 40, no. 19 (August 5, 1947): 411.
———. "A Special Missions Week-December 5–12." 47, no. 44, (November 2, 1954): 1033.
Mumaw, John R. "Editorial." 31, no. 27 (October 6, 1938): 585–86.
———. "For China." 34, no. 49 (March 6, 1942): 1050.
Musser, Shelly. "Correspondence: New Holland." 25, no. 44 (February 2, 1933): 937, 940.
"Notes from Our Mission." 24, no. 6 (May 7, 1931): 133.

"Obituary of Daniel Graber." 23, no. 28 (October 9, 1930): 607.
"Obituary of Elias Swartzendruber." 28, no. 43 (January 23, 1936): 928.
"Obituary of Fanny Graber." 36, no. 14 (July 1, 1943): 294.
"Obituary of Joy Ellen Nase." 56, no. 34 (August 27, 1963): 767.
"Obituary of Richard Nase." 55, no. 2 (January 9, 1962): 47.
"Obituary of Sarah Knepp Swartzendruber." 32, no. 11 (June 15, 1939): 238.
"Our Schools: Goshen College." 49, no. 24 (June 12, 1956): 560.
Peachey, J. Lorne. "The Case of the New Board Member Part II." 55, no. 40 (October 9, 1962): 892–93.
Peachey, Paul. "Why Europe?" 44, no. 14 (April 10, 1951): 350–52.
"Program on Relief." 43, no. 26 (June 27, 1950): 621.
"Redeeming Heathen Words." 34, no. 45 (February 5, 1942): 956.
Reiff, Vernon E. "The Board's Finance Problem." 25, no. 1 (April 7, 1932): 25–27.
———. "Funds for Our General Mission Board." 23, no. 51 (March 19, 1931): 1085–86.
———. "India Support Reductions, 1933." 25, no. 47 (February 23, 1933): 996–97.
———. "Special Needs for Missions." 24, no. 52 (March 24, 1932): 1116–17.
———. "Twenty-Eighth Annual Financial Report." 27, no. 27 (October 4, 1934): 588–94.
"Relief Notes." 36, no. 52 (March 23, 1944): 1102.
"Report of the Forty-Third Annual Meeting of the Mennonite Board of Missions and Charities." 42, no. 28 (July 12, 1949): 674–87.
"Report of the Thirtieth Annual Meeting of the Mennonite Board of Missions and Charities." 29, no. 11 (June 18, 1936): 268–70.
"Report of the Thirty-Fifth Annual Meeting of the Mennonite Board of Missions and Charities." 34, no. 10 (June 1941): 210–12, 223–29.
"Report of the Thirty-First Annual Meeting of the Mennonite Board of Missions and Charities." 30, no. 14 (July 1, 1937): 305–12.
"Report of the Thirty-Second Annual Meeting of the Mennonite Board of Missions and Charities." 31, no. 14 (July 7, 1938): 297–300.
"Report of the Thirty-Sixth Annual Meeting of the Mennonite Board of Missions and Charities." 35, no. 15 (July 9, 1942): 323–30.
"Report of the Thirty-Third Annual Meeting of the Mennonite Board of Missions and Charities." 32, no. 14 (July 6, 1939): 299–301.
"Report of the Twenty-Fifth Annual Meeting of the Mennonite Board of Missions and Charities." 24, no. 12 (June 18, 1931): 273–85.
"Report of the Twenty-Second Annual Meeting of the Mennonite Board of Missions and Charities." 21, no. 14 (July 5, 1928): 290–304.
"Report of the Twenty-Seventh Annual Meeting of the Mennonite Board of Missions and Charities." 26, no. 20 (August 17, 1933): 433–48.
"Report of the Twenty-Sixth Annual Meeting of the Mennonite Board of Missions and Charities." 25, no. 18 (August 4, 1932): 387–92.
"Report of the Twenty-Third Annual Meeting of the Mennonite Board of Missions and Charities." 22, no. 18 (August 1, 1929): 386–400.
"Report of the Work in Belgium." 40, no. 23 (September 2, 1947): 512.

"Reports from the Annual Mission Board Meeting." 41, no. 41 (October 12, 1948): 967–74.
"Reports from the Home Missions and Institutions." 43, no. 27 (July 4, 1950): 669–75.
Ressler, J. A. "God's Leading in Mission Work." 19, no. 1 (April 1, 1926): 19–23.
Ressler, Lina Z. "Nursing as a Profession." 19, no. 45 (February 3, 1927): 966–67.
———. "Nursing as a Profession." 20, no. 1 (April 7, 1927): 20.
Roth, Willard. "J. D. Graber Leaves Mission Legacy." 71, no. 6 (February 7, 1978): 118.
Shank, J. R., C. D. Eash, and Daniel Kauffman. "Missouri-Iowa Conference Report, Sept. 24, 25, 1908." 1, no. 28 (October 10, 1908): 445.
"Shenk Appointed Overseas Assistant." 57, no. 41 (October 20, 1964): 919.
Shenk, John H. "God Deals with Race Prejudice." 47, no. 48 (November 16, 1954): 1081–82, 1102.
Showalter, Elizabeth. "Women's Missionary Sewing Circle Meet at Goshen, June 13." 43, no. 29 (July 18, 1950): 718–19.
Showalter, Stuart. "Mr. Missions: J. D. Graber." 60, no. 31 (August 8, 1967): 702.
Smeltzer, Walter. "Our Service Approach to Missions in Algeria." 49, no. 18 (May 1, 1956): 422–23.
"Special Foreign Missionary Needs for the Year 1932." 25, no. 5 (May 5, 1932): 116.
"Special Meetings." 36, no. 7 (May 13, 1943): 150.
"Statement of Concerns Adopted at a Study Conference on Christian Community Relations." 44, no. 33 (August 14, 1951): 780–81.
Stoltzfus, Grant M. "Report of the Child Welfare Committee." 45, no. 28 (July 8, 1952): 682.
"Thirty-Ninth Annual Report of the American Mennonite Mission." 32, no. 18 (August 3, 1939): 400–408.
"Thirty-Sixth Annual Report of the American Mennonite Mission." 29, no. 14 (July 2, 1936): 305–14.
"To What Purpose Is This Waste?" 19, no. 6 (May 6, 1926): 129–30.
Troyer, G. D. "The Work of the Bible Women." 20, no. 5 (May 5, 1927): 118–19.
Troyer, Kathryn S. "India Letter." 29, no. 3 (April 16, 1936): 53, 60.
"The Way of the Cross in Race Relations." 48, no. 23 (June 7, 1955): 529–30, 439.
"A Week in Ontario." 35, no. 13 (June 25, 1942): 273–75.
"Women's Activities." 45, no. 50 (December 9, 1952): 1210.
"Women's Activities." 47, no. 1 (January 5, 1954): 18–19.
Yoder, John H. "Islam's Special Challenge to Christian Missions." 50, no. 53 (December 31, 1957): 1142–43.
———. "Missions and Material Aid in Algeria." 51, no. 13 (April 1, 1958): 306–7.
———. "Our First Three Years in Algeria." 51, no. 7 (February 18, 1958): 158–60.

Yoder, Sanford Calvin. "Closing the Year with the Mission Board." 26, no. 37 (December 21, 1933): 805, 816.

———. "The Mission Board and Finances." 26, no. 27 (September 28, 1933): 549.

———. "Mission Problems." 27, no. 32 (November 8, 1934): 697–704.

———. "Our Home Coming Missionaries." 25, no. 37 (December 22, 1932): 813.

———. "Our India Missionaries." 35, no. 40 (August 20, 1942): 436.

———. "Plans for the Return of Missionaries." 26, no. 49 (March 8, 1934): 1052–53.

———. "A Statement from the Mission Board." 23, no. 33 (November 13, 1930): 708.

Zimmerman, Verna. "The Organization of a Mennonite Nurses' Association." 35, no. 23 (September 3, 1942): 490–91.

General Bibliography

Adams, Jay Edward. "The Homiletical Innovations of Andrew W. Blackwood." PhD diss., University of Missouri, 1969.

Afigbo, A. E. "The Missions, the State and Education in South-Eastern Nigeria, 1956-71." In *Christianity in Independent Africa*, ed. Fasholé-Luke, Richard Gray, Adrian Hastings, and Godwin Tasie, 176–92. Indiana University Press, 1978.

Akam, E. J. *Fasting or the School of God*. Ibesikpo, Nigeria: The International Supreme Temple of Prayer Fellowship, n.d.

Allen, Roland. *Missionary Methods, St. Paul's or Ours: A Study of the Church in the Four Provinces*. R. Scott, 1912.

Alpenfels, Ethel. *Sense and Nonsense About Race*. Study and Action Pamphlets on Race Relations. Friendship Press, 1946.

Altman, Agustina. "La disolución de Nam Cum en perspectiva: contextos globales de la misión menonita en el Chaco argentino." In *Los evangelios chaqueños: misiones y estrategias indígenas en el Siglo XX*, ed. César Ceriani Cernadas, 117–43. Asociación Civil Rumbo Sur, 2017.

———. "The Dissolution of Nam Cum in Perspective: Global Contexts of the Mennonite Mission in the Chaco, Argentina." *Mennonite Quarterly Review* 94, no. 3 (July 2020): 347–79.

Andrews, C. F. "India and Segregation." *International Review of Mission* 29, no. 1 (January 1940): 140–42.

———. "Missions in India To-Day." *International Review of Mission* 22, no. 2 (April 1933): 189–200.

Azariah, V. S. "The Problem of Co-Operation Between Foreign and Native Workers." In *World Missionary Conference, 1910, Vol. 9: To Consider Missionary Problems in Relation to the Non-Christian World*, 306–15. Oliphant Anderson and Ferrier, Fleming H. Revell Company, 1910.

Baker, Oliver Edwin. "The Effects of Urbanization on American Life and on the Church." *Mennonite Quarterly Review* 19, no 2 (April 1945): 117–42;

Bassham, Rodger C. "Mission Theology: 1948–1975." *International Bulletin of Mission Research* 4, no. 2 (April 1980): 52–58.

Beaver, R. Pierce. "The Expansion of American Foreign Missionary Activities Since 1945." *Occasional Bulletin of Missionary Research* 5, no. 7 (June 4, 1954): 2–7.

———. "The History of Mission Strategy." In *Perspectives on the World Christian Movement*, ed. Steven C. Hawthorne and Ralph D. Winter, Rev., B58–72. William Carey Library, 1992.

Becoming God's People Today 1967, General Mission Handbook Including Annual Reports. Mennonite Board of Missions and Charities, 1967.

Belawa, Mukut. "India Mennonite Church Report – 1939." In *Thirty-Fourth Annual Report of the Mennonite Board of Missions and Charities*. Mennonite Board of Missions and Charities, 1940.

Bender, Harold S. "The Anabaptist Vision." *Church History* 13, no. 1 (1944): 3–24.

Beyerhaus, Peter, and Henry Lefever. *The Responsible Church and the Foreign Mission*. Eerdmans, 1964.

Bianchi, Susana. *Historia de las religiones en la Argentina: Las minorías religiosas*. Random House Mondadori, 2012.

Bingle, E. J. "On Being Evangelized." *World Dominion*, April 1953.

Blosser Yoder, Holly. *The Same Spirit: History of Iowa-Nebraska Mennonites*. Central Plains Mennonite Conference, 2003.

Blough, Neal. "Mission Efforts in Europe; New Congregations, New Questions." In *Testing Faith and Tradition: Global Mennonite History Series: Europe*, 233–54. Good Books, 2006.

Bonk, Jonathon J. *The Theory and Practice of Missionary Identification, 1860–1920*. Edwin Mellen, 1989.

Brunk, A. C. "Reports from Foreign Missions, India." In *Thirtieth Annual Report of the Mennonite Board of Missions and Charities*, 13–14. Mennonite Board of Missions and Charities, 1936.

Brunner, Emil. *The Word and the World*. Student Christian Movement Press, 1931.

Buckwalter, Albert S. "Conversion in the Chaco, 1954." In *Report of the Forty-Ninth Annual Meeting of the Mennonite Board of Missions and Charities*, 43–45. Mennonite Board of Missions and Charities, 1955.

———. *Vocabulario Toba*. Talleres Gráficos Grancharoff, 1980.

Cabrita, Joel, and David Maxwell. "Introduction: Relocating World Christianity." In *Relocating World Christianity: Interdisciplinary Studies in Universal and Local Expressions of the Christian Faith*, 7:1–44. Theology and Mission in World Christianity. Brill, 2017.

Casas, Bartolomé de las. *A Short Account of the Destruction of the Indies*. Translated and edited by Nigel Griffin. Penguin, 1992.

Ceriani Cernadas, César. "Misión, nación y religión. Las fronteras del *dios Chur* entre los tobas formoseños." In *Los evangelios chaqueños: Misiones y estrategias indígenas en el Siglo XX*, edited by César Ceriani Cernadas, 71–89. Asociación Civil Rumbo Sur, 2017.

Ceriani Cernadas, César, and Silvia Citro. "El movimiento del evangelio entre los Toba del Chaco argentino: Una revisión histórica y etnográfica." In *De indio a hermano: Pentecostalismo indígena en América Latina*, ed. Jean

Pierre Bastian and Bernardo Guerrero Jiménez, 111–70. Ediciones Campus: Universidad Arturo Prat: El Jote Errante, 2005.

"Chaco Mission Directory." In *Report of the Forty-Seventh Annual Meeting of the Mennonite Board of Missions and Charities*, 133. Mennonite Board of Missions and Charities, 1953.

Charles, Roland W. *Troopships of World War II*. The Army Transportation Association, 1947.

Church Missionary Society. *The Church Missionary Atlas: Containing an Account of the Various Countries in Which the Church Missionary Society Labours, and of Its Missionary Operations*. 6th ed. Church Missionary House, 1879.

Coffman, Barbara F. *His Name Was John: The Life Story of an Early Mennonite Leader*. Wipf & Stock, 2003.

Comaroff, Jean, and John L. Comaroff. *Of Revelation and Revolution*. Vol. 1. *Christianity, Colonialism, and Consciousness in South Africa*. University of Chicago Press, 1991.

———. *Of Revelation and Revolution*. Vol. 2. *The Dialectics of Modernity on a South African Frontier*. University of Chicago Press, 1997.

"Committee on Affiliation." In *Twenty-Eighth Annual Report of the Mennonite Board of Missions and Charities*, 25–26. Mennonite Board of Missions and Charities, 1934.

Council of International Anabaptist Ministries, 1958–2004. X-16. Mennonite Church USA Archives – Elkhart. Elkhart, IN.

Cragg, Kenneth. *The Call of the Minaret*. Oxford University Press, 1956.

———. *Sandals at the Mosque*. Oxford University Press, 1959.

Davis, John Merle. "Mission Strategy in the New Age." *International Review of Mission* 35, no. 3 (1946): 303–13.

Dennis, James S., Harlan P. Beach, and Charles H. Fahs, eds. *World Atlas of Christian Missions*. Student Volunteer Movement for Foreign Missions, 1911.

Donohugh, Thomas S. "Caste Movements (Commonly Called 'Mass Movements') in India and Their Development, as Illustrated in the Word of the Methodist Episcopal Church in Northern India." *Methodist Review* 95 (1913): 849–67.

Dougall, James Watson Cunningham. "The Reason for Medical Missions." *International Review of Mission* 35, no. 3 (1946): 251–55.

Dube, Saurabh. "Issues of Christianity in Colonial Chhattisgarh." *Sociological Bulletin* 41, no. 1/2 (September 1992): 97–117.

———. "Paternalism and Freedom: The Evangelical Encounter in Colonial Chhattisgarh, Central India." *Modern Asian Studies* 29, no. 1 (February 1995): 171–201.

———. *Untouchable Pasts: Religion, Identity, and Power among a Central India Community, 1780–1950*. SUNY Series in Hindu Studies. State University of New York Press, 1998.

Ellison, Henry Leopold. "The Christian Approach to the Jews: Ambiguities in Terminology." *International Review of Mission* 45, no. 178 (April 1956): 155–60.

Erb, Allen H. "The Mennonite Church and Hospital Work." *Mennonite Quarterly Review* 1, no. 1 (January 1927): 28–33.

Erb, Allen H., and Amos O. Hostetler. *Mennonite General Conference Report*. Mennonite Publishing House, 1948.

Erb, Alta Mae. *The Christian and Race: Outlines for the Second Missionary Study Suggested by the Missionary Education Movement for 1946–47*. Mennonite Commission for Christian Education and Young People's Work and the Mennonite Board of Missions and Charities, 1947.

———. *Studies in Mennonite City Missions*. Mennonite Board of Missions and Charities, 1937.

Fahs, Charles H. "Protestant Benevolent Giving in the United States." *International Bulletin of Mission Research* 18, no. 4 (October 1929): 539–44.

Farquhar, John N. *The Crown of Hinduism*. Oxford University Press, 1913.

Fleming, Daniel Johnson. "Facing World Friction Points." *International Review of Mission* 15, no. 1 (January 1926): 106–19.

Flett, John G. "Tributaries to the IMC Willingen Conference, 1952." In *The Witness of God: The Trinity, Missio Dei, Karl Barth, and the Nature of Christian Community*, 123–62. Eerdmans, 2010.

Forty-Fourth Annual Meeting and Related Conferences of the Mennonite Board of Missions and Charities. Mennonite Board of Missions and Charities, 1950.

Foster, Lance M. *The Indians of Iowa*. University of Iowa Press, 2009.

Frederiks, Martha, and Dorottya Nagy, eds. *World Christianity: Methodological Considerations*. Brill, 2020.

Gerber, Carl R. "Tenth Anniversary at Dillonvale." *Ohio Mission Evangel* 6, no. 6 (December 1952): 15.

Gerdener, G. B. A. "The Crux of the Racial Situation in South Africa." *International Review of Mission* 38, no. 3 (July 1949): 280–94.

Gingerich, Melvin. *The Mennonites in Iowa: Marking the One Hundredth Anniversary of the Coming of the Mennonites to Iowa*. The State Historical Society of Iowa, 1939.

———. "North American Mennonite Overseas Outreach in Perspective, 1890-1965." *Mennonite Quarterly Review* 39, no. 4 (October 1965): 262–79.

Godin, Henri, and Yvan Daniel. *La France, Pays de Mission?* Editions de L'Abeille, 1943.

Goodall, Norman. "The Dilemma of Race Relations." *International Review of Mission* 43, no. 3 (July 1954): 323–29.

Graber, Chris L. *Looking Back: An Autobiography*. Self-published, 1982.

Graber, J. D. "Always a Christian." In *They Met God: A Number of Conversion Accounts and Personal Testimonies of God's Presence and Leading in the Lives of His Children*, ed. J. C. Wenger, 52–56. Herald Press, 1964.

———. "Anabaptism Expressed in Missions and Social Service." In *The Recovery of the Anabaptist Vision: A Sixtieth Anniversary Tribute to Harold S. Bender*, ed. Guy F. Hershberger, 152–66. Herald Press, 1957.

———. "By Word and Deed." In *The Church Apostolic: A Discussion of Modern Missions*, 45–67. Herald Press, 1960.

———. "The Changeless Gospel in a Changing World." In *The Church Apostolic: A Discussion of Modern Missions*, 78–93. Herald Press, 1960.

———. "The Christian Sense of Mission." *The Youth's Christian Companion* 21 (November 21, 1948): 370–71.

———. "A Christian Witness Through Hospital Service." *Christian Monitor* 38 (March 1946): 78, 96.

———. *The Church Apostolic: A Discussion of Modern Missions.* Herald Press, 1960.

———. "The Church at Work Through the Mennonite Board of Missions and Charities." *Christian Ministry* 43 (November 1951): 335.

———. "The Church in the World." Seminary Commencement. Goshen, IN, 1960. Mennonite Historical Library.

———. "The Deed and the Declaration." *Report*, summer 1959.

———. "Field Reports of Missions, India." In *Thirty-Third Annual Report of the Mennonite Board of Missions and Charities*, 16–18. Mennonite Board of Missions and Charities, 1939.

———. "General Secretary's Message." In *Sharing the Living Christ 1963*, 13–20. Mennonite Board of Missions and Charities, 1963.

———. "General Secretary's Message." In *The Church in Mission 1961*, 17–23. Mennonite Board of Missions & Charities, 1961.

———. "A Half Century of Missionary Progress." *Christian Monitor* 45 (December 1953): 372–73.

———. "Hospital Planning Committee." In *Report of the Fortieth Annual Meeting of the Mennonite Board of Missions and Charities*, 30–32. Mennonite Board of Missions and Charities, 1946.

———. "Israel: Striving for a Foothold in Israel." In *Reports of the Fifty-First Annual Meeting of the Mennonite Board of Missions and Charities*, 76–77. Mennonite Board of Missions and Charities, 1957.

———. "Motivating for Mission." *Mission Focus* 1, no. 4 (March 1973): 1–5.

———. *100 Years Prairie Street Mennonite Church*. Ed. John Bender. Prairie Street Mennonite Church, 1971.

———. "Partners in World Mission." In *Partners in World Mission 1965: General Mission Handbook Including Annual Reports*, 242–53. Mennonite Board of Missions & Charities, 1965.

———. "The Plan of Advance." *The Youth's Christian Companion* 28, no. 45 (November 9, 1947): 680.

———. "The Present Missionary Task." *Christian Monitor*, November 1949, 335–36.

———. "Putting the Church in the Center." In *The Church Apostolic: A Discussion of Modern Missions*, 25–44. Herald Press, 1960.

———. "Race Relations in World Evangelism." In *Christ, the Mennonite Churches, and Race*, 37–44. Mennonite Central Committee, 1959.

———. "Report of Christian Work in Chattisgarh Area." *The National Christian Council Review*, June 1931.

———. "Report of the Secretary." In *Report of the Fiftieth Annual Meeting of the Mennonite Board of Missions and Charities*, 19–21. Mennonite Board of Missions and Charities, 1956.

———. "Report of the Secretary." In *Report of the Fortieth Annual Meeting of the Mennonite Board of Missions and Charities*, 7–11. Mennonite Board of Missions and Charities, 1946.

———. "Report of the Secretary." In *Report of the Forty-Third Annual Meeting of the Mennonite Board of Missions and Charities*, 17–27. Mennonite Board of Missions and Charities, 1949.

———. "Report of the Secretary of Missionary Education." In *Report of the Fortieth Annual Meeting of the Mennonite Board of Missions and Charities*, 36–37. Mennonite Board of Missions and Charities, 1946.

———. "Report on Trip to Latin America." In *Report of the Forty-Sixth Annual Meeting of the Mennonite Board of Missions and Charities*, 83–88. Mennonite Board of Missions and Charities, 1952.

———. "Reports from Foreign Missions and the Mexican Border Work, India." In *Thirty-Second Annual Report of the Mennonite Board of Missions and Charities*, 8–10. Mennonite Board of Missions and Charities, 1938.

———. "To All Lands and Peoples." In *The Church Apostolic: A Discussion of Modern Missions*, 68–77. Herald Press, 1960.

———. "To Proclaim or to Serve?" *Mission Focus* 3, no. 3 (January 1975): 1–8.

———. "Transfer of India Church Properties." In *Thirty-Fourth Annual Report of the Mennonite Board of Missions and Charities*, 22–23. Mennonite Board of Missions and Charities, 1940.

———. "Utilizing Our Resources for the Building of the Church and the Community." *Mennonite Quarterly Review* 19, no. 2 (April 1945): 171–76.

———. *We Enter China*. E. V. Publishing House, 1947.

———. *We Enter Japan: A Statement of Historical Development, Present Progress, Plans, Ideals, and Descriptions of Our Mennonite Mission in Japan*. Mennonite Board of Missions and Charities, 1950.

———. "What Is Today the Task of Missions in Asia and Africa?" *Mennonite Observer*, January 10, 1958, 10–11. Paper given also at the Sixth Mennonite World Conference, Karlsruhe, Germany, 1957.

———. "Why Not a Youth Missionary Project?" *The Youth's Christian Companion* 29, no. 12 (March 21, 1948): 92.

Graber, Minnie. "A Hundred Things Concerning One Subject." *The Youth's Christian Companion* 28, no. 45 (November 9, 1947): 677.

Gray, G. Francis S. "The New Relationship Between Church and Missionary." *International Review of Mission* 27, no. 2 (April 1938): 239–44.

Grundmann, Christoffer H. "The Role of Medical Missions in the Missionary Enterprise: A Historical and Missiological Survey." *Mission Studies* 2, no. 1 (1985): 39–48.

Grundmann, Christoffer H. *Sent to Heal! Emergence and Development of Medical Missions*. University Press of America, 2005.

Hanciles, Jehu J. "World Christianity Interrupted: Green Shoots and Growing Pains." In *World Christianity: History, Methodologies, Horizons*, ix–xxiv. Orbis Books, 2021.

Harper, Susan Billington. *In the Shadow of the Mahatma: Bishop V. S. Azariah and the Travails of Christianity in British India*. Eerdmans, 2000.

Hartley, Benjamin L. "'Apostle of Ethnology': Agnes C. L. Donohugh's Missiological Anthropology Between the World Wars." *International Bulletin of Mission Research* 40, no. 2 (April 2016): 106–18.

———. "Mission: Agnes C. L. Donohugh, Early 'Apostle of Ethnography.'" In *On Knowing Humanity: Insights from Theology for Anthropology*, edited by Eloise Hiebert Meneses, and David Bronkema. Routledge, 2017.

Hedenquist, Göte. "The Christian Approach to the Jews." *International Review of Mission* 43, no. 2 (April 1954): 141–45.

———. "The 'Dialogue' Between the Christians and Jews: A New Emphasis in the Christian Approach to the Jews." *International Review of Mission* 47, no. 2 (April 1958).

Hershberger, Emily. "A Neo-Anabaptist Approach to Missions: Ralph and Genevieve Buckwalter and the Hokkaido Mennonite Church, 1949–1980." *Mennonite Quarterly Review* 78, no. 2 (July 2004): 385–414.

Hershberger, Guy F. "Historical Background to the Formation of the Mennonite Central Committee." *Mennonite Quarterly Review* 44, no. 3 (July 1970): 213–44.

———. "Maintaining the Mennonite Rural Community." *Mennonite Quarterly Review* 14, no. 4 (Oct. 1940): 214–23.

Hesselink, John. "The Future of the Christian World Mission." *Reformed Journal* 21, no. 8 (October 1971): 14–17.

Hinojosa, Felipe. "Making Noise Among the 'Quiet in the Land': Mexican American and Puerto Rican Ethno-Religious Identity in the Mennonite Church, 1932–1982." PhD diss., University of Houston, 2009.

Hoffman, Ronan. "The Development of Mission Theology in the Twentieth Century." *Theological Studies* 23, no. 3 (September 1962): 419–41.

Hogg, William Richey. *One World, One Mission*. Friendship Press, 1960.

Hollinger-Janzen, Lynda. *"A New Day in Mission" Irene Weaver Reflects on Her Century of Mission*. Missio Dei: Exploring God's Work in the World 8. Mennonite Mission Network, 2005.

Homan, Gerlof D. "Orie Benjamin Gerig: Mennonite Rebel, Peace Activist, International Civil Servant, and American Diplomat, 1894–1976." *Mennonite Quarterly Review* 73, no. 4 (1999): 751–82.

Hostetler, Beulah Stauffer. "Defensive Structuring and Codification of Practice: Franconia Mennonite Conference." *Mennonite Quarterly Review* 60, no. 3 (July 1986): 429–44.

Hostetler, John A. *God Uses Ink: The Heritage and Mission of the Mennonite Publishing House After Fifty Years*. Herald Press, 1958.

———. *The Sociology of Mennonite Evangelism*. Herald Press, 1954.

———. "The Sociology of Mennonite Evangelism." Ph.D., Pennsylvania State College, 1953.

Hostetler, Marian E. "Algeria." In *Anabaptists Meeting Muslims: A Calling for Presence in the Way of Christ*, edited by James R. Krabill, David W. Shenk, and Linford Stutzman. Herald Press, 2005.

Hostetler, S. Jay. "Soul Winning Methods That Have Proved Successful in India." In *Thirtieth Annual Report of the Mennonite Board of Missions and Charities*, 94–101. Mennonite Board of Missions and Charities, 1936.

Howell, Brian M. "Anthropology and the Making of Billy Graham: Evangelicalism and Anthropology in the 20th Century United States." *American Anthropologist* 117, no. 1 (March 2015): 59–70.

Hutchison, William R. "A Moral Equivalent for Imperialism." In *Errand to the World: American Protestant Thought and Foreign Missions*. University of Chicago Press, 1987.

Ilogu, Edumnd. "The Biblical Idea of Partnership and the Modern Missionary Task." *International Review of Mission* 44, no. 4 (October 1, 1955): 404–7.

International Missionary Council. "The Indigenous Church—the Universal Church in Its Local Setting." In *The Missionary Obligation of the Church*. Edinburgh House Press, 1952.

———. "Partners in Obedience." In *The Witness of a Revolutionary Church*, 23–34. International Missionary Council, 1947.

———. *The Relation Between the Younger and the Older Churches*, vol. 3. Reports of the Jerusalem Meeting of the International Missionary Council, March 24 – April 8, 1928. Oxford University Press, 1928.

———. *The Witness of a Revolutionary Church*. International Missionary Council, 1947.

———. *The World Mission of the Church: Findings and Recommendations of the International Missionary Council*. International Missionary Council, 1939.

Irvin, Dale T. "What Is World Christianity?" In *World Christianity: Perspectives and Insights, Essays in Honor of Peter C. Phan*, edited by Jonathan Y. Tan and Anh Q. Tran. Orbis Books, 2016.

Jackson, John. "Missions and Lepers." *International Review of Mission* 4, no. 4 (October 1915): 584–95.

Jayakumar, Samuel. "The Work of God as Holistic Mission: An Asian Perspective." *Evangelical Review of Theology* 35, no. 3 (July 2011): 227–41.

Johnston, Todd M., and Kenneth R. Ross, eds. *Atlas of Global Christianity 1910–2010*. Edinburgh University Press, 2009.

Juhnke, James C. *Vision, Doctrine, War: Mennonite Identity and Organization in America, 1890–1930*. Vol. 3. Mennonite Experience in America. Herald Press, 1989.

Kanagy, Conrad, Elizabeth Miller, and John D. Roth. *Global Anabaptist Profile: Belief and Practice in 24 Mennonite World Conference Churches*. Institute for the Study of Global Anabaptism, 2017.

Kasdorf, Hans. "The Anabaptist Approach to Mission." In *Anabaptism and Mission*, edited by Wilbert R. Shenk, 51–69. Herald Press, 1984.

Kauffman, Daniel, ed. *Bible Doctrine: A Treatise on the Great Doctrines of the Bible, Pertaining to God, Angels, Satan, the Church, and the Salvation, Duties and Destiny of Man*. Mennonite Pub. House, 1914.

———, ed. *Doctrines of the Bible, a Brief Discussion of the Teachings of God's Word*. Mennonite Pub. House, 1928.

———. *Manual of Bible Doctrines: Setting Forth the General Principles of the Plan of Salvation, Explaining the Symbolical Meaning and Practical Use of the Ordinances Instituted by Christ and His Apostles, and Pointing Out*

Specifically Some of the Restrictions Which the New Testament Scriptures Enjoin upon Believers. Mennonite Pub. Co., 1898.

———, ed. *Mennonite Cyclopedic Dictionary: A Compendium of the Doctrines, History, Activities, Literature, and Environments of the Mennonite Church, Especially in America*. Mennonite Publishing House, 1937.

———. *Mennonite History, Including a Brief Sketch of the Church from the Time of Christ*. Mennonite Publishing House, 1927.

Keay, John. *India: A History: From the Earliest Civilizations to the Boom of the Twenty-First Century*. William Collins, 2022.

Kirkpatrick, David C. "C. René Padilla and the Origins of Integral Mission in Post-War Latin America." *The Journal of Ecclesiastical History* 67, no. 2 (April 2016): 351–71.

Koop, Allen V. *American Evangelical Missionaries in France, 1945–1970*. University Press of America, 1986.

Kraemer, Hendrik. *The Christian Message in a Non-Christian World*. International Missionary Council, 1947.

Kreider, Roy H. *Land of Revelation: A Reconciling Presence in Israel*. Herald Press, 2004.

Lambert, George. *Around the Globe and through Bible Lands: Notes and Observations on the Various Countries Through Which the Writer Traveled*. Mennonite Publishing Co., 1896.

Lambert, George, and Abram B. Kolb. *India, the Horror-Stricken Empire: Containing a Full Account of the Famine, Plague, and Earthquake of 1896–7; Including a Complete Narrative of the Relief Work Through the Home and Foreign Commission*. Mennonite Pub. Co., 1898.

Lamott, Willis C. *Revolution in Missions: From Foreign Missions to the World Mission*. Macmillan, 1954.

Lapp, George Jay. *The Christian Church and Rural India: A Report on Christian Rural Reconstruction and Welfare Service*. Calcutta: Y.M.C.A. Pub., 1938.

Lapp, John A. *The Mennonite Church in India, 1897–1962*. Herald Press, 1972.

Latourette, Kenneth Scott. *A History of Christianity: Volume I: Beginnings to 1500*. Rev. ed. Harper & Row, 1975.

———. "The Need for Missions in the New Day." *Review & Expositor* 33, no. 2 (April 1936): 146–57.

———. "A Suggestion Toward a Reorientation of Mission Policy." *International Review of Mission* 23, no. 3 (July 1934): 405–13.

Latourette, Kenneth Scott, and William Richey Hogg. *Tomorrow Is Here: The Mission and World of the Church as Seen from the Meeting of the International Missionary Council at Whitby, Ontario, July 5–24, 1947*. Friendship Press, 1948.

Lederach, John M. "The History of the Young People's Bible Meeting in the Mennonite Church." *Mennonite Quarterly Review* 26, no. 3 (July 1952): 216–31.

Lehman, M. C. *Our Mission Work in India*. Mennonite Board of Missions and Charities, 1939.

Leiper, Henry Smith. *Blind Spots: Experiments in the Self-Cure of Race Prejudice*. 2nd ed. Friendship Press, 1944.

Levai, Blaise. "The Christian World Mission at This Hour." *International Review of Mission* 50, no. 4 (October 1961): 464–66.

Littell, Franklin H. "The Anabaptist Theology of Mission." In *Anabaptism and Mission*, edited by Wilbert R. Shenk, 13–23. Herald Press, 1984.

Löffler, Paul. *The Layman Abroad in the Mission of the Church: A Decade of Discussion and Experiment.* Edinburgh House Press, 1962.

MacMaster, Richard K. *Land, Piety, Peoplehood: The Establishment of Mennonite Communities in America, 1683–1790.* Vol. 1. Mennonite Experience in America. Herald Press, 1985.

Marshal, David. "The World Council of Churches and the Theology of Christian-Jewish Relations." *The Ecumenical Review* 72, no. 5 (December 2020): 861–94.

McCarley, Rebecca Lawin. "Reconnaissance Level Historical and Architectural Survey of Jefferson Township, Henry County, Iowa." Survey Prepared for the Henry County Historic Preservation Commission. Spark Consulting, June 30, 2016. https://www.waylandiowa.com/index.asp?SEC=21DC23C7-1A6E-4B86-B381-4D9729ED692B.

McGavran, Donald A. "Missionaries and Indigenous Standards of Living." *International Review of Mission* 22, no. 1 (January 1933): 33–40.

———. "My Pilgrimage in Mission." *International Bulletin of Missionary Research* 10, no. 2 (April 1986): 53–58.

Menzel, Emil W. *A Missionary's Leisure in the Indian Jungle*. Christian Education Press, 1942.

Metcalf, Barbara D., and Thomas R. Metcalf. *A Concise History of Modern India*. 2nd ed. Cambridge University Press, 2006.

Meyer, Jacob C. "The Origin of the Young People's Conference Movement of 1918." *Mennonite Historical Bulletin* 28, no. 2 (April 1967): 4–5.

Miller, Mary. *A Pillar of Cloud: The Story of Hesston College*. Mennonite Press, 1959.

Miller Shearer, Tobin. "A Pure Fellowship: The Danger and Necessity of Purity in White and African-American Mennonite Racial Exchange, 1935–1971." Ph.D., Northwestern University, 2008.

Miller, Susan Fisher. *Culture for Service: A History of Goshen College,1894–1994*. Goshen College, 1994.

Mokitimi, Seth M. "Apartheid and the Christian Spirit." *International Review of Mission* 38, no. 3 (July 1949): 276–79.

Mumaw, John R. "Current Forces Adversely Affecting the Life of the Mennonite Community." *Mennonite Quarterly Review* 19, no 2 (April 1945): 101–16

Nasaw, David. "Historians and Biography: Introduction." *The American Historical Review* 114, no. 3 (June 2009): 573–78.

Newbigin, Lesslie. *Unfinished Agenda: An Autobiography*. WCC Publications, 1985.

Nichols, James T. *Birdseye View of Far Lands*. Nichols, 1922.

Nida, Eugene A. "Identification, a Major Problem of Modern Missions." *Practical Anthropology* 2, no. 4 (July 1, 1955): 90–95.

Oldham, J. H. "A Missionary Survey of the Year 1912, British India and Ceylon." *International Review of Mission* 2, no. 1 (1913): 28–41.

"Our Growing Mission Program." *Ohio Mission Evangel* 4, no. 1 (March 1950): 8.

Owen, Robert C. "Air Transport in World War II." In *Air Mobility*, 33–42. Potomac Books, 2013.

Padilla, C. René. "Wholistic Mission: Evangelical and Ecumenical." *International Review of Mission* 81, no. 323 (July 1992): 381–82.

Partners in World Mission 1965: General Mission Handbook Including Annual Reports. Mennonite Board of Missions & Charities, 1965.

Paton, William. "The Indian Mission of Fellowship." *International Review of Mission* 22, no. 2 (April 1933): 215–24.

Patterson, James Alan. "The Loss of a Protestant Missionary Consensus: Foreign Missions and the Fundamentalist-Modernist Conflict." In *Earthen Vessels: American Evangelicals and Foreign Missions, 1880–1980,* edited by Joel A. Carpenter and Wilbert R. Shenk. Eerdmans, 1990.

Pellman, Hubert R. *Mennonite Broadcasts: The First 25 Years*. Mennonite Broadcasts Inc., 1978.

Philip, P. O. "The Indigenous Church: An Indian View." In *The Relation Between the Younger and the Older Churches*, vol. 3. Reports of the Jerusalem Meeting of the International Missionary Council, March 24 – April 8, 1928. Oxford University Press, 1928.

Pickett, Jarrell Waskom. *Christian Mass Movements in India, a Study with Recommendations*. Abingdon Press, 1933.

Pickett, Jarrell Waskom, D. A. McGavran, and G. H. Singh. *Christian Missions in Mid India*. The Mission Press, 1938.

Pierard, Richard V. "Pax Americana and the Evangelical Missionary Advance." In *Earthen Vessels: American Evangelicals and Foreign Missions, 1880–1980*, 155–79. William B. Eerdmans, 1990.

Preheim, Rich. *In Pursuit of Faithfulness: Conviction, Conflict, and Compromise in Indiana-Michigan Mennonite Conference*. Herald Press, 2016.

Presler, Titus. "Mission Is Ministry in the Dimension of Difference: A Definition for the Twenty-First Century." *International Bulletin of Mission Research* 34, no. 4 (October 2010): 195–204.

"Quarterly Notes IMC October 1940." *International Review of Mission* 29, no. 4 (October 1940): i–viii.

"Quarterly Notes." *International Review of Mission* 29, no. 2 (April 1940): i–viii.

Race, Alan. *Christians and Religious Pluralism: Patters in the Christian Theology of Religions*. SCM Press, 1993.

Rankin, M. Theron. "New and Old in Missions in the Orient." *Review & Expositor* 40, no. 4 (October 1943): 436–48.

Redekop, Calvin Wall. *The Pax Story: Service in the Name of Christ 1951–1976*. Pandora Press, 2001.

Report of the Forty-Eighth Annual Meeting of the Mennonite Board of Missions and Charities. Mennonite Board of Missions and Charities, 1954.

Report of the Forty-First Annual Meeting of the Mennonite Board of Missions and Charities. Mennonite Board of Missions and Charities, 1947.

Report of the Forty-Fourth Annual Meeting of the Mennonite Board of Missions and Charities. Mennonite Board of Missions and Charities, 1950.

Report of the Forty-Sixth Annual Meeting of the Mennonite Board of Missions and Charities. Mennonite Board of Missions and Charities, 1952.

Report of the Thirty-Eighth Annual Meeting of the Mennonite Board of Missions and Charities. Mennonite Board of Missions and Charities, 1944.

Report of the Thirty-Ninth Annual Meeting of the Mennonite Board of Missions and Charities. Mennonite Board of Missions and Charities, 1945.

Report of the Twenty-Fifth Annual Meeting of the Mennonite Board of Missions and Charities. Mennonite Board of Missions and Charities, 1931.

"Resolutions." In *Report of the Thirty-Ninth Annual Meeting of the Mennonite Board of Missions and Charities*, 35–37. Mennonite Board of Missions and Charities, 1945.

"Resolutions, Our Mission Outreach." In *Report of the Forty-Seventh Annual Meeting of the Mennonite Board of Missions and Charities*, 113–14. Mennonite Church in India, 1953.

Reyburn, William David. "Identification in the Missionary Task." *Practical Anthropology* 7, no. 1 (February 1960): 1–15.

———. *The Toba Indians of the Argentine Chaco, an Interpretive Report*. Mennonite Board of Missions and Charities, 1954.

Rich, Elaine Sommers. *Mennonite Women: A Story of God's Faithfulness, 1683-1983*. Herald Press, 1983.

Robert, Dana L. *Christian Mission: How Christianity Became a World Religion*. Wiley-Blackwell, 2009.

———. "Christianity in the Wider World." In *Christianity: A Social and Cultural History*, 2nd ed., edited by Howard Clark Kee. Prentice Hall, 1998.

———. "Cooperation, Christian Fellowship, and Transnational Networking: The Birth of the International Missionary Council." In *Together in the Mission of God: Jubilee Reflections on the International Missionary Council*, edited by Risto Jukko. World Council of Churches, 2022.

———. "Cross-Cultural Friendship in the Creation of Twentieth-Century World Christianity." *International Bulletin of Missionary Research* 35, no. 2 (April 2011): 100–107.

———. "Forty Years of the American Society of Missiology: Retrospect and Prospect." *Missiology: An International Review* 42, no. 1 (2013): 1–20.

———. "World Christianity as a Revitalization Movement." In *World Christianity: History, Methodologies, Horizons*, edited by Jenu J. Hanciles. Orbis Books, 2021.

Ruth, John L. *Maintaining the Right Fellowship: A Narrative Account of the Oldest Mennonite Community in North America*. Herald Press, 1984.

Sanneh, Lamin O. *Translating the Message: The Missionary Impact on Culture*. 2nd ed. Revised and expanded. Orbis, 2009.

Schäufele, Wolfgang. "The Missionary Vision and Activity of the Anabaptist Laity." In *Anabaptism and Mission*, edited by Wilbert R. Shenk, 70–87. Herald Press, 1984.

Schlabach, Theron F. "Gospel at Home (I)." In *Gospel Versus Gospel: Mission and the Mennonite Church, 1863–1944*, 224–62. Herald Press, 1980.

———. *Gospel Versus Gospel: Mission and the Mennonite Church, 1863–1944*. Herald Press, 1980.

———. "The Humble Become 'Aggressive Workers': Mennonites Organize for Mission, 1880–1910." *Mennonite Quarterly Review* 52, no. 23 (April 1978): 113–26.

———. *A New Rhythm for Mennonites: The Mennonite Church and the Missionary Movement, 1860–1890*. Mennonite Board of Missions, 1975.

———. *Peace, Faith, Nation: Mennonites and Amish in Nineteenth-Century America*. Vol. 2. Mennonite Experience in America. Herald Press, 1988.

———. "Reveille for Die Stillen Im Lande: A Stir among Mennonites in the Late Nineteenth Century: Awakening or Quickening, Revival or Acculturation?" *Mennonite Quarterly Review* 51, no. 3 (July 1, 1977): 213–26.

———. *War, Peace, and Social Conscience: Guy F. Hershberger and Mennonite Ethics*. Herald Press, 2009.

Schlesinger, Arthur, Jr. "The Missionary Enterprise and Theories of Imperialism." In *The Missionary Enterprise in China and America*, edited by John K. Fairbank. Harvard University Press, 1974.

Scott, H. S. "The Christian Churches and the Colour Bar." *International Review of Mission* 31, no. 3 (July 1942): 301–7.

Shank, David A. "A Missionary Approach to a Dechristianized Society." *Mennonite Quarterly Review* 28, no. 1 (January 1954): 39–55.

Shank, J. W., and Selena Shank. "Mission to the South American Indians." In *Report of the Thirty-Eighth Annual Meeting of the Mennonite Board of Missions and Charities*, 118–19. Mennonite Board of Missions and Charities, 1944.

Sharp, John E. *My Calling to Fulfill: The Orie O. Miller Story*. Kindle edition. Herald Press, 2015.

———. *A School on the Prairie: A Centennial History of Hesston College 1909–2009*. Cascadia, 2009.

Sharvananda, Swami. *Taittiriya-Upanishad, with Sanskrit Text, Paraphrase with Word-for-Word Literal Translation, English Rendering and Comments*. The Ramakrishna Math, 1921. https://estudantedavedanta.net/Taittiriya Upanishad - Swami Sarvanand [Sanskrit-English].pdf.

Shenk, Wilbert R. ed. *Being God's Missionary Community: Reflections on Mennonite Missions 1945–1975*. Mennonite Board of Missions, 1975.

———, ed. *The Challenge of Church Growth*. Institute of Mennonite Studies, Missionary Studies 1. Herald Press, 1973.

———. *By Faith They Went Out: Mennonite Missions 1850–1999*. Occasional Papers, Institute of Mennonite Studies 20. Institute of Mennonite Studies, 2000.

———. *Henry Venn: Missionary Statesman*. Orbis Books, 1983.

———. "Henry Venn's Legacy." *Occasional Bulletin of Missionary Research* 1, no. 2 (1977): 16–19.

———. "Mennonites and the Evangelical Network." In *By Faith They Went Out: Mennonite Missions 1850–1999*, 29–49. Occasional Papers, Institute of Mennonite Studies 20. Institute of Mennonite Studies, 2000.

———. "Mission Agency and African Independent Churches." *International Review of Mission* 63, no. 252 (1974): 475–91.

———. "Rufus Anderson and Henry Venn: A Special Relationship?" *International Bulletin of Missionary Research* 5, no. 4 (1981): 168–72.

Showalter, Mary Emma. *Mennonite Community Cookbook: Favorite Family Recipes* (Mennonite Community Association, 1950).

Sinclaire, Margaret. "A Survey of the Year 1943." *International Review of Mission* 33, no. 1 (January 1944): 13–86.

Smith, A. Christopher. *International Review of Mission: Index 1912–1990.* Geneva: International Review of Mission, 1993.

Smith, Willard H. *The Social and Religious Thought of William Jennings Bryan.* Coronado Press, 1975.

———. *The Trail to Santa Fe: A Pilgrim's Progress*. Self-published, 1985.

———. "William Jennings Bryan and the Social Gospel." *The Journal of American History* 53, no. 1 (June, 1966): 41–60

———. *William Jennings Bryan Christian Reformer*. Bryan College, 1967.

Snead, Alfred C., and Christian and Missionary Alliance. *Missionary Atlas: A Manual of the Foreign Work of the Christian and Missionary Alliance.* Christian Publications, 1950.

Soltau, T. Stanley. *Missions at the Crossroads; the Indigenous Church–a Solution for the Unfinished Task.* Baker Book House, 1955.

"Special Actions and Resolutions." In *Report of the Forty-Seventh Annual Meeting of the Mennonite Board of Missions and Charities*, 109–10. Mennonite Board of Missions and Charities, 1953.

"Special Actions: Belgium Mennonite Center." In *Report of the Forty-Third Annual Meeting of the Mennonite Board of Missions and Charities*, 63–64. Mennonite Board of Missions and Charities, 1949.

"Special Actions: London Mennonite Center." In *Report of the Forty-Third Annual Meeting of the Mennonite Board of Missions and Charities*, 64. Mennonite Board of Missions and Charities, 1949.

"Special Committees and Reports." In *Report of the Forty-Seventh Annual Meeting of the Mennonite Board of Missions and Charities*, 98–100. Mennonite Board of Missions and Charities, 1953.

Stevens, George H. "The Christian Approach to the Jew." *International Review of Mission* 48, no. 4 (October 1959): 427–32.

Stoneman, Timothy. "Preparing the Soil for Global Revival: Station HCJB's Radio Circle, 1949–59." *Church History* 76, no. 1 (March 2007): 114–55.

———. "Radio: Missions: Station ELWA in West Africa." *International Bulletin of Missionary Research* 36, no. 4 (October 2012): 200–204.

"A Survey of the Year 1936." *International Review of Mission* 26, no. 1 (January 1937): 3–106.

"A Survey of the Year 1953." *International Review of Mission* 43, no. 1 (January 1954): 3–76.

Thompson, W. J. "A New Approach in a New Day." *International Review of Mission* 34, no. 3 (1945): 280–87.

Toews, Paul. *Mennonites in American Society, 1930–1970: Modernity and the Persistence of Religious Community*. Herald Press, 1996.

Tucker, Ruth. "The Role of Bible Women in World Evangelism." *Missiology* 13, no. 2 (April 1985): 133–46.

Umble, John S. *Goshen College, 1894–1954: A Venture in Christian Higher Education*. Goshen College, 1955.

Vinson, Bill, and Ginger Quering Casey. "Moore-McCormack Lines, S.S. Brazil, Timeline (1928–1964)," nd. In possession of the author.

Walls, Andrew F. "The American Dimension in the History of the Missionary Movement." In *Earthen Vessels: American Evangelicals and Foreign Missions, 1880-1980*, edited by Joel A. Carpenter and Wilbert R. Shenk. Eerdmans, 1990.

Ward, Arthur Marcus. "Towards a Theology of Missions." *International Review of Mission* 37, no. 3 (July 1948): 249–55.

Warren, Max A. C. *Partnership: The Study of an Idea*. S.C.M. Book Club, 1956.

Weaver, Alain Epp. "'A Habit of Social Concern': Anxieties about the Relationship between MCC's Relief and Service Programs and Mennonite Missions from the 1950s to the 1970s." *Journal of Mennonite Studies* 40, no. 1 (2022): 109–26.

Weaver, Edwin I., and Irene Weaver. *The Uyo Story*. Mennonite Board of Missions and Charities, 1970.

Weaver, Irene. *Irene Weaver, Reminiscing for MBM*. Transcript. Elkhart, IN, 1983. Mennonite Mission Network.

Wenger, Linden M. "A Study of Rural Missions in the Mennonite Church." ThM Thesis, Union Theological Seminary, 1955.

Whiteman, Darrell L. "Anthropology and Mission: The Incarnational Connection." *Missiology: An International Review* 31, no. 4 (October 2003): 397–415.

Wittner, Lawrence S. "MacArthur and the Missionaries: God and Man in Occupied Japan." *Pacific Historical Review* 40, no. 1 (February 1971): 77–98.

Yates, Timothy. *Christian Mission in the Twentieth Century*. Cambridge University Press, 1996.

Yoder, John Howard, Papers, 1944–2013. HM1-048. Mennonite Church USA Archives—Elkhart. Elkhart, IN.

Yoder, Robert Bruce. "Mennonite Missionaries and African Independent Churches: The Development of an Anabaptist Missiology in West Africa: 1958–1967." PhD diss., Boston University, 2016.

Yoder, Sanford Calvin. *The Days of My Years*. Herald Press, 1959.

Zijpp, N. van der. "From Anabaptist Missionary Congregation to Mennonite Seclusion." In *Anabaptism and Mission*, edited by Wilbert R. Shenk, 119–36. Herald Press, 1984.

Index

N

O

P

R

S

Studies in Anabaptist and Mennonite History Series

1. Harold S. Bender. *Two Centuries of American Mennonite Literature, 1727–1928*. 1929.
2. John Horsch. *The Hutterian Brethren, 1528–1931: A Story of Martyrdom and Loyalty*. 1931. Reprint, Macmillan Hutterite Colony, Cayley, Alberta, 1985.
3. Harry F. Weber. *Centennial History of the Mennonites in Illinois, 1829–1929*. 1931.
4. Sanford Calvin Yoder. *For Conscience' Sake: A Study of Mennonite Migrations Resulting from the World War*. 1940.
5. John S. Umble. *Ohio Mennonite Sunday Schools*. 1941.
6. Harold S. Bender. *Conrad Grebel, c. 1498–1526, Founder of the Swiss Brethren*. 1950.
7. Robert Friedmann. *Mennonite Piety Through the Centuries: Its Genius and Its Literature*. 1949.
8. Delbert L. Gratz. *Bernese Anabaptists and Their American Descendants*. 1953.
9. A. L. E. Verheyden. *Anabaptism in Flanders, 1530–1650: A Century of Struggle*. 1961.
10. J. C. Wenger. *The Mennonites in Indiana and Michigan*. 1961.
11. Rollin Stely Armour. *Anabaptist Baptism: A Representative Study*. 1966.

12. John B. Toews. *Lost Fatherland: The Story of Mennonite Emigration from Soviet Russia, 1921–1927*. 1967.
13. Grant M. Stoltzfus. *Mennonites of the Ohio and Eastern Conference, from the Colonial Period in Pennsylvania to 1968*. 1969.
14. John A. Lapp. *The Mennonite Church in India, 1897–1962*. 1972.
15. Robert Friedmann. *The Theology of Anabaptism: An Interpretation*. 1973.
16. Kenneth R. Davis. *Anabaptism and Asceticism: A Study in Intellectual Origins*. 1974.
17. Paul Erb. *South Central Frontiers: A History of the South Central Mennonite Conference*. 1974.
18. Fred R. Belk. *The Great Trek of the Russian Mennonites to Central Asia, 1880–1884*. 1976.
19. Werner O. Packull. *Mysticism and the Early South German-Austrian Anabaptist Movement, 1525–1531*. 1976.
20. Richard K. MacMaster, with Samuel L. Horst and Robert F. Ulle. *Conscience in Crisis: Mennonites and Other Peace Churches in America, 1739–1789*. 1979.
21. Theron F. Schlabach. *Gospel Versus Gospel: Mission and the Mennonite Church, 1863–1944*. 1980.
22. Calvin Wall Redekop. *Strangers Become Neighbors: Mennonite and Indigenous Relations in the Paraguayan Chaco*. 1980.
23. Leonard Gross. *The Golden Years of the Hutterites: The Witness and Thought of the Communal Moravian Anabaptists during the Walpot Era, 1565–1578*. 1980. Rev. ed., Pandora Press Canada, 1998.
24. Willard H. Smith. *Mennonites in Illinois*. 1983.
25. Murray L. Wagner. *Petr Chelcický: A Radical Separatist in Hussite Bohemia*. 1983.
26. John L. Ruth. *Maintaining the Right Fellowship: A Narrative Account of Life in the Oldest Mennonite Community in North America*. 1984.
27. C. Arnold Snyder. *The Life and Thought of Michael Sattler*. 1984.
28. Beulah Stauffer Hostetler. *American Mennonites and Protestant Movements: A Community Paradigm*. 1987.
29. Daniel Liechty. *Andreas Fischer and the Sabbatarian Anabaptists: An Early Reformation Episode in East Central Europe*. 1988.
30. Hope Kauffman Lind. *Apart and Together: Mennonites in Oregon and Neighboring States, 1876–1976*. 1990.
31. Paton Yoder. *Tradition and Transition: Amish Mennonites and Old Order Amish, 1800–1900*. 1991.
32. James R. Coggins. *John Smyth's Congregation: English Separatism, Mennonite Influence, and the Elect Nation*. 1991.
33. John D. Rempel. *The Lord's Supper in Anabaptism: A Study in the Theology of Balthasar Hubmaier, Pilgram Marpeck, and Dirk Philips*. 1993.
34. Gerlof D. Homan. *American Mennonites and the Great War, 1914–1918*. 1994.

35. J. Denny Weaver. *Keeping Salvation Ethical: Mennonite and Amish Atonement Theology in the Late Nineteenth Century*. 1997.
36. Wes Harrison. *Andreas Ehrenpreis and Hutterite Faith and Practice*. 1997. Copublished with Pandora Press Canada.
37. John D. Thiesen. *Mennonite and Nazi? Attitudes among Mennonite Colonists in Latin America, 1933–1945*. 1999. Copublished with Pandora Press Canada.
38. Perry Bush. *Dancing with the Kobzar: Bluffton College and Mennonite Higher Education, 1899–1999*. 2000. Copublished with Pandora Press U.S. and Faith & Life Press.
39. John L. Ruth. *The Earth Is the Lord's: A Narrative History of the Lancaster Mennonite Conference*. 2001.
40. Melanie Springer Mock. *Writing Peace: The Unheard Voices of Great War Mennonite Objectors*. 2003. Copublished with Cascadia Publishing House.
41. Mary Jane Lederach Hershey. *This Teaching I Present: Fraktur from the Skippack and Salford Mennonite Meetinghouse Schools, 1747–1836*. 2003. Published by Good Books.
42. Edsel Burdge Jr. and Samuel L. Horst. *Building on the Gospel Foundation: The Mennonites of Franklin County, Pennsylvania, and Washington County, Maryland, 1730–1970*. 2004.
43. Ervin Beck. *MennoFolk: Mennonite and Amish Folk Traditions*. 2004.
44. Walter Klaassen and William Klassen. *Marpeck: A Life of Dissent and Conformity*. 2008.
45. Theron F. Schlabach. *War, Peace, and Social Conscience: Guy F. Hershberger and Mennonite Ethics*. 2009.
46. Ervin R. Stutzman. *From Nonresistance to Justice: The Transformation of Mennonite Church Peace Rhetoric, 1908–2008*. 2011.
47. Nathan E. Yoder. *Together in the Work of the Lord: A History of the Conservative Mennonite Conference*. 2014.
48. Samuel J. Steiner. *In Search of Promised Lands: A Religious History of Mennonites in Ontario*. 2015.
49. Perry Bush. *Peace, Progress, and the Professor: The Mennonite History of C. Henry Smith*. 2015.
50. Rich Preheim. *In Pursuit of Faithfulness: Conviction, Conflict, and Compromise in Indiana-Michigan Mennonite Conference*. 2016.
51. Anita Hooley Yoder. *Circles of Sisterhood: A History of Mission, Service, and Fellowship in Mennonite Women's Organizations*. 2017.
52. Jo Anne Kraus. *Holy Experiment: The Warwick River Mennonite Colony, 1897–1970*. 2021.
53. Stuart Murray. *The Legacy of Melchior Rinck: Anabaptist Pioneer in Hesse*. 2022.
54. R. Bruce Yoder. *Sowing Seeds: J. D. Graber and the Vision for Global Anabaptism*. 2025.

The Author

R. BRUCE YODER has served as co-executive coordinator of African Inter-Mennonite Mission for four years. He has lived and worked in intercultural settings in Latin America and West Africa for over two decades, serving in the areas of community development, theological education, and church development. His research and writing is focused on the history of twentieth-century North American Anabaptist mission engagement and the emergence of world Christianity. He has a PhD in church history and world Christianity from Boston University School of Theology as well as degrees from Goshen College and Anabaptist Mennonite Biblical Seminary.